Frommer's

DISCARD

Denver,
Boulder &
Colorado
Springs

8th Edition

by Eric Peterson and Don & Barbara Laine

Here's what the critics say about Frommer's:

"Amazingly easy to use. Very portable, very complete."
—*Booklist*

"Detailed, accurate, and easy-to-read information for all price ranges."
—*Glamour Magazine*

"Hotel information is close to encyclopedic."
—*Des Moines Sunday Register*

"Frommer's Guides have a way of giving you a real feel for a place."
—*Knight Ridder Newspapers*

D1534257

Wiley Publishing, Inc.

Published by:

Wiley Publishing, Inc.

111 River St.
Hoboken, NJ 07030-5774

ISBN 0-7645-7430-2

Editor: Cate Latting
Production Editor: Donna Wright
Cartographer: Nick Trotter
Photo Editor: Richard Fox
Production by Wiley Indianapolis Composition Services

Front cover photo: Cowboy & horse sculpture at the Denver Civic Center.
Back cover photo: Golfers on the green at the Broadmoor Hotel, Colorado Springs.

For information on our other products and services or to obtain technical support, please contact our Customer Care Department within the U.S. at 800/762-2974, outside the U.S. at 317/572-3993 or fax 317/572-4002.

Wiley also publishes its books in a variety of electronic formats. Some content that appears in print may not be available in electronic formats.

Manufactured in the United States of America

5 4 3 2 1

Contents

List of Maps

About the Authors

A Denver-based freelance writer, **Eric Peterson** has contributed to Frommer's guides to Colorado, Texas, and the National Parks of the American West, and has written *Frommer's Yellowstone & Grand Teton National Parks* and a coffee-table book, *Roadside Americana* (www.roadsideamericanabook.com). When he's not on the road or writing about travel, Peterson covers Colorado's high-tech business scene and Denver's punk-rock underbelly. He's also an avid camper and hiker who enjoys long weekends in the Colorado Rockies with his antique boots, his campfire-cooked delicacies, and his faithful mutt, Giblet.

Residents of northern New Mexico since 1970, **Don and Barbara Laine** have traveled extensively throughout the Rocky Mountains and the Southwest, spending as much time as possible in the outdoors, and especially in the region's national parks and monuments. They have written Frommer's guides to Utah, Colorado, and the National Parks of the American West. The Laines have also authored *Little-Known Southwest* and *New Mexico & Arizona State Parks* for The Mountaineers; and *The New Mexico Guide* for Fulcrum Publishing.

Acknowledgments

The authors wish to thank for their help Rich Grant and Jill Strunk with the Denver Metro Convention and Visitors Bureau, Nancy Kern with the Boulder Convention and Visitors Bureau, and Elizabeth Youngquist with the Colorado Springs Convention and Visitors Bureau.

An Invitation to the Reader

In researching this book, we discovered many wonderful places—hotels, restaurants, shops, and more. We're sure you'll find others. Please tell us about them, so we can share the information with your fellow travelers in upcoming editions. If you were disappointed with a recommendation, we'd love to know that, too. Please write to:

Frommer's Denver, Boulder & Colorado Springs, 8th Edition
Wiley Publishing, Inc. • 111 River St. • Hoboken, NJ 07030-5774

An Additional Note

Please be advised that travel information is subject to change at any time—and this is especially true of prices. We therefore suggest that you write or call ahead for confirmation when making your travel plans. The authors, editors, and publisher cannot be held responsible for the experiences of readers while traveling. Your safety is important to us, however, so we encourage you to stay alert and be aware of your surroundings. Keep a close eye on cameras, purses, and wallets, all favorite targets of thieves and pickpockets.

Other Great Guides for Your Trip:

Frommer's Colorado

Frommer's National Parks of the American West

Frommer's Rocky Mountain National Park

Frommer's Arizona

Frommer's New Mexico

Frommer's Utah

Frommer's Star Ratings, Icons & Abbreviations

Every hotel, restaurant, and attraction listing in this guide has been ranked for quality, value, service, amenities, and special features using a **star-rating system.** In country, state, and regional guides, we also rate towns and regions to help you narrow down your choices and budget your time accordingly. Hotels and restaurants are rated on a scale of zero (recommended) to three stars (exceptional). Attractions, shopping, nightlife, towns, and regions are rated according to the following scale: zero stars (recommended), one star (highly recommended), two stars (very highly recommended), and three stars (must-see).

In addition to the star-rating system, we also use seven feature icons that point you to the great deals, in-the-know advice, and unique experiences that separate travelers from tourists. Throughout the book, look for:

Finds	Special finds—those places only insiders know about
Fun Fact	Fun facts—details that make travelers more informed and their trips more fun
Kids	Best bets for kids, and advice for the whole family
Moments	Special moments—those experiences that memories are made of
Overrated	Places or experiences not worth your time or money
Tips	Insider tips—great ways to save time and money
Value	Great values—where to get the best deals

The following **abbreviations** are used for credit cards:

AE	American Express	DISC	Discover	V	Visa
DC	Diners Club	MC	MasterCard		

Frommers.com

Now that you have the guidebook to a great trip, visit our website at **www.frommers.com** for travel information on more than 3,000 destinations. With features updated regularly, we give you instant access to the most current trip-planning information available. At Frommers.com, you'll also find the best prices on airfares, accommodations, and car rentals—and you can even book travel online through our travel booking partners. At Frommers.com, you'll also find the following:

- Online updates to our most popular guidebooks
- Vacation sweepstakes and contest giveaways
- Newsletter highlighting the hottest travel trends
- Online travel message boards with featured travel discussions

What's New in Denver, Boulder & Colorado Springs

Colorado's Front Range cities of Denver, Boulder, and Colorado Springs offer a rich combination of old and new. They lure us with both their city attractions, such as museums, galleries, and historic sites, and their outdoor recreation opportunities and proximity to some of America's most beautiful mountains. Here you can sleep in a grand historic hotel, awake to a gourmet breakfast, hike or ride to the top of a spectacular mountain, and be back in town in time for the ballet.

Growth, which Coloradans see as both a blessing and a curse, is the main agent of change in the area. And for at least the next few years, outdoor recreationists who venture into the mountains will see the damage done by major forest fires in the summer of 2002. Following are some of the changes, including some exciting new things to watch for in Denver, Boulder, and Colorado Springs.

SETTLING INTO DENVER Using a car in Denver will be a bit of a challenge for the next few years while a major **road construction** project is underway, slated for completion in 2006. But at least you have some great places to stay while waiting for the traffic to ease up. The first hotel in the ritzy Cherry Creek area, the **JW Marriott,** 150 Clayton Lane (✆ **303/316-2700**), rivals Denver's best downtown luxury hotels and has a restaurant, **Mirepoix,** to match. Denver also boasts some fine new restaurants. These include the **Bistro Vendome,** 1424-H Larimer Sq.

(✆ **303/825-3232**), serving what chef-owner Eric Roeder describes as "French soul food"; **Red Square Euro Bistro,** 1512 Larimer St. at Writer Square (✆ **303/595-8600**), with 100 brands of vodka behind the bar and excellent food that isn't purely Russian in lineage; **MAX Burgerworks,** 1512 Lawrence St. at Writer Square (✆ **303/ 534-0944**), which brings an upscale attitude to the art of burger-making (20 varieties in all); and the **Tom Tom Room,** 1432 Market St. (✆ **303/534- 5050**), a hip and romantic Japanese eatery specializing in sushi and robata, skewers grilled over Japanese charcoal. See chapter 4 for details.

WHAT TO SEE & DO IN DENVER The **Vance Kirkland Museum,** 1311 Pearl St. (✆ **303/832-8576**), greatly expanded its hours, and features remarkable collections of the work of Vance Kirkland (Colorado's most renowned painter) and other Colorado artists, as well as a superlative collection of decorative arts. The **Denver Museum of Nature and Science,** City Park, 2001 Colorado Blvd. (✆ **303/ 322-7009**) has added an exciting new "Space Odyssey" exhibit. Improvements have also been made at the **Butterfly Pavilion & Insect Center,** 6252 W. 104th Ave., Westminster (✆ **303/ 469-5441**), with a 31,000-square-foot expansion that was completed in 2004, housing "Shrunk!"—giant robotic insects and exhibits about the biomechanics of bugs. The south suburbs also have a relatively new museum—**The**

Wildlife Experience, 10035 S. Peoria St. (© 720/488-3300), which specializes in art with a nature theme. The **Larimer Lounge,** 2721 Larimer St. (© 303/291-1007) opened in 2003, delivering punk and indie rock in a barroom that's been open for more than a century.

BOULDER The **St. Julien,** 900 Walnut St. (© 877/303-0900), is the first hotel to open in downtown Boulder since the Boulderado did in 1909. Elegant, with an excellent spa and incredible views, the hotel is Boulder's most upscale property. On the budget end of the spectrum, local entrepreneurs recycled a former "Holidome" into the colorful **Boulder Outlook,** 800 28th St. (© 800/542-0304), with such unique perks as two bouldering rocks (one is 11 ft. high, the other 4 ft.) and a fenced, 4,000-square-foot dog run. Best of all, the rates are typically cheaper than its chain counterparts. On the culinary side of things, John Bizzarro handed the reins of **John's Restaurant,** 2328 Pearl St. (© 303/444-5232), to longtime Flagstaff House chef Corey Buck in 2004. The proprietors of **The Mediterranean** opened a French bistro across the street in **Brasserie Ten Ten,** 1011 Walnut St. (© 303/998-1010), which serves up delectable oysters as well as a nice selection of simple, fresh French stalwarts.

COLORADO SPRINGS The Antlers Adam's Mark is now the **Antlers Hilton,** 4 S. Cascade Ave. (© 719/473-5600), after changing flags in fall 2004. It remains the cornerstone hotel of downtown Colorado Springs. **Walter's Bistro,** 136 E. Cheyenne Mountain Ave. (© 719/630-0201), relocated to a wonderful new space at the foot of Cheyenne Mountain and continues to deliver some of the best meals in town.

The Best of Denver, Boulder & Colorado Springs

The old and the new, the rustic and the sophisticated, the urban and the rural—you'll find all these elements practically side by side in and immediately adjacent to the cities of Denver, Boulder, and Colorado Springs.

Founded in the mid–19th century by both East Coast gold-seekers and European and Asian immigrants in search of a better life, these cities on the Front Range of the majestic Rocky Mountains weren't as wild as Colorado's mountain towns (such as Telluride and Creede), but they did have their day. According to historian Thomas Noel, in 1890 Denver had more saloons per capita than Kansas City, St. Louis, New Orleans, or Philadelphia. But these Colorado cities soon became home to a more sophisticated westerner—the mine owner instead of the prospector, the business owner rather than the gambler.

Today, the thoroughly modern cities have virtually all the amenities you'd expect to find in New York or Los Angeles: opera, theater, modern dance, art, excellent restaurants, and sophisticated hotels and convention centers. You'll also find historic Victorian mansions, working steam trains, and old gold mines. You can go horseback riding, hiking, skiing, or shopping; do the Texas two-step to a live country band; or spend hours browsing through a huge four-story book-store, a gigantic model-train shop, or the world's largest hardware store. You might also join the locals at what many of them enjoy most: being outdoors under the warm Colorado sun—so don't forget your hiking boots, mountain bike, skis, sunscreen, and sunglasses.

Although Denver is certainly a city, bustling and growing, it's still comfortable and fairly easy to explore. Boulder and Colorado Springs call themselves cities, but we like to think of them more as big Western towns, where the buildings aren't very tall and there's lots of open space. In all three, the residents are friendly, relaxed, and casual.

In this book, we'll be putting Denver, Boulder, and Colorado Springs under a magnifying glass, but that's not all. We'll also look at some of the nearby attractions where the locals spend their weekends, including the state's premier natural wonder, Rocky Mountain National Park.

1 Frommer's Favorite Denver, Boulder & Colorado Springs Experiences

- **Lower Downtown and Larimer Square (Denver):** Once neglected and even a bit dangerous, Lower Downtown (LoDo) and Larimer Square are now well-preserved historic gems, heavy with redbricks and activity of all kinds. LoDo is home to Coors Field (home of baseball's Colorado Rockies), plus galleries, nightspots, restaurants, and Mayor John Hickenlooper's longstanding microbrewery, the Wynkoop Brewing Company, right across from Union Station. Larimer Square is abuzz with commercial activity and has more good restaurants than any other block in Denver. See p. 92.

- **Denver Art Museum (Denver):** In the midst of a major expansion slated for completion in 2006, the Denver Art Museum has one of the country's top collections of Western art, ranging from 19th century to contemporary, as well as an excellent American Indian collection. The in-progress expansion features jagged, avant-garde by renowned architect Daniel Libeskind. See p. 86.

- **Shopping for Duds at Rockmount Ranch Wear (Denver):** The inventors of the Western snap shirt have gone into the retail business after sticking strictly to manufacturing and wholesale since 1946. Their downtown store is a three-generation family operation and browsing the racks is something of an education on the history of Western wear. Rock stars regularly stop by while in Denver; Bob Dylan wears Rockmount's dusters onstage. See p. 113.

- **People-Watching on Pearl Street Mall (Boulder):** This 4-block-long tree-lined pedestrian mall marks Boulder's downtown core and its center for dining, shopping, strolling, and loafing in the sun. It's also the best spot in Colorado for observing your fellow humans. Here you'll see students, local businesspeople, and tourists as they watch the musicians, mimes, jugglers, and other street entertainers who hold court on the landscaped mall day and night, year-round. See p. 150.

- **Celestial Seasonings Tour (Boulder):** The nation's leading producer of herbal teas offers a tour that excites the senses as it takes you behind the scenes into the world of tea. The company, which began in a Boulder garage in the 1970s, now produces more than 50 varieties of tea from more than 75 different herbs and spices, imported from 35 countries. Guided tours move from a consumer taste test in the lobby to marketing displays, and finally into the production plant, where the overpowering "Mint Room" is a highlight. See p. 151.

- **Colorado Shakespeare Festival (Boulder):** Among the top Shakespearean festivals in the United States, this 2-month event offers more than a dozen performances of each of four Shakespearean plays each summer. Actors, directors, designers, and everyone associated with the productions are fully schooled Shakespearean professionals. During the festival, company members conduct 1-hour backstage tours before each show. See p. 163.

- **Hiking the Mills Lake Trail in Rocky Mountain National Park:** Although it's packed at first, this moderately rated trail usually becomes much less crowded after you've logged a few miles. At trail's end (elevation 10,000 ft.), towering peaks surround a gorgeous mountain lake. The lake is an excellent spot for photographing dramatic Longs Peak, especially in late afternoon or early evening, and it's the perfect place for a picnic. See chapter 6.

- **Garden of the Gods (Colorado Springs):** There's nothing like sunrise at Garden of the Gods, with its fantastic and sometimes fanciful red-sandstone formations sculpted by wind and water over hundreds of thousands of years. Although

Colorado

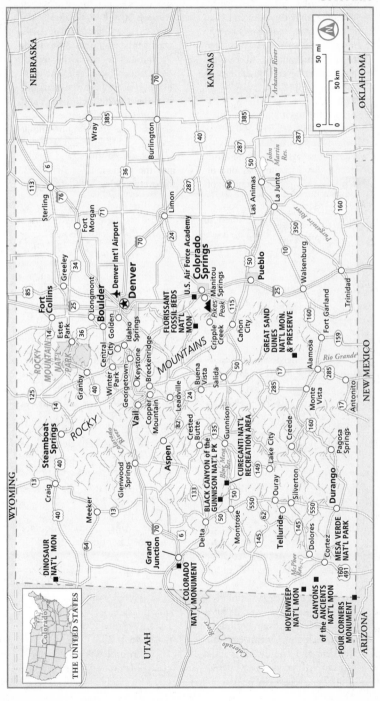

you can see a great deal from the marked view points, it's worth spending some time and energy to get away from the crowds on one of the park's many trails, to listen to the wind, and to imagine the gods cavorting among the formations. See p. 198.

• **Pikes Peak Cog Railway (Colorado Springs):** Perhaps no view in Colorado equals the 360-degree panorama from the summit of Pikes Peak. For those who enjoy rail travel, spectacular scenery, and the thrill of mountain climbing without all the work, this is the trip to take. The 9-mile route, with grades of up to 25%, takes 75 minutes to reach the top of 14,110-foot Pikes Peak. The journey is exciting from the start, but passengers really begin to ooh and aah when the track leaves the forest, creeping above timberline at about 11,500 feet. See p. 199.

2 Best Hotel Bets

• **Best Historic Hotels:** From its spacious, well-appointed lobby to the richly polished wood of its elegant Victorian and almost whimsical Art Deco rooms, the **Brown Palace Hotel,** 321 17th St., Denver (© **800/228-2917** or 303/297-3111), has an air of sophistication, refinement, and class. The Brown has operated continuously since August 1892. See p. 66.

A handsome downtown establishment, the **Hotel Boulderado,** 2115 13th St., Boulder (© **800/433-4344** or 303/442-4344), has been skillfully renovated and restored. It retains its original Otis elevator, lovely leaded-glass ceiling, and spectacular cherrywood staircase, which caused quite a stir when the hotel opened in 1909. See p. 139.

Designed by New York City architects in the Italian Renaissance style, **The Broadmoor,** Lake Circle, at Lake Avenue, Colorado Springs (© **800/634-7711** or 719/634-7711), opened in 1918. Colorado's most elegant and best-preserved hotel of the era, it's filled with objets d'art from around the world, including Oriental art from the Ming and Tsin dynasties and a huge carved wooden bar from an 1800s British pub. See p. 184.

• **Best for Business Travelers:** All rooms at **Loews Denver Hotel,** 4150 E. Mississippi Ave., Denver (© **800/345-9172** or 303/782-9300), are spacious and provide at least three phones. Furthermore, two floors are designed for business travelers: All rooms have modem hookups and in-room fax and receive complimentary newspapers. See p. 72.

• **Best for a Romantic Getaway:** Housed in a magnificent historic stone mansion, the **Castle Marne Bed & Breakfast,** 1572 Race St., Denver (© **800/92-MARNE** or 303/331-0621), is furnished with antiques and reproductions. Three suites feature whirlpool tubs for two, and three rooms offer private balconies equipped with delightful outdoor hot tubs for two. See p. 71.

The Alps, 38619 Boulder Canyon Dr., Boulder (© **800/414-2577** or 303/444-5445), nestles among trees on a hillside outside of town; you won't find a TV in your room, but you will have a cozy fireplace, and there might be a whirlpool tub for two or a private porch. See p. 138.

The Two Sisters Inn, 10 Otoe Place, Manitou Springs, outside

Colorado Springs (℃ **800/2SISINN** or 719/685-9684), offers a cozy honeymoon cottage complete with fresh flowers, a big feather bed, a gas log fireplace, and lots of privacy. What more could you ask for? See p. 187.

- **Best Hotel Lobby for Pretending You're Rich:** The lobby of the **Brown Palace Hotel** (Denver; see address and telephone above) features walls of Mexican onyx and a floor of white marble. The elaborate cast-iron grillwork surrounding the six tiers of balconies draws your eye to the stained-glass ceiling. Luncheon and afternoon tea are served in the lobby nearly every day.

  The first guests at **The Broadmoor** (Colorado Springs; see address and telephone above) when it opened in 1918 were millionaire John D. Rockefeller, Jr., and his party. It's easy to imagine yourself here, surrounded by priceless 17th-century art, mingling with the wealthy, reading the financial news, and sipping a cognac by the hotel's elegant marble staircase.

- **Best Moderately Priced Hotels:** The colorful **Boulder Outlook,** 800 28th St. (℃ **800/542-0304** or 303/443-3322), is fun, fresh, and definitively Boulder, with such unique perks as two bouldering rocks (one is 11 ft. high, the other 4 ft.) and a fenced, 4,000 square foot dog run. Best of all, the rates are typically cheaper than its chain counterparts. See p. 140.

  You can enjoy the best of two worlds at the **Hearthstone Inn,** 506 N. Cascade Ave., Colorado Springs (℃ **800/521-1885** or 719/473-4413): the intimacy and personal attention of a bed-and-breakfast plus the privacy and services of a small hotel. See p. 190.

- **Best Inexpensive Lodging:** For those who appreciate small mom-and-pop establishments, the **Cameron Motel**, 4500 E. Evans Ave., Denver (℃ **303/757-2100**), offers a quiet alternative to budget chains. See p. 73.

  In a converted sorority near the University of Colorado campus, **Boulder International Hostel,** 1107 12th St. (℃ **888/442-0522** or 303/442-0522), is well kept, reputable, and perfect for those traveling on a budget. See p. 141.

- **Best Service:** Dedicated to providing guests with the best possible service, the **Brown Palace Hotel** (Denver; see address and telephone above) succeeds extremely well, and without pretension. Among other things, it offers 24-hour room service, concierge, and in-room massage.

  Taking good care of its guests is a point of pride for **The Broadmoor** (Colorado Springs; see address and telephone above): It offers 24-hour room service, a concierge, in-room massage, valet laundry, a shuttle bus between buildings, and a multitude of recreational activities, as well as almost anything else you might ask for.

- **Best Bed-and-Breakfast:** A great location and oodles of historic ambience are only two reasons to stay at the **Queen Anne Bed & Breakfast Inn,** 2147–51 Tremont Place, Denver (℃ **800/432-4667** or 303/296-6666), a pair of Victorian homes on the edge of downtown. The inn is furnished mostly with antiques, and fresh flowers and piped-in music enhance the rooms. See p. 71.

  At **Old Town GuestHouse,** 115 S. 26th St., Colorado Springs (℃ **888/375-4210** or 719/632-9194), each room is delightfully decorated around a theme, ranging from Saharan to Victorian. This B&B also has just enough in the way of modern convenience. See p. 185.

- **Best Views:** The gorgeous new **St. Julien,** 900 Walnut St., Boulder (© **877/303-0900** or 720/406-9696), is the nearest hotel to Boulder's even more gorgeous foothills. Rooms don't come cheap, but the views rival those from the windows of Colorado's ritziest mountain resorts. See p. 138.

The **JW Marriott,** 150 Clayton Lane, Denver (© **303/316-2700**), the first and only hotel in the tony Cherry Creek shopping district, looks out over the treed Denver Country Club and the creek itself. See p. 72.

- **Best for Families:** Two swimming pools, water slides, and a fabulous summer kids' program at **The Broadmoor** (Colorado Springs; see address and telephone above) will help keep youngsters busy while parents enjoy the golf courses, spa, and seemingly countless other facilities.

3 Best Dining Bets

- **Best Spots for a Romantic Dinner: Bistro Vendome,** 1424-H Larimer Sq., Denver © 303/825-3232), is a quiet, charming restaurant with a refined but casual atmosphere, a sublime patio, and cuisine dubbed "French soul food." See p. 75.

John's Restaurant, 2328 Pearl St., Boulder (© **303/444-5232**), is a small, charming chef-owned spot with a simple elegance that soothes and never intrudes. See p. 142.

One place where locals celebrate anniversaries and other special events, **La Petite Maison,** 1015 W. Colorado Ave., Colorado Springs (© **719/632-4887**), is cozy, intimate, and casually elegant, with soothing chamber music playing in the background. See p. 190.

- **Best Spots for a Celebration:** Denver's most elegant restaurant, the **Palace Arms,** in the Brown Palace Hotel, 321 17th St., Denver (© **303/297-3111**), also serves some of the most elegant food. Try a regional dish, such as roasted rack of Colorado lamb or seared breast of pheasant, or go for one of the more innovative dishes, like fresh lobster enchilada. See p. 74.

When they're not celebrating at La Petite Maison (see above), Colorado Springs locals splurge on a night out at the **Cliff House Dining Room,** Cliff House Inn, 306 Cañon Ave., Manitou Springs (© **719/785-2415**). It offers an elegant Victorian atmosphere, superlative service, and innovative variations on old favorites, such as smoked bacon–scented petite prime-rib roast, with vegetables and potato purée. See p. 189.

- **Best Decor:** Occupying the same premises as when it opened in 1893, the **Buckhorn Exchange,** 1000 Osage St., Denver (© **303/534-9505**), still has a magnificent 19th-century hand-carved oak bar in the upstairs Victorian parlor and saloon. The downstairs features an amazing collection of taxidermy, a menagerie that includes everything from leopard to buffalo. See p. 74.

In a converted Victorian, the Tibetan/Nepalese **Sherpa's,** 825 Walnut St., Boulder (© **303/440-7151**), has no shortage of Himalayan relics, photos, and art to look at, especially in the cozy bar that doubles as a library. See p. 146.

- **Best Values:** The all-you-can-eat buffet at **Govinda's Spiritual Food,** 1400 N. Cherry St., Denver (© **303/333-5461**), has one of the city's best salad bars, plus great soups, fresh-baked bread, and an array of meatless main dishes. See p. 84.

  You'll get fine food at reasonable prices in a casual atmosphere at the **Corner Bar** in the Hotel Boulderado, 2115 13th St., Boulder (© **303/442-4560**). See p. 145.

  It's amazing to find a restaurant that prepares so many different dishes well—candy, ice cream, Southwestern, Greek, basic American—and for such low prices. Perhaps that's why Colorado Springs residents have been coming to **Michelle's,** 122 N. Tejon St. (© **719/633-5089**), since it opened in 1952. See p. 194.

- **Best for Kids:** More a theme park than a restaurant, **Casa Bonita,** in the JCRS Shopping Center, 6715 W. Colfax Ave., Lakewood, west of Denver (© **303/232-5115**), has practically nonstop action, with divers plummeting into a pool beside a 30-foot waterfall, puppet shows, a video arcade, and a fun house. Yes, there's food, too: tacos and other standard Mexican fare, country-fried steak, and fried chicken, served cafeteria-style. See p. 84.

  There's something about trains that brings out the kid in all of us. **Giuseppe's Old Depot Restaurant,** 10 S. Sierra Madre St., Colorado Springs (© **719/635-3111**), has one parked outside the door and plenty more rolling by just outside the large windows. See p. 192.

- **Best Burgers & Beer:** Making a great burger is something of a science at **MAX Burgerworks,** 1512 Larimer St. at Writer Square, Denver (© **303/534-0944**), with a menu that has no less than 20 burger options. See p. 79.

  A full ⅓ pound of good ground beef is the foundation of a great burger at **Tom's Tavern,** 1047 Pearl St., Boulder (© **303/443-3893**). Choose from a variety of beers to wash it all down. See p. 146.

- **Best People-Watching:** With outdoor seating just 2 blocks from home plate of Coors Field in downtown Denver, **Wynkoop Brewing Company,** 1634 18th St. (© **303/297-2700**), is the place to sit and watch the world stroll by. See p. 80.

  Sitting inside or outside, you'll get a great view of the Pearl Street Mall at **14th Street Bar & Grill,** 1400 Pearl St., Boulder (© **303/444-5854**). You'll see all kinds of people passing by—students and families, old and young, and even street entertainers, from musicians to mimes. See p. 144.

- **Best View:** Perched on the side of a mountain above Boulder, with a wall of windows framing the city below and plains beyond, **Flagstaff House Restaurant,** 1138 Flagstaff Rd. (© **303/442-4640**), offers extraordinary views, especially as the sun sets or the city gradually disappears in a swirling snowstorm. See p. 142.

  Large picture windows at **Charles Court,** in The Broadmoor, Lake Circle, Colorado Springs (© **719/634-7711**), afford diners a splendid vista out over The Broadmoor's personal lake. Shouldn't everyone have one? See p. 189.

- **Best Wine List:** With more than 2,000 well-chosen selections, **Flagstaff House Restaurant** (Boulder; see address and telephone above) wins this category without question. See p. 142.

- **Best Desserts:** Homemade desserts at **John's Restaurant** (Boulder; see address and telephone above) include two house specialties: transcendent caramel cheesecake and strongly flavored Italian ice cream.

  With all the fine restaurants that seem to specialize in desserts, the **Craftwood Inn,** 404 El Paso Blvd., Colorado Springs (© **719/ 685-9000**), stands out, particularly for the way it combines raspberries and chocolate. See p. 189.

- **Best Fast Food:** At **Illegal Pete's,** 1447 Pearl St., Boulder (© **303/ 440-3955**), you'll get a choice of unique burritos that are both mouthwatering and massive, as well as salads, chile, fish, chicken, and vegetarian tacos. See p. 145.

- **Best Natural Foods:** The ingredients at **Sunflower,** 1701 Pearl St. (© **303/440-0220**), include certified organic produce and free-range, hormone-free poultry and game. Owner-chef Jon Pell takes a multicultural approach, with influences ranging from Asian to Cajun. See p. 145.

  Fresh and healthy are the key words at **Adam's Mountain Cafe,** 110 Cañon Ave., Manitou Springs, outside Colorado Springs (© **719/ 685-1430**), which serves interesting dishes with a decidedly Mediterranean flair. See p. 193.

- **Best Chinese Cuisine:** Ask any Denver resident: The **Imperial Chinese Restaurant,** 431 S. Broadway (© **303/698-2800**), is the place to go for Chinese food. Choose from classic and innovative Szechuan, Hunan, Mandarin, and Cantonese dishes. Items such as Nanking pork loin, seafood bird's nest, and sesame chicken are the specials of the house.

- **Best Italian Cuisine:** Traditional and innovative Italian flavors blissfully meet at **Panzano,** in

Hotel Monaco, 909 17th St., Denver (© **303/296-3525**). Try the restaurant's specialty, *buridda,* a Genovese seafood stew with mussels, calamari, and shrimp in a savory lobster broth. See p. 75.

- **Best Seafood: McCormick's Fish House & Bar,** in the Oxford Hotel, 1659 Wazee St., Denver (© **303/825-1107**), flies in fresh seafood daily. Choices often include salmon from Alaska, mussels from Maine and Florida, and yellowfin tuna from Hawaii. See p. 80.

- **Best Vietnamese Cuisine:** The original Vietnamese restaurant in Denver, **T-Wa Inn,** 555 S. Federal Blvd., Denver (© **303/922-2378**), is the place to come for genuine Vietnamese cooking. The perfectly cooked and spiced entrees include several vegetarian plates, incredible shrimp and pork loin, and a number of spicy Thai dishes to boot. See p. 85.

- **Best American Cuisine:** The specifics change daily at **Flagstaff House Restaurant** (Boulder; see address and telephone above), but Rocky Mountain game highlights many of the dishes, each individually and creatively prepared with the freshest ingredients.

  It certainly isn't cheap, but the creative and exquisitely prepared American cuisine served at **Charles Court** (Colorado Springs; see address and telephone above) is tough to beat.

- **Best Continental Cuisine:** Bone-in filet mignon with an imaginative wild mushroom and bleu cheese bread pudding at **Walter's Bistro,** 136 E. Cheyenne Mountain Ave., Colorado Springs (© **719/630- 0201**), is just one highlight of this chic eatery at the foot of Cheyenne Mountain. See p. 189.

- **Best Mexican Cuisine:** In a city brimming with Mexican restaurants, the food at **Tosh's Hacienda,** 3090 Downing St., Denver (© **303/295-1861**), stands out. You can't go wrong with enchiladas, burritos, or rellenos, and the margaritas are both tart and strong. See p. 80.

- **Best Regional Cuisine:** For carefully prepared Colorado game and other Western cuisine (such as venison, pheasant, and trout), visit the **Craftwood Inn** (Colorado Springs; see address and telephone above).

2

Planning Your Trip to Denver, Boulder & Colorado Springs

I t's important to prepare for any trip, including one to Colorado's major cities. This chapter offers a variety of planning tools—information on when to go, how to get there, how to get around, and other tips.

1 Visitor Information

Start by contacting the **Colorado Tourism Office,** 1625 Broadway, Denver, CO 80202 (© **800/ COLORADO;** www.colorado.com), for a free copy of the official state vacation guide, which includes a state map and describes attractions, activities, and lodgings throughout Colorado. Another good source for Colorado information is the website of the *Denver Post,* the state's major daily newspaper, at **www.denverpost.com**.

The **Colorado Hotel and Lodging Association,** 999 18th St., Suite 1240, Denver, CO 80202 (© **303/ 297-8335;** www.coloradolodging. com), offers a free guide to lodging across the state. The nonprofit **Bed and Breakfast Innkeepers of Colorado,** P.O. Box 38416, Colorado Springs, CO 80937 (©**800/265-7696;** www.innsofcolorado.org), distributes a free directory describing about 100 B&Bs across the state, including a number of historic inns in Denver, Boulder, and Colorado Springs.

Hostelling International-USA, 8401 Colesville Rd., Suite 600, Silver Spring, MD 20910 (© **301/495-1240;** www.hiayh.org), has a computerized system for making reservations in hostels worldwide, and also has a print directory of U.S. hostels.

A free copy of *Colorado State Parks,* which contains details on the state's 40 parks, is available from state park offices at 1313 Sherman St., Suite 618, Denver, CO 80203 (© **303/866-3437;** www.parks.state.co.us). State park offices can also provide information on boating and snowmobiling.

2 Money

Generally, Colorado is not particularly expensive, especially compared to destinations on the East and West coasts. In Denver, Boulder, and Colorado Springs, you'll find a wide range of prices for lodging and dining; admission to most attractions is less than $10 (it's sometimes free, especially in Boulder). Those traveling away from the major cities will discover prices in small towns are usually quite reasonable, but ski resorts such as Vail and Aspen can be rather pricey, especially during winter holidays. Traveler's checks and credit cards are accepted at almost all hotels, restaurants, shops, and attractions, plus many grocery stores; and automated teller machines for all the major national networks are practically everywhere.

Destination: Denver, Boulder, Colorado Springs— Red Alert Checklist

- Some attractions (such as the U.S. Mint and the top of the dome in the Colorado State Capitol in Denver, and the U.S. Air Force Academy and Peterson Air & Space Museum in Colorado Springs) have been closed for security reasons, and are reopening slowly or with special restrictions. Call ahead for specifics.
- If you want to attend a Denver Broncos game, call early—home games sell out months ahead.
- If you purchased traveler's checks, have you recorded the check numbers and stored the documentation separately from the checks?
- Did you pack your camera and an extra set of camera batteries, and purchase enough film? If you packed film in your checked baggage, did you invest in protective pouches to shield film from airport X-rays?
- Do you have a safe, accessible place to store money?
- Did you bring your ID cards that could entitle you to discounts, such as AAA and AARP cards and student IDs?
- Did you bring emergency drug prescriptions and extra glasses or contact lenses?
- Do you have your credit card personal identification numbers (PINs)?
- If you have an e-ticket, do you have documentation?
- Did you leave a copy of your itinerary with someone at home?

ATMs

The easiest and best way to get cash away from home is from an ATM (automated teller machine). The **Cirrus** (© **800/424-7787**; www.mastercard.com) and **PLUS** (© **800/843-7587**; www.visa.com) networks span the globe; look at the back of your bank card to see which network you're on, then call or check online for ATM locations at your destination. Be sure you know your personal identification number (PIN) before you leave home and be sure to find out your daily withdrawal limit before you depart. Also keep in mind that many banks impose a fee every time a card is used at a different bank's ATM, and that fee can be higher for international transactions (up to $5 or more) than for domestic ones (where they're rarely more than $1.50). On top of this, the bank from which you withdraw cash may charge its own fee. To compare banks' ATM fees within the U.S., use www.bankrate.com. For international withdrawal fees, ask your bank.

You can also get cash advances on your credit card at an ATM. Keep in mind that credit card companies try to protect themselves from theft by limiting the funds someone can withdraw outside their home country, so call your credit card company before you leave home.

TRAVELER'S CHECKS

Traveler's checks are something of an anachronism from the days before the ATM made cash accessible at any time. Traveler's checks used to be the only sound alternative to traveling with dangerously large amounts of cash. They were as reliable as currency, but, unlike cash, could be replaced if lost or stolen.

> **Tips Small Change**
>
> When you change money, ask for some small bills or loose change. Petty cash will come in handy for tipping and public transportation. Consider keeping the change separate from your larger bills, so that it's readily accessible and you'll be less of a target for theft.

These days, traveler's checks are less necessary because most cities have 24-hour ATMs that allow you to withdraw small amounts of cash as needed. However, keep in mind that you will likely be charged an ATM withdrawal fee if the bank is not your own, so if you're withdrawing money every day, you might be better off with traveler's checks—provided that you don't mind showing identification every time you want to cash one.

You can get traveler's checks at almost any bank. **American Express** offers denominations of $20, $50, $100, $500, and (for cardholders only) $1,000. You'll pay a service charge ranging from 1% to 4%. You can also get American Express traveler's checks over the phone by calling ✆ **800/221-7282;** Amex gold and platinum cardholders who use this number are exempt from the 1% fee. AAA members can obtain checks without a fee at most AAA offices.

Visa offers traveler's checks at Citibank locations nationwide, as well as at several other banks. The service charge ranges between 1.5% and 2%; checks come in denominations of $20, $50, $100, $500, and $1,000. Call ✆ **800/732-1322** for information. **MasterCard** also offers traveler's checks. Call ✆ **800/223-9920** for a location near you.

If you choose to carry traveler's checks, be sure to keep a record of their serial numbers separate from your checks in the event that they are stolen or lost. You'll get a refund faster if you know the numbers.

CREDIT CARDS

Credit cards are a safe way to carry money, they provide a convenient record of all your expenses, and they generally offer good exchange rates. You can also withdraw cash advances from your credit cards at banks or ATMs, provided you know your PIN. If you've forgotten yours, or didn't even know you had one, call the number on the back of your credit card and ask the bank to send it to you. It usually takes 5 to 7 business days, though some banks will provide the number over the phone if you tell them your mother's maiden name or some other personal information.

For tips and telephone numbers to call if your wallet is stolen or lost, go to "Lost & Found" in the Fast Facts section of this chapter.

Practically all businesses in Colorado's major cities accept MasterCard and Visa, and many also accept American Express and Discover. Large hotels and restaurants also often accept Diners Club.

3 When to Go

Colorado has two tourist seasons: warm and cold. Those who want to see the state's parks and other scenic wonders, hike, mountain-bike, or raft will usually visit from May through

October; those who prefer skiing, snowboarding, and snowmobiling will obviously have to wait for winter, usually from late November through March or April, depending on snow

> **⌐Tips Dear Visa: I'm Off to Kilarnney!**
>
> Some credit card companies recommend that you notify them of any impending trip abroad so that they don't become suspicious when the card is used numerous times in a foreign destination and your charges are blocked. Even if you don't call your credit card company in advance, you can always call the card's toll-free emergency number (see "Fast Facts," later in this chapter) if a charge is refused—a good reason to carry the phone number with you. But perhaps the most important lesson here is to carry more than one card with you on your trip; a card might not work for any number of reasons, so having a backup is the smart way to go.

levels. Although you can visit most major museums year-round, some, especially in smaller communities, close in winter. The best way to avoid crowds at the more popular destinations is to try to visit from March through May and October through mid-December.

To hear Coloradans tell it, the state has perfect weather all the time. Although they may be exaggerating just a bit, the weather is usually quite pleasant, with an abundance of sun and relatively mild temperatures in most places—just avoid those winter snowstorms that come sweeping out of the mountains.

Along the Front Range, including Denver, Boulder, and Colorado Springs, summers are hot and dry, with mild evenings and cool nights. Humidity is low, and temperatures seldom rise above the 90s. Evenings start to get cooler by mid-September, but even as late as November the days are often sunny and warm. Surprisingly, winters are milder and less snowy than those in the Great Lakes region or New England; many golf courses remain open year-round. The accompanying chart lists average temperatures and precipitation for Denver and Colorado Springs; Denver and Boulder are so close that their statistics are virtually identical.

Average Monthly High/Low Temperatures (°F & °C) & Precipitation (Inches):

		Jan	Feb	Mar	Apr	May	June	July	Aug	Sept	Oct	Nov	Dec
Denver	Temp. (°F)	43/16	47/20	52/26	62/35	71/44	81/52	88/59	86/57	77/48	66/36	53/25	45/17
	Temp. (°C)	6/–9	8/–7	11/–3	17/2	22/7	27/11	31/15	30/14	25/9	19/2	12/–4	7/–8
	Precip. (in.)	0.5	0.6	1.3	1.7	2.4	1.8	1.9	1.5	1.2	1.0	0.9	0.6
elev. 5,280'													
Colorado	Temp. (°F)	41/16	45/20	49/24	60/33	69/43	80/52	85/57	82/56	75/47	66/37	50/25	44/19
Springs	Temp. (°C)	5/–9	7/–7	9/–4	16/1	21/6	27/11	29/14	28/13	24/8	19/3	10/–4	7/–7
	Precip. (in.)	0.3	0.4	0.9	1.2	2.2	2.3	2.9	3.0	1.3	0.8	0.5	0.5
elev. 6.035'													

Most of Colorado is considered semiarid, and overall the state has almost 300 sunny days a year—more sunshine than San Diego or Miami Beach. The prairies average about 16 inches of precipitation annually; the Front Range, 14 inches; the western slope, only 8 inches. Rain, when it falls, is commonly a short deluge—a summer afternoon thunderstorm. However, if you want to see snow, simply head to the mountains, where snowfall is measured in feet instead of inches, and mountain peaks may still be white in July. Mountain temperatures can be bitterly cold, especially if

Lighten Up

Denver has more days of sunshine each year than San Diego or Miami Beach.

---

it's windy, but even at the higher elevations of Colorado's top ski resorts, you'll find plenty of sunshine.

CALENDAR OF EVENTS

Below are some of the major annual events in Denver, Boulder, Colorado Springs, and the surrounding area. You'll find additional events on the Internet at **www.colorado. com** and **www.coloradofestival.com**, as well as on each city's website. We strongly recommend, however, that if a particular event is especially important to your visit, you confirm the date by telephone before you leave home.

January

- **Great Fruitcake Toss,** Colorado Springs. This zany event, where contestants compete to see who can throw a fruitcake the farthest, has been covered by national media and is among the most outlandish and festive spectacles of the year. It takes place in Manitou Springs' Memorial Park, 5 miles west of downtown Colorado Springs. Call ✆ **800/642-2567** or 719/685-5089 for more information. Early January.

- **Mahlerfest,** Boulder. This may be the only festival celebrating the work of Gustav Mahler. Attend a full orchestra concert, free chamber concerts, or the free symposium. Call ✆ **303/447-0513** or visit www.mahlerfest.org for more information. Early January.

- **National Western Stock Show and Rodeo,** Denver. This is the world's largest livestock show and indoor rodeo, with about two dozen rodeo performances, a trade exposition, Western food and crafts booths, and livestock auctions. Call ✆ **303/297-1166** for details. Second and third weeks in January.

- **Boulder Bach Festival,** Boulder. Music of the master baroque composer. Call ✆ **303/652-9101** or visit www.boulderbachfest.org for details. Last weekend in January.

February

- **Buffalo Bill's Birthday Celebration,** Golden. Ceremonies and live entertainment that commemorate the life of the legendary scout and entertainer take place at the Buffalo Bill Memorial Museum. Call ✆ **303/526-0744** or 303/526-0747 or check www. buffalobill.org for further information. Late February.

March

- **Colorado Springs Dance Theatre Wine Festival,** Colorado Springs. Sample the best wines at this 3-day benefit for the Colorado Springs Dance Theatre. Call ✆ **719/630-7434** for further information. Early March.

- **Pow Wow,** Denver. More than 1,500 American Indians (as well as 60 drum groups), representing some 85 tribes from 32 states, perform traditional music and dances. Arts and crafts are also sold. Call ✆ **303/934-8045** for details. Mid-March.

- **Saint Patrick's Day,** Denver. Among the largest Irish holiday parades in the United States, with floats, marching bands, and more than 5,000 horses. Call ✆ **303/ 892-1112** for further information. Saturday before March 17.

April

- **Easter Sunrise Service,** Colorado Springs and Denver. Worshippers watch the rising sun light red sandstone formations in the Garden of the Gods in Colorado

Springs. For details, call ℭ **719/ 634-3144.** Denver's Easter Sunrise Service takes place at Red Rocks Amphitheatre, also in the midst of stunning geological formations. Call ℭ **303/295-4444** or visit **www.redrocksonline.com** for further information. Easter Sunday.

May

• **Cinco de Mayo,** Denver and Colorado Springs. More than 250,000 people from around the Denver metro area celebrate this annual Hispanic event centered on north Federal Boulevard with mariachi bands, dancers, Mexican food, and other activities. Call ℭ **303/534-8342** for information. Memorial Park is the site for the Colorado Springs celebration. Call ℭ **719/635-5001** for information. May 5.

• **Plant and Book Sale,** Denver. The largest volunteer-run plant and book sale in the nation, this event at Denver Botanic Gardens offers more than 250,000 plants, thousands of new and used books, and free gardening advice. Call ℭ **720/865-3500** or visit www. botanicgardens.org for details. Early May.

• **Boulder Kinetic Fest,** Boulder. A wacky event that's a real crowd pleaser. Most years an average of 70 teams race over land and water at Boulder Reservoir in a variety of imaginative human-powered conveyances. Activities include the kinetic parade, kinetic concerts, the kinetic ball, and a hot-air-balloon launch. Call ℭ **303/ 444-5600** for details. Early May.

• **Bolder Boulder,** Boulder. This footrace attracts some 40,000 entrants each year, plus numerous spectators. Participants walk, jog, or run the 10K course. Call ℭ **303/444-RACE** or visit www.

bolderboulder.com for details. Memorial Day.

June

• **International Buskerfest,** Denver. An international street performers' festival featuring amazing shows by world-class jugglers, sword swallowers, magicians, tightrope artists, mimes, and acrobats! Call ℭ **303/478-7878** or go to www.buskerfest.com for more information. Mid-June.

• **Wool Market,** Estes Park. This huge natural-fiber show boasts contests, demonstrations, a children's tent, and sale of animals plus products made from their wool. Kids love it. Call ℭ **970/ 586-5800** or go to www.estes net.com for details. Mid-June.

• **Colorado Shakespeare Festival,** Boulder. Considered among the top Shakespeare festivals in the country, with most performances in an outdoor theater. Call ℭ **303/ 492-0554** for details. Late June through late August.

• **Garden Concerts,** Denver. Jazz, blues, and folk concerts take place in the outdoor amphitheater at **Denver Botanic Gardens.** Call ℭ **720/865-3500** or visit www. botanicgardens.org for information. June through September.

July

• **Pikes Peak Auto Hill Climb,** Colorado Springs. This "race to the clouds," held annually since 1916, takes drivers to the top of 14,110-foot Pikes Peak. Call ℭ **719/685-4400** for additional information. Saturday close to July 4th.

• **Rooftop Rodeo & Parade,** Estes Park. Award-winning rodeos Tuesday through Sunday evenings. A grand parade kicks it all off on Tuesday morning. Call ℭ **970/ 586-5800** or visit www.estesnet. com for details. Mid-July.

- **Art Fair,** Boulder. Some 150 local and regional artists display their works in downtown Boulder, offering "fine art to fun art" plus live musical performances. Call ℭ **303/449-3774** or visit www.boulderdowntown.com for more information. Third weekend in July.
- **Buffalo Bill Days,** Golden. A parade, kids' rides, burro race, arts and crafts displays, petting zoo, car show, and a pancake breakfast mark Golden's largest event. Call ℭ **303/384-0003** or visit www.buffalobilldays.com for more information. Late July.

August

- **Pikes Peak or Bust Rodeo,** Colorado Springs. Colorado's largest outdoor rodeo, and a popular stop on the professional rodeo circuit. Call ℭ **719/635-3547** or visit www.coloradospringsrodeo.org for details. Early August.
- **Colorado State Fair,** Pueblo. National professional rodeo, carnival rides, food booths, industrial displays, horse shows, animal exhibits, and entertainment by top-name performers. Call ℭ **800/876-4567,** ext. 2028, or visit www.coloradostatefair.com for additional information. Mid-August through Labor Day.

September

- **Colorado Springs Balloon Classic,** Colorado Springs. More than 100 colorful hot-air balloons launch from Memorial Park, making this one of the largest balloon rallies in the country. Call ℭ **719/471-4833** or visit www.balloonclassic.com for more information. Labor Day weekend.
- **A Taste of Colorado,** Denver. This is Denver's largest celebration, with an annual attendance of about 400,000. Local restaurants serve house specialties; there are also crafts exhibits and free concerts. Call ℭ **303/295-6330** or visit www.atasteofcolorado.com for details. Labor Day weekend.
- **Colorado Performing Arts Festival,** Denver. This celebration of performing arts, which takes place at the Denver Performing Arts Complex, includes dance, music, theater, and storytelling. Call ℭ **303/640-6943** or visit www.denvergov.org/performingartsfest for information. Mid-September.
- **Fall Festival,** Boulder. An Oktoberfest celebration in downtown Boulder, this festival includes polka bands, food, carnival rides, and an art fair. Call ℭ **303/449-3774** or visit www.boulderdowntown.com for more information. Late September or early October.

October

- **Great American Beer Festival,** Denver. Hundreds of American beers are available for sampling, and seminars are presented at what is considered the largest and most prestigious beer event in the United States. Call ℭ **303/447-0816** or visit www.beertown.org for information. Early October.
- **Pumpkin Festival,** Denver. This family event, sponsored by Denver Botanic Gardens and held at Chatfield Nature Preserve southwest of town, includes pumpkin picking, food, crafts, hayrides, and other activities. Call ℭ **720/865-3500** or visit www.botanicgardens.org for details. Mid-October.

November

- **Holiday Gift & Garden Market,** Denver. Handmade Christmas ornaments, gifts, dried-flower arrangements, and food items are among the unique merchandise at this annual sale at Denver Botanic Gardens. Call ℭ **720/865-3500** or visit www.botanicgardens.org for information. Mid-November.

Tips **Quick ID**

Tie a colorful ribbon or piece of yarn around your luggage handle, or slap a distinctive sticker on the side of your bag. This makes it less likely that someone will mistakenly appropriate it. And if your luggage gets lost, it will be easier to find.

December

- **World's Largest Christmas Lighting Display,** Denver. Some 40,000 colored floodlights illuminate the Denver City and County Building. All month.
- **Blossoms of Light,** Denver. Over 12,000 sparkling lights cascade through the Botanic Gardens. Grand topiaries, nightly entertainment, "kissing spots," whimsical displays, and warm treats make for an unforgettable winter evening. Call ✆ **303/865-3500** or visit www.botanicgardens.org for information. All month.
- **Parade of Lights,** Denver. A holiday parade winds through downtown Denver, with floats, balloons, and marching bands. Call ✆ **303/478-7878** or visit www.denverparadeoflights.com for information. Early December.
- **Festival of Lights Parade,** Colorado Springs. A nighttime parade kicks off this month-long celebration of the holidays. Features include decorated live trees and holiday scenes from cultures around the world. Call ✆ **719/ 634-5581** or visit www.csfinearts center.org for information. Early December.
- **Christmas with Cody,** Golden. Buffalo Bill Cody playing Santa? He sure did, and a reenactor continues the tradition, with gifts for the kids at the Buffalo Bill Memorial Museum. Call ✆ **303/526-0744** or 303/526-0747 or check www.buffalobill.org for further information. First Sunday in December.
- **Olde Golden Christmas,** Golden. Come to Golden for an old-fashioned candlelight walk on the first Friday in December, and stay for weekend festivities throughout the town. Call ✆ **303/279-3113** or visit www.goldencochamber.org for information. Begins in early December.
- **Pikes Peak Summit Fireworks,** Colorado Springs. A wondrous fireworks display to ring in the New Year. Call (✆ **800/888-4748** or 719/635-7506 or check out www.coloradosprings-travel.com. December 31.

---

4 Travel Insurance

Check your existing insurance policies and credit card coverage before you buy travel insurance. You may already be covered for lost luggage, cancelled tickets, or medical expenses. The cost of travel insurance varies widely, depending on the cost and length of your trip, your age, health, and the type of trip you're taking.

TRIP-CANCELLATION INSURANCE

Trip-cancellation insurance helps you get your money back if you have to back out of a trip, if you have to go home early, or if your travel supplier goes bankrupt. Allowed reasons for cancellation can range from sickness to natural disasters to the State

Department declaring your destination unsafe for travel. (Insurers usually won't cover vague fears, though, as many travelers discovered who tried to cancel their trips in October 2001 because they were wary of flying.) Trip-cancellation insurance is a good buy if you're getting tickets well in advance—who knows what the state of the world, or of your airline, will be in 9 months? Insurance policy details vary, so read the fine print—and especially make sure that your airline or cruise line is on the list of carriers covered in case of bankruptcy. For information, contact one of the following insurers: **Access America** (② 866/ 807-3982; www.accessamerica.com); **Travel Guard International** (② 800/ 826-4919; www.travelguard.com); **Travel Insured International** (② 800/ 243-3174; www.travelinsured.com); and **Travelex Insurance Services** (② 888/457-4602; www.travelex-insurance.com).

MEDICAL INSURANCE

Most health insurance policies cover you if you get sick away from home—but check, particularly if you're insured by an HMO.

LOST-LUGGAGE INSURANCE

On domestic flights, checked baggage is covered up to $2,500 per ticketed passenger. On international flights (including U.S. portions of international trips), baggage is limited to approximately $9.07 per pound, up to approximately $635 per checked bag. If you plan to check items more valuable than the standard liability, see if your valuables are covered by your homeowner's policy, get baggage insurance as part of your comprehensive travel-insurance package, or buy Travel Guard's "BagTrak" product. Don't buy insurance at the airport, as it's usually overpriced. Be sure to take any valuables or irreplaceable items with you in your carry-on luggage, as many valuables (including books, money, and electronics) aren't covered by airline policies.

If your luggage is lost, immediately file a lost-luggage claim at the airport, detailing the luggage contents. For most airlines, you must report delayed, damaged, or lost baggage within 4 hours of arrival. The airlines are required to deliver luggage, once found, directly to your house or destination free of charge.

5 Health & Safety

STAYING HEALTHY

About two-thirds of Colorado is more than a mile above sea level, which means there is less oxygen and lower humidity than many travelers are accustomed to. This creates a unique set of problems for short-term visitors, such as the possibility of shortness of breath, fatigue, and other physical concerns.

Those not used to higher elevations should get sufficient rest, avoid large meals, and drink plenty of nonalcoholic fluids, especially water. Individuals with heart or respiratory problems should consult their personal physicians before planning a trip to the Colorado mountains. Those in generally

good health need not take any special precautions, but it is best to ease the transition to high elevations by changing altitude gradually. For instance, spend a night or two in Denver (elevation 5,280 ft.) or Colorado Springs (elevation 6,035 ft.) before driving or taking the cog railway to the top of Pikes Peak (elevation 14,110 ft.).

Lowlanders can also help their bodies adjust to higher elevations by taking it easy for their first few days in the mountains, cutting down on cigarettes and alcohol, and avoiding sleeping pills and other drugs. Your doctor can provide prescription drugs to help prevent and relieve symptoms of altitude sickness.

Because the sun's rays are more direct in the thinner atmosphere, they cause sunburn more quickly. The potential for skin damage increases when the sun reflects off snow or water. A good sunblock is strongly recommended, as are good-quality ultraviolet-blocking sunglasses. Remember that children need more protection than adults.

COMMON AILMENTS

HANTAVIRUS State health officials warn outdoor enthusiasts to take precautions against the Hantavirus, a rare but often fatal respiratory disease first recognized in 1993. About half of the country's confirmed cases have been reported in the Four Corners states of Colorado, New Mexico, Arizona, and Utah. The disease is usually spread by the urine and droppings of deer mice and other rodents, and health officials recommend that campers avoid areas with signs of rodent droppings. Symptoms of Hantavirus are similar to flu and lead to breathing difficulties and shock.

WEST NILE VIRUS Colorado is also one of the worst places in the United States for the West Nile virus, reporting more than 3,000 of the 9,800 cases of infection in the U.S. during 2003. The best prevention is mosquito repellant and keeping mosquito populations across the state in check. The virus can be fatal, but is typically not. Symptoms include fever, headache, and body aches.

WHAT TO DO IF YOU GET SICK AWAY FROM HOME

You'll find excellent hospitals in all of Colorado's major cities, and in most cases, your existing health plan will provide the coverage you need. But double-check; you may want to buy **travel medical insurance** instead. (See the section on insurance, above.) Bring your insurance ID card with you when you travel.

If you suffer from a chronic illness, consult your doctor before your departure. For conditions like epilepsy, diabetes, or heart problems, wear a **Medic Alert Identification Tag** (© 800/825-3785; www.medicalert. org), which will immediately alert doctors to your condition and give them access to your records through Medic Alert's 24-hour hotline.

Pack **prescription medications** in your carry-on luggage, and carry prescription medications in their original containers, with pharmacy labels—otherwise they won't make it through airport security. Also bring along copies of your prescriptions in case you lose your pills or run out. Don't forget an extra pair of contact lenses or prescription glasses.

STAYING SAFE

While there are many reasons to visit Colorado and its major cities, two of the reasons most often cited are its historic sites and magnificent outdoor activities. However, visiting historic sites and participating in outdoor activities can lead to accidents.

When visiting such historic sites as ghost towns, gold mines, and railroads, keep in mind that they were probably built more than 100 years ago, at a time when safety standards were extremely lax, if they existed at all. Never enter abandoned buildings, mines, or railroad equipment on your own. When you're visiting commercially operated historic tourist attractions, use common sense and don't be afraid to ask questions.

High & Mighty

Colorado boasts 75% of the land in the continental United States above 10,000 feet in elevation.

Walkways in mines are often uneven and poorly lit, and are sometimes slippery due to seeping groundwater that can also stain your clothing with its high iron content. When entering old buildings, be prepared for steep, narrow stairways, creaky floors, and low ceilings and doorways. Steam trains are a wonderful experience as long as you remember that steam is very hot, and that oil and grease can ruin your clothing.

When heading to the great outdoors, keep in mind that injuries often occur when people fail to follow instructions. Pay attention when the experts tell you to stay on established ski trails, hike only in designated areas, carry rain gear, and wear a life jacket when rafting. Mountain weather can be fickle, and many of the most beautiful spots are in remote areas. Be prepared for extreme changes in temperature at any time of year, and watch out for sudden summer-afternoon thunderstorms that can leave you drenched and shivering in minutes.

6 Specialized Travel Resources

TRAVELERS WITH DISABILITIES

Most disabilities shouldn't stop anyone from traveling. There are more options and resources out there than ever before. Travelers with disabilities will find the cities of Colorado fairly accessible, although some historic buildings are not wheelchair accessible, so you should check before going.

The U.S. National Park Service offers a **Golden Access Passport** that gives free lifetime entrance to all properties administered by the National Park Service—national parks, monuments, historic sites, recreation areas, and national wildlife refuges—for persons who are blind or permanently disabled, regardless of age. You may pick up a Golden Access Passport at any NPS entrance-fee area by showing proof of medically determined disability and eligibility for receiving benefits under federal law. Besides free entry, the Golden Access Passport also offers a 50% discount on federal-use fees charged for such facilities as camping, swimming, parking, boat launching, and tours. For more information, go to www.nps.gov/fees_passes.htm or call © 888/467-2757.

Many travel agencies offer customized tours and itineraries for travelers with disabilities. **Flying Wheels Travel** (© 507/451-5005; www.flyingwheelstravel.com) offers escorted tours and cruises that emphasize sports and private tours in minivans with lifts. **Accessible Journeys** (© 800/846-4537 or 610/521-0339; www.disabilitytravel.com) caters specifically to slow walkers and wheelchair travelers and their families and friends.

Organizations that offer assistance to travelers with disabilities include the **MossRehab Hospital** (www.mossresourcenet.org), which provides a library of accessible-travel resources online; the **Society for Accessible Travel and Hospitality** (© 212/447-7284; www.sath.org; annual membership fees: $45 adults, $30 seniors and students), which offers a wealth of travel resources for all types of disabilities and informed recommendations on destinations, access guides, travel agents, tour operators, vehicle rentals, and companion services; and the **American Foundation for the Blind** (© 800/232-5463; www.afb.org), which provides information on traveling with Seeing Eye dogs.

For more information specifically targeted to travelers with disabilities, the community website **iCan** (www.icanonline.net/channels/travel/index.cfm) has destination guides and several regular columns on accessible travel.

Also check out the quarterly magazine *Emerging Horizons* ($14.95 per year, $19.95 outside the U.S.; www.emerginghorizons.com); **Twin Peaks Press** (© 360/694-2462), offering travel-related books for travelers with special needs; and *Open World Magazine,* published by the Society for Accessible Travel and Hospitality (see above; subscription: $18 per year, $35 outside the U.S.).

GAY & LESBIAN TRAVELERS

In general, gay and lesbian travelers will find they are treated just like any other travelers in Colorado. Even cities such as Colorado Springs, home of Focus on the Family and other conservative groups, have become somewhat more open-minded about alternative lifestyles recently. Those with specific concerns can contact **Gay, Lesbian, Bisexual, and Transgender Community Services Center of Colorado** (© 303/733-7743) in Denver; the organization can also provide information on events and venues of interest to gay and lesbian visitors.

The International Gay & Lesbian Travel Association (IGLTA) (© 800/448-8550 or 954/776-2626; www.iglta.org) is the trade association for the gay and lesbian travel industry, and offers an online directory of gay- and lesbian-friendly travel businesses; go to their website and click on "Members."

Many agencies offer tours and travel itineraries specifically for gay and lesbian travelers. **Above and Beyond Tours** (© 800/397-2681; www.abovebeyondtours.com) is the exclusive gay and lesbian tour operator for United Airlines. **Now, Voyager** (© 800/255-6951; www.nowvoyager.com) is a well-known San Francisco–based gay-owned and operated travel service. **Olivia Cruises & Resorts** (© 800/631-6277 or 510/655-0364; www.olivia.com) charters entire resorts and ships for exclusive lesbian vacations and offers smaller group experiences for both gay and lesbian travelers.

The following travel guides are available at most travel bookstores and gay and lesbian bookstores, or you can order them from **Giovanni's Room** bookstore, 1145 Pine St., Philadelphia, PA 19107 (© 215/923-2960; www.giovannisroom.com): *Frommer's Gay & Lesbian Europe,* an excellent travel resource; *Out and About* (© 800/929-2268 or 415/644-8044; www.outandabout.com), which offers guidebooks and a newsletter 10 times a year packed with solid information on the global gay and lesbian scene; *Spartacus International Gay Guide* and *Odysseus,* both good, annual English-language guidebooks focused on gay men; the *Damron* guides, with separate, annual books for gay men and lesbians; and *Gay Travel A to Z: The World of Gay & Lesbian Travel Options at Your Fingertips* by Marianne Ferrari (Ferrari Publications; Box 35575, Phoenix, AZ 85069), a very good gay and lesbian guidebook series.

SENIOR TRAVEL

Mention the fact that you're a senior citizen when you first make your travel reservations. Although all of the major U.S. airlines except America West have cancelled their senior discount and coupon book programs, many hotels still offer discounts for seniors. In most cities, people over the age of 60 (sometimes 62 or 65) qualify for reduced admission to theaters, museums, and other attractions, as well as discounted fares on public transportation.

Many Colorado hotels and motels offer special rates to senior citizens, and an increasing number of restaurants, attractions, and public transportation systems offer discounts as well, some for "oldsters" as young as 55.

Members of **AARP** (formerly known as the American Association of Retired Persons), 601 E St. NW,

Washington, DC 20049 (© **800/ 424-3410** or 202/434-2277; www. aarp.org), get discounts on hotels, air-fares, and car rentals. AARP offers members a wide range of benefits, including *AARP: The Magazine* and a monthly newsletter. Anyone over 50 can join.

The **U.S. National Park Service** offers a **Golden Age Passport** that gives seniors 62 years or older lifetime entrance to all properties administered by the National Park Service—national parks, monuments, historic sites, recreation areas, and national wildlife refuges—for a one-time pro-cessing fee of $10, which must be pur-chased in person at any NPS facility that charges an entrance fee. Besides free entry, a Golden Age Passport also offers a 50% discount on federal-use fees charged for such facilities as camping, swimming, parking, boat launching, and tours. For more infor-mation, go to www.nps.gov/fees_ passes.htm or call © **888/467-2757.**

Many reliable agencies and organi-zations target the 50-plus market. **Elderhostel** (© **877/426-8056;** www. elderhostel.org) arranges study pro-grams for those aged 55 and over (and a spouse or companion of any age) in the U.S. and in more than 80 coun-tries around the world. Most courses last 5 to 7 days in the U.S. (2–4 weeks abroad), and many include airfare, accommodations in university dormi-tories or modest inns, meals, and tuition. **ElderTreks** (© **800/741-7956;** www.eldertreks.com) offers small-group tours to off-the-beaten-path or adventure-travel locations, restricted to travelers 50 and older.

Recommended publications offer-ing travel resources and discounts for seniors include: the quarterly maga-zine *Travel 50 & Beyond* (www.travel 50andbeyond.com); *Travel Unlim-ited: Uncommon Adventures for the Mature Traveler* (Avalon); *101 Tips for Mature Travelers,* available from Grand Circle Travel (© **800/221-2610** or 617/350-7500; www.gct. com); *The 50+ Traveler's Guidebook* (St. Martin's Press); and *Unbelievably Good Deals and Great Adventures That You Absolutely Can't Get Unless You're Over 50* (McGraw Hill).

TRAVELING WITH PETS

Many of us wouldn't dream of going on vacation without our pets. Under the right circumstances, it can be a wonderful experience for both you and your animals. Dogs and cats are accepted at many lodgings in Col-orado, but not as universally in resorts and at the more expensive hotels. Throughout this book, we've tried to consistently note those lodgings that take pets. Some properties require you to pay a fee or damage deposit in advance, and most insist they be noti-fied at check-in that you have a pet.

Be aware, however, that national parks and monuments and other fed-eral lands administered by the National Park Service are not pet-friendly. Dogs are usually prohibited on all hiking trails, must always be leashed, and in some cases cannot be taken more than 100 feet from estab-lished roads. On the other hand, U.S. Forest Service and Bureau of Land Management areas and most state parks are pro-pet, allowing dogs on trails and just about everywhere except inside buildings. State parks require that dogs be leashed; regulations in national forests and BLM lands are generally looser.

Aside from regulations, though, you need to be concerned with your pet's well-being. Just as people need extra water in Colorado's dry climate, so do pets. We especially like those clever spill-resistant travel water bowls sold in pet shops. And keep in mind that many trails are rough, and jagged rocks can cut the pads on your dog's feet.

> **Tips   The Peripatetic Pet**
>
> Never leave your pet inside a parked car with the windows rolled up. It's never a good idea to leave a pet inside a hot car, even with the windows rolled down, for any length of time.
>
>   Make sure your pet is wearing a name tag with the name and phone number of a contact person who can take the call if your pet gets lost while you're away from home.

An excellent resource is www.pets welcome.com, which dispenses medical tips, names of animal-friendly lodgings and campgrounds, and lists of kennels and veterinarians. Also check out *The Portable Petswelcome. com: The Complete Guide to Traveling with Your Pet* (Howell Book House), which features the best selection of pet travel information anywhere. Another resource is *Canine Colorado: Where to Go and What to Do with Your Dog* (Fulcrum Publishing).

If you plan to fly with your pet, the FAA has compiled a list of all requirements for transporting live animals at http://airconsumer.ost.dot.gov/ publications/animals.htm. You may be able to carry your pet onboard a plane if it's small enough to put inside a carrier that can slip under the seat. Pets usually count as one piece of carry-on luggage. Note that many airlines will not check pets as baggage in the hot summer months. The ASPCA discourages travelers from checking pets as luggage at any time, as storage conditions on planes are loosely monitored, and fatal accidents are not unprecedented. Your other option is to ship your pet with a professional carrier, which can be expensive. Ask your veterinarian whether you should sedate your pet on a plane ride or give it anti-nausea medication. Never give your pet sedatives used by humans.

7 Planning Your Trip Online

SURFING FOR AIRFARES

The "big three" online travel agencies, **Travelocity.com**, **Expedia.com,** and **Orbitz.com**, sell most of the air tickets bought on the Internet. (Canadian travelers should try Travelocity.ca and expedia.ca; U.K. residents can go for expedia.co.uk and opodo.co.uk.) Each has different business deals with the airlines and may offer different fares on the same flights, so it's wise to shop around. Expedia and Travelocity will also send you **e-mail notification** when a cheap fare becomes available to your favorite destination. Of the smaller travel agency websites, **Side-Step** (www.sidestep.com) has gotten the best reviews from Frommer's authors. It's a browser add-on that purports to "search 140 sites at once," but in reality only beats competitors' fares as often as other sites do.

Also remember to check **airline websites,** especially those for low-fare carriers such as Southwest, JetBlue, AirTran, WestJet, or Ryanair, whose fares are often misreported or simply missing from travel agency websites. Even with major airlines, you can often shave a few bucks from a fare by booking directly through the airline and avoiding a travel agency's transaction fee. But you'll get these discounts only by **booking online:** Most airlines now offer online-only fares that even their phone agents know nothing about. For the websites of airlines that fly to and from your destination, go to "Getting There," later in this chapter.

Great **last-minute deals** are available through free weekly e-mail services provided directly by the airlines. Most of these are announced on Tuesday or Wednesday and must be purchased online. Most are only valid for travel that weekend, but some (such as Southwest's) can be booked weeks or months in advance. Sign up for weekly e-mail alerts at airline websites or check mega-sites that compile comprehensive lists of last-minute specials, such as **Smarter Living** (smarterliving.com). For last-minute trips, **site59.com** in the U.S. and **lastminute.com** in Europe often have better deals than the major-label sites.

If you're willing to give up some control over your flight details, use an **opaque fare service** like **Priceline** (www.priceline.com; www.priceline.co.uk for Europeans) or **Hotwire** (www.hotwire.com). Both offer rock-bottom prices in exchange for travel on a "mystery airline" at a mysterious time of day, often with a mysterious change of planes en route. The mystery airlines are all major, well-known carriers—and the possibility of being sent from Philadelphia to Chicago via Tampa is remote; the airlines' routing computers have gotten a lot better than they used to be. But your chances of getting a 6am or 11pm flight are pretty high. Hotwire tells you flight prices before you buy; Priceline usually has better deals than Hotwire, but you have to play their "name our price" game. If you're new at this, the helpful folks at **BiddingForTravel** (www.biddingfortravel.com) do a good job of demystifying Priceline's prices. Priceline and Hotwire are great for flights within North America and between the U.S. and Europe. But for flights to other parts of the world, consolidators will almost always beat their fares.

For much more about airfares and savvy air-travel tips and advice, pick up a copy of *Frommer's Fly Safe, Fly Smart* (Wiley Publishing, Inc.).

SURFING FOR HOTELS

Shopping online for hotels is much easier in the U.S., Canada, and certain parts of Europe than it is in the rest of the world. Of the "big three" sites, **Expedia** may be the best choice, thanks to its long list of special deals. **Travelocity** runs a close second. Hotel specialist sites **hotels.com** and **hotel discounts.com** are also reliable. An excellent free program, **TravelAxe** (www.travelaxe.net), can help you search multiple hotel sites at once, even ones you may never have heard of.

Booking lodging online in Denver, Boulder, and Colorado Springs (and throughout Colorado, for that matter) is generally easy. Most of the chamber of commerce and visitor bureau websites are lodging links, and most B&Bs in the area are members of Bed & Breakfast Innkeepers of Colorado, which has an excellent website: www.innsofcolorado.com.

Priceline and Hotwire are even better for hotels than for airfares; with both, you're allowed to pick the neighborhood and quality level of your hotel before offering up your money. Priceline's hotel product even covers Europe and Asia, though it's much better at getting five-star lodging for three-star prices than at finding anything at the bottom of the scale. *Note:* Hotwire overrates its hotels by one star—what Hotwire calls a four-star is a three-star anywhere else.

SURFING FOR RENTAL CARS

For booking rental cars online, the best deals are usually found at rental-car company websites, although all the major online travel agencies also offer rental-car reservations services. Priceline and Hotwire work well for rental cars, too; the only "mystery" is which major rental company you get, and for most travelers the difference between Hertz, Avis, and Budget is negligible.

Frommers.com: The Complete Travel Resource

For an excellent travel-planning resource, we highly recommend **Frommers.com** (www.frommers.com). We're a little biased, of course, but we guarantee that you'll find the travel tips, reviews, monthly vacation giveaways, and online-booking capabilities thoroughly indispensable. Among the special features are our popular **Message Boards,** where Frommer's readers post queries and share advice (sometimes even our authors show up to answer questions); **Frommers.com Newsletter,** for the latest travel bargains and insider travel secrets; and **Frommer's Destinations Section,** where you'll get expert travel tips, hotel and dining recommendations, and advice on the sights to see for more than 3,000 destinations around the globe. When your research is done, the **Online Reservations System** (www.frommers.com/book_a_trip) takes you to Frommer's preferred online partners for booking your vacation at affordable prices.

8 The 21st-Century Traveler

INTERNET ACCESS AWAY FROM HOME

Travelers have any number of ways to check their e-mail and access the Internet on the road. Of course, using your own laptop—or even a PDA (personal digital assistant) or electronic organizer with a modem—gives you the most flexibility. But even if you don't have a computer, you can still access your e-mail and even your office computer from cybercafes.

WITHOUT YOUR OWN COMPUTER

It's hard nowadays to find a city that *doesn't* have a few cybercafes. Although there's no definitive directory for cybercafes—these are independent businesses, after all—three places to start looking are **www.cybercaptive. com**, **www.netcafeguide.com**, and **www.cybercafe.com**.

Aside from formal cybercafes, most **youth hostels** nowadays have at least one computer you can use to get onto the Internet. And most **public libraries** across the world offer Internet access free or for a small charge.

Avoid **hotel business centers,** which often charge exorbitant rates.

Most major airports now have **Internet kiosks** scattered throughout their gates. These kiosks, which you'll also see in shopping malls, hotel lobbies, and tourist information offices around the world, give you basic Web access for a per-minute fee that's usually higher than cybercafe prices. The kiosks' clunkiness and high price means they should be avoided whenever possible.

To retrieve your e-mail, ask your **Internet Service Provider (ISP)** if it has a Web-based interface tied to your existing e-mail account. If your ISP doesn't have such an interface, you can use the free **mail2web** service (www.mail2web.com) to view (but not reply to) your home e-mail. For more flexibility, you may want to open a free, Web-based e-mail account with **Yahoo! Mail** (http://mail.yahoo.com). (Microsoft's Hotmail is another popular option, but Hotmail has severe spam problems.) Your home ISP may be able to forward your e-mail to the Web-based account automatically.

If you need to access files on your office computer, look into a service called **GoToMyPC** (www.gotomypc. com). The service provides a Web-based interface for you to access and manipulate a distant PC from any-where—even a cybercafe—provided your "target" PC is on and has an always-on connection to the Internet (such as with Road Runner cable). The service offers top-quality security, but if you're worried about hackers, use your own laptop rather than a cybercafe to access the GoToMyPC system.

WITH YOUR OWN COMPUTER

Major Internet Service Providers (ISP) have **local access numbers** around the world, allowing you to go online by simply placing a local call. Check your ISP's website or call its toll-free number and ask how you can use your current account away from home, and how much it will cost.

Most business-class hotels offer dataports for laptop modems, and many properties in Colorado now offer high-speed Internet access using an Ethernet network cable. You'll have to bring your own cables either way, so **call your hotel in advance** to find out what the options are.

Many business-class hotels in the U.S. also offer a form of computer-free Web browsing through the room TV set. We've successfully checked Yahoo! Mail and Hotmail on these systems.

If you have an 802.11b/**Wi-fi** card for your computer, several commercial companies have made wireless service available in airports, hotel lobbies, and coffee shops, primarily in the U.S. **T-Mobile Hotspot** (www.t-mobile. com/hotspot) serves up wireless connections at more than 1,000 Starbucks coffee shops nationwide. **Boingo** (www.boingo.com) and **Wayport** (www.wayport.com) have set up networks in airports and high-class hotel lobbies. IPass providers (see above) also give you access to a few hundred wireless hotel lobby setups. Best of all, you don't need to be staying at the Four Seasons to use the hotel's network; just set yourself up on a nice couch in the lobby. Unfortunately, the companies' pricing policies are byzantine, with a variety of monthly, per-connection, and per-minute plans.

Community-minded individuals have also set up **free wireless networks** in major cities around the world. These networks are spotty, but you get what you (don't) pay for. Each network has a home page explaining how to set up your computer for their particular system; start your explorations at www.personaltelco.net/index.cgi/WirelessCommunities.

USING A CELLPHONE ACROSS THE U.S.

Just because your cellphone works at home doesn't mean it'll work elsewhere in the country (thanks to our nation's fragmented cellphone system). It's a good bet that your phone will work in major cities. But take a look at your wireless company's coverage map on its website before heading out—T-Mobile, Sprint, and Nextel are particularly weak in rural areas; Verizon and AT&T work pretty well in Colorado's major cities, but neither one is perfect. If you need to stay in touch at a destination where you know your phone won't work, **rent** a phone that does from **InTouch USA** (*©* **800/872-7626;** www.intouch global.com) or a rental car location, but beware that you'll pay $1 a minute or more for airtime.

If you're venturing deep into the mountains or backcountry, you may want to consider renting a **satellite phone ("satphones"),** which are different from cellphones in that they connect to satellites rather than ground-based towers. A satphone is more costly than a cellphone but works where there's no cellular signal and no towers. Unfortunately, you'll

Online Traveler's Toolbox

Veteran travelers usually carry some essential items to make their trips easier. Throughout this book you'll find websites pertinent to this part of Colorado. Following is a selection of other online tools to bookmark.

- **Visa ATM Locator** (www.visa.com), for locations of PLUS ATMs worldwide, or **MasterCard ATM Locator** (www.mastercard.com), for locations of Cirrus ATMs worldwide.
- **Intellicast** (www.intellicast.com) and **Weather.com** (www.weather.com). Give weather forecasts for all 50 states and for cities around the world.
- **Mapquest** (www.mapquest.com). This best of the mapping sites lets you choose a specific address or destination, and in seconds, it will return a map and detailed directions.
- **Universal Currency Converter** (www.xe.com/ucc). See what your dollar or pound is worth in more than 100 other countries.
- **Travel Warnings** (http://travel.state.gov/travel_warnings.html, www.fco.gov.uk/travel, www.voyage.gc.ca, www.dfat.gov.au/consular/advice). These sites report on places where health concerns or unrest might threaten American, British, Canadian, and Australian travelers. Generally, U.S. warnings are the most paranoid; Australian warnings are the most relaxed.

pay at least $2 per minute to use the phone, and it only works where you can see the horizon (i.e., usually not indoors). In North America, you can rent Iridium satellite phones from **RoadPost** (www.roadpost.com; © **888/290-1606** or 905/272-5665). InTouch USA (see above) offers a wider range of satphones but at higher rates. As of this writing, satphones were amazingly expensive to buy, so don't even think about it.

If you're not from the U.S., you'll be appalled at the poor reach of our **GSM (Global System for Mobiles) wireless network,** which is used by much of the rest of the world (see below). Your phone will probably work in most major U.S. cities; it definitely won't work in many rural areas. (To see where GSM phones work in the U.S., check out www.t-mobile.com/coverage/national_popup.asp.) And you may or may not be able to send SMS (text messaging) home—something Americans tend not to do anyway, for various cultural and technological reasons. (International budget travelers like to send text messages home because it's much cheaper than making international calls.) Assume nothing—call your wireless provider and get the full scoop. In a worst-case scenario, you can always rent a phone; InTouch USA delivers to hotels.

9 Getting There

BY CAR

An excellent road system, connecting to interstate highways heading in all directions, makes driving a good and economical choice. This is especially true for those planning excursions out of the Denver, Boulder, or Colorado Springs city limits. Although these cities have good public transportation within their boundaries, a car (either

> **Fun Fact Take the High Road**
>
> The world's highest automobile tunnel, the Eisenhower Tunnel, crosses the Continental Divide 65 miles west of Denver, at an elevation of 11,000 feet.

your own or a rental) is practically mandatory for those intent on getting out into the country.

Some 1,000 miles of interstate highways form a star on the map of Colorado, with its center at Denver. (See the state map in chapter 1.) **I-25** crosses the state from south to north, extending from New Mexico to Wyoming; over its 300 miles; it goes through nearly every major city of the Front Range, including Pueblo, Colorado Springs, Denver, and Fort Collins. **I-70** crosses from west to east, extending from Utah to Baltimore, Maryland. It enters Colorado near Grand Junction, passes through Glenwood Springs, Vail, and Denver, and exits just east of Burlington, a distance of about 450 miles. **I-76** is an additional 190-mile spur that begins in Denver and extends northeast to Nebraska, joining I-80 just beyond Julesburg.

Denver is about 1,025 miles from Los Angeles, 780 miles from Dallas, 600 miles from Kansas City, 510 miles from Salt Lake City, 440 miles from Albuquerque, 750 miles from Las Vegas, 820 miles from Phoenix, 1,010 miles from Chicago, and 1,800 miles from New York.

BY PLANE

Those flying to Colorado will probably land at Denver International Airport or Colorado Springs Airport. Both offer car rentals and shuttle services to their city's hotels.

Denver International Airport (DIA) is 23 miles northeast of downtown Denver, about a 35- to 45-minute drive. It is the sixth-busiest airport in the nation, with six runways and 94 gates. An information line (© **800/AIR-2-DEN;** TDD 800/688-1333; www.flydenver.com) provides data on flight schedules and connections, parking, ground transportation, current weather conditions, and local accommodations. The local airport information and paging number is © **303/342-2300.** Airlines serving Denver include **Air Canada** (© 888/247-2262; www.aircanada.ca), **Alaska Airlines** (© **877/502-5357;** www.alaskaair.com), **American** (© 800/433-7300; www.aa.com), **America West** (© 800/235-9292; www.americawest.com), **Continental** (© 800/525-0280; www.continental.com), **Delta** (© 800/221-1212; www.delta.com), **Frontier** (© 800/432-1359; www.frontierairlines.com), **Korean Air** (© 800/438-5000; www.koreanair.com), **Martinair** (© 800/366-4655; www.martinair.com), **Mesa** (© 800/637-2247; www.mesa-air.com), **Mexicana** (© 800/531-7921; www.mexicana.com), **Midwest Airlines** (© 800/452-2022; www.midwestairlines.com), **Northwest** (© 800/225-2525; www.nwa.com), **Sun Country** (© 800/359-6786; www.suncountry.com), **United and United Express** (© 800/241-6522; www.ual.com), and **US Airways** (© 800/428-4322; www.usair.com).

Colorado Springs Airport (© 719/550-1900), located in the southeast corner of Colorado Springs, has nearly 100 flights each day, with connections to most major U.S. cities. **American, America West, Continental, Mesa, Northwest,** and **United** serve Colorado Springs.

FLIGHTS FROM THE UNITED KINGDOM

British Airways (© **800/247-9297,** 0845/773-3377 in London; www. british-airways.com) offers one daily nonstop flight between London and Denver. Travelers from the United Kingdom can also take British Airways to other U.S. cities and make connecting flights to Denver or Colorado Springs.

GETTING INTO TOWN FROM THE AIRPORT

Bus, taxi, and limousine services shuttle travelers between the airport and downtown, and most major car-rental companies have outlets at the airport. Many major hotels are some distance from the airport, so travelers should check on the availability and cost of hotel shuttle services when making reservations.

The cost of a **city bus** ride from the airport to downtown Denver is $8; from the airport to Boulder and suburban Park-n-Ride lots, it is about $10. The **SuperShuttle** (© **800/525-3177** or 303/370-1300; www.super shuttle.com) provides transportation to and from a number of hotels downtown and in the Denver Tech Center. The **SuperShuttle** has frequent scheduled service between the airport and downtown hotels for $18 each way; door-to-door service is also available.

Taxi companies are another option, with fares generally in the $30-to-$50 range, and you can often share a cab and split the fare by calling the cab company ahead of time. For instance, **Yellow Cab** (© **303/777-7777**) will take up to five people from DIA to most downtown hotels for a flat rate of $43. **Metro Taxi** (© **303/333-3333**) is the other service in Denver.

GETTING THROUGH THE AIRPORT

With the federalization of airport security, security procedures at U.S. airports are more stable and consistent than ever. Generally, you'll be fine if you arrive at the airport **1 hour** before a domestic flight and **2 hours** before an international flight; if you show up late, tell an airline employee and he or she will probably whisk you to the front of the line.

Bring a **current, government-issued photo ID** such as a driver's license or passport, and if you've got an e-ticket, print out the **official confirmation page;** you'll need to show your confirmation at the security checkpoint, and your ID at the ticket counter or the gate. (Children under 18 do not need photo IDs for domestic flights, but the adults checking in with them need them.)

Security lines are getting shorter than they were during 2001 and 2002,

---

⌒Tips Don't Stow It—Ship It

If ease of travel is your main concern and money is no object, you can ship your luggage with one of the growing number of luggage-service companies that pick up, track, and deliver your luggage (often through couriers such as Federal Express) with minimum hassle for you. Traveling luggage-free may be ultra-convenient, but it's not cheap: One-way overnight shipping can cost from $100 to $200, depending on what you're sending. Still, for some people, especially seniors or the infirm, it's a sensible solution to lugging heavy baggage. Specialists in door-to-door luggage delivery are **Virtual Bellhop** (www.virtualbellhop.com), **SkyCap International** (www.skycapinternational.com), and **Luggage Express** (www.usxpluggageexpress.com).

but some doozies remain. If you have trouble standing for long periods of time, tell an airline employee; the airline will provide a wheelchair. Speed up security by **not wearing metal objects** such as big belt buckles or clanky earrings. If you've got metallic body parts, a note from your doctor can prevent a long chat with the security screeners. Keep in mind that only **ticketed passengers** are allowed past security, except for folks escorting passengers with disabilities or children.

Federalization has stabilized **what you can carry on** and **what you can't.** The general rule is that sharp things are out, nail clippers are okay, and food and beverages must be passed through the X-ray machine—but that security screeners can't make you drink from your coffee cup. Bring food in your carry-on rather than checking it, as explosive-detection machines used on checked luggage have been known to mistake food (especially chocolate, for some reason) for bombs. Travelers in the U.S. are allowed one carry-on bag, plus a "personal item" such as a purse, briefcase, or laptop bag. Carry-on hoarders can stuff all sorts of things into a laptop bag; as long as it has a laptop in it, it's still considered a personal item. The Transportation Security Administration (TSA) has issued a list of restricted items; check its website (www.tsa.gov/public/index.jsp) for details.

Passengers with e-tickets and without checked bags can beat the ticket-counter lines by using **electronic kiosks** or even **online check-in.** Ask your airline which alternatives are available, and if you're using a kiosk, bring the credit card you used to book the ticket. If you're checking bags, you will still be able to use most airlines' kiosks; again, call your airline for up-to-date information. **Curbside check-in** is also a good way to avoid lines, although a few airlines still ban curbside check-in entirely; call before you go.

FLYING FOR LESS: TIPS FOR GETTING THE BEST AIRFARE

Passengers sharing the same airplane cabin rarely pay the same fare. Travelers who need to purchase tickets at the last minute, change their itinerary at a moment's notice, or fly one-way often get stuck paying the premium rate. Here are some ways to keep your airfare costs down.

- Passengers who can book their ticket **long in advance,** who can **stay over Saturday night,** or who **fly midweek** or **at less-trafficked hours** will pay a fraction of the full fare. If your schedule is flexible, say so, and ask if you can secure a cheaper fare by changing your flight plans.
- You can also save on airfares by keeping an eye out in local newspapers for **promotional specials** or **fare wars,** when airlines lower prices on their most popular routes. You rarely see fare wars offered for peak travel times, but if you can travel in the off-months, you may snag a bargain.
- Search **the Internet** for cheap fares (see "Planning Your Trip Online").
- **Consolidators,** also known as bucket shops, are great sources for international tickets, although they usually can't beat the Internet on fares within North America. Start by looking in Sunday newspaper travel sections; U.S. travelers should focus on the *New York Times, Los Angeles Times,* and *Miami Herald.* For less-developed destinations, small travel agents who cater to immigrant communities in large cities often have the best deals. *Beware:* Bucket shop tickets are usually nonrefundable or rigged with stiff cancellation penalties, often as high as 50% to 75% of the ticket price, and some put you on charter airlines with

Travel in the Age of Bankruptcy

Airline bankruptcies have been in the news lately. To protect yourself, **buy your tickets with a credit card,** as the Fair Credit Billing Act guarantees that you can get your money back from the credit card company if a travel supplier goes under (and if you request the refund within 60 days of the bankruptcy). **Travel insurance** can also help, but make sure it covers against "carrier default" for your specific travel provider. And be aware that if a U.S. airline goes bust mid-trip, a 2001 federal law requires other carriers to take you to your destination (albeit on a space-available basis) for a fee of no more than $25, provided you rebook within 60 days of the cancellation.

questionable safety records. Several reliable consolidators are worldwide and available on the Net. **STA Travel** is now the world's leader in student travel, thanks to their purchase of Council Travel. It also offers good fares for travelers of all ages. **Flights. com** (© 800/TRAV-800; www. flights.com) started in Europe and has excellent fares worldwide, but particularly to that continent. It also has "local" websites in 12 countries. **FlyCheap** (© 800/FLY-CHEAP; www.1800flycheap.com) is owned by package-holiday megalith MyTravel and so has especially good access to fares for sunny destinations. **Air Tickets Direct** (© 800/778-3447; www.airtickets direct.com) is based in Montreal and leverages the currently weak Canadian dollar for low fares.

• Join **frequent-flier clubs.** Accrue enough miles, and you'll be rewarded with free flights and elite status. It's free, and you'll get the best choice of seats, faster response to phone inquiries, and prompter service if your luggage is stolen,

your flight is canceled or delayed, or if you want to change your seat. You don't need to fly to build frequent-flier miles—**frequent-flier credit cards** can provide thousands of miles for doing your everyday shopping.

• For many more tips about air travel, including a rundown of the major frequent-flier credit cards, pick up a copy of *Frommer's Fly Safe, Fly Smart* (Wiley Publishing, Inc.).

GETTING THERE BY TRAIN

Amtrak (© 800/USA-RAIL; www. amtrak.com) has two routes through Colorado. The California Zephyr, which links San Francisco and Chicago, passes through Grand Junction, Glenwood Springs, Granby, Winter Park, Denver, and Fort Morgan en route to Omaha, Nebraska. The Southwest Chief, which runs between Los Angeles and Chicago, travels from Albuquerque, New Mexico, via Trinidad, La Junta, and Lamar before crossing the southeastern Colorado border into Kansas.

10 Packages for the Independent Traveler

Before you start your search for the lowest airfare, you may want to consider booking your flight as part of a travel package. Package tours are not the same thing as escorted tours. Package tours are simply a way to buy the airfare, accommodations, and other elements of your trip (such as car rentals, airport transfers, and some-times even activities) at the same time and often at discounted prices—kind of like one-stop shopping. Packages are sold in bulk to tour operators—who resell them to the public at a cost that usually undercuts standard rates.

One good source of package deals is the airlines themselves. Most major airlines offer air/land packages, including **American Airlines Vacations** (© 800/321-2121; www.aavacations. com), **Delta Vacations** (© 800/221-6666; www.deltavacations.com), **Continental Airlines Vacations** (© 800/301-3800; www.coolvacations.com), and **United Vacations** (© 888/854-3899; www.unitedvacations.com). Several big **online travel agencies**—Expedia, Travelocity, Orbitz, Site59, and Lastminute.com—also do a brisk business in packages. If you're unsure about the pedigree of a smaller pack-ager, check with the Better Business Bureau in the city where the company is based, or go online at www.bbb.org. If a packager won't tell you where it's based, don't fly with them.

One company that puts together packages for trips to several resort communities of Colorado, including Vail, Aspen, Steamboat Springs, and Durango (but not to Denver, Boulder, and Colorado Springs), is **Mountain Vacations** (© **800/754-3704;** www.mountainvacations.com).

Travel packages are also listed in the travel section of your local Sunday newspaper. Or check ads in the national travel magazines such as *Arthur Frommer's Budget Travel Magazine, Travel & Leisure, National Geographic Traveler,* and *Condé Nast Traveler.*

Package tours can vary by leaps and bounds. Some offer a better class of hotels than others. Some offer the same hotels for lower prices. Some offer flights on scheduled airlines, while others book charters. Some limit your choice of accommodations and travel days. You are often required to make a large payment up front. On the plus side, packages can save you money, offering group prices but allowing for independent travel. Some even let you add on a few guided excursions or escorted day trips (also at prices lower than if you booked them yourself) without booking an entirely escorted tour.

Before you invest in a package tour, get some answers. Ask about the **accommodations choices** and prices for each. Then look up the hotels' reviews in a Frommer's guide and check their rates for your specific dates of travel online.

Finally, look for **hidden expenses.** Ask whether airport departure fees and taxes, for example, are included in the total cost.

11 Escorted General-Interest Tours

Escorted tours are structured group tours, with a group leader. The price usually includes everything from air-fare to hotels, meals, tours, admission costs, and local transportation. Below are some of the better companies that offer escorted tours in the Denver, Boulder, and Colorado Springs areas.

Gray Line, 5855 E. 56th Ave. (P.O. Box 646), Denver, CO 80217 (© **303/289-2841**), provides traditional bus and van tours to the U.S. Air Force

Academy, Pikes Peak, Rocky Mountain National Park, and historic sites of Denver.

Maupintour, 1515 St. Andrews Dr., Lawrence, KS 66047 (© **800/255-4266;** www.maupintour.com), offers a variety of tours, including well-planned multiday tours of Rocky Mountain National Park and other scenic and historic areas.

Sample Colorado Tour Company and Travel Club, P.O. Box 621906,

Littleton, CO 80162-1906 (© **303/ 904-2376**), offers scheduled and custom tours with a historic theme throughout the state—both day trips from Denver and multiday excursions.

See also the "Organized Tours" section in chapter 5 for Denver and chapter 7 for Colorado Springs.

Many people derive a certain ease and security from escorted trips. Escorted tours let travelers sit back and enjoy their trip without having to spend lots of time behind the wheel. All the little details are taken care of; you know your costs up front; and there are few surprises. Escorted tours can take you to the maximum number of sights in the minimum amount of time with the least amount of hassle— you don't have to sweat over the plotting and planning of a vacation schedule. Escorted tours are particularly convenient for people with limited mobility.

On the downside, an escorted tour often requires a big deposit up front, and lodging and dining choices are predetermined. As part of a cloud of tourists, you'll get little opportunity for serendipitous interactions with locals. The tours can be jam-packed with activities, leaving little room for individual sightseeing, whim, or adventure—plus they also often focus only on the heavily touristed sites, so you miss out on the lesser-known gems.

Before you invest in an escorted tour, ask about the **cancellation policy**: Is a deposit required? Can they cancel the trip if they don't get enough people? Do you get a refund if they cancel? If *you* cancel? How late can you cancel if you are unable to go?

When do you pay in full? *Note:* If you choose an escorted tour, think strongly about purchasing trip-cancellation insurance, especially if the tour operator asks you to pay up front. See the section on "Travel Insurance," earlier in this chapter.

You'll also want to get a complete **schedule** of the trip to find out how much sightseeing is planned each day and whether enough time has been allotted for relaxing or wandering solo.

The **size** of the group is also important to know up front. Generally, the smaller the group, the more flexible the itinerary, and the less time you'll spend waiting for people to get on and off the bus. Find out the **demographics** of the group as well. What is the age range? What is the gender breakdown? Is this mostly a trip for couples or singles?

Discuss what is included in the **price.** You may have to pay for transportation to and from the airport. A box lunch may be included in an excursion, but drinks might cost extra. Tips may not be included. Find out if you will be charged if you decide to opt out of certain activities or meals.

Before you invest in a package tour, get some answers. Ask about the **accommodations choices** and prices for each. Then look up the hotels' reviews in a Frommer's guide and check their rates for your specific dates of travel online.

Finally, if you plan to travel alone, you'll need to know if a **single supplement** will be charged and if the company can match you up with a roommate.

12 Special-Interest Trips

Hikers, bikers, and other outdoor recreationists can head into the mountains with **The World Outdoors,** 2840 Wilderness Place, Suite F, Boulder, CO 80301 (© **800/488-8483** or 303/413-0938; fax 303/413-0926; www.theworldoutdoors.com), which leads hiking and multisport adventures throughout the West, including trips into Rocky Mountain National Park. Most trips are 6 days long and include transportation, lodging, and dining.

13 Tips on Accommodations

Denver, Boulder, and Colorado Springs offer a variety of lodging options, from typical American chain motels to luxury hotels, cozy bed-and-breakfasts to inexpensive mom-and-pop independent motels, cabins to magnificent grande-dame hotels.

The chains here are the same ones you see everywhere else in America: Best Western, Comfort, Days Inn, Embassy Suites, Hampton Inn, Hilton, Holiday Inn, Motel 6, Quality Inn, Sheraton, Super 8, Travelodge, and so on. They look just about the same as those found elsewhere, and have the same levels of service. In most cases their rooms are little more than boring boxes of various sizes, with beds and the appropriate plumbing and heating fixtures, and, if you're lucky, a decent view out the window. These chains, even the high-end ones like Hilton and Sheraton, are fine if you just want a place to sleep and plan to take advantage of their swimming pools, exercise rooms, and other facilities. However, they do very little to enhance your vacation experience, to let you know you're in Colorado.

To make your lodging an integral part of your Colorado experience, we suggest choosing a historic property. We discuss numerous historic bed-and-breakfast inns in the following pages, and—especially when you take into consideration the wonderful breakfasts most of them serve—the rates are fairly reasonable. Why spend $90 for a boring motel room and then another $10 to $15 for breakfast when for just a bit more you can sleep in a handsome, antique-decorated Victorian home and enjoy a home-cooked breakfast?

This area of Colorado also has several magnificent but pricey historic hotels, including the absolutely wonderful Brown Palace in Denver and the family-friendly Broadmoor in Colorado Springs. These hotels are as much attractions as lodgings, and what better way to see them than to book a room for the night, just as others have done for the better part of a century?

Other lodging choices here include cabins and a handful of small independent motels. Both are usually fairly inexpensive, although they often lack the facilities, such as pools, spas, and exercise equipment that you'll find in most chains. We still prefer the cabins and independents, though, because they're often a very good value and the rooms usually have at least some personality (can anybody actually describe the decor of the last Super 8 or Days Inn they stayed at?), and cabins, although sometimes a bit primitive, are often in beautiful settings.

SAVING ON YOUR HOTEL ROOM

The **rack rate** is the official rate, usually (but always) the maximum rate that a hotel charges for a room. Hardly anybody pays these prices, however, and there are many ways around them.

- **Don't be afraid to bargain.** Most rack rates include commissions of 10% to 25% for travel agents, which some hotels may be willing to give you if you make your own reservations and haggle a bit. Always ask whether a room less expensive than the first one quoted is available, or whether any special rates apply to you. You may qualify for corporate, student, military, senior, or other discounts. Be sure to mention membership in AAA, AARP, frequent-flier programs, or trade unions, which may entitle you to special deals as well. Find out the hotel policy on children—do kids stay free in the room or is there a special rate?

- **Watch for coupon books and advertised discounts.** State welcome centers, community visitor centers, and a variety of businesses (but not hotels) distribute free booklets that contain nothing but discount lodging coupons. These are usually for chains, and usually are for walk-ins only, so you won't be able to make a reservation. They also do not usually apply during special events. But if you can use one of these coupons, you can often save 20% to 40% off the rack rate. These coupons are also available online: try www.hotelcoupons.com, and www.roomsaver.com. Also check ads in your local Sunday newspaper travel section, a good source for up-to-the-minute hotel deals, especially for lodging in resort areas.
- **Dial direct.** When booking a room in a chain hotel, you'll often get a better deal by calling the individual hotel's reservation desk than at the chain's main number.
- **Book online.** Many hotels offer Internet-only discounts, or supply rooms to Priceline, Hotwire, or Expedia at rates much lower than the ones you can get through the hotel itself.
- **Remember the law of supply and demand.** Resort hotels are most crowded and therefore most expensive on weekends, so discounts are usually available for midweek stays. Business hotels in downtown locations are busiest during the week, so you can expect big discounts over the weekend. Many hotels have high-season and low-season prices, and booking the day after 'high season' ends can mean big discounts.
- **Look into group or long-stay discounts.** If you come as part of a large group, you should be able to negotiate a bargain rate, since the hotel can then guarantee occupancy in a number of rooms. Likewise, if you're planning a long stay (at least 5 days), you might qualify for a discount. As a general rule, expect 1 night free after a 7-night stay.
- **Avoid excess charges and hidden costs.** When you book a room, ask whether the hotel charges for parking. Use your own cellphone, pay phones, or prepaid phone cards instead of dialing direct from hotel phones, which usually have exorbitant rates. And don't be tempted by the room's minibar offerings: Most hotels charge through the nose for water, soda, and snacks. Finally, ask about local taxes and service charges, which can increase the cost of a room by 15% or more. If a hotel insists upon tacking on a surprise "energy surcharge" that wasn't mentioned at check-in or a "resort fee" for amenities you didn't use, you can often make a case for getting it removed.
- **Book an efficiency.** A room with a kitchenette allows you to shop for groceries and cook your own meals. This is a big money saver, especially for families on long stays.

LANDING THE BEST ROOM

Somebody has to get the best room in the house. It might as well be you. You can start by joining the hotel's frequent-guest program, which may make you eligible for upgrades. A hotel-branded credit card usually gives it owner "silver" or "gold" status in frequent-guest programs for free. Always ask about a corner room. They're often larger and quieter, with more windows and light, and they often cost the same as standard rooms. When you make your reservation, ask if the hotel is renovating; if it is, request a room away from the construction. Ask about nonsmoking rooms, rooms with views, rooms with twin, queen- or king-size beds. If you're a light sleeper, request a quiet room away from vending machines, elevators, restaurants, bars, and discos. Ask for one of the rooms that have been most recently renovated or redecorated.

If you aren't happy with your room when you arrive, say so. If another room is available, most lodgings will be willing to accommodate you.

14 Recommended Reading

Those planning vacations in Denver, Boulder, and Colorado Springs and the nearby mountains can turn to a number of sources for background on the state and its major cities. Among our favorites is *A Lady's Life in the Rocky Mountains,* a fascinating compilation of Isabella L. Bird's letters to her sister; they were written in the late 1800s as she traveled alone through the Rockies, usually on horseback. Those who enjoy lengthy novels will want to get their hands on a copy of James Michener's 1,000-page *Centennial,* inspired by the northeastern plains of Colorado. For a more bohemian point of view, look no further than Jack Kerouac's classic, *On the Road.* Also engrossing is Wallace Stegner's Pulitzer Prize–winning 1971 novel, *Angle of Repose.* Horror fans will surely appreciate a pair of Stephen King classics with Colorado ties: *The Stand* is set in Boulder and *The Shining* was inspired by the writer's stay at the Stanley Hotel in Estes Park.

Travelers interested in seeing wildlife will likely be successful with help from the *Colorado Wildlife Viewing Guide,* by Mary Taylor Gray. You'll likely see a lot of historical sights here, so it's good to first get some background from the short, easy-to-read *Colorado: A History,* by Marshall Sprague.

3

For International Visitors

Whether it's your first visit or your tenth, a trip to the United States may require an additional degree of planning. This chapter will provide you with essential information, helpful tips, and advice for the more common problems that some international visitors encounter.

1 Preparing for Your Trip

ENTRY REQUIREMENTS

Check at any U.S. embassy or consulate for current information and requirements. You can also obtain a visa application and other information online at the **U.S. State Department**'s website, at **www.travel.state.gov**.

VISAS The U.S. State Department has a **Visa Waiver Program** allowing citizens of certain countries to enter the United States without a visa for stays of up to 90 days. At press time these included Andorra, Australia, Austria, Belgium, Brunei, Denmark, Finland, France, Germany, Iceland, Ireland, Italy, Japan, Liechtenstein, Luxembourg, Monaco, the Netherlands, New Zealand, Norway, Portugal, San Marino, Singapore, Slovenia, Spain, Sweden, Switzerland, and the United Kingdom. Citizens of these countries need only a valid passport and a round-trip air or cruise ticket in their possession upon arrival. If they first enter the United States, they may also visit Mexico, Canada, Bermuda, and/or the Caribbean islands and return to the United States without a visa. Further information is available from any U.S. embassy or consulate. Canadian citizens may enter the United States without visas; they need only proof of residence.

Citizens of all other countries must have (1) a valid passport that expires at least 6 months later than the scheduled end of their visit to the United States, and (2) a tourist visa, which may be obtained without charge from any U.S. consulate.

To obtain a visa, the traveler must submit a completed application form (either in person or by mail) with a 1½-inch-square photo, and must demonstrate binding ties to a residence abroad. Usually you can obtain a visa at once or within 24 hours, but it may take longer during the summer rush from June through August. If you cannot go in person, contact the nearest U.S. embassy or consulate for directions on applying by mail. Your travel agent or airline office may also be able to provide you with visa applications and instructions. The U.S. consulate or embassy that issues your visa will determine whether you will be issued a multiple- or single-entry visa and any restrictions regarding the length of your stay.

British subjects can obtain up-to-date visa information by calling the **U.S. Embassy Visa Information Line** (𝄐 **0891/200-290**) or by visiting the "Consular Services" section of the American Embassy London's website at www.usembassy.org.uk.

Irish citizens can obtain up-to-date visa information through the **Embassy of USA Dublin,** 42 Elgin

Rd., Dublin 4, Ireland (© **353/1-668-8777**) or by checking the "Consular Services" section of the website at www.usembassy.ie.

Australian citizens can obtain up-to-date visa information by contacting the **U.S. Embassy Canberra,** Moonah Place, Yarralumla, ACT 2600 (© **02/6214-5600**) or by checking the U.S. Diplomatic Mission's website at http://usembassy-australia.state.gov/consular.

Citizens of **New Zealand** can obtain up-to-date visa information by contacting the **U.S. Embassy New Zealand,** 29 Fitzherbert Terr., Thorndon, Wellington (© **644/472-2068**), or get the information directly from the "Services to New Zealanders" section of the website at http://usembassy.org.nz.

MEDICAL   REQUIREMENTS

Unless you're arriving from an area known to be suffering from an epidemic (particularly cholera or yellow fever), inoculations or vaccinations are not required for entry into the United States. If you have a medical condition that requires **syringe-administered medications,** carry a valid signed prescription from your physician—the Federal Aviation Administration (FAA) no longer allows airline passengers to pack syringes in their carry-on baggage without documented proof of medical need. If you have a disease that requires treatment with **narcotics,** you should also carry documented proof with you—smuggling narcotics aboard a plane is a serious offense that carries severe penalties in the U.S.

For **HIV-positive visitors,** requirements for entering the United States are somewhat vague and change frequently. According to the latest publication of *HIV and Immigrants: A Manual for AIDS Service Providers,* the Immigration and Naturalization Service (INS) doesn't require a medical exam for entry into the United States, but INS officials may stop individuals because they look sick or because they are carrying AIDS/HIV medicine.

If an HIV-positive non-citizen applies for a non-immigrant visa, the question on the application regarding communicable diseases is tricky no matter which way it's answered. If the applicant checks "no," INS may deny the visa on the grounds that the applicant committed fraud. If the applicant checks "yes" or if INS suspects the person is HIV-positive, it will deny the visa unless the applicant asks for a special waiver for visitors. This waiver is for people visiting the United States for a short time, to attend a conference, for instance, to visit close relatives, or to receive medical treatment. It can be a confusing situation. For up-to-the-minute information, contact the Centers for Disease Control's **National Center for HIV** (© **404/332-4559;** www.hivatis.org) or the **Gay Men's Health Crisis** (© **212/367-1000;** www.gmhc.org).

DRIVER'S   LICENSES Foreign driver's licenses are mostly recognized in the U.S., although you may want to get an international driver's license if your home license is not written in English.

PASSPORT INFORMATION

Safeguard your passport in an inconspicuous, inaccessible place like a money belt. Make a copy of the critical pages, including the passport number, and store it in a safe place, separate from the passport itself. If you lose your passport, visit the nearest consulate of your native country as soon as possible for a replacement. Passport applications are downloadable from the websites listed below.

Note that the International Civil Aviation Organization (ICAO) has recommended a policy requiring that *every* individual who travels by air have his or her own passport. In response, many countries are now requiring that children must be issued their own passports to travel internationally, where before those under 16 or so may have been allowed to travel on a parent or guardian's passport.

FOR RESIDENTS OF CANADA

You can pick up a passport application at one of 28 regional passport offices or most travel agencies. Canadian children who travel must have their own passport. However, if you hold a valid Canadian passport issued before December 11, 2001, that bears the name of your child, the passport remains valid for you and your child until it expires. Passports cost C$85 for those 16 years and older (valid 5 years), C$35 for children ages 3 to 15 (valid 5 years), and C$20, children under 3 (valid for 3 years). Applications, which must be accompanied by two identical passport-sized photographs and proof of Canadian citizenship, are available at travel agencies throughout Canada or from the central **Passport Office,** Department of Foreign Affairs and International Trade, Ottawa, ON K1A 0G3 (© **800/567-6868;** www.dfait-maeci. gc.ca/passport). Processing takes 5 to 10 days if you apply in person, or about 3 weeks by mail.

FOR RESIDENTS OF THE UNITED KINGDOM

As a member of the European Union, you need only an identity card, not a passport, to travel to other EU countries. However, if you already possess a passport, it's always useful to carry it. To pick up an application for a standard 10-year passport (5-year passport for children under 16), visit the nearest Passport Office, major post office, or travel agency. You can also contact the **United Kingdom Passport Service** at © **0870/571-0410** or visit its website at www.passport.gov.uk. Passports are £33 for adults and £19 for children under 16, with an additional £30 fee if you apply in person at a Passport Office. Processing takes

about 2 weeks (1 week if you apply at the Passport Office).

FOR RESIDENTS OF IRELAND

You can apply for a 10-year passport, costing €57, at the **Passport Office,** Setanta Centre, Molesworth Street, Dublin 2 (© **01/671-1633;** www. irlgov.ie/iveagh). Those under age 18 and over 65 must apply for a €12 3-year passport. You can also apply at 1A South Mall, Cork (© **021/272-525**) or over the counter at most main post offices.

FOR RESIDENTS OF AUSTRALIA

You can pick up an application from your local post office or any branch of **Passports Australia,** but you must schedule an interview at the passport office to present your application materials. Call the **Australian Passport Information Service** at © **131-232,** or visit the government website at www.passports.gov.au. Passports for adults are A$144 and for those under 18 are A$72.

FOR RESIDENTS OF NEW ZEALAND

You can pick up a passport application at any New Zealand Passports Office or download it from their website. Contact the **Passports Office** at © **0800/225-050** in New Zealand or 04/474-8100, or log on to www.passports.govt. nz. Passports for adults are NZ$80 and for children under 16, NZ$40.

CUSTOMS
WHAT YOU CAN BRING IN

Every visitor more than 21 years of age may bring in, free of duty, the following: (1) 1 liter of wine or hard liquor; (2) 200 cigarettes, 100 cigars (but not from Cuba), or 3 pounds of smoking tobacco; and (3) $100 worth of gifts. These exemptions are offered to travelers who spend at least 72 hours in the United States and who have not claimed them within the preceding 6 months. It is altogether forbidden to bring into the country foodstuffs (particularly fruit, cooked meats, and canned goods) and plants (vegetables, seeds, tropical plants, and the like). Foreign tourists may bring in or take out up to $10,000 in U.S. or foreign currency with no formalities; larger sums must be declared to U.S. Customs on entering or leaving, which includes filing form CM 4790. For more specific information regarding U.S. Customs, contact your nearest U.S. embassy or consulate, or the **U.S. Customs** office (© **202/927-1770** or www.customs.ustreas.gov).

WHAT YOU CAN TAKE HOME

U.K. citizens returning from a non-EU country have a customs allowance of: 200 cigarettes; 50 cigars; 250g of smoking tobacco; 2 liters of still table wine; 1 liter of spirits or strong liqueurs (over 22% volume); 2 liters of fortified wine, sparkling wine or other liqueurs; 60cc (ml) perfume; 250cc (ml) of toilet water; and £145 worth of all other goods, including gifts and souvenirs. People under 17 cannot have the tobacco or alcohol allowance. For more information, contact HM Customs & Excise at © **0845/010-9000** (from outside the U.K., 020/8929-0152), or consult their website at www.hmce.gov.uk.

For a clear summary of **Canadian** rules, request the booklet *I Declare,* issued by the **Canada Customs and Revenue Agency** (© **800/461-9999** in Canada, or 204/983-3500; www.ccra-adrc.gc.ca). Canada allows its citizens a C$750 exemption, and you're allowed to bring back duty-free 1 carton of cigarettes, 1 can of tobacco, 40 imperial ounces of liquor, and 50 cigars. In addition, you're allowed to mail gifts to Canada valued at less than C$60 a day, provided they're unsolicited and don't contain alcohol or tobacco (write on the package "Unsolicited gift, under $60

value"). All valuables should be declared on the Y-38 form before departure from Canada, including serial numbers of valuables you already own, such as expensive foreign cameras. *Note:* The $750 exemption can only be used once a year and only after an absence of 7 days.

The duty-free allowance in **Australia** is A$400 or, for those under 18, A$200. Citizens age 18 and over can bring in 250 cigarettes or 250 grams of loose tobacco, and 1,125 milliliters of alcohol. If you're returning with valuables you already own, such as foreign-made cameras, you should file form B263. A helpful brochure available from Australian consulates or Customs offices is *Know Before You Go.* For more information, call the **Australian Customs Service** at © **1300/363-263,** or log on to www.customs.gov.au.

The duty-free allowance for **New Zealand** is NZ$700. Citizens over 17 can bring in 200 cigarettes, 50 cigars, or 250 grams of tobacco (or a mixture of all 3 if their combined weight doesn't exceed 250g); plus 4.5 liters of wine and beer, or 1.125 liters of liquor. New Zealand currency does not carry import or export restrictions. Fill out a certificate of export, listing the valuables you are taking out of the country; that way, you can bring them back without paying duty. Most questions are answered in a free pamphlet available at New Zealand consulates and Customs offices: *New Zealand Customs Guide for Travellers, Notice no. 4.* For more information, contact **New Zealand Customs,** The Customhouse, 17–21 Whitmore St., Box 2218, Wellington (© **0800/428-786** or 04/473-6099; www.customs.govt.nz).

HEALTH INSURANCE

Although it's not required of travelers, health insurance is highly recommended. Unlike many European countries, the United States does not usually offer free or low-cost medical care to its citizens or visitors. Doctors and hospitals are expensive, and in most cases will require advance payment or proof of coverage before they render their services. Policies can cover everything from the loss or theft of your baggage and trip cancellation to the guarantee of bail in case you're arrested. Good policies will also cover the costs of an accident, repatriation, or death. See "Travel Insurance" in chapter 2 for more information. Packages such as **Europ Assistance's "Worldwide Healthcare Plan"** are sold by European automobile clubs and travel agencies at attractive rates. **Worldwide Assistance Services, Inc.** (© **800/821-2828;** www.worldwide assistance.com) is the agent for Europ Assistance in the United States.

Though lack of health insurance may prevent you from being admitted to a hospital in non-emergencies, don't worry about being left on a street corner to die: The American way is to fix you now and bill the living daylights out of you later.

INSURANCE FOR BRITISH TRAVELERS   Most big travel agents offer their own insurance and will probably try to sell you their package when you book a holiday. Think before you sign. **Britain's Consumers' Association** recommends that you insist on seeing the policy and reading the fine print before buying travel insurance. **The Association of British Insurers** (© **020/7600-3333;** www.abi.org.uk) gives advice by phone and publishes *Holiday Insurance,* a free guide to policy provisions and prices. You might also shop around for better deals: Try **Columbus Direct** (© **020/7375-0011;** www.columbusdirect.net).

INSURANCE FOR CANADIAN TRAVELERS   Canadians should check with their provincial health plan offices or call **Health Canada** (© **613/957-2991;** www.hc-sc.gc.ca) to find out the extent of their coverage and what documentation and receipts they

must take home in case they are treated in the United States.

MONEY

CURRENCY   The U.S. monetary system is very simple: The most common **bills** are the $1 (colloquially, a "buck"), $5, $10, and $20 denominations. There are also $2 bills (seldom encountered), $50 bills, and $100 bills (the last two are usually not welcome as payment for small purchases). All the paper money was recently redesigned, making the famous faces adorning them disproportionately large. The old-style bills are still legal tender.

There are seven denominations of coins: 1¢ (1 cent, or a penny); 5¢ (5 cents, or a nickel); 10¢ (10 cents, or a dime); 25¢ (25 cents, or a quarter); 50¢ (50 cents, or a half dollar); the new gold "Sacagawea" coin worth $1; and, prized by collectors, the rare, older silver dollar.

Note: The "foreign-exchange bureaus" so common in Europe are rare even at airports in the United States, and nonexistent outside major cities. It's best not to change foreign money (or traveler's checks denominated in a currency other than U.S. dollars) at a small-town bank, or even a branch in a big city; in fact, leave any currency other than U.S. dollars at home—it may prove a greater nuisance to you than it's worth.

TRAVELER'S CHECKS   Though traveler's checks are widely accepted, make sure that they're denominated in U.S. dollars, as foreign-currency checks are often difficult to exchange. The three traveler's checks that are most widely recognized—and least likely to be denied—are **Visa, American Express,** and **Thomas Cook.** Be sure to record the numbers of the checks, and keep that information in a separate place in case they get lost or stolen. Most businesses are pretty good about taking traveler's checks, but you're better off cashing them in

Travel Tip

Be sure to keep a copy of all your travel papers separate from your wallet or purse, and leave a copy with someone at home should you need it faxed in the event of an emergency.

at a bank (in small amounts, of course) and paying in cash. *Remember:* You'll need identification, such as a driver's license or passport, to change a traveler's check.

CREDIT CARDS & ATMs Credit cards are the most widely used form of payment in the United States: **Visa** (Barclaycard in Britain), **MasterCard** (EuroCard in Europe, Access in Britain, Chargex in Canada), **American Express, Diners Club, Discover,** and **Carte Blanche.** There are, however, a handful of stores and restaurants that do not take credit cards, so be sure to ask in advance. Most businesses display a sticker near their entrance to let you know which cards they accept. (*Note:* Businesses may require a minimum purchase, usually around $10, to use a credit card.)

It is strongly recommended that you bring at least one major credit card— Visa and MasterCard are the most widely accepted in Colorado, with American Express and Discover next. You must have a credit or charge card to rent a car. Hotels and airlines usually require a credit card imprint as a deposit against expenses, and in an emergency a credit card can be priceless.

You'll find **automated teller machines (ATMs)** on just about every block—at least in almost every town— across the country. Some ATMs will allow you to draw U.S. currency against your bank and credit cards. Check with your bank before leaving home, and remember that you will need your personal identification number (PIN) to do so. Most accept Visa, MasterCard, and American Express, as well as ATM cards from other U.S. banks. Expect to be charged up to $3

per transaction, however, if you're not using your own bank's ATM.

One way around these fees is to ask for cash back at grocery stores that accept ATM cards and don't charge usage fees. Of course, you'll have to purchase something first.

ATM cards with major credit card backing, known as "debit cards," are now a commonly acceptable form of payment in most stores and restaurants. Debit cards draw money directly from your checking account. Some stores enable you to receive "cash back" on your debit card purchases as well.

SAFETY

GENERAL SAFETY SUGGESTIONS Although tourist areas are generally safe, U.S. urban areas tend to be less safe than those in Europe or Japan. You should always stay alert. This is particularly true of large American cities such as Denver. If you're in doubt about which neighborhoods are safe, don't hesitate to ask the hotel front-desk staff or at the local tourist office.

Avoid deserted areas, especially at night, and don't go into public parks after dark unless there's a concert or similar occasion that will attract a crowd.

Avoid carrying valuables with you on the street, and keep expensive cameras or electronic equipment bagged up or covered when not in use. If you're using a map, try to consult it inconspicuously—or better yet, study it before you leave your room. Hold onto your pocketbook, and place your billfold in an inside pocket. In theaters, restaurants, and other public places, keep your possessions in sight.

Always lock your room door—don't assume that once you're inside the hotel you are automatically safe and no longer need to be aware of your surroundings. Hotels are open to the public, and in a large hotel, security may not be able to screen everyone who enters.

DRIVING SAFETY Driving safety is important too, and carjacking is not unprecedented. Question your rental agency about personal safety and ask for a traveler-safety brochure when you pick up your car. Obtain written directions—or a map with the route clearly marked—from the agency showing how to get to your destination. (Many agencies now offer the option of renting a cellphone for the duration of your car rental; check with the rental agent when you pick up the car. Otherwise, contact **InTouch USA** at ⓒ **800/872-7626** or www.intouchusa.com for short-term cellphone rental.) And, if possible, arrive and depart during daylight hours.

If you drive off a highway and end up in a dodgy-looking neighborhood, leave the area as quickly as possible. If you have an accident, even on the highway, stay in your car with the doors locked until you assess the situation or until the police arrive. If you're bumped from behind on the street or are involved in a minor accident with no injuries, and the situation appears to be suspicious, motion to the other driver to follow you. Never get out of your car in such situations. Go directly to the nearest police precinct, well-lit service station, or 24-hour store.

Park in well-lit and well-traveled areas whenever possible. Always keep your car doors locked, whether the vehicle is attended or unattended. Never leave any packages or valuables in sight. If someone attempts to rob you or steal your car, don't try to resist the thief/carjacker. Report the incident to the police department immediately by calling ⓒ **911.**

2 Getting to the U.S.

Most international visitors will fly to **Denver International Airport (DIA)** (ⓒ **800/AIR-2-DEN;** www.flydenver.com). Airlines offering flights into Denver include **Air Canada** (ⓒ 888/247-2262; www.aircanada.ca), **Alaska Airlines** (ⓒ **877/502-5357;** www.alaskaair.com), **American** (ⓒ 800/433-7300; www.aa.com), **America West** (ⓒ 800/235-9292; www.americawest.com), **Continental** (ⓒ 800/525-0280; www.continental.com), **Delta** (ⓒ 800/221-1212; www.delta.com), **Frontier** (ⓒ 800/432-1359; www.frontierairlines.com), **Korean Air** (ⓒ 800/438-5000; www.koreanair.com), **Martinair** (ⓒ 800/366-4655; www.martinair.com), **Mexicana** (ⓒ 800/531-7921; www.mexicana.com), **Midwest Airlines** (ⓒ 800/452-2022; www.midwestairlines.com), **Northwest** (ⓒ 800/225-2525; www.nwa.com), **United** (ⓒ 800/241-6522; www.ual.com), and **US**

Airways (ⓒ 800/428-4322; www.usair.com). International travelers can also take flights to O'Hare International Airport in Chicago, LAX in Los Angeles, and JFK International Airport in New York, and catch connecting flights to Denver from there.

British Airways (ⓒ **800/247-9297,** 0845/773-3377 in London; www.british-airways.com) offers one daily nonstop flight between London and Denver. Travelers from the United Kingdom can also take British Airways flights to such cities as Philadelphia or Chicago and make connecting flights to Denver.

AIRLINE DISCOUNTS The smart traveler can find numerable ways to reduce the price of a plane ticket simply by taking time to shop around. For example, overseas visitors can take advantage of the APEX (Advance

Purchase Excursion) reductions offered by all major U.S. and European carriers. For the best rates, compare fares and be flexible with the dates and times of travel.

IMMIGRATION & CUSTOMS CLEARANCE   Visitors arriving by air, no matter what the port of entry, should cultivate patience and resignation before setting foot on U.S. soil. Getting through immigration control can take as long as 2 hours on some days, especially on summer weekends, so be sure to carry this guidebook or something else to read. This is especially true in the aftermath of the World Trade Center attacks, when security clearances have been considerably beefed up at U.S. airports.

People traveling by air from Canada, Bermuda, and certain countries in the Caribbean can sometimes clear Customs and Immigration at the point of departure, which is much quicker.

3 Getting Around the U.S.

BY PLANE   Some large airlines (for example, Northwest and Delta) offer travelers on their transatlantic or transpacific flights special discount tickets under the name **Visit USA,** allowing mostly one-way travel from one U.S. destination to another at very low prices. These discount tickets are not on sale in the United States and must be purchased abroad in conjunction with your international ticket. This system is the best, easiest, and fastest way to see the United States at low cost. You should obtain information well in advance from your travel agent or the office of the airline concerned, since the conditions attached to these discount tickets can be changed without advance notice.

BY TRAIN   Amtrak (© 800/USA-RAIL; www.amtrak.com) connects Denver to both the East and West coasts. International visitors (excluding Canada) can buy a **USA Rail Pass,** good for 15 or 30 days of unlimited travel on Amtrak. The pass is available through many foreign travel agents. Prices in 2004 for a 15-day pass were $295 off-peak, $440 peak; a 30-day pass costs $385 off-peak, $550 peak. With a foreign passport, you can also buy passes at some Amtrak offices in the United States, including locations in San Francisco, Los Angeles, Chicago, New York, Miami, Boston, and Washington, D.C. Reservations are generally required and should be made for each part of your trip as early as possible. Regional rail passes are also available.

BY BUS   Although bus travel is often the most economical form of public transit for short hops between U.S. cities, it can also be slow and uncomfortable. It's certainly not an option for everyone, particularly when Amtrak, which is far more luxurious, offers similar rates. **Greyhound/Trailways** (© 800/231-2222; www.greyhound. com), the sole nationwide bus line, offers an **International Ameripass** that must be purchased before coming to the United States, or by phone through the Greyhound International Office at the Port Authority Bus Terminal in New York City (© 212/971-0492). The pass can be obtained from foreign travel agents and costs less than the domestic version. In 2004, options and prices were: 4 days ($135), 7 days ($183), 10 days ($223), 15 days ($271), 21 days ($319), 30 days ($367), 45 days ($407), or 60 days ($495). You can get more info on the pass at www. greyhound.com, or by calling © 212/ 971-0492 (14:00 to 21:00 GMT) or © 402/330-8552 (all other times). In addition, special rates are available for seniors and students.

BY CAR   Unless you plan to spend the bulk of your vacation time in a city where walking is the best and easiest way to get around (read: New York City, New Orleans, or maybe Denver), the most cost-effective, convenient, and comfortable way to travel around the United States is by car. The interstate highway system connects cities and towns all over the country; in addition to these high-speed, limited-access roadways, there's an extensive network of federal, state, and local highways and roads. Some of the major national car-rental companies with outlets in Denver and Colorado Springs include **Alamo** (© 800/462-5260; www.alamo.com), **Avis** (© 800/331-1212; www.avis.com), **Budget** (© 800/527-0700; www.budget.com), **Dollar** (© 800/800-4000; www.dollar car.com), **Hertz** (© 800/654-3131; www.hertz.com), **National** (© 800/227-7368; www.nationalcar.com), and **Thrifty** (© 800/847-4389; www.thrifty.com).

If you plan to rent a car in the United States, you probably won't need the services of an additional automobile organization. If you're planning to buy or borrow a car, automobile-association membership is recommended. The **American Automobile Association (AAA)** (© 800/222-4357; www.aaa.com), the country's largest auto club, supplies its members with maps, insurance, and, most important, emergency road service. The cost of joining runs from $63 for singles to $95 for two members, but if you're a member of a foreign auto club with reciprocal arrangements, you can enjoy free AAA service in America. See "Getting There," in chapter 2, for more information.

FAST FACTS: For the International Traveler

Automobile Organizations Auto clubs will supply maps, suggested routes, guidebooks, accident and bail-bond insurance, and emergency road service. The **American Automobile Association (AAA),** the major auto club in the United States, has offices nationwide, and in Denver, Boulder, and Colorado Springs. If you belong to an auto club in your home country, inquire about AAA reciprocity before you leave. You may be able to join AAA even if you're not a member of a reciprocal club; to inquire, call AAA (© **800/222-4357;** www.aa.com). AAA is actually an organization of regional auto clubs; so look under "AAA Automobile Club" in the White Pages of the telephone directory.

Business Hours Offices are usually open weekdays from 9am to 5pm. Banks are open weekdays from 9am to 3pm or later, and sometimes Saturday morning. Stores typically open between 9 and 10am and close between 5 and 6pm from Monday through Saturday. Stores in shopping complexes or malls tend to stay open late: often until about 9pm, and many malls and larger department stores are open on Sundays. Discount stores and supermarkets are often open later than other stores, and some supermarkets are open 24 hours a day.

Currency & Currency Exchange See "Entry Requirements" and "Money" under "Preparing for Your Trip," earlier in this chapter.

Drinking Laws The legal age for purchase and consumption of alcoholic beverages is 21; proof of age is required and often requested at bars, nightclubs, and restaurants, so it's always a good idea to carry an ID when you go out. Except for 3.2% beer (sold in supermarkets and convenience stores 7 days a week), alcoholic beverages must be purchased in liquor stores in Colorado. These are open Monday through Saturday. Licensed restaurants, lounges, and bars may serve alcohol Monday through Saturday from 7am to 2am, Sunday from 8am to 2am, and Christmas Day from 8am to midnight. Incidentally, 3.2% beer, which is sold only in Colorado, Utah, Oklahoma, and Kansas, does have less alcohol than the same beer sold elsewhere, despite what some storekeepers may tell you. According to the Budweiser people, 3.2% beer has about 4% alcohol by volume (which is equivalent to 3.2% alcohol by weight), while full-strength American beers have about 5% alcohol by volume. Some microbrews and specialty beers and ales have much higher alcohol content, sometimes even 9% or 10%.

Do not carry open containers of alcohol in your car or any public area that isn't zoned for alcohol consumption. The police can fine you on the spot. And nothing will ruin your trip faster than getting a citation for DUI ("driving under the influence"), so don't even think about driving while intoxicated.

Electricity Like Canada, the United States uses 110 to 120 volts AC (60 cycles), compared to 220–240 volts AC (50 cycles) in most of Europe, Australia, and New Zealand. If your small appliances use 220 to 240 volts, you'll need a 110-volt transformer and a plug adapter with two flat parallel pins. Downward converters that change 220–240 volts to 110–120 volts are difficult to find in the United States, so bring one with you.

Embassies & Consulates All embassies are located in the nation's capital, Washington, D.C. Some consulates are located in major U.S. cities, and most nations have a mission to the United Nations in New York City. If your country isn't listed below, call for directory information in Washington, D.C. (© **202/555-1212**) or log on to **www.embassy.org/embassies**.

The embassy of **Australia** is at 1601 Massachusetts Ave. NW, Washington, DC 20036 (© **202/797-3000;** www.austemb.org). There are consulates in Denver, Honolulu, Houston, Los Angeles, New York, San Francisco, and other cities.

The embassy of **Canada** is at 501 Pennsylvania Ave. NW, Washington, DC 20001 (© **202/682-1740;** www.canadianembassy.org). Other Canadian consulates are in Buffalo (N.Y.), Detroit, Los Angeles, New York, and other cities.

The embassy of **Ireland** is at 2234 Massachusetts Ave. NW, Washington, DC 20008 (© **202/462-3939;** www.irelandemb.org). Irish consulates are in Boston, Chicago, New York, and other cities.

The embassy of **Japan** is at 2520 Massachusetts Ave. NW, Washington, DC 20008 (© **202/238-6700;** www.embjapan.org). Japanese consulates are located in Atlanta, Denver, Kansas City, San Francisco, Washington D.C., and other cities.

The embassy of **New Zealand** is at 37 Observatory Circle NW, Washington, DC 20008 (© **202/328-4800;** www.nzemb.org). New Zealand consulates are in Los Angeles, Salt Lake City, San Francisco, and Seattle.

The embassy of the **United Kingdom** is at 3100 Massachusetts Ave. NW, Washington, DC 20008 (© **202/588-7800;** www.britainusa.com). Other British consulates are in Atlanta, Boston, Chicago, Cleveland, Denver, Houston, Los Angeles, New York, San Francisco, and other cities.

The following countries have consulates in the Denver area: **Australia,** 9200 W. Cross Dr. (☎ 303/321-2234); **Costa Rica,** 3356 S. Xenia (☎ 303/696-8211); **Denmark,** 5353 W. Dartmouth Ave., Lakewood (☎ 303/980-9100); **France,** 1420 Ogden St. (☎ 303/831-8616); **Germany,** 621 17th St. (☎ 303/279-1551); **Japan,** 1225 17th St. (☎ 303/534-1151); **Korea,** 1600 Broadway, Suite 500 (☎ 303/830-0500); **Mexico,** 48 Steele St. (☎ 303/331-1110); **Netherlands,** 1625 Broadway (☎ 303/592-5362); **Norway,** 370 17th St. (☎ 303/592-5930); **Sweden,** 4242 E. Amherst Ave. (☎ 303/758-0999); **Switzerland,** 2810 Iliff St., Boulder (☎ 303/499-5641); **Thailand,** 717 17th St. (☎ 303/312-1934); **United Kingdom,** World Trade Center, 1675 Broadway, Ste. 1030 (☎ 303/592-5200). There are about 100 consulates in Denver in all.

Emergencies Call ☎ **911** to report a fire, call the police, or get an ambulance anywhere in the United States. This is a toll-free call. (No coins are required at public telephones.)

If you encounter serious problems, contact the **Traveler's Aid Society International** (☎ **202/546-1127;** www.travelersaid.org) to help direct you to a local branch, although at this time there are no branches in Colorado. This nationwide, nonprofit, social-service organization geared to helping travelers in difficult straits offers services that might include reuniting families separated while traveling, providing food and shelter to people stranded without cash, or even emotional counseling.

Gasoline (Petrol) Petrol is known as gasoline (or simply "gas") in the United States, and petrol stations are known as both gas stations and service stations. Gasoline costs about half as much here as it does in Europe (about $1.85–$2 per gallon at press time), and the printed price includes taxes. One U.S. gallon equals 3.8 liters or .85 Imperial gallons.

Holidays Banks, government offices, post offices, and many stores, restaurants, and museums are closed on the following legal national holidays: January 1 (New Year's Day), the third Monday in January (Martin Luther King, Jr., Day), the third Monday in February (Presidents' Day, Washington's Birthday), the last Monday in May (Memorial Day), July 4th (Independence Day), the first Monday in September (Labor Day), the second Monday in October (Columbus Day), November 11 (Veterans Day/Armistice Day), the fourth Thursday in November (Thanksgiving Day), and December 25 (Christmas). Also, the Tuesday following the first Monday in November is Election Day and is a federal-government holiday in presidential-election years (held every 4 years, and next in 2008).

Legal Aid If you are "pulled over" for a minor infraction (such as speeding), never attempt to pay the fine directly to a police officer; this could be construed as attempted bribery, a much more serious crime. Pay fines by mail, or directly into the hands of the clerk of the court. If accused of a more serious offense, say and do nothing before consulting a lawyer. Here the burden is on the state to prove a person's guilt beyond a reasonable doubt, and everyone has the right to remain silent, whether he or she is suspected of a crime or actually arrested. Once arrested, a person can make one telephone call to a party of his or her choice. Call your embassy or consulate.

Mail If you aren't sure what your address will be in the United States, mail can be sent to you, in your name, c/o General Delivery at the main post office of the city or region where you expect to be. Contact the U.S. Postal Service at ℂ **800/275-8777** or www.usps.com for information on the nearest post office. In Denver, the main downtown post office is at 951 20th St. The addressee must pick up mail in person and must produce proof of identity (driver's license, passport, or other ID). Most post offices will hold your mail for up to 1 month, and are open Monday to Friday from 8am to 6pm and Saturday from 9am to 3pm.

Generally found at intersections, mailboxes are blue with a red-and-white stripe and carry the inscription U.S. MAIL. If your mail is addressed to a U.S. destination, don't forget to add the five-digit postal code (or ZIP code), after the two-letter abbreviation of the state to which the mail is addressed (CO for Colorado). This is essential for prompt delivery.

At press time, domestic postage rates were 23¢ for a postcard and 37¢ for a letter. For international mail, a first-class letter of up to ½ ounce costs 80¢ (60¢ to Canada and Mexico); a first-class postcard costs 70¢ (50¢ to Canada and Mexico); and a preprinted postal aerogramme costs 70¢.

Measurements See the chart on the inside front cover of this book for details on converting metric measurements to U.S. equivalents.

Taxes The United States has no value-added tax (VAT) or other indirect tax at the national level. Every state, county, and city has the right to levy its own local tax on all purchases, including hotel and restaurant checks, airline tickets, and so on. Sales taxes in Colorado vary, but usually total about 7.5%. An exception is the tax on lodging, which often runs to 10%, and is 14% in Denver. Sales tax is not usually included in the price tags you'll see on merchandise or in the rates you're quoted for lodging. These taxes are not refundable.

Telephone, Telegraph, Telex & Fax Private corporations run the U.S. telephone system, so rates, especially for long-distance service and operator-assisted calls, can vary widely. Generally, hotel surcharges on long-distance and local calls are astronomical, so you're usually better off using a **public pay telephone,** which you'll find clearly marked in most public buildings and private establishments as well as on the street. Convenience (small grocery) stores and gas stations always have them. Many convenience stores and packaging services sell **prepaid calling cards** in denominations up to $50; these can be the least expensive way to call home. Many public phones at airports accept American Express, MasterCard, and Visa credit cards. **Local calls** made from public pay phones usually cost 50¢. Pay phones do not accept pennies, and few will take anything larger than a quarter.

You may want to look into leasing a cellphone for the duration of your trip.

Most long-distance and international calls can be dialed directly from any phone. For calls within the United States and to Canada, dial 1 followed by the area code and the seven-digit number. For other international calls, dial 011 followed by the country code, city code, and the telephone number of the person you are calling.

Calls to area codes 800, 888, 877, and 866 are toll-free. However, calls to numbers in area codes 700 and 900 (chat lines, bulletin boards, "dating" services, and so on) can be very expensive—usually a charge of 95¢ to $3 or more per minute, and they sometimes have minimum charges that can run as high as $15 or more.

For reversed-charge or collect calls, and for person-to-person calls, dial 0 (zero, not the letter O) followed by the area code and number you want; an operator will then come on the line, and you should specify that you are calling collect, or person-to-person, or both. If your operator-assisted call is international, ask for the overseas operator.

For local directory assistance ("information"), dial ℂ **411**; for long-distance information, dial 1, then the appropriate area code and ℂ **555-1212**.

Telegraph and telex services are provided primarily by Western Union. You can bring your telegram into the nearest Western Union office (there are hundreds across the country) or dictate it over the phone (ℂ **800/325-6000**). You can also telegraph money, or have it telegraphed to you, very quickly over the Western Union system, but this service can cost as much as 15% to 20% of the amount sent.

Most hotels have **fax machines** available for guest use (be sure to ask about the charge to use it). Many hotel rooms are even wired for guests' fax machines. A less expensive way to send and receive faxes may be at stores such as Kinko's or The UPS Store. (Look in the Yellow Pages directory under "Fax Transmission Services" or "Packing Services.")

There are two kinds of telephone directories in the United States. The so-called **White Pages** list private households and business subscribers in alphabetical order. The inside front cover lists emergency numbers for police, fire, ambulance, the Coast Guard, poison-control center, crime-victims hot line, and so on. The first few pages usually will tell you how to make long-distance and international calls, complete with country codes and area codes. Government numbers are usually printed on blue paper within the White Pages. Printed on yellow paper, the so-called **Yellow Pages** list all local services, businesses, industries, and houses of worship according to activity, with an index at the front or back. (Drugstores/pharmacies and restaurants are also sometimes listed by geographic location.) The Yellow Pages often also include city maps, postal ZIP codes, and public transportation routes.

Time The continental United States is divided into **four time zones:** Eastern Standard Time (EST), Central Standard Time (CST), Mountain Standard Time (MST)—which includes all of Colorado—and Pacific Standard Time (PST). Alaska and Hawaii have their own zones. For example, noon in New York City (EST) is 11am in Chicago (CST), 10am in Denver (MST), 9am in Los Angeles (PST), 8am in Anchorage (AST), and 7am in Honolulu (HST).

Daylight saving time is in effect in Colorado and most of the country from 1am on the first Sunday in April through 1am on the last Sunday in October. Note that Arizona (except for the Navajo Nation), Hawaii, much of Indiana, and Puerto Rico do not observe DST. Daylight saving time moves the clock 1 hour ahead of standard time.

Tipping Tipping is so ingrained in the American way of life that the annual income tax of tip-earning service personnel is based on how much they should have received in light of their employers' gross revenues. Accordingly, they may have to pay tax on a tip you didn't actually give them.

Here are some rules of thumb:

In hotels, tip **bellhops** at least $1 per bag ($2–$3 per bag if you have a lot of luggage) and tip the **chamber staff** $1 to $2 per day (more if you've left a disaster area, or if you're traveling with kids and/or pets). Tip the **doorman** or **concierge** only if he or she has provided you with some specific service (for example, calling a cab for you or obtaining difficult-to-get theater tickets). Tip the **valet-parking attendant** $1 every time you get your car.

In restaurants, bars, and nightclubs, tip **service staff** 15% to 20% of the check, tip **bartenders** 10% to 15%, tip **checkroom attendants** $1 per garment, and tip **valet-parking attendants** $1 per vehicle. Tip the **doorman** only if he has provided you with some specific service (such as calling a cab for you). Tipping is not expected in cafeterias and fast-food restaurants.

As for other service personnel, tip **cab drivers** 15% of the fare, tip **sky-caps** at airports at least $1 per bag ($2–$3 per bag if you have a lot of luggage) and tip **hairdressers** and **barbers** 15% to 20%.

Tipping ushers at movies and theaters, and gas-station attendants, is not expected.

Toilets You won't find public toilets or "restrooms" on the streets in most U.S. cities, but they can be found in hotel lobbies, bars, restaurants, museums, department stores, railway and bus stations, and service stations. Large hotels, visitor centers, discount stores such as Walmart and Target, and fast-food restaurants are probably the best bet for good, clean facilities. If possible, avoid the toilets at parks and beaches, which tend to be dirty; some may be unsafe. Restaurants and bars in resorts or heavily visited areas may reserve their restrooms for patrons. Some establishments display a notice indicating this. You can ignore this sign or, better yet, avoid arguments by paying for a cup of coffee or a soft drink, which will qualify you as a patron.

4

Settling into Denver

It's no accident that Denver is called "the Mile High City": When you climb up to the State Capitol, you're precisely 5,280 feet above sea level when you reach the 18th step. Denver's location at this altitude was purely coincidental; Denver is one of the few cities that was not built on an ocean, lake, navigable river, or even on an existing road or railroad.

In the summer of 1858, eager prospectors discovered a few flecks of gold where Cherry Creek empties into the shallow South Platte River, and a tent camp quickly sprang up on the site. (The first permanent structure was a saloon.) When militia Gen. William H. Larimer arrived in 1859, he claim-jumped the land on the east side of the Platte, laid out a city, and, hoping to gain political favors, named it after James Denver, governor of the Kansas Territory, which included this area. Larimer was not aware that Denver had recently resigned.

Larimer's was one of several settlements on the South Platte. Three others also sought recognition, but Larimer, a shrewd man, had a solution. For the price of a barrel of whisky, he bought out the other would-be town fathers, and the name "Denver" caught on.

Although the gold found in Denver was but a teaser for much larger strikes in the nearby mountains, the community grew as a shipping and trade center, in part because it had a milder climate than the mining towns it served. A devastating fire in 1863, a deadly flash flood in 1864, and American Indian hostilities in the late 1860s created many hardships. But the establishment of rail links to the east and the influx of silver from the rich mines to the west kept Denver going. Silver from Leadville and gold from Cripple Creek made Denver a showcase city in the late 19th and early 20th centuries. The U.S. Mint, built in 1906, established Denver as a banking and financial center.

In the years following World War II, Denver mushroomed to become the largest city between the Great Plains and the Pacific Coast, with about 500,000 residents within the city limits and more than 2.5 million in the metropolitan area. Today, it's a sprawling and growing city, extending from the Rocky Mountain foothills on the west far into the plains to the south and east. Denver is noted for its dozens of tree-lined boulevards, 200 city parks that cover more than 20,000 acres, and architecture ranging from Victorian to sleek contemporary.

1 Orientation

ARRIVING
BY PLANE
Denver International Airport (DIA) is 23 miles northeast of downtown, usually a 35- to 45-minute drive. Covering 53 square miles (twice the size of Manhattan), DIA boasts one of the tallest flight-control towers in the world, at

327 feet. The airport, which has 94 gates and 6 full-service runways, can handle around 33 million passengers annually.

Major national airlines serving Denver include American, America West, Continental, Delta, Frontier, Northwest, Sun Country, JetBlue, United, and US Airways. **International airlines** include Air Canada, British Airways, Lufthansa, and Mexicana de Aviación.

Regional and **commuter airlines** connecting Denver with other points in the Rockies and Southwest include Alaska Airlines, Aspen Air, Mountain Air Express, and three United Express airlines: Air Wisconsin, Great Lakes Aviation, and Mesa.

For airlines' national reservations phone numbers and websites, see "Getting There," in chapter 2. For other information, call the Denver International Airport **information line** (✆ **800/AIR-2-DEN** or 303/342-2000; TDD 800/688-1333; www.flydenver.com). Other important airport phone numbers include: **administration,** ✆ 303/342-2200; **emergencies,** ✆ 303/342-4211; **ground transportation,** ✆ 303/342-4059; **vehicle assistance,** including emergency car-start, ✆ 303/342-4650; **paging,** ✆ 303/342-2300; **parking,** ✆ 303/342-4086; and **police,** ✆ 303/342-4212.

GETTING TO & FROM THE AIRPORT   Bus, taxi, and limousine services shuttle travelers between the airport and downtown, and most major car-rental companies have outlets at the airport. Because many major hotels are some distance from the airport, travelers should check on the availability and cost of hotel shuttle services when making reservations.

The **city bus** fare from the airport to downtown Denver is $8; from the airport to Boulder and suburban Park-n-Ride lots, it is about $10. The **Super-Shuttle** (✆ **800/525-3177** or 303/370-1300; www.supershuttledenver.com) provides transportation to and from a number of hotels downtown and in the Denver Tech Center. The SuperShuttle has frequent scheduled service between the airport and downtown hotels for $18 per person each way; door-to-door service is also available. **Taxi** companies (see "Getting Around," later in this chapter) are another option, with fares generally in the $30-to-$50 range, and you can often share a cab and split the fare by calling the cab company ahead of time. For instance, **Yellow Cab** (✆ **303/777-7777**) will take up to five people from DIA to most downtown hotels for a flat rate of $45.

Those who prefer a bit of luxury may prefer **Mile Hi City Limousine,** also known as White Dove Limousine (✆ **800/910-7433** or 303/355-5002; www. whitedovelimo.com). Rates to different parts of the Denver metro area start at $65 but vary, so call for prices. The company operates sedan and stretch limousines (as well as a minibus) built to accommodate 3 to 14 people. Charter services are also available.

BY CAR
The principal highway routes into Denver are **I-25** from the north (Fort Collins and Wyoming) and south (Colorado Springs and New Mexico); **I-70** from the east (Burlington and Kansas) and west (Grand Junction and Utah); and **I-76** from the northeast (Nebraska). If you're driving into Denver from Boulder, take **U.S. 36;** from Salida and southwest, **U.S. 285.**

BY TRAIN
Amtrak serves Union Station, 17th and Wynkoop streets (✆ **800/USA-RAIL** or 303/825-2583; www.amtrak.com), in the lower downtown historic district.

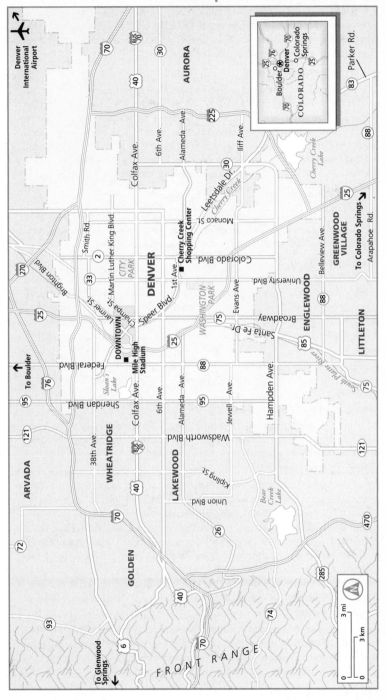

BY BUS

Greyhound, 19th and Arapahoe streets (℗ **800/231-2222;** www.greyhound.
com), is the major bus service in Colorado, with about 60 daily arrivals and
departures to communities in and out of the state.

VISITOR INFORMATION

The **Denver Metro Convention and Visitors Bureau** operates a visitor center
on the 16th Street Mall at 918 16th St. (℗ **303/892-1505**). It's open Monday
through Friday from 8am to 5pm and summer Saturdays from 9:30am to
1:30pm. Visitor information is also available in the Tabor and Cherry Creek
Shopping Centers, and at the Colorado State Capitol and Denver International
Airport. Ask for the *Official Visitors Guide,* a 150-plus-page full-color booklet
with a comprehensive listing of accommodations, restaurants, and other visitor
services in Denver and surrounding areas.

For advance information, contact the Denver Metro Convention and Visitors
Bureau, 1555 California St., Suite 300, Denver, CO 80202-4264 (℗ **800/233-
6837;** www.denver.org). Two other good Internet resources are **www.denver.
citysearch.com** and **www.denvergov.org**.

CITY LAYOUT

It is difficult to get lost in Denver, as long as you remember that the mountains,
nearly always visible, are to the west. All the same, getting around a city of half
a million people can be perplexing. One element of confusion is that Denver has
both an older grid system, which is oriented northeast–southwest to parallel the
South Platte River, and a newer north–south grid system that surrounds the
older one.

The *Official Visitors Guide,* available free of charge from the Denver Metro
Convention and Visitors Bureau (see "Visitor Information," above), contains a
good map.

MAIN ARTERIES & STREETS

It's probably easiest to get your bearings from Civic Center Park. From here,
Colfax Avenue (U.S. 40) extends east and west as far as the eye can see. The same
is true for Broadway, which reaches north and south.

DOWNTOWN DENVER   North of Colfax and west of Broadway is the center of downtown, where the streets follow the old grid pattern. A mile-long
pedestrian mall, **16th Street,** cuts northwest off Broadway just above this intersection. (The numbered streets parallel 16th to the northeast, extending to 44th;
and to the southwest, as far as 5th.) Intersecting the numbered streets at right
angles are **Lawrence Street** (which runs one-way northeast) and **Larimer Street**
(which runs one-way southwest), 12 and 13 blocks north, respectively, of the
Colfax-Broadway intersection.

I-25 skirts downtown Denver to the west, with access from Colfax or **Speer
Boulevard,** which winds diagonally along Cherry Creek past Larimer Square.

OUTSIDE DOWNTOWN   Outside the downtown sector, the pattern is a little less confusing. But keep in mind that the numbered *avenues* that parallel Colfax to the north and south (Colfax is equivalent to 15th Ave.) have nothing in
common with the numbered *streets* of the downtown grid. In fact, any byway
labeled an "avenue" runs east–west, never north–south.

FINDING AN ADDRESS

NORTH–SOUTH ARTERIES   The thoroughfare that divides avenues into
east and west is **Broadway,** which runs one-way south between 19th Street and

I-25. Each block east or west adds 100 to the avenue address; thus, if you wanted to find 2115 E. 17th Ave., it would be a little more than 21 blocks east of Broadway, just beyond Vine Street.

Main thoroughfares that parallel Broadway to the east include **Downing Street** (1200 block), **York Street** (2300 block; it becomes **University Blvd.** south of 6th), **Colorado Boulevard** (4000 block), **Monaco Street Parkway** (6500 block), and **Quebec Street** (7300 block). Colorado Boulevard (Colo. 2) is the most significant commercial artery, intersecting I-25 on the south and I-70 on the north. North–south streets that parallel Broadway to the west include **Santa Fe Drive** (U.S. 85; 1000 block); west of I-25 are **Federal Boulevard** (U.S. 287 North; 3000 block), and **Sheridan Boulevard** (Colo. 95; 5200 block), the boundary between Denver and Lakewood.

EAST–WEST ARTERIES   Denver streets are divided into north and south at **Ellsworth Avenue,** about 2 miles south of Colfax. Ellsworth is a relatively minor street, but it's a convenient dividing point because it's just a block south of **1st Avenue.** With building numbers increasing by 100 each block, that puts an address like 1710 Downing St. at the corner of East 17th Avenue. **First, 6th, Colfax** (1500 block), and **26th** avenues, and **Martin Luther King Jr. Boulevard** (3200 block) are the principal east–west thoroughfares. There are no numbered avenues south of Ellsworth. Major east–west byways south of Ellsworth are **Alameda** (Colo. 26; 300 block), **Mississippi** (1100 block), **Louisiana** (1300 block), **Evans** (2100 block), **Yale** (2700 block), and **Hampden** avenues (U.S. 285; 3500 block).

NEIGHBORHOODS IN BRIEF

Lower Downtown (LoDo) A 25-block area surrounding Union Station, and encompassing **Wynkoop Street** southeast to **Market Street** and **20th Street** southwest to **Speer Boulevard,** this delightful and busy historic district was until recently a somewhat seedy neighborhood of deteriorating Victorian houses and redbrick warehouses. A major restoration effort has brought it back to life. Today it is home to chic shops, art galleries, nightclubs, and restaurants. Listed as both a city and county historic district, it boasts numerous National Historic Landmarks; skyscrapers are prohibited by law. Coors Field, the 50,000-seat home of the Rockies baseball team, opened here in 1995.

Central Business District This extends along **16th, 17th, and 18th streets between Lawrence Street and Broadway.** The ban on skyscrapers certainly does not apply here. In this area you'll find the Brown Palace Hotel, the Westin Hotel at Tabor Center, and other upscale lodgings; numerous restaurants and bars; plus the popular 16th Street Mall.

Far East Center Denver's Asian community is concentrated along this strip of **Federal Boulevard,** between **West Alameda** and **West Mississippi** avenues. It burgeoned in the aftermath of the Vietnam War to accommodate throngs of Southeast Asian refugees, especially Thai and Vietnamese. Look for authentic restaurants, bakeries, groceries, gift shops, and clothing stores. The Far East Center Building at Federal and Alameda is built in Japanese pagoda style.

Five Points The "five points" actually meet at 23rd Street and Broadway, but the cultural and commercial hub of Denver's black community, from **23rd** to **38th** streets, northeast of downtown, covers a much larger area and incorporates four historic districts. Restaurants offer soul food, barbecued ribs, and Caribbean cuisine, while jazz and blues musicians and contemporary dance troupes perform in theaters and nightclubs. The Black American West Museum and Heritage Center is also in this area.

La Alma Lincoln Park/Auraria Hispanic culture, art, food, and entertainment predominate along this strip of **Santa Fe Drive,** between **West Colfax** and **West 6th** avenues. It's notable for its Southwestern character and architecture. This neighborhood is well worth a visit for its numerous restaurants, art galleries, and crafts shops. Denver's annual Cinco de Mayo celebration takes place here.

Uptown Denver's oldest residential neighborhood, from **Broadway** east to **York Street** (City Park) and **23rd Avenue** south to **Colfax Avenue,** is best known today for two things: It's bisected by 17th Avenue, home to many of the city's finest restaurants, and several of its classic Victorian and Queen Anne-style homes have been converted to captivating bed-and-breakfasts (see "Where to Stay," later in this chapter).

Washington Park A grand Victorian neighborhood centered on the lush park of its namesake, "Wash Park" is one of Denver's trendiest and most popular neighborhoods. Bounded by **Broadway** east to **University Boulevard,** and **Alameda Avenue** south to **Evans Avenue,** it features a good deal of dining and recreational opportunities, but little in the way of lodging. It is a great place, however, for architecture and history buffs to drive or walk past the grand rows of houses.

Capitol Hill One of Denver's most diverse and oldest neighborhoods

lies just southeast of downtown. Capitol Hill centers on the gold-domed Capitol Building, encompassing **Broadway** east to **York,** and **Colfax Avenue** south to **6th Avenue.** The north edge is improving after years of neglect and criminal activity, and now features such attractions as the Fillmore Auditorium and a lively restaurant and bar scene. There are several commercial and retail districts in the area, nestled amidst Victorian houses and modern lofts and apartments. Also here are the Molly Brown House Museum (see chapter 5) and several lodging options, ranging from B&Bs to luxury hotels (see "Where to Stay," below). You'll notice that there are no old wooden buildings here. After a disastrous fire in 1863, the government forbade the construction of wooden structures, a ban that stood until after World War II.

Cherry Creek Home of the Cherry Creek Shopping Center and Denver Country Club, this area extends north from **East 1st Avenue** to **East 8th Avenue,** and from **Downing Street** east to **Steele Street.** You'll find huge, ostentatious stone mansions here, especially around Circle Drive (southwest of 6th and University), where many of Denver's wealthiest families have lived for generations.

Glendale Denver surrounds Glendale, an incorporated city. The center of a lively entertainment district that is home to a slew of topless clubs, Glendale straddles Cherry Creek on South Colorado Boulevard south of East Alameda Avenue.

Tech Center At the southern end of the metropolitan area is the Denver Tech Center, along **I-25** between **Belleview Avenue** and **Arapahoe Road.** In this district, about a 25-minute drive from downtown, you

To Boulder↑

To Burlington →

← To Glenwood
Springs

70

25

33

W. 38th Ave.

287

E. 40th Ave.

Brighton Blvd.

38th St.

South Platte River

20th St.

Market St.

30TH-DOWNING

Martin Luther King Blvd.

LODO

FIVE
POINTS

UNION
STATION

PEPSI
CENTER

Wynkoop St.

Welton St.

Park Ave.

Downing St.

City
Park

MILE
HIGH

DOWN-
TOWN

Mile High
Stadium

Auraria Pkwy.

UPTOWN

Colfax Ave.

BUS
70

40

287

State
Capitol

CAPITOL
HILL

2

Speer Blvd.

10TH-OSAGE

Colorado Blvd.

6

6th Ave.

LA ALMA/
LINCOLN
PARK

←

Cherry Creek

CHERRY
CREEK

Santa Fe Dr.

Broadway

1st Ave.

Federal Blvd.

26

Alameda Ave.

South Platte River

ALAMEDA

Cherry Creek
Shopping Center

FAR EAST
CENTER
→

To Glendale →

Washington
Park

I-25–BROADWAY

University Blvd.

Mississippi Ave.

WASHINGTON
PARK

85

Jewell Ave.

EVANS

To Colorado
Springs ↘

25

88

Evans Ave.

RTD Light Rail

C line   D line

10TH-OSAGE

*Note: Downtown
stations not shown*

Santa Fe Dr.

25   76

Boulder ⊛

70   Denver   70

COLORADO   ○ Colorado
Springs

25

0   1 mi
0   1 km

N

ENGLEWOOD

ENGLEWOOD

Hampden Ave.

will find the headquarters of several international and national companies, high-tech businesses, and a handful of upscale hotels heavily oriented toward business travelers.

2 Getting Around

BY PUBLIC TRANSPORTATION

The **Regional Transportation District,** or **RTD** (© **800/366-7433,** 303/299-6000, or TDD 303/299-6089 for route and schedule information; 303/299-6700 for other business; www.rtd-denver.com) calls itself "The Ride." It operates bus routes and a light-rail system, with free transfer tickets available. It provides good service within Denver and its suburbs and outlying communities (including Boulder, Longmont, and Evergreen), as well as free parking at 65 Park-n-Ride locations throughout the Denver-Boulder metropolitan area. The light-rail service is designed to get buses and cars out of congested downtown Denver; many of the bus routes from outlying areas deliver passengers to light-rail stations rather than downtown.

The local one-way fare is $1.25; seniors and passengers with disabilities pay 60¢, and children age 5 and under travel free. Regional bus fares vary (for example, Denver to Boulder costs $3.75). Exact change is required for buses, and train tickets can be purchased at vending machines beneath light-rail station awnings.

Depending on the route, the departure time of the last bus or train varies from 9pm to 2am. Maps for all routes are available at any time at the RTD **Civic Center Station,** 16th Street and Broadway; and the **Market Street Station,** Market and 16th streets. RTD also provides special service to Colorado Rockies (baseball) and Denver Broncos (football) games. All RTD buses and trains are completely wheelchair accessible.

Free buses run up and down the 16th Street Mall between the Civic Center and Market Street every 75 seconds during peak hours (less frequently at other times), daily from 6am to 1am.

Visitors should take particular note of the light-rail **C Line.** After diverting from the main north–south light-rail line at Colfax Avenue, it veers west and stops at Invesco Field at Mile High, the Pepsi Center, and Six Flags Elitch Gardens before chugging into Union Station at 17th and Wynkoop streets in lower downtown. The fare is the same as on any other local route, but the schedule is extended, with the last train leaving Union Station at about 2am. By the end of 2006, a new train along I-25 from Broadway to Mineral Avenue in the south suburbs will begin running.

The open-air **Platte Valley Trolley** (© **303/458-6255;** www.denvertrolley. org) operates year-round. From June through October between noon and 4pm Thursday through Sunday, there's a half-hour "Denver Sightseeing Route" ride ($3 adults, $1 seniors and children), which operates from 15th Street at Confluence Park, south to Decatur Street along the west bank of the Platte River. Different routes are offered at other times.

BY TAXI

The main companies are **Yellow Cab** (© **303/777-7777**) and **Metro Taxi** (© **303/333-3333**). Taxis can be hailed on the street, though it's preferable to telephone for a taxi or wait for one at a taxi stand outside a major hotel. On weekends, however, hailing a taxi can be difficult when the bars close down for the night.

For the traveler seeking true luxury, Denver has several limousine services, including **Presidential Limousines** (© 800/828-8680 or 303/320-1101), and **Executive Transportation** (© 800/546-6120 or 303/755-5089), which covers the entire state, offering Suburbans, 15-passenger vans, town cars, and limos.

BY CAR

Because cars are not really necessary downtown, visitors can save the cost of renting and parking by arranging to stay downtown while in Denver, then renting a car to leave the area.

The Denver office of the **American Automobile Association (AAA)** is at 4100 E. Arkansas Ave., Denver, CO 80222-3405 (© **800/222-4357** or 303/753-8800); there are several other locations in the Denver area.

T-Rex, a major highway and light-rail project, began in 2001 and will slow traffic on I-25 until 2006. The area affected is south of downtown, so travelers to the Denver Technological Center and other environs south of Denver should expect delays and possible closures. For more information, call © **303/786-8739** for recorded information or visit **www.trexproject.com**.

CAR RENTALS   Most major car-rental agencies have outlets in or near downtown Denver, as well as at Denver International Airport. These include **Alamo,** 24530 E. 78th Ave. (© 800/462-5266 or 303/342-7373); **Avis,** 1900 Broadway (© 800/831-2847 or 303/839-1280; 303/342-5500 at DIA); **Dollar,** 10343 N. Federal Blvd., Westminster (© 800/800-4000 or 303/790-0970; 303/317-1142 at DIA); **Enterprise,** 5179 S. Broadway (© 800/736-8222 or 303/794-3333; 303/342-7350 at DIA); **Hertz,** 2001 Welton St. (© 800/654-3131 or 303/297-9400; 303/342-3800 at DIA); **National,** at Denver International Airport (© 800/227-7368 or 303/342-0717); and **Thrifty,** 8006 E. Arapahoe Ave. (© 800/847-4389 or 303/220-1020; 303/342-9400 at DIA). You can rent campers, travel trailers, motor homes, and motorcycles from **Cruise America,** 8950 N. Federal Blvd. (© 800/327-7799 or 303/426-6699; www.cruiseamerica.com).

Per-day rentals for midsize cars range from $30 to $60, although AAA and other discounts are often available, and weekend and multiday rates can also save money. Four-wheel-drive vehicles, trucks, and campers cost more.

PARKING   Downtown parking-lot rates vary from 75¢ per half-hour to $15 per full day. Rates are higher near the 16th Street Mall, in the central business district, and in hotel lots (some downtown hotels charge as much as $26 per night). Keep a handful of quarters if you plan to use on-street parking meters.

FAST FACTS: Denver

American Express The American Express travel agency, 555 17th St. (© **303/383-5050**), is open Monday through Friday from 8am to 5pm. It offers full member services and currency exchange. To report a lost card, call © **800/528-4800**; to report lost traveler's checks, call © **800/221-7282**.

Area Code Area codes are **303** and **720,** and local calls require 10-digit dialing. See the "Telephone, Telegraph, Telex & Fax" section under "Fast Facts," in chapter 3.

Babysitters Front desks at major hotels can often arrange for babysitters for their guests.

Business Hours   Generally, business offices are open weekdays from 9am to 5pm and government offices are open from 8am until 4:30 or 5pm. Stores are open 6 days a week, with many also open on Sunday; department stores usually stay open until 9pm at least 1 day a week. Discount stores and supermarkets are often open later than other stores, and some supermarkets are open 24 hours a day.

Banks are usually open weekdays from 9am to 5pm, occasionally a bit later on Friday, and sometimes on Saturday. There's 24-hour access to automated teller machines (ATMs) at most banks, plus in many shopping centers and other outlets.

Car Rentals   See "Getting Around," above.

Doctors & Dentists   Doctor and dentist referrals are available by calling ✆ **800/DOCTORS. Centura Health Advisor** (✆ **800/327-6877** or 303/777-6877) provides free physician referrals and answers health questions; the **Parent Smart Health Line** (✆ **303/861-0123**) specializes in referrals to children's doctors and dentists, and also has staff on hand to provide advice.

Drugstores   Throughout the metropolitan area, you will find Walgreens and other chain pharmacies, as well as Safeway and King Soopers grocery stores (which also have drugstores). The **Walgreens** at 2000 E. Colfax Ave. (✆ **303/331-0917**) is open 24 hours a day. For the locations of other Walgreens, call ✆ **800/WALGREENS.**

Emergencies   Call ✆ **911.** For the **Rocky Mountain Poison Center,** call ✆ **800/323-3073** or 303/739-1123. For the **Rape Crisis and Domestic Violence Hotline,** call ✆ **303/318-9989.**

Eyeglasses   One-hour replacements and repairs are usually available at **Pearle Vision,** 2720 S. Colorado Blvd. at Yale Avenue (✆ **303/758-1292**), and **LensCrafters,** in Cherry Creek Shopping Center (✆ **303/321-8331**).

Hospitals   Among Denver-area hospitals are **St. Joseph's,** 1835 Franklin St. (✆ **303/837-7111**), just east of downtown, and **Children's Hospital,** 1056 E. 19th Ave. (✆ **303/861-8888**).

Maps   Denver's largest map store, **Mapsco Map and Travel Center,** 800 Lincoln St., Denver, CO 80203 (✆ **800/456-8703** or 303/830-2373; www.mapsco.com), offers USGS and recreation maps, state maps and travel guides, raised relief maps, and globes.

Newspapers & Magazines   The *Denver Post* (www.denverpost.com) is Colorado's largest daily newspaper. The *Rocky Mountain News* (www.rockymountainnews.com) also covers the metropolitan area. Under a joint operating agreement, each publishes a separate weekday edition, only the *News* prints on Saturday, and only the *Post* appears on Sunday. A widely read free weekly, *Westword* (www.westword.com), is known as much for its controversial jibes at local politicians and celebrities as it is for its entertainment listings. National newspapers such as *USA Today* and the *Wall Street Journal* can be purchased at newsstands and at major hotels.

Photographic Needs   For photographic supplies, equipment, 1-hour processing, and repairs, visit **Wolf Camera** at 1 of its 15 Denver locations; its downtown branch, at 1545 California St. (✆ **303/623-1155,** or 888/644-WOLF for other locations; www.wolfcamera.com), claims to be the biggest single-floor camera store in the world. Check Sunday's *Denver Post* for discount coupons for Wolf Camera's services. Another good source for photo supplies and film processing is **Mike's Camera,** 759 S. Colorado Blvd. (© 303/733-2121; www.mikescamera.com).

Post Office The main downtown post office, 951 20th St., is open Monday through Friday from 7am to 10:30pm, Saturday and Sunday from 8:30am to 10:30pm. For full 24-hour postal service, go to the General Mail Facility, 7500 E. 53rd Place. For other post office locations and hours, call the U.S. Postal Service (© 800/275-8777; www.usps.com).

Safety Although Denver is a relatively safe city, it is not crime-free. Safety is seldom a problem on the 16th Street Mall, but even streetwise Denverites avoid late-night walks along certain sections of East Colfax Avenue, just a few blocks away. If you are unsure of the safety of a particular area you wish to visit, ask your hotel concierge or desk clerk.

Taxes State and local sales tax in Denver is about 7% (it varies slightly in neighboring counties and suburbs). The hotel tax is about 7%, bringing the total tax on accommodations to nearly 14%.

Useful Telephone Numbers For a weather report, time, and temperature, call © 303/337-2500. Statewide road condition reports are available by calling © 303/639-1111. For information on possible road construction delays in the Denver area and statewide, see www.cotrip.org. Information on the T-Rex (the highway-widening and rail-expansion project that's slowing Denver's traffic through 2006) is available by calling © 303/786-8739 or browsing www.trexproject.com.

3 Where to Stay

Although most hotels and motels in the Denver area do not have seasonal rates (as you'll find in many other parts of Colorado), hotels that cater to business travelers, such as the **Brown Palace** and the **Warwick** (see below), often offer substantial weekend discounts, sometimes as much as 50% off the regular rates. Rates listed below do not include the 13.55% accommodations tax.

The lodging industry is still trying to catch up with the construction of Denver International Airport several years ago, and you'll find that many of the major chains and franchises have built or are in the process of constructing facilities near the new airport. Among those now open are **Courtyard by Marriott at DIA,** 6901 Tower Rd., Denver, CO 80249 (© 800/321-2211 or 303/371-0300), with rates of $69 to $149 for a double; **Fairfield Inn–DIA,** 6851 Tower Rd., Denver, CO 80249 (© 800/228-2800 or 303/576-9640), which charges $79 to $109 for a double; and **Hampton Inn DIA,** 6290 Tower Rd., Denver CO 80249 (© 800/426-7866 or 303/371-0200), with a rate of $100 for a double.

Reliable chain hotels in the downtown area include: **Comfort Inn,** 401 17th St., Denver, CO 80202 (© 800/228-5150 or 303/296-0400), with a convenient location and rates of $149 double and $189 to $289 suite; **Embassy Suites,** 1881 Curtis St. (© 800/733-3366 or 303/297-8888), with suites for $129 to $159 on weekend nights and $175 to $250 during the week; **La Quinta Inn Downtown,** 3500 Park Ave. W. (at I-25 exit 213), Denver, CO 80216 (© 800/531-5900 or 303/458-1222), charging $90 to $100 for a double; and **Red Lion**

Denver Accommodations

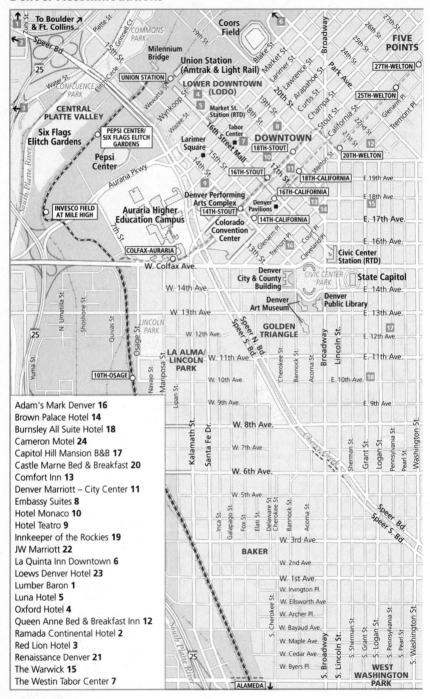

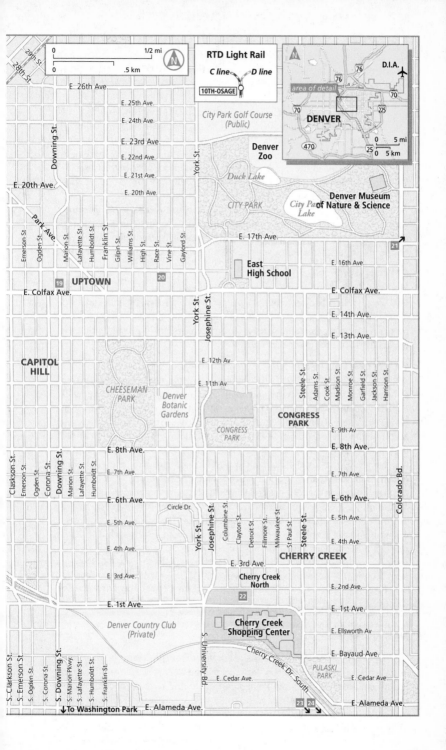

Hotel at Invesco Field, 1975 Bryant St. (at I-25 exit 210B), Denver, CO 80204 (✆ **800/388-5381** or 303/433-8331), with rates of $79 to $129 double. A budget option is the **Ramada Continental Hotel,** 2601 Zuni St. (at I-25 exit 212B for Speer Blvd.), Denver, CO 80211 (✆ **800/2RAMADA** or 303/433-6677), which charges $79 for a double.

Outside downtown, chain lodgings include: **Hampton Inn,** 4685 Quebec St., Denver, CO 80216 (✆ **800/HAMPTON** or 303/388-8100), with a double rate of $59 to $84; and **Motel 6,** 480 Wadsworth Blvd., Lakewood, CO 80226 (✆ **800/466-8356** or 303/232-4924), charging $44 to $54 double. Among the four Best Westerns in the metro area is **Best Western Denver Stapleton,** 3535 Quebec St., Denver, CO 80207 (✆ **800/328-2268** or 303/333-7711), which has double rates from $69 to $89.

These official, or "rack," rates do not take into consideration any discounts, such as those offered to members of AAA or AARP. Be sure to ask if you qualify for a reduced rate. Because a chain hotel's national reservation service may not be able to offer discounts, your best bet may be to call the hotel directly.

DOWNTOWN

Hotels in downtown Denver, "the central business district of the Rocky Mountain West," generally cater to businesspeople, with high-tech amenities and locations convenient to the Convention Center or the financial district. These properties are more than adequate for leisure travelers, and especially enticing on weekends when they lower their rates.

VERY EXPENSIVE

Adam's Mark Denver ⭐   This striking, sprawling complex consists of two buildings that were designed by onetime Denver resident I. M. Pei in the 1950s, joined as Denver's first convention hotel in the mid-1990s. Linked by a pedestrian bridge that crosses Court Place, it combines the 22-floor Tower Building (a former Hilton and Radisson property) and the Plaza Building (a former May D & F department store) into the largest hotel in the Rocky Mountain region. From the upper floors of the Tower Building, the west-facing rooms have marvelous views of the Front Range, and it's a real treat to relax and watch the lights of the city come on as the sun makes a graceful exit behind the curtain of mountains.

Rooms, on average, are larger than the norm in downtown Denver, and the range of suites is dizzying. The decor of both guest rooms and public areas is classical, with an emphasis on brass, marble, and solid woods such as oak and mahogany. Colors are muted and restful.

1550 Court Place, Denver, CO 80202. ✆ 800/444-2326 or 303/893-3333. Fax 303/626-2542. www.adamsmark. com. 1,225 units. $165–$249 double; $375–$1,200 suite. AE, DC, DISC, MC, V. Underground valet parking $22, self-parking $15; 6 ft. 4 in. height limit. **Amenities:** 3 restaurants (1 Italian, 2 cafes); 3 lounges; heated outdoor pool; health club (weight room, cardiovascular machines); sauna; business center; 24-hr. room service; coin-op washers and dryers; dry cleaning; executive level (concierge and business services, full breakfast, local and national newspapers, and happy hour w/hors d'oeuvres, coffee, and desserts). *In room:* A/C, TV w/pay movies, high-speed Internet, minibar, fridge, coffeemaker, hair dryer, iron.

Brown Palace Hotel ⭐⭐⭐ (Moments   For more than 100 years, the city's finest hotel has been the place to stay for anyone who is anyone. It combines great rooms and amenities with the intangibles: interesting history, romantic atmosphere, regional personality, and impeccable service. A National Historic Landmark, the Brown Palace has operated continuously since it opened in 1892. Designed with an odd triangular shape by the renowned architect Frank Edbrooke, it was built of Colorado red granite and Arizona sandstone. The lobby's walls are paneled with Mexican onyx, and elaborate cast-iron grillwork surrounds six tiers of balconies up to the stained-glass ceiling. Every president since 1905 (except Calvin Coolidge) has visited the hotel, and Dwight Eisenhower made the Brown his home away from the White House. His former room, now known as the Eisenhower Suite, is a vision of stately elegance, with a preserved dent in the fireplace trim that is the alleged result of an errant golf swing. There are also lavish, unique suites named after Teddy Roosevelt, Ronald Reagan, and The Beatles, each recently redecorated.

Standard rooms are also lush and comfortable, either Victorian or Art Deco in style with reproduction furnishings and fixtures. Each has a desk, a duvet, and individual climate control. The clientele is a mix of leisure travelers and businesspeople with a taste—and a budget—for luxury. The staterooms on the ninth floor are especially enticing, with cordless phones, big-screen TVs, fridges, fax/printers, and safes. The water's great here: The Brown Palace has its own artesian wells!

321 17th St., Denver, CO 80202. ✆ 800/321-2599 or 303/297-3111. Fax 303/312-5900. www.brownpalace. com. 241 units. $279–$339 double; $359–$1,159 suite. Weekend rates from $169 double. AE, DC, DISC, MC, V. Valet parking $22 overnight. Pets up to 20 lb. accepted. **Amenities:** 3 restaurants (all Continental; see "Where to Dine," later in this chapter); 2 lounges; exercise room; concierge, courtesy car; business center; 24-hr. room service; in-room massage (for an extra charge). *In room:* A/C, TV w/pay movies, 2-line phone w/dataport, voice mail, and complimentary high-speed Internet access, hair dryer, iron.

Denver Marriott–City Center ✪   This hotel's location in the heart of the financial district makes it a great choice for both business and leisure travelers. Totally renovated in 2001–02, it's just 2 blocks from the 16th Street Mall, and convenient to Larimer Square, the Convention Center, Coors Field, Elitch Gardens amusement park, the U.S. Mint, and the Denver Art Museum. Each room has one king-size or two double beds, a desk, and typically great views. Some suites have small kitchenettes, making this one of the few properties in downtown Denver with such an amenity.

1701 California St., Denver, CO 80202. ✆ 800/228-9290 or 303/297-1300. Fax 303/298-7474. www.marriott hotels.com/DENDT. 613 units. $179–$235 double; $1,000 suite. AE, DC, DISC, MC, V. Parking $19–$23. Small pets accepted with deposit. **Amenities:** 2 restaurants (eclectic, American), lounge; small indoor pool; fitness center; spa; wet/dry saunas; business center; limited room service; massage (by appointment); coin-op laundry; laundry service; concierge level. *In room:* A/C, cable TV w/pay movies, dataport, kitchenettes, coffeemaker, hair dryer, iron.

Hotel Monaco ✪✪ *(Kids)*   Billing itself as "Denver's hippest high-style luxury hotel," the Hotel Monaco is a standout for the Kimpton Group chain. With eye-catching interiors inspired equally by Art Deco and French design, the hotel occupies a pair of renovated historic buildings in the heart of the central business district. This is one of the few downtown hotels that is 100% pet-friendly—the staff even delivers guests a named goldfish upon request. (The establishment also has a mascot, a Jack Russell terrier named Lily Sopris.) Rooms have a rich style, equal parts sinful red and snazzy yellow, with perks such as CD stereos, terry-cloth robes, and Starbucks coffee. With jetted tubs, wet bars, and VCRs, the generously sized suites are even more luxurious. You might

---

Fun Fact On the Hoof

If you're in town for the National Western Stock Show, make sure to visit the Brown Palace Hotel for a study in contrasts—the champion steer is traditionally corralled in the lobby during one of the event's final mornings.

bump into a celebrity here—the Monaco is a favorite of pro sports teams, rock bands, and Hollywood types, who often stay in the "music suites," named for and decorated after John Lennon, Janis Joplin, and Miles Davis. Another perk is the nightly "Altitude Adjustment Hour" in the lobby, where guests enjoy complimentary glasses of wine along with 5-minute massages from the employees of the on-site Aveda Spa.

1717 Champa St. (at 17th St.), Denver, CO 80202. ℭ **800/397-5380** or 303/296-1717. Fax 303/296-1818. www.monaco-denver.com. 189 units. $170–$205 double; $215–$970 suite; call for weekend rates. AE, DC, DISC, MC, V. Valet parking $19. Pets accepted. **Amenities:** Restaurant (Panzano; see "Where to Dine," later in this chapter); lounge; exercise room; spa; concierge; 24-hr. room service; in-room massage (for an extra charge); laundry service. *In room:* A/C, TV w/pay movies, fax, dataport (high-speed Internet access), minibar, fridge, coffeemaker, hair dryer, iron, safe.

Hotel Teatro ★★ *Finds*   Hotel Teatro is one of Denver's newest hotels. It's also the most dramatic: The Denver Center for the Performing Arts (across the street) inspired the decor, which features masks, playbills, and wardrobe from past productions of its resident theater company. The hotel caters to both business and leisure travelers with exquisitely furnished guest rooms that hold Indonesian marble, cherrywood desks and fixtures, and frette linens and towels. The nine-story building is a historic landmark, constructed as the Denver Tramway Building in 1911. The $18 million restoration brought 21st-century perks, such as free high-speed Web access and a combination fax/scanner/copier/printer in each room. Each room also features Aveda amenities and a shower massager. Kevin Taylor, one of Denver's best-known chefs, runs both restaurants and the room service.

1100 14th St. (at Arapahoe St.), Denver, CO 80202. ℭ **303/228-1100.** Fax 303/228-1101. www.hotel teatro.com. 111 units. $195–$325 double; $345–$1,400 suite. AE, DC, DISC, MC, V. Valet parking $24 overnight. Pets accepted. **Amenities:** 2 restaurants (American bistro, French); lounge; concierge; courtesy car; 24-hr. room service; massage; laundry service; dry cleaning. *In room:* A/C, TV w/pay movies, fax, dataport (w/high-speed Internet access), minibar, fridge, coffeemaker, hair dryer, iron.

The Westin Tabor Center ★★   The focal point of the 2-square-block Tabor Center shopping-and-office complex, the 19-story Westin bridges the gap between the central business district and lower downtown, and is conveniently located near Coors Field. Its contemporary design incorporates architectural elements of nearby Victorian-era structures. The elegant second-floor lobby features three-dimensional murals and modern fountains. The workout room is downtown Denver's best.

The spacious guest rooms, three-quarters of which contain king-size beds, were renovated with a contemporary flair in 2003–04. Every room has Westin's trademark pillow-topped mattresses and deluxe showerheads. The Executive Club on the top three floors provides upgraded features and amenities, including an in-room wet bar, continental breakfast, afternoon cocktails, and a resident concierge.

1672 Lawrence St., Denver, CO 80202. ℭ **800/228-3000** or 303/572-9100. Fax 303/572-7288. www. westin.com. 430 units. $219–$279 double; $400–$1,400 suite; call for weekend rates and packages. Children under 18 stay free in parent's room. AE, DC, DISC, MC, V. Valet parking $24; self-parking $12. **Amenities:** 2 restaurants (American, steakhouse); lounge; heated indoor/outdoor pool; health club (w/weight room and racquetball courts); Jacuzzi; sauna; concierge; business center; shopping arcade; limited room service; massage; laundry service; dry cleaning; executive level. *In room:* A/C, TV w/pay movies, dataport, minibar, coffeemaker, hair dryer, iron, safe.

EXPENSIVE

Burnsley All Suite Hotel ★★   This small, elegant hotel offers suites with private balconies and separate living, bedroom, dining, and fully stocked kitchen areas. The units are handsomely furnished, featuring marble entrance floors and antiques. The suites are expansive (averaging 700 sq. ft.) and popular with travelers who prefer to be a bit away from the hubbub of downtown. The hotel sits on a relatively quiet one-way street a few blocks southeast of the State Capitol.

The restaurant serves breakfast, lunch, and dinner on weekdays, and breakfast and dinner on weekends. The menu features fresh salmon, tenderloin, Colorado game plate, and vegetarian dishes. The lounge is a local favorite, a swank space with live jazz on Thursdays and Fridays. The hotel is conveniently situated near the Cherry Creek shopping areas and is only 5 blocks from downtown.

1000 Grant St. (at E. 10th Ave.), Denver, CO 80203. (C) 800/231-3915 or 303/830-1000. Fax 303/830-7676. www.burnsley.com. 80 suites. $109–$209 double. Weekend rates available. AE, DC, MC, V. Free covered parking. **Amenities:** Restaurant (Continental); lounge; seasonal outdoor pool; access to nearby health club; business center; room service until 10pm; laundry service. *In room:* A/C, TV, dataport, kitchen, coffeemaker, hair dryer, iron.

Luna Hotel ★★   This contemporary boutique hotel is one of the few lodging options in the lively LoDo neighborhood. Formerly the LoDo Inn, the property changed hands and underwent a metamorphosis in 2002. Today it's sleek and smart, combining the personal service of a B&B with the conveniences of a full-service hotel. Featuring spare yet inviting decor, the guest rooms are studies in efficiency, with perks like CD and DVD players, unique art prints, and large armoires. Some rooms have private balconies and others have jetted tubs; the suite has a copper-topped table and a small kitchen. The property is also the first in downtown Denver to set up a Wi-Fi network, affording guests a high-speed Internet connection in their rooms, the lobby, the Manhattan-esque Flow Lounge, and the restaurants without any pesky cables. The hotel is entirely nonsmoking.

1612 Wazee St., Denver, CO 80202. (C) 303/572-3300. Fax 303/623-0773. www.thelunahotel.com. 19 units. $169–$219 double; $249–$299 suite. AE, DC, DISC, MC, V. Parking $10. **Amenities:** 2 restaurants (cafe, eclectic); lounge; exercise room; concierge. *In room:* A/C, TV w/DVD player, dataport, kitchenette, coffeemaker, hair dryer, iron.

Oxford Hotel ★★ *Finds*   Designed by the architect Frank Edbrooke, this is one of Denver's few hotels that has survived from the 19th century (another being the Brown Palace, described earlier in this chapter). The facade is simple red sandstone, but the interior boasts marble walls, stained-glass windows, frescoes, and silver chandeliers, all of which were restored between 1979 and 1983 using Edbrooke's original drawings. The hotel is listed on the National Register of Historic Places.

Antique pieces imported from England and France furnish the large rooms, which were created by combining smaller rooms during the restoration. No two units are alike (they're either Art Deco or Victorian in style), but all are equipped with one king or queen bed, individual thermostats, dressing tables, and large closets.

An Art Deco gem, the Cruise Room Bar boasts perhaps the swankest cocktail atmosphere in Denver, and the spa is the largest in the area.

1600 17th St. (at Wazee St.), Denver, CO 80202. (C) 800/228-5838 or 303/628-5400. Fax 303/628-5413. www.theoxfordhotel.com. 80 units. $189–$229 double; $369 suite. Children under 18 stay free in parent's room. AE, DC, DISC, MC, V. Valet parking $21. **Amenities:** Restaurant (McCormick's Fish House & Bar; see "Where to Dine," below); 2 lounges; exercise room; spa (w/Jacuzzi and sauna); complimentary access to a nearby health club; concierge; courtesy car; salon; 24-hr. room service; massage; laundry service; dry cleaning. *In room:* A/C, TV, dataport, minibar, hair dryer, iron.

The Warwick ★★   One of four Warwicks in the United States (the others are in New York, San Francisco, and Seattle), this handsome midsize choice boasts an exterior and rooms reminiscent of hotels in Paris, where the corporate office is located. In contrast, the earth-tone lobby stylishly reflects the region, with classic European design, contemporary Western furnishings, and slate and red-stone stonework. The hotel completed a $20 million renovation in 2000 that updated the property and cemented its status as one of the city's finest.

Every room features a full private balcony with a great city view, and most are equipped with a fridge and wet bar. Each has one king- or two queen-size beds, contemporary mahogany furniture, floral prints on the walls, cable TV (with pay-per-view movies), and two incoming phone lines—as well as wireless high-speed Internet access. There's also a phone in each bathroom. The standard rooms are very spacious, averaging 750 square feet each, and the 42 suites, which range from two-room parlor suites to grand luxury suites, are even more so.

1776 Grant St. (at E. 18th Ave.), Denver, CO 80203. ✆ **800/525-2888** or 303/861-2000. Fax 303/832-0320. www.warwickdenver.com. 220 units. $139–$210 double; $129–$650 suite. Weekend rates $79–$99 double; from $129 suite. Children under 18 stay free in parent's room. AE, DC, DISC, MC, V. Valet parking $16 per day, self-parking $10 per day, both underground. **Amenities:** Restaurant (contemporary); lounge; rooftop heated pool; exercise room; concierge; courtesy town car; business center; limited room service; laundry service. *In room:* A/C, cable TV w/pay movies, dataport, coffeemaker, hair dryer, iron, safe.

INEXPENSIVE

Innkeeper of the Rockies *(Value)*   A member of Hostelling International, this centrally located hostel is in a bustling urban area just off Colfax Avenue, within walking distance of more than 50 restaurants as well as all the major downtown attractions. Facilities include a community kitchen, lockers, laundry machines, Internet access, and a cafe. Each dorm room has no more than four beds; there are also five private bed-and-breakfast rooms in two adjacent houses. The front door is always locked and someone is on the premises all night. Under the same ownership are a nearby B&B and guesthouse, and a lodge in the Rockies.

1530 Downing St., Denver, CO 80218. ✆ **800/909-4776,** PIN 67, or 303/861-7777. www.innkeeperrockies. com. 80 beds, 5 private units. $19 per person ($16 for Hostelling International members); $40 private unit. Rates include full breakfast. AE, DISC, MC, V. **Amenities:** Free pickup and delivery at bus and train stations; coin-op laundry. *In room:* No phone.

BED & BREAKFASTS

Those seeking an alternative to a hotel or motel might consider one of Denver's many bed-and-breakfast inns. Often located in historic 19th-century homes, bed-and-breakfasts offer a more personalized lodging experience than you could expect in all but the very best hotels, because you rarely find more than 10 rooms in a B&B, and you are, literally, a guest in someone's home.

Capitol Hill Mansion Bed & Breakfast ★★   Located on Denver's "Mansion Row" just southeast of downtown and the State Capitol, this turreted B&B exemplifies Richardsonian Romanesque design with its ruby sandstone exterior and curving front porch. The mansion, built in 1891, is listed on the National Register of Historic Places and boasts the original woodwork and stained glass.

The inn is outfitted for the 21st century, with refrigerators, color TVs, and wireless high-speed Web access. Each individually decorated room is named after a Colorado wildflower; some feature two-person Jacuzzi tubs, fireplaces, and private balconies. The elegant Elk Thistle Suite on the third floor features a panoramic view of the Rockies, a claw-foot tub, and a kitchen. Honeymooners might enjoy the second floor Shooting Star Balcony Room, which has a separate whirlpool tub and shower, and a private balcony with a city view.

Breakfasts include such items as crème brûlée French toast and pecan bread pudding. Smoking is not permitted inside the inn.

1207 Pennsylvania St., Denver, CO 80203. ℂ **800/839-9329** outside 303 and 720 area codes or 303/839-5221. Fax 303/839-8046. www.capitolhillmansion.com. 8 units. $95–$175 double; $145–$175 suite. Rates include full breakfast and evening wine and refreshments. AE, DC, DISC, MC, V. Free off-street parking. *In room:* A/C, cable TV, dataport, fridge, coffeemaker, hair dryer, iron.

Castle Marne Bed & Breakfast ★★   A National Historic Landmark, Castle Marne is an impressive stone fortress designed and built in 1889 by the renowned architect William Lang for a contemporary silver baron. It was so named because a subsequent owner's son fought in the Battle of the Marne during World War I.

The inn is furnished with antiques, fine reproductions, and family heirlooms. Several rooms have private balconies with hot tubs, and 2002 saw the addition of a second suite with an outdoor hot tub for two. Three rooms have old-fashioned bathrooms with pedestal sinks and cast-iron claw-foot tubs. A gourmet breakfast (two seatings) is served in the original formal dining room, and a proper afternoon tea is served daily in the parlor. Smoking is not permitted.

1572 Race St., Denver, CO 80206. ℂ **800/92-MARNE** or 303/331-0621 for reservations. Fax 303/331-0623. www.castlemarne.com. 9 units. $105–$170 double; $200–$255 suite. Rates include full breakfast and afternoon tea. AE, DC, DISC, MC, V. Free off-street parking. *In room:* A/C.

Lumber Baron ★★ *Finds*   After buying this turreted mansion in Denver's Highlands neighborhood on April Fool's Day 1991, Walt Keller began a 4-year, $1.5 million renovation. Built in 1890 by lumber baron John Mouat (hence the name), the 8,500-square-foot house held many surprises: a myriad of ornate wood fixtures (cherry, poplar, maple, and oak, to name a few) and a once-hidden third-story ballroom under an ornate pyramidal dome. The rooms feature antique furnishings from around the world and unique themes: the Honeymoon Suite has a neoclassical bent, a four-poster mahogany queen bed, and a gargantuan mirror; and the Helen Keller Suite (named for Walt's distant relative) has a garden motif with historic photos and intricate Anglo-Japanese wallpapering. For those seeking entertainment, the Lumber Baron hosts 50 "murder mystery parties" annually for $37 (dinner included; two-for-one pricing for guests), comedic events with a handful of actors amongst the 50 to 100 partygoers. Candlelit dinners are available in-room for $45 to $65.

2555 W. 37th Ave., Denver, CO 80211. ℂ **303/477-8205.** Fax 303/477-0269. www.lumberbaron.com. 5 units. $145 double; $195–$235 suite. Rates include full breakfast. AE, DISC, MC, V. *In room:* A/C, hair dryer, iron.

Queen Anne Bed & Breakfast Inn ★★   A favorite of both business travelers and couples, the Queen Anne might be considered the perfect bed-and-breakfast in the perfect home. It consists of two Victorian houses: one built by the well-known architect Frank Edbrooke in 1879, and the other built in 1886. Innkeeper extraordinaire Tom King provides piped-in chamber music, fresh flowers, and fax services. Each of the 10 double rooms in the 1879 Pierce-Tabor House is decorated with period antiques. Three rooms boast original murals: All four walls of the Aspen Room are filled with (what else?) aspen trees; the third-floor Park Room overlooks a park and has a mural depicting the view that visitors would have seen in 1879. Each of the four two-room suites in the adjacent 1886 Roberts house is dedicated to a famous artist (Norman Rockwell, Frederic Remington, John Audubon, and Alexander Calder). The suites have deep soaking tubs, and the Remington suite has a hot tub. Half of the rooms have cable television.

Located in the Clements Historic District, the Queen Anne borders downtown Denver and is within easy walking distance of the major attractions. Smoking is not permitted.

2147–51 Tremont Place, Denver, CO 80205. ℂ **800/432-4667** or 303/296-6666. Fax 303/296-2151. www. queenannebnb.com. 14 units. $85–$165 double; $145–$175 suite. Rates include hot breakfast and Colorado wine each evening. AE, DC, DISC, MC, V. Free off-street parking. *In room:* A/C, dataport.

OUTSIDE DOWNTOWN
VERY EXPENSIVE

JW Marriott ★★ *Kids*   Opening in summer 2004, the high-end JW Marriott is the first hotel in the Cherry Creek neighborhood, and it was well worth the wait. Sumptuous interiors and bold primary colors make for a distinctive ambience, and the attention to detail is excellent. The little touches are what this hotel is all about: jumbo flatscreen TVs with DVD players, spectacular views, big bathrooms with granite aplenty, user-friendly thermostats, and excellent service. For shoppers, it's beyond ideal, a block from the Cherry Creek Mall and surrounded by chic retailers of all stripes. The standout amenities: Mirepoix, the sleek eatery; a huge exercise room; and an upscale shopping arcade. Conveniently, the hotel is next door to the Cherry Creek Bike Rack, where you can rent bikes and also park them for free, and very close to the Cherry Creek bike path.

150 Clayton Lane, Denver, CO 80206. ℂ **800/228-9290** or 303/316-2700. Fax 303/316-4697. www.jwmarriott denver.com. 196 units. $189–$229 double; $349–$1,099 suite; weekend rates from $159. AE, DC, DISC, MC, V. Free valet and self-parking. Pets accepted. **Amenities:** Restaurant (Mirepoix; see "Where to Dine," below); lounge; exercise room; concierge; courtesy car; business center; shopping arcade; 24-hr. room service; massage; coin-op washers and dryers; dry cleaning; executive level. *In room:* A/C, TV w/pay movies and DVD player, dataport (w/high-speed Internet access), minibar, coffeemaker, hair dryer, iron, safe.

EXPENSIVE

Loews Denver Hotel ★ *Kids*   Located just east of Colorado Boulevard and south of Cherry Creek, the Loews Denver's sleek, towering exterior is black steel with a reflecting glass tower. Inside, it's bella Italia, with columns finished in imitation marble, and Renaissance-style murals and paintings that look 500 years old. The location, about a 15-minute drive from downtown, is good for those who want access to scattered attractions or the Denver Tech Center. Throughout the hotel, much use has been made of floral patterns, Italian silk wall coverings, and marble-top furnishings. All of the spacious rooms have elegant decor, along with all of the business perks any traveler could want: at least three phones, high-speed Internet access, and a fax machine. The resident eatery, The Tuscany, is also excellent.

4150 E. Mississippi Ave., Denver, CO 80246. ℂ **800/345-9172** or 303/782-9300. Fax 303/758-6542. www. loewshotels.com. 200 units. $109–$189 double; $209–$1,000 suite; weekend rates from $89. Children under 18 stay free in parent's room. AE, DC, DISC, MC, V. Free valet and self-parking. Pets accepted. **Amenities:** Restaurant (Mediterranean); lounge; exercise room; access to nearby health club; concierge; courtesy van; business center; secretarial services; 24-hr. room service; massage; laundry service; dry cleaning; business-traveler rooms. *In room:* A/C, TV w/pay movies, fax, dataport (w/high-speed Internet access), minibar, coffeemaker, hair dryer, iron.

Kids Family-Friendly Hotels

Hotel Monaco (p. 67)   Kids get a kick out of the colorful decor, the complimentary goldfish, and the house mascot, a Jack Russell terrier named Lily Sopris.

Loews Denver Hotel (see above)   Kids get a teddy bear and coloring books when they arrive; the Tuscany Restaurant has a special children's menu.

MODERATE

Renaissance Denver ★   About midway between downtown and Denver International Airport, the Renaissance is our pick for a comfortable but still somewhat elegant hotel that offers all the amenities we might want. Particularly impressive is the architecture—a white double pyramid 12 stories high. The 10-story atrium lobby has tropical palms and fig trees growing beneath the central skylight, fountains, lots of marble and brass, and plants draping down from the balconies. Each spacious room—among the largest you'll find in Denver—is decorated in a contemporary style and includes an easy chair and ottoman, two phones, and a private balcony. The hotel is adjacent to now-closed Stapleton Airport, and most of its patrons are businesspeople. It's also a good choice for budget-minded tourists looking for a convenient stopover between the mountains and DIA, with lower rates than comparable downtown properties, and a location closer to the airport.

3801 Quebec St., Denver, CO 80207. ✆ 800/HOTELS-1 or 303/399-7500. Fax 303/321-1966. www.renaissance hotels.com. 400 units. $99 double; $195–$650 suite. Weekend rates from $64 double. AE, DC, DISC, MC, V. Free self-parking; valet parking $5. **Amenities:** Restaurant (American); lounge; indoor and outdoor pools; exercise room; 2 Jacuzzis; sauna; concierge; business center; 24-hr. room service; complimentary washers and dryers; dry cleaning; executive level. *In room:* A/C, cable TV w/pay movies, dataport, minibar, coffeemaker, hair dryer, iron.

INEXPENSIVE

Cameron Motel *Value*   A small mom-and-pop motel located about 10 minutes from downtown, the Cameron provides a quiet alternative to some of the more expensive chains. Built in the 1940s, the property has been completely renovated. The walls of the average-size rooms are glazed brick; remote-control cable TVs offer 60 channels. Three rooms are equipped with kitchenettes, and some also have dataports. The owners live on-site, and their pride of ownership shows.

4500 E. Evans Ave. (I-25 exit 203), Denver, CO 80222. ✆ 303/757-2100. Fax 303/757-0974. 35 units (14 with shower only). $45–$58 double; $72 suite. AE, DISC, MC, V. Free off-street parking. Pets accepted with $5 nightly fee. *In room:* A/C, cable TV.

CAMPING

Chatfield State Park ★   On the south side of Denver, 1 mile south of the intersection of Colo. 121 (Wadsworth) and Colo. 470, Chatfield has a 1,550-acre reservoir with ample opportunities for boating, water-skiing, fishing, and swimming, plus around 20 miles of trails for horseback riding, mountain biking, and hiking. Facilities include hot showers, picnic areas, a dump station, boat ramps and rentals, and electric hookups. The campground is open from May to October.

11500 N. Roxborough Park Rd., Littleton, CO 80125. ✆ 303/791-7275, or 800/678-2267 for state park reservation service. www.parks.state.co.us. 197 sites. $16–$22, plus $5–$6 day-use fee. MC, V only for advance reservations.

Delux R.V. Park   The only RV campground actually in Denver city limits, this campground has shaded sites, hot showers, laundry, a dumpsite, and full hookups. It's convenient to buses (no. 31 RTD), shopping, and recreational facilities. Open year-round, the campground is 5 blocks north of I-70 exit 272, and 2 blocks south of I-76 exit 3, on the east side of Federal Boulevard.

5520 N. Federal Blvd., Denver, CO 80221. ✆ 303/433-0452. www.deluxrvpark.com. 51 sites. $25–$31. MC, V.

Chief Hosa Campground   Those seeking the amenities and easy accessibility of a commercial campground close to Denver will find a nice (but often quite busy) campground at this longstanding establishment 20 miles west of Denver.

There are tent and RV sites, and most of the latter have electric and water hookups. When it opened in 1913, the south campground here was dubbed "America's First Motor-Camping Area." The campground is open year-round. The amenities include showers, grills, and a volleyball court.

27661 Genessee Dr., Golden, CO 80401. ℭ **800/244-3346** or 303/526-0242. www.campdenver.com. 87 sites. $22–$28. AE, DC, DISC, MC, V. Just off I-70 exit 253, 20 miles west of Denver.

4 Where to Dine

Denver abounds with Mexican hole-in-the-walls, chain eateries, steak joints, and even a few bison joints, and the restaurants in LoDo and Cherry Creek become more like those in Los Angeles and Manhattan every year. The restaurants we've listed here are mostly independent, unique to this area, and a cut above others in their price ranges.

DOWNTOWN
VERY EXPENSIVE

Broker Restaurant ★★ STEAK/SEAFOOD   The historic Denver National Bank building, with its circular 23-ton door still in place, is the site of the Broker. Patrons sit in cherry-wood booths once used by bank customers to inspect safe-deposit boxes, and historic photos of Denver line the walls. Famous for its generous portions, the Broker's at its best with beef: New York steaks, beef Wellington, and prime rib are all excellent. Rocky Mountain trout, rack of lamb, and Alaskan king crab legs round out the menu, and vegetarians can select from a small roster of meatless offerings, including an interesting vegetable Wellington. The Broker's trademark is a complimentary large bowl of steamed gulf shrimp with a tasty and tangy sauce. The popular new lunch menu is among the cheapest downtown; they rolled the prices back to what they were in 1972.

821 17th St. (near Champa St.). ℭ **303/292-5065**. Reservations recommended. Main courses $3–$7 lunch, $26–$40 dinner. AE, DC, DISC, MC, V. Tues–Fri 11am–2pm; daily 4:30–10pm.

Buckhorn Exchange ★★★ ROCKY MOUNTAIN   In the same rickety premises where it was established in 1893, this landmark restaurant displays its Colorado Liquor License No. 1 above the 140-year-old bar in the upstairs saloon. On the first level, the densely decorated dining room, dominated by a daunting menagerie of taxidermy, will alarm vegetarians, but meat lovers will not be disappointed one bit. The Buckhorn's game dishes (slow-roasted buffalo prime rib, lean and served medium rare, elk, pheasant, and quail) are the best in the city. The beefsteaks, ranging from 8-ounce tenderloins to 64-ounce table steaks for five, are also quite good. With fried alligator tail, Rocky Mountain oysters, and smoked buffalo sausage among the options, the appetizers will surely broaden one's palate. Our recommendation: rattlesnake, served in cream cheese–chipotle dip with tricolor tortilla chips. For dessert, try a slab of hot Dutch apple pie—if you have room. Lunch is lighter and more affordable, with an assortment of charbroiled meat entrees, sandwiches, and hearty homemade soups. A mile southwest of the State Capitol, the Buckhorn sits adjacent to a light-rail stop, making it an easy trip from downtown.

1000 Osage St. (at W. 10th Ave.). ℭ **303/534-9505**. Reservations recommended. Main courses $8–$16 lunch, $18–$44 dinner. AE, DC, DISC, MC, V. Mon–Fri 11am–2pm; Mon–Thurs 5:30–9pm; Fri–Sat 5–10pm; Sun 5–9pm. Bar open all day. Light-rail: Osage.

Palace Arms ★★★ CONTINENTAL/REGIONAL   Despite its dramatic Napoleonic decor—antiques dating from 1670 include a dispatch case and a pair of dueling pistols that may have belonged to Napoleon—the Palace Arms' cuisine is a combination of traditional American, new American, and classical French. To begin, the sherry-braised rabbit loin is a special treat, or maybe you'd rather have the superb Caesar salad, prepared tableside for two. For an excellent main course, try the bison steak, horseradish-crusted veal loin, or roasted rack of Colorado lamb. There are a number of tasty "heart healthy" items on the menu, and the wine list has received *Wine Spectator*'s "Best of" award.

If you're short a coat, try the **Ship Tavern,** also in the hotel (© **303/297-3111**), with a similar, less expensive menu. The lunch menu at the Brown's third restaurant, **Ellyngton's,** has some great gourmet sandwiches, and is also the site of the Brown's luxuriant Sunday brunch.

In the Brown Palace Hotel, 321 17th St. © 303/297-3111. Reservations recommended. Jacket and tie required at dinner. Main courses $29–$42 dinner. AE, DC, DISC, MC, V. Daily 6–10pm.

EXPENSIVE

Bistro Vendome ★★ FRENCH BISTRO   Chef-owner Eric Roeder serves up splendid interpretations of Gallic standbys (dubbing it "French soul food") at his intimate space on Larimer Square, which opened in 2003. The steak tartare, which we loved for its spicy kick and flavors of beef, onions, cumin, and sweet soy, is the perfect starting point. Bistro Vendome is also known for having some of Denver's best mussels, prepared three ways. The menu changes regularly, but you can expect excellent seafood—say, trout amandine with caviar or slow-roasted salmon with French lentils—as well as a succulent seared duck breast and some creative game dishes. The salty-sweet steak frites (aka French fries) are also beloved by locals, and the side dishes and desserts don't disappoint. The patio is one of the best in Denver.

1424-H Larimer Square. © 303/825-3232. Reservations accepted. Main courses $7–$14 brunch, $15–$23 dinner. AE, DC, DISC, MC, V. Sun and Tues–Thurs 5–10pm; Fri–Sat 5–11pm; brunch Fri–Sun 10am–2pm. Closed Mon.

Denver ChopHouse & Brewery ★ STEAKS   A LoDo mainstay since it opened alongside Coors Field in 1995, this is one of the Mile High City's best places for carnivores. Set in the steeped brick-and-wood atmosphere of a restored early-19th-century train depot, the ChopHouse does classic meat and potatoes (not to mention microbrews) as well as anybody in town. Our picks are always juicy steaks, from filet mignon to New York strip, and the other hearty classics, such as huge, cheese-stuffed pork chops and herb-crusted racks of lamb; white cheddar mashers are our side of choice. The restaurant also serves a nice selection of fresh seafood and some less expensive sandwiches and pizzas, and even a few vegetarian items. There is also a **Boulder ChopHouse,** 921 Walnut St. (© **303/443-1188**).

1735 19th St. © 303/296-0800. Reservations recommended for dinner. Main courses $10–$27. AE, DC, MC, V. Sat–Thurs 11am–2:30pm; Mon–Thurs 5–11pm; Fri–Sat 4:30pm–midnight; Sun 4:30pm–10pm.

Panzano ★★ CONTEMPORARY ITALIAN   The Hotel Monaco's resident eatery is a standout, one of the best Italian restaurants in town and also one of the best in a hotel. Served in a densely decorated dining room with a busy open kitchen, the dishes emphasize fresh, often seasonal ingredients, attractive presentation, and traditional Italian flavors. The menu changes every 3 months, but you'll likely find the signature *buridda,* a Genovese seafood stew with mussels, calamari, and shrimp in a savory lobster broth; *osso buco di pesce,* braised monkfish wrapped in pancetta, served with mascarpone polenta; and an array of pastas

Denver Dining

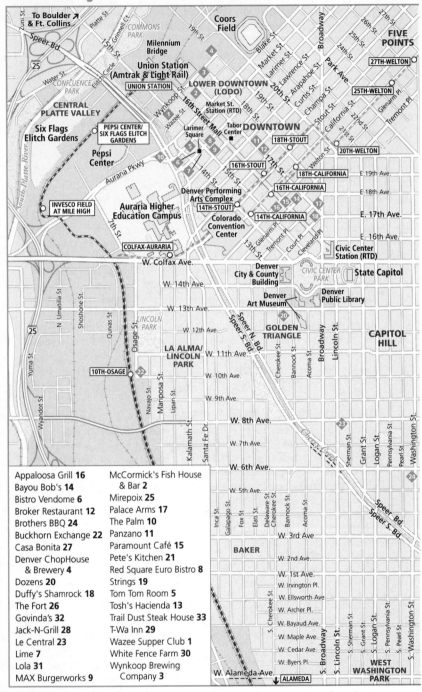

Appaloosa Grill **16**
Bayou Bob's **14**
Bistro Vendome **6**
Broker Restaurant **12**
Brothers BBQ **24**
Buckhorn Exchange **22**
Casa Bonita **27**
Denver ChopHouse
  & Brewery **4**
Dozens **20**
Duffy's Shamrock **18**
The Fort **26**
Govinda's **32**
Jack-N-Grill **28**
Le Central **23**
Lime **7**
Lola **31**
MAX Burgerworks **9**

McCormick's Fish House
  & Bar **2**
Mirepoix **25**
Palace Arms **17**
The Palm **10**
Panzano **11**
Paramount Café **15**
Pete's Kitchen **21**
Red Square Euro Bistro **8**
Strings **19**
Tom Tom Room **5**
Tosh's Hacienda **13**
Trail Dust Steak House **33**
T-Wa Inn **29**
Wazee Supper Club **1**
White Fence Farm **30**
Wynkoop Brewing
  Company **3**

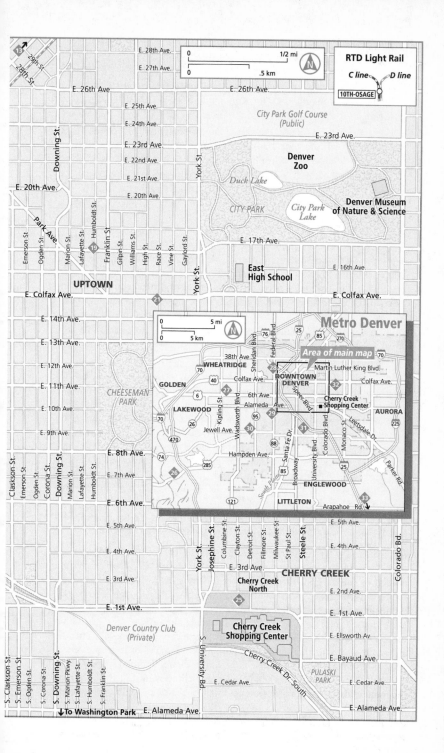

E. 28th Ave.
E. 27th Ave.

0   1/2 mi
0   .5 km

RTD Light Rail
C line   D line
10TH-OSAGE

29th St.
28th St.

E. 26th Ave.   E. 26th Ave.

City Park Golf Course
(Public)

E. 25th Ave.
E. 24th Ave.

Downing St.

E. 23rd Ave   E. 23rd Ave.
E. 22nd Ave.

**Denver
Zoo**

E. 21st Ave.

Duck Lake

E. 20th Ave.   E. 20th Ave.

Park Ave.

Emerson St.
Ogden St.
Marion St.
Lafayette St.
Humboldt St.
Franklin St.
Gilpin St.
Williams St.
High St.
Race St.
Vine St.
Gaylord St.

19

CITY PARK

City Park
Lake

**Denver Museum
of Nature & Science**

York St.

E. 17th Ave.

**East
High School**

E. 16th Ave.

UPTOWN

E. Colfax Ave.   E. Colfax Ave.

21

E. 14th Ave.

0   5 mi
0   5 km

Metro Denver

E. 13th Ave.

Federal Blvd.
76
25
85
270

E. 12th Ave.

Area of main map

70

CHEESEMAN
PARK

E. 11th Ave.

38th Ave.
WHEATRIDGE
70
Sheridan Blvd.
28
Martin Luther King Blvd.
32
Colfax Ave.

E. 10th Ave.

GOLDEN
40
Colfax Ave.
**DOWNTOWN
DENVER**
Speer Blvd.

E. 9th Ave.

6
27
Kipling St.
6th Ave.
**Cherry Creek
Shopping Center**
Colfax Ave.
AURORA
225

E. 8th Ave.

LAKEWOOD
Wadsworth Blvd.
Alameda Ave.
29
Colorado Blvd.
Monaco St.
Leetsdale Dr.

26
95

E. 7th Ave.

470
Jewell Ave.
30
31
Santa Fe Dr.
University Blvd.

E. 6th Ave.

74
88

Parker Rd.

E. 5th Ave.

285
Hampden Ave.
Broadway
85
25

E. 4th Ave.

121
ENGLEWOOD
33
Arapahoe Rd.

York St.
Josephine St.
Columbine St.
Clayton St.
Detroit St.
Fillmore St.
Milwaukee St.
St Paul St.
Steele St.

South Platte River
LITTLETON

E. 5th Ave.

E. 3rd Ave.

E. 4th Ave.

Colorado Bd.

CHERRY CREEK

Clarkson St.
Emerson St.
Ogden St.
Corona St.
Downing St.
Marion St.
Lafayette St.
Humboldt St.

E. 3rd Ave.

**Cherry Creek
North**

E. 2nd Ave.

E. 1st Ave.

25

E. 1st Ave.

*Denver Country Club
(Private)*

**Cherry Creek
Shopping Center**

E. Ellsworth Av.

E. Bayaud Ave.

S. University Bd.

Cherry Creek Dr. South

*PULASKI
PARK*

E. Cedar Ave.

S. Clarkson St.
S. Emerson St.
S. Ogden St.
S. Corona St.
S. Downing St.
S. Marion Pkwy.
S. Lafayette St.
S. Humboldt St.
S. Franklin St.

↓To Washington Park   E. Alameda Ave.

E. Cedar Ave.

E. Alameda Ave.

Kids **Family-Friendly Restaurants**

Casa Bonita (p. 84)   If the kids aren't concentrating on the tacos, the puppet shows, high divers, fun house, and video arcade will enthrall them.

White Fence Farm (p. 84)   Meals are served family-style, with Mom or Dad doling out the vegetables to live musical entertainment, but the best part is outside, with live farm animals and a playground.

Wynkoop Brewing Company (p. 80)   With a dining area separate from the bar, this pub and restaurant has a loud, bustling atmosphere and plenty of kid-friendly menu options.

---

prepared fresh in-house daily. There are also innovative variations on steak, seafood, soups, and salads, which change according to available ingredients: In the summer, for example, a sweet corn soup appears on the menu. For dessert, don't pass on the tiramisu, which manages to be heavenly and sinful at once. With lighter, similar fare (including killer salads), lunch attracts power meetings.

In Hotel Monaco, 909 17th St. ✆ **303/296-3525.** Reservations recommended. Main courses $7–$15 lunch, $13–$25 dinner. AE, DC, DISC, MC, V. Mon–Fri 7–10am and 11am–2:30pm; Mon–Thurs 5–10pm; Fri–Sat 5–11pm; Sun 4:30–9:30pm. Closed Thanksgiving and Dec 25.

Strings ★★ CONTEMPORARY   Modern and sleek in its decor, Strings attracts a hip crowd of loyal locals, as well as visiting celebrities who contribute to a wall of autographed photos. Popular and typically crowded, the restaurant welcomes guests in T-shirts as well as tuxedos; it's especially busy during the before- and after-theater hours. The menu focuses on fusion cuisine, creative noodle dishes, and fresh seafood, such as cashew-crusted sea bass. Another popular entree is Rocky Mountain lamb chops with a cool cucumber-mint sauce with lemon mashed potatoes. Lunch and dinner specials change weekly to match the season and the mood of the chef. Strings has an outdoor patio for summer dining and four private rooms.

1700 Humboldt St. (at E. 17th Ave.). ✆ **303/831-7310.** Reservations recommended. Main courses $11–$18 lunch, $14–$30 dinner. AE, DISC, MC, V. Mon–Thurs 11am–10pm; Fri–Sat 5–11pm; Sun 5–9pm.

The Palm ★★ ITALIAN/STEAK/SEAFOOD   Pio Bozzi and John Ganzi opened the first Palm restaurant in New York City in 1926. It originally specialized in cuisine from their hometown of Parma, Italy, but whenever a customer requested steak, Ganzi ran to a nearby butcher shop, bought a steak, and cooked it to order. This eventually led to The Palm's having its own meat wholesale company to ensure the quality of its steaks. The current third-generation owners introduced seafood to the menu and expanded the business by opening a dozen more restaurants across the country. Most famous for its prime cuts of beef and live Nova Scotia lobsters, The Palm celebrates tradition, with some of Ganzi's original Italian dishes still popular (and cheaper) menu items. The dining room is plastered with caricatures of local celebrities; customers are seated at either booths or tables.

In the Westin at Tabor Center, 1672 Lawrence St. ✆ **303/825-7256.** www.thepalm.com. Reservations recommended. Main courses $8.50–$18 lunch, $17–$40 dinner. AE, DC, DISC, MC, V. Mon–Fri 11am–11pm; Sat 5–11pm; Sun 5–10pm.

Tom Tom Room ★★ JAPANESE   An über-trendy new spot in LoDo, the Tom Tom Room is one of just a handful of restaurants in the entire country that specializes in *robata:* skewers of meat, seafood, and veggies placed over bin-chotan charcoal, served in the center of the table to be shared. The Tom Tom Room also does some excellent sushi rolls, a spicy calamari that defies expectations, and offers kobe beef that you grill yourself as an appetizer. The decor and atmosphere are slick, sleek, and ultra contemporary; the bar features a video wall that resembles flowing water, beaded curtains, and a TV with constant marine wildlife videos playing. There are private rooms, canopied tables, and a sushi and robata bar to choose from, each distinct in personality.

1432 Market St. ✆ 303/534-5050. Reservations accepted. Robata items $1–$7, sushi rolls $1–$5.50. AE, DC, DISC, MC, V. Sun and Tues–Thurs 5–10pm; Fri–Sat 5pm–midnight. Lounge and sushi/robata bar open later.

MODERATE

Appaloosa Grill ★ CONTEMPORARY/ECLECTIC   One of beermaker/ restaurateur-turned-mayor John Hickenlooper's downtown eateries, the Appaloosa features an eclectic menu, merging Asian, Southwestern, and bar grub. The ribs are a good bet, as are the tamales. The lunch menu includes salads, sandwiches, and assorted lighter entrees. With a casual, semi-intimate atmosphere and a handsome antique bar, this is a good place for dinner to morph into a night on the town. It doesn't hurt that there is live musical entertainment nightly.

535 16th St. Mall (at Welton St.). ✆ 720/932-1700. Main courses $7–$10 lunch, $9–$25 dinner. AE, DISC, MC, V. Daily 11am–1am. Bar open later.

Le Central ★★ (*Value*) FRENCH   Seven blocks south of the Colorado State Capitol, Le Central is a romantic restaurant that prides itself on creating French dishes that are both top-quality and affordable. Housed in an aged urban structure with a distinctive European vibe, the restaurant changes its menus daily, but you can always expect to find a selection of fresh chicken, pork, beef, lamb, and seafood. They're available grilled, sautéed, or roasted and finished with some of the tastiest sauces this side of Provence. Bouillabaisse and paella are usually available, and every menu features a vegetarian dish. Shellfish fanatics, take note: Le Central's mussel-and-clam menu is legendary, and served with all the french fries you can eat.

112 E. 8th Ave. (at Lincoln St.). ✆ 303/863-8094. Reservations recommended. Main courses $7–$9 lunch, $14–$22 dinner. AE, DC, DISC, MC, V. Mon–Fri 11:30am–2:15pm; Sat–Sun 11am–2pm; Mon–Thurs 5:30–10pm; Fri–Sat 5–10pm; Sun 5–9pm.

MAX Burgerworks (*Kids*) BURGERS   Founders Greg Waldbaum and Gerard Rudofsky wanted to "take a standard food group and raise the bar," and they've accomplished that with this bright and modern burger joint. The menu lists no less than 20 varieties of burger, with veggie burgers, salmon burgers, bison burgers, Italian sausage burgers, and myriad beef options. (The beef is top-grade stuff from Niman Ranch, typically reserved for steaks.) We like the Southwestern Burger, with pepper jack, chipotle mayonnaise, and onion rings. Also of note are a nice selection of upscale salads, Big City Reds hot dogs, the shakes and malts, and the draft beers and martinis.

1512 Larimer St. at Writer Square. ✆ 303/534-0944. Reservations accepted. Main courses $7.50–$13. AE, MC, V. Mon–Wed 11am–9pm; Thurs–Sat 11am–10pm. Closed Sun. Shorter winter hours.

McCormick's Fish House & Bar ✦ SEAFOOD In lower downtown's historic Oxford Hotel, McCormick's maintains a late-19th-century feel with stained-glass windows, oak booths, and a fine polished-wood bar. Come here for the best seafood in town—it's flown in daily, and might include Alaskan salmon and halibut, mussels from Florida, lobsters from Maine, Hawaiian mahimahi, red rockfish from Oregon, and trout from Idaho. The menu also offers pasta, chicken, and a full line of prime beef.

In the Oxford Hotel, 1659 Wazee St. ☎ 303/825-1107. Reservations recommended. Lunch and light dishes $6–$12; dinner $12–$24. AE, DC, DISC, MC, V. Mon–Fri 11am–2pm; Sun brunch 10am–2pm; Sun–Thurs 5–10pm; Fri–Sat 5–11pm.

Red Square Euro Bistro ✦✦ RUSSIAN/CONTEMPORARY After the Little Russian Café closed in 2003, its all-Russian staff reunited under owner Steve Ryan and opened Red Square. They did their old place one better, with a rich red interior, contemporary Russian art, and a vodka bar stocked with infusions made in-house (ranging from raspberry to garlic) and about 100 brands from 17 countries, including Russia, Holland, Poland, Sweden, and even Mexico. Chef Maxim Ionikh's excellent entrees are not purely Russian: the steak stroganoff has a salmon counterpart, the menu has Asian and French influences, and the appetizers include pâté and goat cheese ravioli. But there is cold borsht, a roasted Russian wild boar chop, golubtsi (a meat-filled cabbage roll), and, of course, the vodka. Lots and lots of vodka.

1512 Larimer St. at Writer Square. ☎ 303/595-8600. Main courses $7.50–$14 lunch, $13–$20 dinner. AE, DC, DISC, MC, V. Mon–Fri 11am–2pm; daily 5–10pm. Bar open later.

Tosh's Hacienda ✦ *Finds* MEXICAN In a city brimming with Mexican restaurants, the food here stands out. Open for more than half a century in the Five Points neighborhood, Tosh's has an easygoing atmosphere, and tile and redbrick decor. The reasonably priced combination plates feature one or two main dishes with rice and beans. You can't go wrong with enchiladas, burritos, or rellenos, and the margaritas are both tart and strong.

3090 Downing St. ☎ 303/295-1861. Main courses $7–$14. AE, DC, DISC, MC, V. Sun–Thurs 11am–9pm; Fri–Sat 11am–10pm.

Wynkoop Brewing Company ✦ *Kids* REGIONAL AMERICAN/PUB When the Wynkoop opened its doors in 1988 as Denver's first new brewery in more than 50 years, it started a minirevolution: Since then, about 75 microbreweries have opened in Colorado. Wynkoop occupies a renovated warehouse across from Union Station and close to Coors Field. The menu offers pub fare, sandwiches, soups, and salads, plus dinners of steak, Denver cut elk medallions, and honey-beer-mustard chicken breast. A hearty option is buffalo sirloin steak with spicy, buffalo-wing-style shrimp. See also "Denver After Dark," in chapter 5.

1634 18th St. (at Wynkoop St.). ☎ 303/297-2700. Reservations recommended for large parties. Main courses $8–$16. AE, DC, DISC, MC, V. Mon–Thurs 11am–11pm; Fri–Sat 11am–midnight; Sun 11am–10pm. Bar open later.

INEXPENSIVE

In addition to the options listed below, there are a number of great breakfast spots in the downtown area. **Dozens,** 236 W. 13th Ave. (☎ **303/572-0066**), is a local favorite of everyone from plumbers to politicians with a beloved breakfast menu: One omelet is named after former Denver Broncos quarterback and local legend John Elway. Established in 1942, **Pete's Kitchen,** 1962 E. Colfax Ave. (☎ **303/321-3139**), is a prototypical urban diner, with checkerboard floors, a breakfast bar, booths, plenty of local color, and killer breakfast burritos. The menu has a nice selection of Greek, Mexican, and American standbys. Pete's is open 24 hours on weekends, making it a favorite of the barhopping crowd. For Denver's best barbecue, hit **Brothers BBQ,** 568 Washington St. (© **720/ 570-4227**) for brisket, links, chicken, and other dishes coated with a thick, sweet sauce that is seriously habit-forming.

Bayou Bob's CAJUN   Fishnets, street signs, and Southern-tinged bric-a-brac cover the walls of Bayou Bob's, which serves Denverites reasonably priced Cajun food in its bar and dining room. Gumbo, red beans and rice, fresh crawfish étouffée, and jambalaya are all favorites, as are the huge Mardi Gras–style Hurricanes. The spicy fried alligator is a great starter, and the many combination plates are a good bet for almost any taste. Catfish, po' boys, and hamburgers are also available.

1635 Glenarm St. (in the Paramount Theatre Building). © **303/573-6828.** Main courses $6–$14. AE, DC, DISC, MC, V. Mon–Sat 11am–10pm; Sun 4–9pm.

Duffy's Shamrock ★ *Finds* AMERICAN   This traditional Irish bar and restaurant with fast, cheerful service has been thriving since the late 1950s. Drink specialties include Irish coffees and imported Irish beers, but the food is mostly American. Daily specials may include prime rib, fried Louisiana prawns, low-carb plates, or grilled liver and onions. Sandwiches, on practically every kind of bread imaginable, include corned beef, Reuben, roast beef with gravy, and BLT.

1635 Court Place. © **303/534-4935.** Main courses $2–$6 breakfast, $5–$8 lunch, $5–$11 dinner. AE, DC, DISC, MC, V. Mon–Fri 7am–1:30am; Sat 7:30am–1:30am; Sun 11am–1:30am.

Lime ★ MEXICAN   When you first take your seat at the Lime, your server promptly delivers a basket of homemade chips and salsa along with halved limes filled with tequila. This is a pretty good indication of what to expect: a festive atmosphere, affordable and creative Mexican fare, and a serious emphasis on tequila. The house specialties are "Scorpions": flash-fried jalapeño halves stuffed with shrimp and cream cheese. These spicy little numbers are our favorites, but the fare is uniformly good. The menu runs to creative updates on Mexican standbys, including a zesty green chile with shredded chicken instead of pork. In contrast to the sleek dining room, the bar is one of Denver's liveliest and loudest, and the wait for a table can seem an eternity if you're looking for an intimate evening. But the bar mixes seven types of margaritas to help while away the time; the potent Mi-T Marg is the one to watch out for—it's about 50% tequila.

1424 Larimer St. © **303/893-5463.** Main courses $7.50–$13. AE, MC, V. Mon–Tues 4–9pm; Wed–Thurs 4–10pm; Fri–Sat 4–11pm. Bar open later. Closed Sun.

Paramount Cafe AMERICAN   Housed in the restored lobby of Denver's historic Paramount Theatre on the 16th Street Mall, this bar and grill is popular, lively, and a bit noisy. It's got a plethora of televisions, a poolroom with five tables plus satellite trivia games, and a year-round patio on the mall makes this a good choice for people-watching. The menu features exotic subs, excellent burgers, large salads, and some Tex-Mex fare.

519 16th St. (at Glenarm St.). © **303/893-2000.** Main courses $6–$10. AE, DC, DISC, MC, V. Mon–Sat 11am–2am; Sun 11am–midnight. Bar open later.

Wazee Supper Club ★ *Finds* PIZZA/SANDWICHES   A former plumbing-supply store in lower downtown, the Wazee is a Depression-era relic with a black-and-white tile floor and a bleached mahogany burl bar—a magnificent

(Tips **A Good City for Green Chile Fiends**

Green chile (green *chil*-ee) *n.* a fiery-sweet stew made of chile peppers and other ingredients, often but not always including chunks of pork, tomato, and onion. Denver's eateries serve bowl after bowl of good green chile, stuff that ranges from merely spicy to flat-out nuclear. If you—like us—have a serious weakness for a bowl of green, here are five hotspots in the Mile High City, in no particular order.

1. **Campus Lounge,** 701 S. University Blvd. (© **303/722-9696**): Near the University of Denver, this first-rate hockey bar also serves a mean green that is good by itself or for quesadilla dipping.
2. **Brewery Bar II,** 150 Kalamath St. (© **303/893-0971**): Inconspicuously nestled in a warehouse district, the Brewery Bar serves up some of the hottest green chile in Denver. It also happens to be some of the tastiest.
3. **Jack-N-Grill,** 2524 N. Federal Blvd. (© **303/964-9544**): Sweet and typically served in a bowl with beans, Jack Martinez's green chile is excellent, as is his red.
4. **Little Anita's,** 1550 S. Colorado Blvd. (© **303/691-3337**): Relatively new in Denver, this longtime Albuquerque eatery cooks up wicked green chile from a strip mall in southeast Denver.
5. **Lime,** 1424 Larimer St. (© **303/893-5463**): Almost too hip for its own good, Larimer Square's Lime eschews pork for chicken and dresses up the bowl with tortilla strips. Defying tradition tastes pretty good.

example of 1930s Art Deco. It's been popular for more than 20 years with artists, architects, theatergoers, entertainers, businesspeople, and just about everybody else. Pizza lovers throng the place (some believe the pizza here is the best in town, if not the world), but you'll also find an array of overstuffed sandwiches, from turkey and Swiss to Philly cheese steaks, plus buffalo burgers, and about a dozen draft beers. Don't miss the dumbwaiter used to shuttle food and drinks to the mezzanine floor—it's a converted 1937 garage-door opener.

1600 15th St. (at Wazee St.). © 303/623-9518. Most menu items $3.50–$9; large pizzas $14 and up. AE, MC, V. Mon–Sat 11am–2am; Sun noon–midnight.

OUTSIDE DOWNTOWN
VERY EXPENSIVE

The Fort ★★★ *Moments* ROCKY MOUNTAIN   There are several reasons to drive 18 miles southwest (and 800 ft. up) from downtown to The Fort in Denver's foothills. First, the atmosphere: The building was hand-constructed of adobe bricks in 1962 as a full-scale reproduction of Bent's Fort, Colorado's first fur-trading post. The equally authentic interior boasts striking views of Denver's city lights. Second: owner Sam Arnold, a local celeb and master chef who has been known to open champagne bottles with a tomahawk. Third: The Fort's impeccable, gracious service might just be the best in town.

The fourth and best reason to go is the food. The Fort built its reputation on high-quality, low-cholesterol buffalo, of which it claims to serve the largest variety and greatest quantity of any restaurant in the world. There's steak, roast marrow, tongue, and even "bison eggs"—hard-boiled quail eggs wrapped in buffalo sausage. Our pick is the game plate, with elk chop, teriyaki-style quail, and buffalo filet, served with a salad (and extraordinary homemade dressings), rice, and vegetables. Other house specialties include Rocky Mountain Oysters and elk medallions with wild-huckleberry sauce. Diehards can get good ol' beefsteak.

19192 Colo. 8 (just north of the intersection of Colo. 8 and W. Hampden Ave./U.S. 285), Morrison. ℰ 303/697-4771. Reservations recommended. Main courses $20–$45. AE, DC, DISC, MC, V. Mon–Thurs 6–9:30pm; Fri 5:30–9:30pm; Sat 5–9:30pm; Sun 5–8:30pm. Call for special holiday hours.

Mirepoix ★★★ CONTEMPORARY AMERICAN   Located in the JW Marriott in Cherry Creek, Mirepoix is dark, intimate, and stunningly contemporary. The eye-catching back wall is adorned with purple neon and displays the restaurant's impressive wine racks. But the food is the real centerpiece: impeccable presentation, an obvious thirst for experimentation, and contrasting flavors that work unexpectedly well together. Locally lauded Chef Bryan Moscatello employs vegetable stocks as few other chefs can, although Mirepoix is far from vegetarian. A few examples of Moscatello's creativity: grilled beef ribeye with sheep's milk ricotta ravioli and cauliflower poached in herb-infused cream with a sea scallop. The breakfast and lunch menus also contain quite a few quirky but wonderfully realized dishes (such as, Applewood smoked bacon crisp and a crab-and-ham Monte Cristo sandwich). Most of the items on the menu are "small plates;" entrees are on the small side and they beg to be shared.

In JW Marriott Hotel, 150 Clayton Lane. ℰ 303/253-3000. Reservations recommended. Breakfast $9–$15, lunch $7–$15, dinner $9–$30. AE, DC, DISC, MC, V. Daily 6am–2pm and 5–10pm.

EXPENSIVE

Lola ★★ MEXICAN SEAFOOD   A new trend in Denver dining of late are upscale Mexican restaurants with hipper and pricier dishes than most of their older, simpler cousins—often too hip and too pricey to attract average burrito aficionados. Of them, we like the striking Lola, about 4 miles southeast of downtown. Start off with some guacamole, prepared fresh tableside, before moving onto a bowl of yellow tomato gazpacho, served cold and nicely spiced with near-microscopic amounts of habanero peppers. The entrees, such as albacore tuna fajitas and succulent grilled shrimp, served with squash enchiladas, come mainly from the sea. Sunday brunch means that the guacamole cart is serving as a Bloody Mary cart. The brunch favorite is chicken-fried steak smothered in chorizo gravy, which can sweep away even the most twisted of Saturday night's cobwebs. On Saturday night, however, Lola's margaritas and caipirinhas, sweet Brazilian cocktails with entire quartered limes, are quite good at spinning them.

1469 S. Pearl St. ℰ 720/570-8686. Main courses $15–$23. AE, DC, MC, V. Mon–Sat 5–10pm; Sun 10am–2pm and 5–9pm.

MODERATE

Trail Dust Steak House STEAK   Country-music lovers flock to the Trail Dust, which serves up live dance music along with mesquite-grilled steaks and ribs. Steaks range from 7 to 30 ounces and come with salad, beans, and bread. Chicken, fish, pasta, and a smattering of Mexican dishes are also available. The decor is made up of necktie tips and Western antiques interspersed with large photos of Hollywood western heroes. The necktie tips are the result of a Trail Dust tradition: Wear a tie and the staff will snip it off with scissors, then buy you a drink.

There's a second **Trail Dust** at the north end of Denver, at 9101 Benton St., Westminster (✆ **303/427-1446**), next to the Westminster Mall.

7101 S. Clinton St., Tech Center, Englewood. ✆ 303/790-2420. Reservations accepted. Main courses $5–$15 lunch, $10–$28 dinner. AE, DC, DISC, MC, V. Mon–Fri 11am–2pm; Sun–Thurs 11am–10pm; Fri–Sat 11am–11pm. Exit I-25 south at Dry Creek Rd., drive 1 block east, and turn left onto Clinton St.

White Fence Farm ⭐ 〈Kids〉 AMERICAN   Locals come to this seemingly rural spot in suburban Lakewood for family-style fried-chicken dinners—a delicately fried half chicken per person, plus heaping bowls of potatoes, corn fritters, homemade gravy, coleslaw, cottage cheese, pickled beets, and bean salad. Also available are T-bone steaks, pork chops, deep-fried shrimp, roast turkey, and liver and onions. For dessert, try the fresh pies. A children's menu is available, as are a children's playground, farm animals, carriage rides, and a unique gift shop, all in a beautiful country setting a 20-minute drive from downtown Denver.

6263 W. Jewell Ave., Lakewood. ✆ 303/935-5945. Reservations accepted for parties of 15 or more. Complete meals $12–$21. DISC, MC, V. Tues–Sat 4:30–8:30pm; Sun 11:30am–8pm. Closed Jan.

INEXPENSIVE

Casa Bonita 〈Kids〉 MEXICAN/AMERICAN   A west Denver landmark, Casa Bonita is more of a theme park than a restaurant. A pink Spanish cathedral-type bell tower greets visitors, who discover nonstop action inside: divers plummeting into a pool below a 30-foot waterfall, puppet shows, a video arcade, "Black Bart's Cave," and strolling mariachi bands. The cafeteria-style service is quite an undertaking for a restaurant that seats 1,100! There's standard Mexican fare— enchiladas, tacos, and fajitas—along with country-fried steak and fried chicken dinners. While the food is average at best, many plates are all-you-can-eat, and patrons need only raise a miniature flag to get another round of tacos. Meals include hot *sopaipillas* (deep-fried sweet dough), served with honey.

In the JCRS Shopping Center, 6715 W. Colfax Ave., Lakewood. ✆ 303/232-5115. Reservations not accepted. Main courses $7–$13; children's meals around $3. DISC, MC, V. Mon–Thurs 11am–9:30pm; Fri–Sat 11am–10pm.

Jack-N-Grill 〈Finds〉 NEW MEXICAN   "We are not fast food," reads a sign at Jack-N-Grill, and it's spot on: This is clearly a restaurant that takes its time, and its food is worth the wait. Named for Jack Martinez and his ever-present grill, the food reflects Jack's father's motto: "Comida sin chile, no es comida," or "A meal without chile is not a meal." Not surprisingly, just about everything at Jack-N-Grill has chile in it, which are roasted by the Martinez family on-site. Both the green and red chile are top notch, as are the Mexican dishes and the fresh homemade salsa. Also popular: Frito pies and calabasitas, bowls with squash, zucchini, corn, green chile, and onions. Don't expect Jack to add any chile-free dishes to the menu. "What's the use?" he says.

2524 N. Federal Blvd. ✆ 303/964-9544. Plates $5–$10, a la carte dishes $2–$4.50. AE, MC, V. Tues–Thurs 11am–3pm and 5–8pm; Fri 11am–3pm and 5–9pm; Sat–Sun 9am–9pm.

Govinda's Spiritual Food 〈Finds〉 VEGETARIAN   Attached to—and operated by—a Hare Krishna temple, Govinda's is a surprising gem of a restaurant and a godsend to vegetarians and vegans. With a different all-you-can-eat buffet every day, patrons can select from one of the city's best salad bars, great soups, fresh-baked bread, and an array of meatless main dishes, from enchiladas to casseroles to stir-fry dishes, with a good deal of Indian and Middle Eastern fare. The atmosphere is basic, and the seasonal patio is a pleasant, breezy spot for a meal.

There are free Sunday dinners in the attached temple at 6pm, if you're on an extremely tight budget.

1400 N. Cherry St. ☎ **303/333-5461**. Buffet $5–$8. MC, V. Mon–Fri 11:30am–2:30pm; Mon–Sat 5–8pm.

T-Wa Inn ★★ *Finds* VIETNAMESE   Denver's oldest Vietnamese restaurant is still the best. With simple, pleasant decor and relics from the Far East on display, it looks the part, but the food is what makes it work. Everything is excellent, but we especially like the succulent shrimp, perfect pork tenderloin, and the attention to authentic Vietnamese flavors. T-Wa also serves several spicy Thai dishes, as well as Asian beers and a whole rainbow of neon-colored specialty drinks.

555 S. Federal Blvd. (2 blocks south of Alameda Ave.) ☎ **303/922-2378**. Most main courses $6–$13. AE, DISC, MC, V. Sun–Thurs 11am–9:30pm; Fri–Sat 11am–10pm.

What to See & Do in Denver

Denver, an intriguing combination of modern American city and sprawling Old West town, offers a wide variety of attractions, activities, and events. You'll discover art, history, sports, recreation, shopping, and, of course, dining. It is quite easy to spend a week in the city and never be bored. Denver also makes a convenient base for easy day trips to Boulder, to Colorado Springs, or up into the mountains.

SUGGESTED ITINERARIES

If You Have 1 Day

Start at Larimer Square, Denver's birthplace, with a self-guided walking tour of the historic sites (p. 100). Then stroll the 16th Street pedestrian mall and head toward the State Capitol, just across Broadway. En route, take a 1-block detour for an early lunch or a cup of tea at the Brown Palace Hotel. After seeing the capitol, explore other Civic Center sites, including the Denver Art Museum.

If You Have 2 Days

Spend your first day as suggested above. On day 2, drive west (and up). Venture into the old Rocky Mountain foothill mining towns of Idaho Springs and Georgetown. En route, visit the Red Rocks Amphitheatre near Morrison, where numerous hiking trails originate. On your return, stop in Golden at Coors Brewery or visit Buffalo Bill's grave on Lookout Mountain.

If You Have 3 Days

Spend your first 2 days as suggested above. On day 3, explore more of Denver. The city has numerous historic homes, beautiful parks, attractive shopping centers, and several highly touted museums (for example, the Denver Museum of Nature and Science, the Botanic Gardens, and the Black American West Museum).

If You Have 4 Days or More

Spend days 1 to 3 as suggested above. On day 4, plan a daylong excursion to a nearby city, such as Colorado Springs (home of the Air Force Academy and the Pikes Peak Cog Railway) or Boulder.

For your fifth day, climb higher into the Rockies to resort communities such as Estes Park (the gateway to Rocky Mountain National Park), or venture west on I-70, uphill toward the renowned ski resorts that dot Colorado's high country.

1 The Top Attractions

Denver Art Museum ★★ Founded in 1893, this seven-story museum is wrapped by a thin 28-sided wall faced with one million sparkling tiles. Construction on a jagged, avant-garde addition, designed by renowned architect Daniel Libeskind, began in 2003. When finished in fall 2006, the unique structure will double the size of the museum and give Denver its most distinctive building by a long shot.

The museum's collection of Western and regional works is its cornerstone. Included are Frederic Remington's bronze *The Cheyenne,* Charles Russell's painting *In the Enemy's Country,* plus 19th-century photography, historical pieces, and works by Georgia O'Keeffe. In 2001, Dorothy and William Harmsen, longtime Colorado residents and founders of the Jolly Rancher Candy Company, donated their prestigious Western art collection to the museum. Assembled over 40 years, the collection immediately made the museum's inventory of Western art one of the most impressive in the nation.

The American Indian collection is also excellent, consisting of more than 17,000 pieces from 150 tribes of North America, spanning nearly 2,000 years. The collection is growing through the acquisition of historic pieces as well as the commissioning of works by contemporary artists. Other collections include architecture and design; graphics; and Asian, African, Oceanic, modern and contemporary, pre-Columbian, and Spanish Colonial art.

Overview tours are available Tuesday through Sunday at 1:30pm, plus 11am on Saturday; an in-depth tour of a different area of the museum is offered each Wednesday and Friday at noon and 1pm; and a variety of child-oriented and family programs are scheduled regularly. There is also a gift shop. Allow 2 to 3 hours.

100 W. 14th Ave. (at Civic Center Park). ⓒ 720/865-5000. www.denverartmuseum.org. Admission $6 adults, $4.50 students and seniors, free for children under 12; free for Colorado residents Sat. Tues and Thurs–Sat 10am–5pm; Wed 10am–9pm; Sun noon–5pm. Bus: 5, 7, 8, 9, or 50.

Denver Museum of Nature & Science ★★ *(Kids*   The largest museum of its kind in the Rocky Mountain region, the Denver Museum of Nature & Science features scores of world-renowned dioramas, an extensive gems and minerals display, a pair of Egyptian mummies, a terrific fossil collection, and several other award-winning exhibitions. The museum focuses on six areas of science: anthropology, health science, geology, paleontology, space science, and zoology.

The newest permanent exhibition, "Space Odyssey," opened in 2003. Visitors experience a carefully crafted mix of exhibits, live programming, digital multimedia, and interactive modules that engage them in contemporary stories of space exploration. The Gates Planetarium, which also reopened in 2003 after renovations, has been transformed into a state-of-the-art digital planetarium. The new facility has an advanced computer graphics and video system, unlike any planetarium in the world.

The "Prehistoric Journey" exhibit traces the history of life on earth through 3.5 billion years. Dinosaur skeletons, fossils, interactive exhibits, and dioramas of ancient ecologies make this one of the museum's most popular attractions, especially with children.

Another popular exhibit is the "Hall of Life," which focuses on the science of the human body. Using a magnetic card, visitors gather information on themselves as they move through the interactive exhibits. When finished, they receive a printout about their own physical condition.

An **IMAX theater** (ⓒ **303/322-7009**) presents science, nature, or technology-oriented films with surround-sound on a screen that measures four and a half stories tall. Allow 2 to 4 hours.

City Park, 2001 Colorado Blvd. ⓒ 800/925-2250 outside Metro Denver, or 303/322-7009; 303/370-8257 for the hearing impaired. www.dmns.org. Admission to museum $9 adults, $6 children 3–18, seniors 65 and older; IMAX $8 adults, $5.50 children and seniors; planetarium $4 additional adults, $3 additional children and seniors. Daily 9am–5pm. Closed Dec 25. Bus: 24, 32, or 40.

Denver Attractions

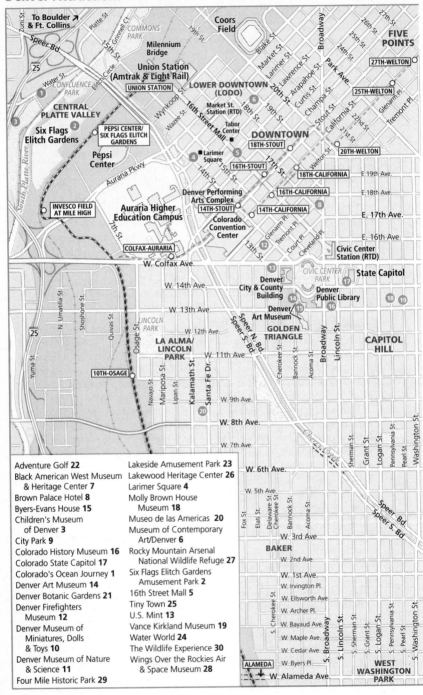

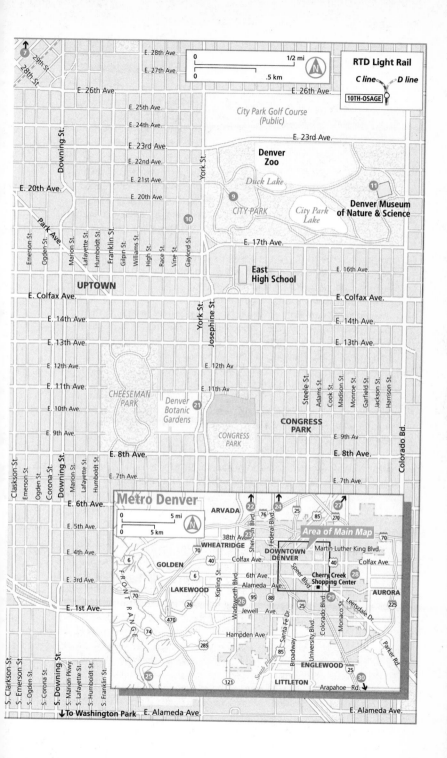

Page content (labels visible on the map):

E. 28th Ave.
E. 27th Ave.
E. 26th Ave.
E. 26th Ave.

0 | 1/2 mi
0 | .5 km

RTD Light Rail
C line   D line
10TH-OSAGE

E. 25th Ave.
E. 24th Ave.
E. 23rd Ave.
E. 23rd Ave.
E. 22nd Ave.
E. 21st Ave.
E. 20th Ave.
E. 20th Ave.

City Park Golf Course (Public)

Denver Zoo

Duck Lake

Downing St.
Park Ave.
York St.

11

Denver Museum of Nature & Science

9
CITY PARK

City Park Lake

10

E. 17th Ave.

Emerson St., Ogden St., Marion St., Lafayette St., Humboldt St., Franklin St., Gilpin St., Williams St., High St., Race St., Vine St., Gaylord St.

UPTOWN

E. 16th Ave.

East High School

E. Colfax Ave.
E. Colfax Ave.

E. 14th Ave.
E. 13th Ave.
E. 12th Ave.
E. 11th Ave.
E. 10th Ave.
E. 9th Ave.
E. 8th Ave.
E. 7th Ave.

York St.
Josephine St.

E. 14th Ave.
E. 13th Ave.
E. 12th Av
E. 11th Av

CHEESEMAN PARK

Denver Botanic Gardens
21

CONGRESS PARK

CONGRESS PARK

Steele St., Adams St., Cook St., Madison St., Monroe St., Garfield St., Jackson St., Harrison St.

Colorado Bd.

E. 9th Av
E. 8th Ave.
E. 7th Ave.

Clarkson St., Emerson St., Ogden St., Corona St., Downing St., Marion St., Lafayette St., Humboldt St., Franklin St.

E. 6th Ave.
E. 5th Ave.
E. 4th Ave.
E. 3rd Ave.
E. 1st Ave.

Metro Denver

0 | 5 mi
0 | 5 km

ARVADA
22 **24** 25 85 270 **27**

76

Sheridan Blvd.
Federal Blvd.

Area of Main Map

70

WHEATRIDGE
38th Ave.
70

Martin Luther King Blvd.
Colfax Ave.
40

GOLDEN
6
40
Colfax Ave.
DOWNTOWN DENVER

FRONT RANGE
6

LAKEWOOD
26
470

6th Ave.
Alameda Ave.

Speer Blvd.

Cherry Creek Shopping Center
28

AURORA
225

Kipling St.
Wadsworth Blvd.
95
88
Jewell Ave.
26

25
Colorado Blvd.
29
Monaco Blvd.

Leetsdale Dr.

74

Hampden Ave.
285

South Platte

Santa Fe Dr.
Broadway
University Blvd.

85
25
ENGLEWOOD
25

Parker Rd.

25
121

LITTLETON
Arapahoe Rd.

30

S. Clarkson St., S. Emerson St., S. Ogden St., S. Corona St., S. Downing St., S. Marion Pkwy., S. Lafayette St., S. Humboldt St., S. Franklin St.

↓To Washington Park   E. Alameda Ave.
E. Alameda Ave.

(Fun Fact **Robbery at the Mint**

A daring armed robbery took place at the Denver Mint in 1922, just 1 week before Christmas, and although police were certain they knew who the culprits were, no one ever served a day in jail for the crime. The most secure building in Denver, the Mint seemed an unlikely target for a robbery. In fact, the thieves did not rob the Mint itself—they simply waited for guards to carry the money out the front door.

A Federal Reserve Bank truck was parked outside the Mint on West Colfax Avenue at about 10:30am on December 18. It was being loaded with $200,000 worth of brand-new $5 bills, to be taken to a bank about 12 blocks away, when a black Buick touring car pulled up. Two men jumped out and began firing sawed-off shotguns, killing one guard and spraying the Mint and nearby buildings, while a third robber grabbed the bags of money. Guards inside the Mint quickly pulled their guns and returned fire, but within a minute and a half the robbers were gone—$200,000 richer.

Mint guards were certain they had hit one of the thieves, and 4 weeks later the Buick turned up in a dusty Denver garage. Lying in the front seat was the frozen, bloody body of Nick Trainor, a convicted criminal who had recently been released on parole from the Nebraska State Penitentiary. Trainor had been shot several times.

Secret Service agents recovered $80,000 of the missing loot the following year in St. Paul, Minnesota, but no arrests were made, and little more was mentioned until 1934, when Denver police announced that they knew the identities of the other men involved. Still, no charges were filed. Two of the suspects were already serving life sentences for other crimes.

At the time, police said a Midwest gang had pulled off the robbery and immediately fled to the Minneapolis–St. Paul area. The robbers gave the money to a prominent Minneapolis attorney, who also was never charged.

U.S. Mint ★★   Whether we worship it or simply consider money a necessary commodity, we all have to admit a certain fascination with the coins and bills that seem to make the world turn. There are four mints in the United States, but the Denver Mint is one of only two (the other is the Philadelphia Mint) where we can actually see the process of turning lumps of metal into shiny coins.

Opened in 1863, the Mint originally melted gold dust and nuggets into bars. In 1904 the office moved to this site, and 2 years later began making gold and silver coins. Copper pennies were added a few years later. The last silver dollars (containing 90% silver) were coined in 1935. In 1970, all silver was eliminated from dollars and half dollars (today they're made of a copper-nickel alloy). The Denver Mint stamps billions of coins each year, and each has a small D on it.

Although visitors today don't get as close as they once did, a self-guided tour along the visitors' gallery provides a good look at the process, with a bird's-eye view from the mezzanine of the actual coin-minting process. A variety of displays help explain the minting process, and an adjacent **gift shop** on Cherokee Street (© **303/572-9500**) offers a variety of souvenirs. Allow 1 hour.

Note: Due to greatly increased security, individuals are now required to arrange tours at least 3 weeks in advance

with their congressional representatives at www.senate.gov or www.house.gov, and there are quite a few requirements for entering the mint. It is uncertain that walk-in visitors will be allowed in the future.

320 W. Colfax Ave. (between Cherokee and Delaware sts.). © **303/405-4757** or 303/405-4761. www.usmint. gov. Free admission. Tours Mon–Fri 8am–1pm. Gift shop 8am–3:30pm. Closed 1–2 weeks in summer for audit; call for exact date. Bus: 7.

Colorado State Capitol ★★   Built to last 1,000 years, the capitol was constructed in 1886 of granite from a Colorado quarry. The dome, which rises 272 feet above the ground, was first sheathed in copper, then replaced with gold leaf after a public outcry: Copper was not a Colorado product.

Murals depicting the history of water in the state adorn the walls of the first-floor rotunda, which offers a splendid view upward to the underside of the dome. The rotunda resembles the layout of the U.S. Capitol in Washington, D.C. South of the rotunda is the governor's office, paneled in walnut and lit by a massive chandelier.

On the first floor, the west lobby hosts revolving temporary exhibits. To the right of the main lobby is the governor's reception room. The second floor has main entrances to the House, Senate, and old Supreme Court chambers. On the third floor are entrances to the public and visitor galleries for the House and Senate (open to the public during legislative session from January through early May).

Lincoln St. and Colfax Ave. © **303/866-2604.** Free admission. 1-hr. tours offered year-round (more frequently in summer), Memorial Day to Labor Day Mon–Fri 9am–3:30pm; rest of year Mon–Fri 9:15am–2:30pm. Bus: 2, 7, 8, 12, or 15.

2 More Attractions

HISTORIC BUILDINGS

Denver encompasses 17 recognized historic districts, including Capitol Hill, the Clements District (around 21st St. and Tremont St., just east of downtown), and 9th Street Park in Auraria (off 9th St. and West Colfax Ave.). **Historic Denver,** P.O. Box 480491, Denver, CO 80248-0491 (© **303/534-5288;** www.historic denver.org), offers walking-tour maps of many of these areas and organizes several annual events. The **Colorado Historical Society** (© **303/866-3682**) also arranges free tours of historic mansions in July and August. For additional information on some of Denver's historic areas, also see the "Neighborhoods in Brief" section in chapter 4.

Byers-Evans House   This elaborate Victorian home, built by *Rocky Mountain News* founding editor William Byers in 1883, has been restored to its appearance of 1912–24, when it was owned by William Gray Evans, son of Colorado's second territorial governor. (The Evans family continued to reside here until 1981.) Guided tours describe the architecture and explain the fascinating lives of these prominent Denver families. There is a gift shop. Allow 45 minutes.

1310 Bannock St. (in front of the Denver Art Museum). © **303/620-4933.** Admission $3 adults, $2.50 seniors, $1.50 children 6–16, free for children under 6. Tues–Sun 11am–3pm. Closed state holidays. Bus: 8.

Larimer Square ⭐ This is where Denver began. Larimer Street between 14th and 15th streets was the entire community of Denver City in 1858, with false-fronted stores, hotels, and saloons to serve gold-seekers and other pioneers. In the mid-1870s it was the main street of the city and the site of Denver's first post office, bank, theater, and streetcar line. By the 1930s, however, this part of Larimer Street had deteriorated so much that it had become a skid row of pawn-shops, gin mills, and flophouses. Plans had been made to tear these structures down, when a group of investors purchased the entire block in 1965.

The Larimer Square project became Denver's first major historic preservation effort. All 16 of the block's commercial buildings, constructed in the 1870s and 1880s, were renovated, providing space for street-level retail shops, restaurants, and nightclubs, as well as upper-story offices. A series of courtyards and open spaces was created, and in 1973 it was added to the National Register of Historic Places. Allow at least a half-hour.

Larimer Square hosts numerous special events, many tied to local sporting occasions (the National Western Stock Show, the Denver Grand Prix, and so forth). Oktoberfest (Sept) features German music, dancing, heritage booths, and authentic *bier;* June's La Piazza dell'Arte features 200 artists creating pastel masterpieces on the street.

1400 block of Larimer St. ℂ 303/534-2367 or 303/685-8143 (events line). www.larimersquare.com. Bus: 2, 7, 12, 15, 16, 28, 31, 32, 38, or 44.

Molly Brown House Museum ⭐ Built in 1889 of Colorado rhyolite with sandstone trim, this was the residence of J.J. and Margaret (Molly) Brown from 1894 to 1932. The "unsinkable" Molly Brown became a national heroine in 1912 when the *Titanic* sank. She took charge of a group of immigrant women in a lifeboat and later raised money for their benefit.

Restored to its 1910 appearance, the Molly Brown House has a large collection of early-20th-century furnishings and art objects, many of which belonged to the Brown family. There are also temporary exhibits (recent ones detailed the lives of servants in Brown's day and trends in Victorian undergarments), and a carriage house with a museum store at the rear is open to visitors. The house can be seen on guided tours. Allow 1 hour.

1340 Pennsylvania St. ℂ 303/832-4092. www.mollybrown.org. Guided tour $6.50 adults, $5 seniors over 65, $3 children 6–12, free for children under 6. June–Aug Mon–Sat 10am–4pm, Sun noon–4pm; Sept–May Tues–Sat 10am–4pm, Sun noon–4pm. Guided tours every 30 min.; last tour of the day begins at 3:30pm. Closed major holidays. Bus: 2 on Logan St. to E. 13th, then 1 block east to Pennsylvania.

MUSEUMS & GALLERIES

Black American West Museum & Heritage Center ⭐ Nearly one-third of the cowboys in the Old West were black, and this museum chronicles their little-known history, along with that of black doctors, teachers, miners, farmers, newspaper reporters, and state legislators. The extensive collection occupies the Victorian home of Dr. Justina Ford, the first black woman licensed to practice medicine in Denver. Known locally as the "Lady Doctor," Ford (1871–1951) delivered more than 7,000 babies—most of them at home because she was denied hospital privileges—and consistently served the disadvantaged and underprivileged of Denver.

The museum's founder and curator emeritus, Paul Stewart, loved to play cowboys and Indians as a boy, but his playmates always chose him to be an Indian because "There was no such thing as a black cowboy." He began researching the history of blacks in the West after meeting a black cowboy who had led cattle drives in the early 20th century. Stewart explored almost every corner of the American West, gathering artifacts, memorabilia, photographs, oral histories—anything to document the existence of black cowboys—and his collection served as the nucleus for this museum when it opened in 1971. Allow 1 hour.

3091 California St. (at 31st St.). ℭ 303/292-2566. Admission $6 adults, $5.50 seniors, $4 children 5–12, free for children under 5. June–Sept daily 10am–5pm; Oct–May Wed–Fri 10am–2pm, Sat–Sun 10am–5pm. Light Rail: Stop no. 1.

Colorado History Museum ★ The Colorado Historical Society's permanent exhibits include "The Colorado Chronicle," an 1800-to-1949 timeline that uses biographical plaques and a remarkable collection of photographs, news clippings, and paraphernalia to illustrate Colorado's past. Dozens of dioramas portray episodes in state history, including an intricate re-creation of 19th-century Denver. There's also a life-size display on early transportation and industry.

The first major new permanent exhibit at the museum in some time, "Ancient Voices," is slated to open in early 2005, a $400,000 multimedia exhibit dedicated to Colorado's native tribes and their history. It will be followed by another new exhibit, "Confluence of Cultures," which will depict the Pioneer era when it opens in 2006. The museum offers a series of lectures and statewide historical and archaeological tours. Its gift shop is also worth a visit. Allow 1 hour.

1300 Broadway. ℭ 303/866-3682. www.coloradohistory.org. Admission $5 adults, $4.50 seniors and students, $3.50 children 6–12, free for children under 6. Mon–Sat 10am–4:30pm; Sun noon–4:30pm. Bus: 8.

Denver Firefighters Museum *(Kids)* The history of the Denver Fire Department is preserved and displayed here, in historic Fire Station No. 1. Built in 1909 for Engine Company No. 1, it was one of the largest firehouses in Denver, occupying 11,000 square feet on two floors. In its early years, it lodged men, fire engines, and horses. Motorized equipment replaced horse-drawn engines by 1923, and in 1932 the firehouse was "modernized." Concrete replaced the wooden floor, the stables and hayloft were removed, and the plumbing was improved. Visitors today see firefighting equipment dating to 1866, as well as historic photos and newspaper clippings. Allow 45 minutes.

1326 Tremont Place. ℭ 303/892-1436. www.denverfirefightersmuseum.org. Admission $4 adults, $3 seniors, $2 children under 15. Mon–Sat 10am–4pm. Closed major holidays. Located 2 blocks west of Civic Center Park on the north side of Colfax.

Denver Museum of Miniatures, Dolls & Toys *(Finds)* This late-19th-century property is home to an intriguing collection of antique and collectible dolls, from rag and wood to exquisite German and French bisque. Also on display are dollhouses, from a Santa Fe adobe with hand-carved furniture to a replica of a 16-room home in Newport, Rhode Island. The museum also displays wonderful old toys, from teddy bears to model cars. The gift shop is equally delightful. Allow 45 to 60 minutes.

1880 Gaylord St. (just west of City Park). ℭ 303/322-1053. www.dmmdt.com. Admission $5 adults, $4 seniors and children 5–16, free for children under 5. Tues–Sat 10am–4pm; Sun 1–4pm.

Four Mile Historic Park ★ Four miles southeast of downtown Denver—thus the name—the oldest log home (1859) still standing in Denver serves as the centerpiece for this 12-acre open-air museum. Everything is authentic to the period from 1859 to 1883, including the house (a former stagecoach stop), its furnishings, outbuildings, and farm equipment. There are draft horses and chickens in the barn, and crops in the garden. Weekend visitors can enjoy horse-drawn carriage rides ($2), weather permitting. Seasonal "Heritage Events" feature pioneer-era musicians and actors as well as many food and craft demonstrations. Big events include July 4th and an outdoor theater series. Allow 1 hour.

715 S. Forest St. (at Exposition Ave.). ℂ 303/399-1859. www.fourmilepark.org. Free admission; museum tours $3.50 adults, $2 seniors and children 6–15, free for children under 6. Apr–Sept Wed–Fri noon–4pm, Sat–Sun 10am–4pm; Oct–Mar Sat–Sun noon–4pm.

Lakewood's Heritage Center at Belmar Park   In Denver's early days, many wealthy residents maintained summer estates in the rural Lakewood area, and this historic village tells their story as well as that of others who lived and worked here. Your first stop should be the visitor center, for an introduction to the museum; you can begin a personalized guided or self-guided tour here. The village includes an 1870s farmhouse, a 1920s one-room school, a 1950s variety store, and the Barn Gallery. There's an exhibit on "Lakewood People and Places," antique and vintage farm machinery, self-guided history walks through the surrounding 127-acre park, changing art exhibits, and a picnic area. On-site are also an amphitheater and festival area, hosting a summer concert series and a slate of seasonal fairs and celebrations. Allow 1 to 2 hours.

801 S. Yarrow Blvd. (near Wadsworth and Ohio), Lakewood. ℂ 303/987-7850. Admission $3 adults, $2 children 4–18, free for children under 4. Mon–Fri 10am–4pm; Sat noon–4pm. Closed Sun. Bus: 76.

Museo de las Americas ⚐ *Finds*   The only museum in the Rocky Mountains focusing exclusively on the art, culture, and history of Latinos, the Museo is worth a stop, as is a stroll through the surrounding gallery-laden neighborhood. The exhibits here change regularly, and a semi-permanent exhibit tells the story of pre-Colombian Latin America, with a replica of an ornate sunstone and exhibits on Tenochtitlan, the Aztec metropolis (on the site of present-day Mexico City) destroyed by invading Spaniards in the 16th century. In 2005, a major exhibit on folk art is being displayed. Allow 1 to 2 hours.

861 Santa Fe Dr. ℂ 303/571-4401. www.museo.org. Admission $4 adults, seniors and students $3, free for children under 13. Tues–Sat 10am–5pm.

Museum of Contemporary Art/Denver   Rotating avant-garde exhibitions by numerous local and national artists are the main attraction at this downtown museum. Temporary exhibits in the two floors of exhibition space rotate every 5 months. The museum will likely be moving to a new LoDo location in 2006 or 2007. Allow at least 1 hour.

1275 19th St. at Sakura Sq. (19th and Larimer sts.). ℂ 303/298-7554. www.mcartdenver.org. Admission $5 adults, $3 seniors and students, free for children under 12. Tues–Sat 11am–5:30pm; Sun noon–5pm.

Vance Kirkland Museum ⚐⚐ *Finds*   This relatively new museum covers Colorado's most illustrious artist, Vance Kirkland (1904–81), in grand fashion, while also presenting a world-class collection of decorative arts. Kirkland was a watercolor painter focused on Western landscapes when he started experimenting and combined oils and watercolors on one canvas. The traditional arts establishment dropped his modern ideas like a bad habit, but he later won accolades for creating his own artistic universe in his stunning paintings, about 60 of which are on display here. His preserved brick studio (first built in 1911) has an unusual harness he used for painting on flat canvases face down (dating from his "dot" period). The decorative arts collection includes about 3,000 pieces ranging from teacups to armchairs, and there are also over 600 works by notable Colorado artists other than Kirkland.

1311 Pearl St. © **303/832-8576**. www.kirklandmuseum.org. Admission $6 adults, $5 students, teachers, and seniors. No one under 13 permitted due to the fragile nature of the collection. Children 13 to 17 must be accompanied by an adult. Mon–Fri 1–5pm. Guided tour Tues at 1:30pm. Closed major holidays.

The Wildlife Experience ⭑   Opened in 2002 near the Denver Technological Center, this impressive $40 million museum has three foci: natural history, nature films, and wildlife art, with nine galleries of paintings, sculptures, and photography. The museum's aim is to educate visitors about conservation and the delicate balance between people and the environment, and do it in an aesthetically pleasing fashion. They accomplish the task, with such highlights as a National Geographic Channel screening room and an interactive Children's Gallery. Also here are a 315-seat Iwerks Extreme Screen Theater, a restaurant, and a gift shop. Allow 1 hour.

10035 S. Peoria St. © **720/488-3300**. www.thewildlifeexperience.org. Admission or theater tickets $6 adults, $5 seniors, $3 children; combination museum/theater tickets $10 adults, $8 seniors, $5 children. Tues–Sun 9am–5pm. Closed major holidays and non-holiday Mon. Located 1 mile east of I-25 via Lincoln Ave. (exit 193).

Wings Over the Rockies Air & Space Museum ⭑ *Kids*   More than 40 planes and spacecraft occupy cavernous Hangar No. 1, which became a museum when Lowry Air Force Base closed in 1995; now it's a burgeoning residential area about 6 miles southeast of downtown. On display are antique biplanes, a search-and-rescue helicopter, an F-14 Tomcat, a massive B-1A bomber—one of only two in existence—and most of the F-100 fighter series. You can also see a World War II uniform collection, a Norden bombsight, U3A Blue Canoe, and the Freedom space module, plus seasonal exhibits. On each month's second Saturday the museum hosts "Demo Cockpit Day," when visitors get to climb into the planes' cockpits. Sci-fi fans take note: A full-size X-Wing prop used in the filming of *Star Wars* is on permanent display. The store is filled with aviation- and space-oriented souvenirs. Allow 1½ hours.

7711 E. Academy Pkwy., Hangar No. 1. © **303/360-5360**. www.wingsmuseum.org. Admission $6 adults, $5 seniors, $4 children 6–17, free for children under 6. Mon–Sat 10am–5pm; Sun noon–5pm. Bus: 6.

PARKS, GARDENS & ZOOS

Butterfly Pavilion & Insect Center ⭑⭑ *Kids*   A walk through the butterfly conservatory introduces the visitor to a world of grace and beauty. The constant mist creates a hazy habitat to support the lush green plants that are both food and home to the inhabitants. If you stand still for a few minutes, a butterfly might land on you, but don't try to pick them up—the oils on your hands contaminate their senses, interfering with their ability to find food. One display describes the differences among butterflies, moths, and skippers, and color charts help with identification. (A butterfly guide is available for a nominal fee.)

In the insect room you'll discover that honeybees beat their wings some 200 times per second, and beetles comprise one-fifth of all living things on earth. Meet arthropods (the scientific name for insects) that are native to Colorado, and see exotic species from around the world. A fascinating "touch cart" allows you to get up close to a cockroach or tarantula, assuming that you really want to.

A 31,000-square-foot expansion was completed in 2004, housing "Shrunk!"— giant robotic insects (it can be scary for little ones) and nifty interactive exhibits about the biomechanics of bugs. Also on the premises are a large gift shop and snack bar. Outside, a ½-mile nature trail meanders amidst cacti and other desert-friendly plants. Allow 2 to 3 hours.

6252 W. 104th Ave., Westminster. ✆ 303/469-5441. www.butterflies.org. Admission $7.95 adults, $5.95 seniors, $4.95 children 4–12, free for children under 4. Memorial Day to Labor Day daily 9am–6pm; rest of year 9am–5pm. Take the Denver–Boulder Turnpike (U.S. 36) to W. 104th Ave. and go east for about a block. The pavilion is on your right.

City Park   Denver's largest urban park covers 330 acres (96 sq. blocks) on the east side of uptown. Established in 1881, it retains Victorian touches. The park encompasses two lakes (with boat rentals and fishing), athletic fields, jogging and walking trails, a free children's water feature, playgrounds, tennis courts, picnic areas, and an 18-hole municipal golf course. In summer, there are concerts. The park is also the site of the Denver Zoo and the Denver Museum of Nature and Science (including its IMAX Theater), discussed elsewhere in this chapter.

E. 17th to E. 26th aves., between York St. and Colorado Blvd. Free admission to park. Separate admission to zoo, museum, golf course, and other sites. Daily 24 hr. Bus: 24 or 32.

Colorado's Ocean Journey   A decade in the making, Denver's state-of-the-art aquarium—the largest between Chicago and Monterey, California—opened in 1999 as a non-profit, and then nearly went bankrupt, and in 2003 was sold to the for-profit Landry's seafood restaurant chain, who plan to open a theme restaurant once permitting allows. Permanent exhibits include re-creations of two ecosystems that are on opposite sides of the planet: the Colorado River in North America and the Kampar River in Indonesia. The Colorado River path features the greenback cutthroat trout (the Colorado state fish) as well as river otters and innumerable other aquatic denizens. It culminates in a flash-flood simulation and the 187,000-gallon Sea of Cortez display, populated with exotic fish and moray eels. The Kampar River path features endangered Sumatran tigers. Allow 2 hours.

700 Water St., just east of I-25 via 23rd Ave. (exit 211). ✆ 303/561-4450. www.oceanjourney.org. Admission $15 adults, $13 youths 13–17 and seniors, $6.95 children 4–12, free for children under 4. Memorial Day to Labor Day daily 10am–6pm; rest of year daily 10am–5pm. Closed Dec 25.

Denver Botanic Gardens ★★   Twenty-three acres of outstanding outdoor and indoor gardens display plants native to the desert, plains, mountain foothills, and alpine zones. There's also a traditional Japanese garden, herb garden, water garden, fragrance garden, and a garden inspired by the art of Monet. "Romantic Gardens" feature a waterway, and the "Gardens of the World" hold plants from Asia, Europe, Africa, Australia, and the tropics.

Even in the cold of winter, the dome-shaped, concrete-and-Plexiglas Tropical Conservatory houses thousands of species of tropical and subtropical plants. Huge, colorful orchids and bromeliads share space with a collection of plants used for food, fibers, dyes, building materials, and medicines. The Botanic Gardens also have a gift shop, library, and auditorium. Special events are scheduled throughout the year; offerings range from garden concerts in summer to a spring book-and-plant sale to a cornfield maze southwest of Denver in the fall. Allow 1 to 2 hours.

1005 York St. ✆ 720/865-3500. www.botanicgardens.org. Admission May to mid-Sept $8.50 adults, $5.50 seniors, $5 children 4–15; mid-Sept to Apr $7.50 adults, $4.50 seniors, $4 children 4–15; free for children under 4 year-round. May to mid-Sept Sat–Tues 9am–8pm, Wed–Fri 9am–5pm; mid-Sept to Apr daily 9am–5pm. Bus: 2, 6, or 10.

Denver Mountain Parks ★★   Formally established in August 1913, the city's Mountain Parks system immediately began acquiring land in the mountains near Denver to be set aside for recreational use. Today it includes more than 14,000 acres, with 31 developed mountain parks and 16 unnamed wilderness areas that are wonderful places for hiking, picnicking, bird-watching, golfing, or lazing in the grass and sun.

The first and largest, **Genesee Park,** is 20 miles west of Denver off I-70 exit 254; its 2,341 acres contain the Chief Hosa Lodge and Campground (the only overnight camping available in the system), picnic areas with fireplaces, a softball field, a scenic overlook, and an elk-and-buffalo enclosure.

Among the system's other parks is **Echo Lake,** about 45 minutes from downtown Denver on Colo. 103. At 10,600 feet elevation on Mount Evans, the park has good fishing, hiking, and picnicking, plus a restaurant and curio shop. (*Note:* A fee program is being tested here; the charge is $10 per carload.) Other parks include 1,000-acre **Daniels Park** (23 miles south of Denver; take I-25 to Castle Pines Parkway, then go west to the park), which offers picnic areas, a bison enclosure, and a scenic overlook; and **Dedisse Park** (2 miles west of Evergreen on Colo. 74), which provides picnic facilities, a golf course, restaurant, clubhouse, and opportunities for ice-skating, fishing, and volleyball.

Dept. of Parks and Recreation. © 303/697-4545. www.denvergov.org. Free admission.

Denver Zoo ★★ *Kids*   More than 750 species of animals (more than 4,000 individuals) live in this spacious zoological park, home to the rare deer-like okapi as well as endangered cheetahs, Komodo dragons, and western lowland gorillas. The newest (and most ambitious) habitat here is Predator Ridge, a re-created African savannah with lions, hyenas, and other African predators, opening along with a new entrance and parking facility in 2004. The exhibit is modeled after a Kenyan preserve, complete with artificial termite mounds that disperse insects for the banded mongoose that live here. The zoo has long been an innovator in re-creating realistic habitats: Bear Mountain, built in 1918, was the first animal exhibit in the United States constructed of simulated concrete rockwork.

The zoo is home to the nation's first natural gas–powered train ($1). The electric Safari Shuttle ($2.50 adults, $1.50 children) tours all zoo paths from spring through fall. An especially kid-friendly attraction is the Conversation Carousel ($1), featuring wood-carved renditions of such endangered species as okapi, polar bears, Komodo dragons, and hippos. The Hungry Elephant, a cafeteria with an outdoor eating area, serves full meals, and picnicking is popular, too. Feeding times are posted near the zoo entrance so you can time your visit to see the animals at their most active. Allow from 2 hours to a whole day.

City Park, 23rd Ave. and Steele St. (main entrance between Colorado Blvd. and York St.). © 303/376-4800. www.denverzoo.org. Admission $11 adults summer, $9 adults winter; $9 seniors 62 and over summer, $7 seniors winter; $7 children 3–12 (accompanied by an adult) summer, $5 children winter; free for children under 3. Apr–Sept daily 9am–5pm; Oct–Mar daily 10am–4pm. Bus: 24 or 32.

Rocky Mountain Arsenal National Wildlife Refuge   Once a site where the U.S. Army manufactured chemical weapons such as mustard gas and GB nerve agent, and later leased to a private enterprise to produce pesticides, the Rocky Mountain Arsenal has become an environmental success story. The 27-square-mile Superfund cleanup site, an area of open grasslands and wetlands just west of Denver International Airport, is home to more than 330 species, including deer, coyotes, prairie dogs, and birds of prey. An estimated 100 bald eagles make this one of the country's largest eagle-roosting locales during the winter.

The Rocky Mountain Arsenal Wildlife Society Bookstore is at the visitor center, and there are 10 miles of hiking trails and catch-and-release fishing. For a guided tour, it's best to call a day or two in advance. Allow at least an hour.

56th Ave. at Quebec St. © 303/289-0930. Free admission. Sat–Sun 8am–4:30pm. Bus: 48.

3 Amusement Parks & Places Especially for Kids

Denver abounds in child-oriented activities, and the listings below will probably appeal to young travelers of any age. In addition, some sights listed in the previous sections may appeal to families. They include the Butterfly Pavilion and Insect Center; Colorado History Museum; Colorado's Ocean Journey; Denver Art Museum; Denver Museum of Miniatures Dolls & Toys; Denver Museum of Nature and Science; Denver Zoo; Four Mile Historic Park; and the U.S. Mint.

Adventure Golf *Kids*   Each of the 54 holes at this miniature golf course has a theme to challenge you, such as a haunted house, pirate battle, fairy castle, fire-breathing dragon, and fiery volcano. Or perhaps you'd prefer to visit the Lost Continent, with "deadly" piranha pools and quicksand pits. Allow 1 to 2 hours.

9650 N. Sheridan Blvd. (at 96th Ave.). (*C*) **303/650-7587.** 18 holes $5.95 adults, $5.75 seniors over 65, $4.95 children 4–12, free for children under 4. Mar–Nov Sun–Thurs 10am–10pm, Fri–Sat 10am–11pm, weather permitting. Hours may be shorter in spring and fall. Closed Dec–Feb. Bus: 51.

Children's Museum of Denver *Kids*   Denver's best hands-on experience for children, this intriguing museum is both educational and just plain fun. Focusing on the zero-to-8 age bracket, the museum uses educational "playscapes" to entertain and activate young minds.

New playscapes for 2004 are "Fire Station No. 1," which teaches safety with such exhibits as a real fire engine, and "Community Market," a faux supermarket that allows kids to role-play as shoppers and clerks. There are several other playscapes with themes ranging from biology to engineering. There's also a resource center that provides parenting information to adults. And a cafe that serves sandwiches, snacks, and beverages. Allow at least 2 hours.

2121 Children's Museum Dr. (*C*) **303/433-7444.** www.mychildsmuseum.org. Admission $7 ages 1–59, $5 seniors 60 and over, free for children under 1. Mon–Fri 9am–4pm; Sat–Sun 10am–5pm. Take exit 211 (23rd Ave.) east off I-25; turn right on 7th St., and again on Children's Museum Dr.

Fat City *Kids*   This 3.5-acre indoor entertainment mall, completely renovated in 2000, bills itself as "fun for everyone." It's not much of an exaggeration—inside are 40 lanes of bowling, mini-golf, Laser Tag, roller-skating, and a large video arcade for the kids; for the more mature crowd, there's scads of TVs, billiards, a restaurant, and a 50-foot martini bar. Allow 1 to 4 hours.

9670 W. Coal Mine Ave. (at Kipling St.), Littleton. (*C*) **303/972-4344.** www.fatcityinfo.com. Free admission; activities $5–$7; multi-activity tickets available. Sun–Thurs 11am–midnight; Fri–Sat 11am–2am; call for activity availability. About 15 miles southwest of downtown Denver. Bus: 67 or 76.

Lakeside Amusement Park *Kids*   Among the largest amusement parks in the Rocky Mountains, Lakeside has about 40 rides, including a Cyclone roller coaster, a midway with carnival and arcade games, and a rare steam-powered miniature train that circles the lake. There are also food stands and picnic facilities, plus a separate Kiddie's Playland with 15 rides. Allow 3 hours.

4601 Sheridan Blvd. (just south of I-70, exit 271). (*C*) **303/477-1621.** www.lakesideamusementpark.com. Admission $2 to Kiddie's Playland. Ride coupons 50¢ (rides require 1–4 coupons each); unlimited rides $13 Mon–Fri, $18 Sat–Sun and holidays. May Sat–Sun and holidays noon–11pm; June to Labor Day Mon–Fri 6–11pm, Sat–Sun and holidays noon–11pm. Kiddie's Playland Mon–Fri 1–10pm, Sat–Sun and holidays noon–10pm. Closed from the day after Labor Day to Apr.

Six Flags Elitch Gardens Theme Park *Kids*   A Denver tradition established in 1889, this amusement park moved to its present downtown site in 1995. The 45-plus rides include Twister II, an unbelievable 10-story roller coaster with a 90-foot drop and dark tunnel; the Flying Coaster, a one-of-a-kind "hang gliding" experience where passengers lie facedown; the Halfpipe, a snow-boarding-themed thrill ride that involves 16 passengers on a 39-foot board; the 220-foot, free-fall Tower of Doom; and a fully restored 1925 carousel with 67 hand-carved horses and chariots. Patrons of all ages can enjoy the Island Kingdom Water Park while the little ones have fun on pint-sized rides in the Looney Tunes MovieTown. There are also musical revues and stunt shows, games and arcades, food, shopping, and beautiful flower gardens. Allow 3 hours.

Speer Blvd., at I-25 exit 212A. © 303/595-4386. www.sixflags.com/elitchgardens. Gate admission with unlimited rides $37 for those taller than 4 ft., $20 for those 4 ft. and under and seniors 55–69, free for children under 4 and seniors over 69. Memorial Day to Labor Day daily 10am–10pm; Apr to late May and early Sept to Oct weekends, call for hours.

Tiny Town and Railroad *Kids* *Finds* Originally built in 1915 at the site of a Denver-Leadville stagecoach stop, Tiny Town is exactly what its name implies—a one-sixth scale Western village. Nestled in a scenic mountain canyon about 20 miles southeast of downtown Denver, Tiny Town is made up of 100 colorful buildings and a steam-powered locomotive visitors can ride for an additional $1. Allow 1 hour.

6249 S. Turkey Creek Rd., Tiny Town, CO 80465. © 303/697-6829. www.tinytownrailroad.com. Admission $3 adults, $2 children 2–12, free for children under 2. Memorial Day to Labor Day daily 10am–5pm; early to mid-May and early Sept to Oct Sat–Sun 10am–5pm. Closed Nov–Apr.

Water World *★* *Kids* This 64-acre complex, billed as America's largest family water park, has two ocean-like wave pools, river rapids for inner-tubing, twisting water slides, a small children's play area, plus other attractions—more than 40 in all. Allow at least 3 hours.

88th Ave. and Pecos St., Federal Heights. © 303/427-SURF. www.waterworldcolorado.com. Admission $28 adults, $24 children 4–12, free for seniors and children under 4. Memorial Day to Labor Day daily 10am–6pm. Closed rest of year and some school days in Aug. Take the Thornton exit (exit 219, 84th Ave.) off I-25 north.

WALKING TOUR	DOWNTOWN DENVER

Start:	Denver Information Center, Civic Center Park.
Finish:	State Capitol, Civic Center Park.
Time:	2 to 8 hours, depending on how much time you spend shopping, eating, and sightseeing.
Best Times:	Any Tuesday through Friday in late spring.
Worst Times:	Monday and holidays, when the museums are closed.

Start your tour of the downtown area at Civic Center Park, on West Colfax Avenue at 14th Street.

❶ Civic Center Park

This 2-square-block oasis features a Greek amphitheater, fountains, statues, flower gardens, and 30 different species of trees, 2 of which (it is said) were originally planted by Abraham Lincoln at his Illinois home.

Overlooking the park on its east side is the State Capitol. On its south side is the:

❷ Colorado History Museum

The staircase-like building houses exhibits that make the state's colorful history come to life.

Also on the south side of the park are the Denver Public Library and the:

❸ Denver Art Museum

Designed by Gio Ponti of Milan, Italy, the art museum is a 28-sided, 10-story structure that resembles a medieval fortress with a skin of more than a million tiny glass tiles. Inside are more than 35,000 works of art, including renowned Western and American Indian collections.

On the west side of Civic Center Park is the:

4 City and County Building

During the Christmas season, a rainbow of colored lights decorates it in spectacular fashion.

A block farther west is the:

5 U.S. Mint

Modeled in Italian Renaissance style, the building resembles the Palazzo Riccardi in Florence. More than 60,000 cubic feet of granite and 1,000 tons of steel went into its construction in 1904.

Cross over Colfax and go diagonally northwest up Court Place. Two blocks ahead is the:

6 Denver Pavilions

The city's newest retail hot spot sits at the south end of the 16th Street Mall, featuring a Hard Rock Cafe, a 15-screen movie theater, and a Barnes & Noble Superstore.

Three blocks up the 16th Street Mall, head southwest 2 blocks on California Street past the Colorado Convention Center and turn right on 14th Street. Walk 2 blocks to the:

7 Denver Center for the Performing Arts

The complex covers 4 square blocks between 14th Street and Cherry Creek, Champa Street and Arapahoe Street. The entrance is under a block-long, 80-foot-high glass archway. The center includes seven theaters, a symphony hall in the round, a voice research laboratory, and a smoking solar fountain. Free tours are offered.

Two more blocks up 14th past the arts center is:

8 Larimer Square

This is Denver's oldest commercial district. Restored late-19th-century Victorian buildings accommodate more than 30 shops and a dozen restaurants and clubs. Colorful awnings, hanging flower baskets, and quiet open courtyards accent the square, once home to such notables as Buffalo Bill Cody and Bat Masterson. Horse-drawn carriage rides originate here for trips up the 16th Street Mall or through lower downtown.

TAKE A BREAK
Stop at **Lime,** 1424 Larimer St., between 14th and 15th sts. (☎ **303/893-5463**), for some great Mexican food. (See full review on p. 81.)

A walkway at the east corner of Larimer and 15th leads through:

9 Writer Square

Quaint gas lamps, brick walkways, and outdoor cafes dot this shopping-and-dining complex.

At 16th Street, cross to the:

10 Tabor Center

The glass-enclosed shopping complex spreads over three levels. In effect a 2-block-long greenhouse (with the Westin Hotel within), the Tabor Center was developed by the Rouse Company, the same firm that created Faneuil Hall Marketplace in Boston, South Street Seaport in New York, and Harborplace in Baltimore.

To the east, the Tabor Center is anchored by the:

11 D & F Tower

The city landmark was patterned after the campanile of St. Mark's Basilica in Venice, Italy, in 1910.

Here, with the State Capitol building to the southeast, begin a leisurely stroll down the:

12 16th Street Mall

The $76-million pedestrian path affords the finest people-watching spot in the city. You'll see everyone

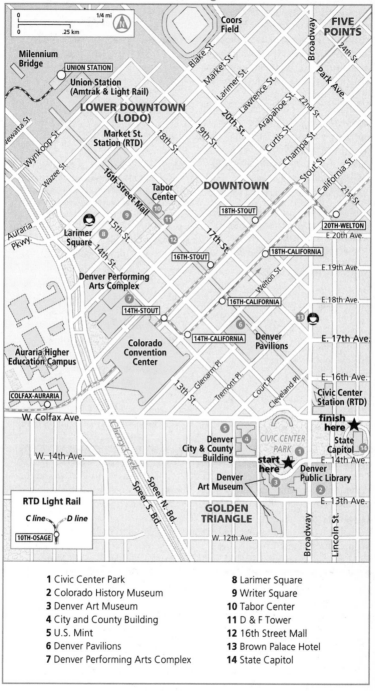

0   1/4 mi
0   .25 km

Coors Field

FIVE POINTS

Milennium Bridge

UNION STATION

Union Station (Amtrak & Light Rail)

LOWER DOWNTOWN (LODO)

Market St. Station (RTD)

Blake St.
Market St.
Larimer St.
Lawrence St.
Arapahoe St.
Curtis St.
Champa St.
Stout St.
California St.
Broadway
24th St.
22nd St.
21st St.
Park Ave.

Wynkoop St.
Newatta St.
Wazee St.
20th St.
19th St.
18th St.
16th Street Mall

Tabor Center

DOWNTOWN

Auraria Pkwy.

Larimer Square

15th St.
14th St.

18TH-STOUT
20TH-WELTON
E.20th Ave.

Denver Performing Arts Complex

17th St.
16TH-STOUT
18TH-CALIFORNIA
E.19th Ave.

Welton St.

14TH-STOUT
16TH-CALIFORNIA
18TH-CALIFORNIA
E.18th Ave.

Auraria Higher Education Campus

Colorado Convention Center

14TH-CALIFORNIA
Denver Pavilions

E. 17th Ave.

COLFAX-AURARIA

13th St.
Glenarm Pl.
Tremont Pl.
Court Pl.
Cleveland Pl.

E. 16th Ave.

Civic Center Station (RTD)

W. Colfax Ave.

Cherry Creek

finish here

Denver City & County Building

CIVIC CENTER PARK

State Capitol

W. 14th Ave.

Speer N. Bd.
Speer S. Bd.

start here

Denver Public Library
E. 14th Ave.

RTD Light Rail

C line   D line

10TH-OSAGE

Denver Art Museum

GOLDEN TRIANGLE

E. 13th Ave.

Broadway
Lincoln St.

W. 12th Ave.

1 Civic Center Park	**8** Larimer Square
2 Colorado History Museum	**9** Writer Square
3 Denver Art Museum	**10** Tabor Center
4 City and County Building	**11** D & F Tower
5 U.S. Mint	**12** 16th Street Mall
6 Denver Pavilions	**13** Brown Palace Hotel
7 Denver Performing Arts Complex	**14** State Capitol

from street entertainers to lunching office workers to travelers like yourself. Built of red and gray granite, it is lined with 200 red oak trees, a dozen fountains, and a lighting system straight out of *Star Wars*. You'll also see outdoor cafes, restored Victorian buildings, modern skyscrapers, and hundreds of shops—with an emphasis on sports—plus restaurants and department stores. Sleek European-built shuttle buses run through, offering free transportation up and down the mall as often as every 90 seconds.

You'll walk 7 blocks down 16th Street from the Tabor Center before reaching Tremont Place. Turn left, go 1 block farther, and across the street, on your right, you'll see the:

⑬ Brown Palace Hotel

One of the most beautiful grande-dame hotels in the United States, it was built in 1892 and features a nine-story atrium lobby topped by a Tiffany stained glass ceiling. Step into the lobby for a look, and if you're hungry . . .

TAKE A BREAK
The **Brown Palace Hotel,** 321 17th St. (© 303/297-3111), serves lunch in several restaurants and also offers afternoon tea in its elegant lobby. Reservations are recommended for the English tea, which includes sandwiches and pastries from the Brown Palace bakery. (See full review on p. 66.)

Continue across Broadway on East 17th Avenue. Go 2 blocks to Sherman Street, turn right, and proceed 2 blocks south on Sherman to East Colfax Avenue. You're back overlooking Civic Center Park, but this time you're at the:

⑭ State Capitol

If you stand on the 18th step on the west side of the building, you're exactly 5,280 feet (1 mile) above sea level. Architects modeled the Colorado capitol after the U.S. Capitol in Washington, D.C., and used the world's entire known supply of rare rose onyx in its interior wainscoting. A winding 93-step staircase leads to an open-air viewing deck beneath the capitol dome; on a clear day, the view can extend from Pikes Peak near Colorado Springs to the Wyoming border.

4 Organized Tours

Visitors who want to be personally guided to the attractions of Denver and the surrounding areas by those in the know have a variety of choices. In addition to the following, see "Escorted General-Interest Tours" and "Special-Interest Trips," in chapter 2.

Half- and full-day bus tours of Denver and the nearby Rockies are offered by the ubiquitous **Gray Line,** P.O. Box 17646, Denver, CO 80217 (© **800/348-6877** for information only; 303/289-2841 for reservations and information; www.coloradograyline.com). Fares for children 12 and under are half the adult prices listed below. Prices include entry fees but usually no food. Tours depart the Cherry Creek Shopping Center at 1st Avenue and Milwaukee Street, as well as local hotels and hostels on a reservation basis.

A 4-hour tour (no. 27), leaving at 1:30pm, takes in Denver's mountain parks: Red Rocks Park, Bergen Park, and Buffalo Bill's grave atop Lookout Mountain. It costs $30 for adults. The Denver city tour (no. 28), which departs daily at 8:30am and takes about 3½ hours, gives you a taste of both old Denver—through Larimer Square and other historic buildings—and the modern-day city. It's $25 for adults. The city tour combined with the mountain-parks tour costs

$55. Gray Line also offers tours of Rocky Mountain National Park and the Colorado Springs area; call or check the website for information.

The Colorado Sightseer, 6780 W. 84th Circle, Suite 60, Arvada, CO 80003 (② 303/423-8200; www.coloradosightseer.com), offers guided tours of Denver and environs. The Historic Denver tour includes a visit to LoDo and some of the city's earliest buildings, the State Capitol, the Molly Brown House, and Four Mile Historic Park. It lasts about 4 hours and costs $40 for adults, $30 for children 5 to 12. A Rocky Mountain National Park tour, lasting about 9½ hours, costs $75 for adults and $55 for children 5 to 12, including a box lunch. The 4½-hour Foothills Tour includes stops at Coors Brewery, the Buffalo Bill memorial, and scenic Red Rocks Park. The costs are $35 for adults, $25 for children 5 to 12, and free for children 4 and younger.

The **LoDo District** (② 303/628-5428; www.lodo.org) leads guided walking tours of the storied area June to October. Tours depart from Union Station (17th and Wynkoop sts.) on Saturday at 10am; the cost is $7 per person. Take advantage of your cellphone with **Rocky Mountain Audio Guides** (② 303/898-7073; www.rmaguides.com), which delivers 40- and 80-minute walking tours of downtown Denver. Call 24 hours before your tour to buy the tours; then you simply dial a number and walk around town, guided via satellite.

BICYCLING & MULTISPORT TOURS

A few companies operate bicycling and hiking tours out of the Denver area. In and around town, give **RMP&E Bike Tours** (② 720/641-3166; www.mountain biketours.us) a holler. They offer 3-hour custom tours of Denver and the foothills west of town for $50 per person. They also lead annual guided trips to Telluride and Moab, Utah.

The World Outdoors (② 800/488-8483 or 303/413-0938; www.theworld outdoors.com) offers a 6-day, 5-night multi-sport hut-to-hut tour that begins and ends in Vail (100 miles west of Denver). The huts, described by *Mountain Bike Magazine* as "luxurious backcountry accommodations," act as recreational headquarters for guests, who have plenty of hiking, rafting, and sightseeing opportunities between mountain-biking treks.

The trips aren't cheap, running about $1,295 to $1,395 per person, but this might be the best way for the outdoors enthusiast to enjoy the Rockies west of Denver. The trip runs twice each summer, in June and August.

Another company that offers weeklong tours in the area is **Bicycle Tour of Colorado** (② 303/985-1180; www.bicycletourcolorado.com). For about $300, a biker can join a tour involving more than 1,000 riders and 70 volunteers—including medical and bike-tech support as well as guiding services—on a 400-mile journey that hits six different cities each year, crossing the Continental Divide several times in the process. While accommodations can be prearranged at hotels, most riders elect to stay at facilities provided by the city (for example, the local high school). All meals are provided for about $300 for the week.

A good resource for bicyclists is the **Denver Bicycle Touring Club** (② 303/756-7240; www.dbtc.org), which organizes local rides and publishes a monthly newsletter. See also "Bicycling & Skateboarding," below.

5 Outdoor Activities

Denver's proximity to the Rocky Mountains makes it possible to spend a day skiing, snowmobiling, horseback riding, hiking, river running, sailing, fishing, hunting, mountain climbing, or rock-hounding and return to the city by nightfall. Within the city limits and nearby, visitors will find more than 200 miles of jogging and bicycle paths, over 100 free tennis courts, and several dozen public golf courses.

The city has an excellent system of **Mountain Parks** (© 303/697-4545), covering more than 14,000 acres, which are discussed earlier in this chapter in the "Parks, Gardens & Zoos" section.

The Skinny on Denver

According to a federal study, Denver has the highest proportion of thin people of any city in the country.

Campsites are easy to reach from Denver, as are suitable sites for hang gliding and hot-air ballooning. Sailing is popular within the city at Sloan's Lake and in Washington Park (both Denver City Parks), and the Platte River is clear for many miles of river running in rafts, kayaks, and canoes.

The Denver Metro Convention and Visitors Bureau (see "Visitor Information," in chapter 4) can supply detailed information about activities in the city. Information on nearby outdoor activities is available from: **Colorado State Parks,** 1313 Sherman St., Suite 618, Denver, CO 80203 (© **303/866-3437;** www.parks.state.co.us); the **U.S. Forest Service,** Rocky Mountain Region, 740 Sims St., Golden, CO 80401 (© **303/275-5350;** www.fs.fed.us/r2); the **U.S. Bureau of Land Management,** 2850 Youngfield St., Lakewood, CO 80215 (© **303/239-3600;** www.co.blm.gov); and the **National Park Service,** P.O. Box 25287, Denver, CO 80225 (© **303/969-2000;** www.nps.gov).

Visitors who don't bring the necessary equipment have several rental sources. **Sports Rent,** 8761 Wadsworth Blvd., Arvada, (© **303/467-0200;** www.sports rent.net), has just about everything imaginable, including bikes, in-line skates, canoes, camping equipment, skis, snowboards, snowshoes, ski racks, and clothing. The **REI** Flagship store, 1416 Platte St. (© **303/756-3100**) also has a rental department stocked with tents, backpacks, stoves, mountaineering equipment, kayaks, and other gear.

BALLOONING   You can't beat a hot-air balloon ride for viewing the magnificent Rocky Mountain scenery. **Life Cycle Balloon Adventures, Ltd.** (© **800/ 980-9272** or 303/216-1990; www.lifecycleballoons.com), offers sunrise champagne flights daily and has over 30 years of experience. **Colorado Balloon Rides** (© **800/873-8927** or 303/978-1813; www.flywithpride.com) generally schedules daily flights year-round from all over Colorado's Front Range. **Looney Balloons** (© **303/979-9476**) offers daily 1-hour flights year-round, weather permitting. The cost at all three companies is usually $175 to $250 per person.

BICYCLING & SKATEBOARDING   The paved bicycle paths that crisscross Denver include a 12-mile scenic stretch along the bank of the South Platte River and along Cherry Creek beside Speer Boulevard. All told, the city has 85 miles of off-road trails for bikers and runners, and is *Bicycle Magazine's* top city for bicyclists. Bike paths link the city's 205 parks, and many streets have bike lanes. In all, the city has more than 130 miles of designated bike paths and lanes. For more information, contact **Bike Denver** (© **303/322-3320;** www.bike denver.org) or **Bicycle Colorado** (© **303/417-1544;** www.bicyclecolo.org). Bike tours are available from several companies and clubs (see "Organized Tours," above). The **Cherry Creek Bike Rack,** 171 Detroit St. (© **303/388-1630;** www.cherrycreekbikerack.com), opened in 2004, offering rentals, service, and free parking for bikes.

Denver also has the largest free skateboarding park (3 acres) in the country, the **Denver Skatepark,** 19th and Little Raven sts. (© **720/913-0696**). It is quite popular and open between the hours of 6am and 11pm.

BOATING A quiet way to view some of downtown Denver is from a punt on scenic Cherry Creek. **Venice on the Creek** (© **303/893-0750**) operates from May to August, Tuesday through Thursday by reservation, Friday and Saturday from 5 to 10pm and Sunday from 3 to 6:30pm. On weekdays it accommodates only groups of 12 or more; smaller groups are taken on weekends. Guides describe the history of the city while pointing out landmarks. Tickets are available at the kiosk at Creekfront Plaza, at the intersection of Speer Boulevard and Larimer Street. A 1-hour trip costs $15 for adults, $7 for children, and $12 for seniors. Half-hour trips are also available, for about two-thirds the cost.

Commercial rafting companies offer raft trips on the Platte River through Littleton and Englewood in Denver's south suburbs. Water level permitting, **Flexible Flyers Rafting** (© **970/247-4628**) offers 2½-hour trips; call for the current schedule. The cost is $40 for adults and $20 children 12 and under.

You'll find powerboat marinas at **Cherry Creek State Park,** 4201 S. Parker Rd., Aurora, CO 80014 (© **303/699-3860**), 11 miles from downtown off I-225; and **Chatfield State Park,** 11500 N. Roxborough Park Rd., Littleton, CO 80125 (© **303/791-7275**), 16 miles south of downtown Denver off Colo. 470. Jet-skiing and sail-boarding are also permitted at both parks. Sail-boarding, canoeing, and other wakeless boating are popular at **Barr Lake State Park,** 13401 Picadilly Rd., Brighton, CO 80601 (© **303/659-6005**), 21 miles northeast of downtown on I-76.

For a different watersports experience, try river-boarding with **RipBoard** (© **866/311-2627** or 303/904-8367; www.ripboard.com), which entails going down Clear Creek face-first with flippers on your feet and a helmet on your head. It's exciting and exhausting, but can be a lot of fun in the right water. Lessons (including equipment) are $35 for 2 hours; rentals and sales are also available.

For information on other boating opportunities, contact Colorado State Parks, the National Park Service, or the U.S. Forest Service (see above).

FISHING A couple of good bets in the metropolitan area are Chatfield State Park, with trout, bass, and panfish, and Cherry Creek State Park, which boasts trout, walleye pike, bass, and crappie (see "Boating," above). In all, there are more than 7,100 miles of streams and 2,000 reservoirs and lakes in Colorado. For information, contact Colorado State Parks, the Colorado Division of Wildlife (© **303/297-1192**), or the U.S. Fish and Wildlife Service (© **303/ 236-7917**). Within Denver city limits, the **Denver Department of Parks and Recreation** (© **720/913-0696**) stocks 24 lakes with fish.

A number of sporting-goods stores can provide more detailed information. The skilled and experienced staff at **The Flyfisher Ltd.,** 120 Madison St. (© **303/322-5014**), can help with equipment choices and recommendations for where to go. The Flyfisher also offers lessons, seminars, clinics, and guided wade and float trips ($395 a day for two people).

GOLF Throughout the Front Range, it's often said that you can play golf at least 320 days a year, because the sun always seems to be shining, and even when it snows, the little snow that sticks melts quickly. There are more than 50 courses in the Denver area, including seven municipal golf courses, with nonresident greens fees up to $22 for 18 holes. City courses are: **City Park Golf Course,**

East 25th Avenue and York Street (© 303/295-4420); **Evergreen Golf Course,** 29614 Upper Bear Creek Rd., Evergreen (© 303/674-4128); the par-3 **Harvard Gulch Golf Course,** East Iliff Avenue and South Clarkson Street (© 303/698-4078); **Kennedy Golf Course,** 10500 E. Hampden Ave. (© 303/751-0311); **Overland Park Golf Course,** South Santa Fe Drive and West Jewell Avenue (© 303/698-4975); **Wellshire Golf Course,** 3333 S. Colorado Blvd. (© 303/692-5636); and **Willis Case Golf Course,** 4999 Vrain St. near West 50th Avenue (© 303/458-4877). Wellshire is the best overall course, but we prefer Willis Case for its spectacular mountain views.

You can make same-day reservations by calling the course; otherwise, nonresident golfers must purchase a $10 card at any municipal course, then make reservations through the **automated phone system** (© **303/784-4000**). The one exception to this policy is Evergreen Golf Course, where you can call the starter for reservations 3 days in advance. For information on any course, you can also call the **Department of Parks and Recreation** (© 720/913-0696).

For information on the state's major golf courses, contact the **Colorado Golf Resort Association** 2110 S. Ash St., Denver, CO 80222 (© **303/680-9967;** www.coloradogolfresorts.com).

A new Frisbee golf course will open in mid-2005 at Lakewood Gulch, near Federal Boulevard and 12th Street Call the **Department of Parks and Recreation** (© **720/913-0696**) for more information.

HIKING & BACKPACKING   The **Colorado Trail** ★★ is a hiking, horse, and mountain-biking route stretching 500 miles from Denver to Durango. The trail is also open to cross-country skiing, snowshoeing, and llama-pack hiking. Opened in 1988, the trail is still being fine-tuned. It took 15 years to establish, using volunteer labor, and crosses eight mountain ranges and five river systems, winding from rugged terrain to pristine meadows. For information, contact the **Colorado Trail Foundation,** 710 10th St., Room 210, Golden, CO 80401-1022 (© **303/384-3729**; www.coloradotrail.org). Beyond being a source of information, the foundation maintains and improves the trail, publishes relevant guidebooks, and offers supported treks and accredited courses.

For hikes in the Denver area, contact the city **Department of Parks and Recreation** (© **720/913-0696**) for information on Denver's park system. Or contact any of the following agencies: Colorado State Parks, Colorado Division of Wildlife, National Park Service, U.S. Bureau of Land Management, or U.S. Forest Service (see the introduction to this section and "Fishing," above). A good source for the many published area maps and hiking guides is **Mapsco Map and Travel Center,** 800 Lincoln St., Denver (© **800/456-8703** or 303/623-4299; www.mapsco.com). Other sources are local sporting-goods stores and bookstores (see "Shopping," later in this chapter).

Mount Falcon Park ★ offers excellent trails that are easy to moderate in difficulty, making this a good place for families with children. There are also picnic areas, shelters, and ruins of an old castlelike home. From Denver, go west on U.S. 285 and north on Parmalee Gulch Road; the park is open daily from dawn to dusk, and admission is free. Mountain bikes and horseback riding are permitted, as are leashed dogs.

Other relatively easy trails near Denver are in **Roxborough State Park** (© **303/973-3959**), 10 miles south of Littleton—the 1-mile **Willow Creek Trail** and the 2¼-mile **Fountain Valley Trail** ★. There are several more strenuous trails at Roxborough, but worth the effort if you enjoy beautiful red rocks and the chance to see wildlife. To get to Roxborough Park, exit Colo. 470 south onto U.S. 85 and turn west onto Titan Road, then south again at Roxborough Park Road to the main entrance. Admission costs $5 per vehicle. The park is open daily from 8am to 8pm in summer, with shorter hours the rest of the year. Dogs, bikes, and horseback riding are not permitted.

HORSEBACK RIDING   Equestrians can find a mount year-round at **Stockton's Plum Creek Stables,** 7479 W. Titan Rd., Littleton (© **303/791-1966**), near Chatfield State Park, 15 miles south of downtown. Stockton's offers hayrides and barbecue picnics, as well as lessons ($50 an hour). **Paint Horse Stables,** 4201 S. Parker Rd., Aurora (© **303/690-8235**), at Cherry Creek State Park, also rents horses, boards horses, and provides riding lessons, hayrides, and pony rides for kids.

RECREATION CENTERS   The **Denver Department of Parks and Recreation** (© **720/913-0696**) operates about 30 recreation centers around the city, several of which have facilities oriented to seniors. Daily guest passes for all facilities, including swimming pools, cost $5 for adults, $2 for children under 18. Facilities vary but may include basketball courts, indoor or outdoor pools, gyms, and weight rooms. The centers offer fitness classes and other recreation programs, including programs for those with special needs. Call © **720/913-0693** for current program information.

   Among the city's recreation centers are the following: **William Scheitler Recreation Center,** 5031 W. 46th Ave. (© **303/458-4898**), which has indoor and outdoor pools; **Martin Luther King, Jr. Recreation Center,** 3880 Newport St. (© **303/331-4034**), which is the nearest full-service center to Denver International Airport and has an indoor pool, large gym, and racquetball court; **20th Street Recreation Center,** downtown at 1011 20th St., between Arapahoe and Curtis streets (© **303/295-4430**), with an indoor pool and weight room; and **Washington Park Recreation Center,** 701 S. Franklin St. (© **303/698-4960**), with an indoor pool, advanced weight room, large gym, and walking and jogging trails.

SKIING   Several ski resorts are close to Denver. They include **Eldora Mountain Resort,** 45 miles west (© **303/440-8700;** www.eldora.com), which covers almost 700 acres and has 53 trails, with skiing rated 20% beginner, 50% intermediate, and 30% advanced. **Loveland Basin and Valley,** 56 miles west on I-70, exit 216 (© **800/736-3754** or 303/569-3203; fax 303/571-5580; www.skiloveland.com), covers 1,365 acres and has 70 trails, rated 17% beginner, 42% intermediate, and 41% advanced. **Winter Park Resort** ⚐, 73 miles west of Denver on I-70 and U.S. 40 (© **800/729-5813** or 970/726-5514; fax 970/726-1572; www.winterparkresort.com), boasts 2,762 ski-able acres with 134 trails, rated 10% beginner, 36% intermediate, and 54% advanced.

   Eldora and Winter Park offer Nordic as well as alpine terrain.

Tips **Denver's Dog Parks**

New in 2004, Denver allowed canines to roam free at five parks within city limits, and there are dozens of off-leash parks in the metropolitan area as a whole. Contact the Department of Parks and Recreation (© **720/913-0696**) for more information or visit **www.denvergov.org.**

Full information on statewide skiing is available from **Colorado Ski Country USA,** 1507 Blake St., Denver, CO 80202 (© **303/837-0793;** www. coloradoski.com), and the **Colorado Cross Country Ski Association** (www.colorado-xc.org).

Some useful Denver telephone numbers for skiers include: **ski-area information and snow report** (© 303/825-7669), **weather report** (© 303/337-2500), and **road conditions** (© 303/639-1111).

SWIMMING   The Denver Department of Parks and Recreation (© **303/ 458-4795**) operates 17 outdoor swimming pools (open daily mid-June to mid-Aug) and 12 indoor pools (open Mon–Sat year-round). Nonresident fees are $3 for adults and $2 for children. See "Recreation Centers," above.

TENNIS   The Denver Department of Parks and Recreation (© **720/913-0696**) manages or owns close to 150 tennis courts, more than one-third of them lit for night play. Among the most popular courts are those in City Park (York St. and E. 17th Ave.), Berkeley Park (Tennyson St. and W. 17th Ave.), Green Valley East Ranch Park (Jebel St. and E. 45th Ave.), Washington Park (S. Downing St. and E. Louisiana Ave.), and Sloan's Lake Park (Sheridan Blvd. and W. 17th Ave.). The public courts are free. For more information, contact the **Colorado Tennis Association,** 1241 S. Parker Rd., Suite 100, Denver, CO 80231 (© **303/695-4116;** www.coloradotennis.com).

GREAT NEARBY STATE PARKS

Colorado has a number of excellent state parks offering a wide range of activities and scenery. Information on the state's parks is available at **www. parks.state.co.us**.

BARR LAKE STATE PARK   About 25 miles northeast of Denver on I-76 in Brighton, this wildlife sanctuary of almost 2,800 acres comprises a prairie reservoir and surrounding wetlands and uplands. Boats with motors exceeding 10 horsepower are not allowed, but you can sail, paddle, row, and fish. A 9-mile hiking and biking trail circles the lake. A boardwalk from the nature center at the south parking lot leads to a good view of a heron rookery, and bird blinds along this trail allow wildlife observation and photography. Three picnic areas provide tables and grills; there's a commercial campground opposite the park on the west side. The entrance is at 13401 Picadilly Rd. Admission costs $5 per vehicle. Call © **303/659-6005** for more information.

CASTLEWOOD CANYON STATE PARK ⭐   Steep canyons, a meandering stream, a waterfall, lush vegetation, and considerable wildlife distinguish this 2,000-acre park. You can see the remains of Castlewood Canyon Dam, which was built for irrigation in 1890; it collapsed in 1933, killing two people and flooding the streets of Denver. The park, 30 miles south of Denver on Colo. 83, east of Castle Rock in Franktown, provides picnic facilities and hiking trails. The entrance is at 2989 S. State Hwy. 83; admission is $5 per vehicle. Call © **303/688-5242** for more information.

CHATFIELD STATE PARK ⭐   Sixteen miles south of downtown Denver on U.S. 85 in Littleton, this park occupies 5,600 acres of prairie against a backdrop of the steeply rising Rocky Mountains. Chatfield Reservoir, with a 26-mile shoreline, invites swimming, boating, fishing, and other watersports. The area also has 18 miles of paved bicycle trails, plus hiking and horseback-riding paths. In winter, there's ice fishing and cross-country skiing. The park also has a hot-air-balloon launch pad, a radio-controlled model aircraft field, and a 21-acre manmade wetlands area.

Facilities include 197 pull-through campsites, showers, laundry, and a dump station. Admission is $5 to $6 per vehicle; the camping fee is $16 to $22 daily. The entrance is 1 mile south of C-470 on Wadsworth Boulevard (© **303/791-7275**).

CHERRY CREEK STATE PARK   The 880-acre Cherry Creek Reservoir, created for flood control by the construction of a dam in 1950, is the central attraction of this popular park, which draws 1.5 million visitors each year. Located at the southeast Denver city limits (off Parker Rd. and I-225) about 12 miles from downtown, the park encompasses 4,200 acres in all.

Watersports include swimming, water-skiing, boating, and fishing. There's a nature trail, dog-training area, model-airplane field with paved runways, jet-ski rental facility, rifle range, pistol range, and trap-shooting area. Twelve miles of paved bicycle paths and 12 miles of bridle trails circle the reservoir (horse rentals are available). Rangers offer guided walks by appointment, as well as evening campfire programs in an amphitheater. In winter, there's skating, ice fishing, and ice boating.

Each of the park's 102 campsites has access to showers, laundry, and a dump station. Most sites have full hookups with water and electric. Many lakeshore day-use sites have picnic tables and grills.

Admission costs $6 to $7 per vehicle; the camping fee is $12 to $22 daily. Campgrounds are open year-round. The entrance is at 4201 S. Parker Rd. in Aurora. Call © **303/699-3860** for general information or © **800/678-2267** for camping reservations.

GOLDEN GATE STATE PARK ☆   One hour west of Denver, this 14,000-acre park ranges in elevation from 7,400 to 10,400 feet and offers camping, picnicking, hiking, biking, fishing, hunting, and horseback-riding opportunities. A daily vehicle pass costs $5, and camping fees range from $10 to $18 in developed campgrounds, $7 for backcountry camping. There are around 160 developed campsites, with a limited number of electrical hookups. Reverend's Ridge, the park's largest campground, has coin-operated showers and laundry facilities.

To get to Golden Gate, take Colo. 93 north from Golden 1 mile to Golden Gate Canyon Road. Turn left and continue 13 miles to the park. For more information, call © **303/582-3707.**

6 Spectator Sports

Tickets to many sporting events can be obtained from **Ticketville USA,** 101 W. 84th Ave., Denver, CO 80260 (© **303/430-1100;** www.ticketvilleusa.com), which delivers to hotels; or **Ticketmaster** (© **303/830-TIXS**), with several outlets in the Denver area.

AUTO RACING   The **Grand Prix of Denver** (© **303/830-TIXS** for tickets or 720/873-5021 for information; www.denvergrandprix.com) is held over Labor Day weekend in the streets surrounding the Pepsi Center (Speer Blvd. and Chopper Circle). General-admission tickets run $20 to $40 per day for adults, less for children; grandstand seats are more expensive.

For drag racing, head to **Bandimere Speedway,** 3051 S. Rooney Rd., Morrison (© **303/697-6001,** or 303/697-4870 for a 24-hr. recording; www. bandimere.com), with races scheduled from April through October. There are motorcycles, pickup trucks, street cars, and sports cars, plus car shows, swap meets, special events for high school students, and a junior drag-racing series for ages 8 to 17.

BASEBALL   The **Colorado Rockies** (© **800/388-7625** or 303/762-5437; www.coloradorockies.com), who began as a National League expansion team in 1993, initially enjoyed record-breaking fan support, but attendance has fallen recently. The team plays at the attractive Coors Field, in historic lower downtown. The 50,000-seat stadium, with a redbrick exterior and on-site microbrewery, was designed in the style of baseball stadiums of old. Tickets are easy to come by, from either the box office or the gaggle of scalpers on the street.

BASKETBALL   The traditionally floundering **Denver Nuggets** (© **303/405-1111** for ticket information; www.nuggets.com) of the National Basketball Association have skyrocketed in popularity thanks to new superstar Carmelo Anthony. The Nuggets play their home games at the handsome Pepsi Center (downtown at Speer Blvd. and Auraria Pkwy.). There are 41 home games a year between November and April, with playoffs continuing into June.

The **University of Denver** (© **303/871-2336** for ticket office) plays a competitive college basketball schedule from late November through March.

FOOTBALL   The **Denver Broncos** (© **720/258-3333** for tickets; www.denverbroncos.com) of the National Football League make their home at the new Invesco Field at Mile High, after abandoning the legendary Mile High Stadium in 2001. Home games are sold out months in advance, so call early; there are also a few tickets sold on game day. Your best bet may be to find someone hawking tickets outside the stadium entrance on game day. Pricing tickets above face value is technically illegal, but the law is rarely enforced.

You might have better luck getting into a college game. The **University of Colorado Buffaloes** (© **303/492-8337;** www.cu-sports.com) of the Big Twelve Conference play in Boulder. Other top college football teams in the area are Colorado State University, in Fort Collins, and the Air Force Academy, in Colorado Springs.

GREYHOUND RACING   **Wembley Park,** East 62nd Avenue and Dahlia Street, Commerce City (© **303/288-1591**), has pari-mutuel dog races from June to February, as well as simulcast horse racing year-round. Call for the current schedule.

HOCKEY   Denver's National Hockey League team, the **Colorado Avalanche** (© **303/405-1111** for ticket information; www.coloradoavalanche.com), plays in front of sellout crowds at the Pepsi Center (Speer Blvd. and Auraria Pkwy.). The season runs from October through April. Tickets are typically expensive and hard to come by.

For a cheaper ticket (and a fun atmosphere), the **University of Denver** (© **303/871-2336** for ticket office) men's hockey team (the 2004 National Champions) plays a competitive schedule between October and mid-March.

LACROSSE   In sports-crazy Denver, even the pro lacrosse team, the **Colorado Mammoth** (© **303/405-1111**), sells out the 18,000-seat Pepsi Center. Tickets are inexpensive and the atmosphere is festive, to say the least.

HORSE RACING   **Arapahoe Park,** 26000 E. Quincy Ave., Aurora (© **303/690-2400**), offers horse racing each summer, with simulcast wagering the rest of the year.

RODEO   The **National Western Stock Show and Rodeo** (© **303/297-1166;** www.nationalwestern.com) is held the second and third weeks of January.

The rodeo takes place at the Denver Coliseum, and other activities at the National Western Complex and the Event Center. With more than $500,000 available in prize money and 600,000 people in attendance, this is one of the world's richest and largest rodeos.

SOCCER   The **Colorado Rapids** (℅ **303/405-1111;** www.coloradorapids. com) of Major League Soccer play home games at Invesco Field at Mile High.

7 Shopping

If you're in Denver on foot, you'll find that most visitors do their shopping along the **16th Street Mall** (the mile-long pedestrian walkway between Market St. and Tremont Place), and adjacent areas, including **Larimer Square, The Shops at Tabor Center, Writer Square,** and the newest retail development downtown, **Denver Pavilions.**

Outside the downtown area there are more options, primarily the huge **Cherry Creek Shopping Center**—a shopper's dream—south of downtown. There are also numerous funky urban retail areas within city limits, as well as suburban shopping malls.

Business hours vary from store to store and from mall to mall. Generally, stores are open 6 days a week, with many open on Sunday, too; department stores usually stay open until 9pm at least 1 evening a week. Discount stores and supermarkets are often open later than other stores, and some supermarkets are open 24 hours a day.

SHOPPING A TO Z
ANTIQUES

Denver's main antiques area is **Antique Row,** along **South Broadway** between Mississippi and Iowa streets, with some 400 dealers selling all sorts of fine antiques, collectibles, and junk. Wandering through the gigantic rooms, where each dealer has his or her own little space, is great fun. Just remember that prices are often negotiable; unless you're quite knowledgeable about antiques, it wouldn't hurt to do some comparison-shopping before making a major purchase.

Occupying a major part of Antique Row are the **Antique Guild** (℅ **303/ 722-3359**), a dealers' mall in the 1200 block of South Broadway, and the adjacent **Antique Market** (℅ **303/744-0281**). Together they have about 100 dealers selling every type of antique and collectible imaginable.

Serious antiques hunters will also want to explore the **Antique Mall of Lakewood,** 9635 W. Colfax Ave. (℅ **303/238-6940**), which has a 34,000-square-foot showroom where some 130 dealers display a wide variety of items from the 18th and 19th centuries, as well as more recent collectibles. A cafe serves breakfast and lunch.

ART & FINE CRAFTS

The renaissance of Denver's lower downtown (LoDo) has resulted in the creation of the **Lower Downtown Arts District,** where you can explore more than two dozen galleries. The district runs from Larimer to Wynkoop streets between 14th and 20th streets. Call ℅ **303/628-5424** or browse **www.lodo.org** for additional information.

A mile to the southeast, the Golden Triangle neighborhood, bordered by Lincoln Street, Speer Boulevard, and Colfax Avenue, has over 50 galleries. The **Golden Triangle Arts District** (℅ **303/534-0771;** www.gtad.org) puts together an open gallery event the first Friday night of every month, complete with a free shuttle.

Andenken Open weekends, this hip LoDo gallery shows the work of contemporary young artists working in every medium under the sun, usually outside the boundaries of tradition. 2110 Market St. ℂ **303/292-3281.**

Camera Obscura *(Finds)* This highly respected gallery exhibits vintage and contemporary photographs, including works by internationally renowned photographers. Closed Monday. 1309 Bannock St. ℂ **303/623-4059.**

Sandy Carson Gallery Established regional artists are represented at this respected gallery in a burgeoning gallery area on Santa Fe Drive, which is known for showing contemporary works in traditional media. 760 Santa Fe Dr. ℂ **303/ 573-8585.**

Native American Trading Company Older weavings, pottery, baskets, jewelry, and other American Indian works from the Rocky Mountain region are the focus at this fine gallery. Appropriately, it's across the street from the Denver Art Museum. 213 W. 13th Ave. ℂ **303/534-0771.**

Pirate Denver's oldest arts co-op, Pirate has showcased the work of cutting-edge contemporary artists of all kinds for more than 20 years. It's in a funky north Denver neighborhood with several dining options and a theater. 3659 Navajo St. ℂ **303/458-6058.**

Pismo Contemporary Art Glass Nationally renowned glass artists, as well as emerging stars, are represented in this gallery, located in Cherry Creek North. 235 Fillmore St. ℂ **303/333-2879.**

BOOKS

Barnes & Noble Barnes & Noble has a large selection of all kinds of books and music, often at discounted prices. This two-story location opened in 1999 in an increasingly popular retail area on the south side of downtown Denver. There's a particularly good travel section, where you'll find local and regional maps. The store also has a Starbucks attached. 500 16th St. (in the Denver Pavilions). ℂ **303/825-9166.**

Mile High Comics Megastore *(Kids)* One of five Mile High Comics locations in the Denver area, this is the largest comic-book store in the nation. Its 11,000 square feet are packed with comics of all descriptions, plus games, toys, posters, and other books. 9201 N. Washington St., Thornton (10 miles north of downtown Denver). ℂ **303/457-2612.**

Tattered Cover *★★* One of the largest bookstores in the world, this shop is so big it supplies maps to help you find your way through its maze of shelves. Comfortable chairs are placed strategically throughout the building for those who want to check out the first chapter before buying or to rest up after a hike to the fourth floor. The store also provides a wide selection of newspapers and magazines, a bargain-book section, free gift-wrapping, mail order, and out-of-print search services. An elevator serves all four floors. In addition, there's a full-service coffee bar, an excellent restaurant, and occasional storytelling in the children's section. Hours are Monday through Saturday from 9am to 11pm, Sunday from 10am to 6pm. 2955 E. 1st Ave. (opposite Cherry Creek Shopping Center). ℂ **800/833-9327** or 303/322-7727. www.tatteredcover.com. There's a second location at Denver's LoDo at 16th and Wynkoop streets (ℂ **303/436-1070**).

FASHION

Eddie Bauer This is the place to come for good deals on the famous Eddie Bauer line of upscale outdoor clothing. This extra-large store features a wide variety of men's and women's fashions alongside outdoor-oriented gadgetry. 3000 E. Cherry Creek Ave. (in the Cherry Creek Mall). ⓒ 303/377-2100.

Lawrence Covell   This renowned upscale shop, established in 1967 by Lawrence and Cathy Covell, offers the finest men's and women's fashions, including designer clothing by Kiton, John Lobb, Etro, and Paul Smith. 225 Steele St. (in Cherry Creek N.). ⓒ 303/320-1023.

Rockmount Ranch Wear ★★   Founded in 1946 by Jack A. Weil, Rockmount is one of the last real Western landmarks in town. The three-generation family business—which was the first company to put a snap on a shirt!—recently turned its longtime warehouse into a retail store, and it's even got a museum of Western wear and memorabilia. The place sells dusters, shirts, scarves, and everything else anyone might need to dud up like a cowboy or cowgirl. Rock bands and movie stars love the brand, and even stop by the store on a regular basis. 1626 Wazee St. ⓒ 303/629-7777.

FOOD & DRINK

King Soopers, Safeway, and **Albertson's** are the main grocery-store chains.

Applejack Liquors *Value*   This huge store, which covers some 40,000 square feet and claims to be America's largest beer, wine, and liquor supermarket, offers some of the best prices in the area. It also delivers. The store has a wide choice of single-malt scotches; an extensive wine section, which includes a number of Colorado wines; and a good selection of cigars. It's open Monday through Thursday until 10pm, and Friday and Saturday until 11pm. No credit cards. 3320 Youngfield St. (in the Applewood Shopping Center), Wheat Ridge (I-70 exit 264). ⓒ 800/ 879-5225 or 303/233-3331.

Argonaut Wine & Liquor Supermarket   You'll find an excellent selection of wines, as well as beer and liquor, at good prices at this large store 4 blocks east of the State Capitol. It's open Monday through Thursday until 10pm and Friday and Saturday until 11:45pm. 718 E. Colfax Ave. (at Washington St.). ⓒ 303/831-7788.

Stephany's Chocolates   Colorado's largest manufacturer and wholesaler of gourmet confections is best known for its Denver Mint and Colorado Almond Toffee. In business for more than 3 decades, it offers tours twice daily on weekdays, by advance reservation only. Retail outlets are located in malls throughout the city. 6770 W. 52nd Ave., Arvada (north of I-70 via Wadsworth Blvd.). ⓒ 800/888-1522 or 303/421-7229. www.stephanys-chocolates.com.

Whole Foods   This enormous store helps perpetuate Coloradans' healthy lifestyles. No food sold here contains artificial flavoring or preservatives, nor was any grown using pesticides, chemicals, or other additives. There's sushi, a salad bar, and many to-go lunch and dinner offerings as well. This Cherry Creek–area store, part of the national chain, opened in 2001; others are scattered throughout the metropolitan area. 2375 E. 1st Ave. (at University Blvd.). ⓒ 720/941-4100.

GIFTS & SOUVENIRS

Colorado History Museum Store   This museum shop carries unique made-in-Colorado gifts and souvenirs, including American Indian jewelry and sand paintings, plus an excellent selection of books on Colorado. 1300 Broadway. ⓒ 303/ 866-4993.

Where the Buffalo Roam   Here you'll find the gamut of traditional Denver and Colorado souvenirs, from T-shirts to buttons to hats to mugs. 535 16th St. ⓒ 303/260-7347.

JEWELRY

Atlantis Gems   This store features unique custom jewelry plus a large selection of loose gemstones and exotic minerals. It also stocks fossils, estate jewelry, and vintage watches; a gemologist is on site. 910 16th St. Mall. ⓒ **303/825-3366.**

Jeweler's Center at the University Building   Here you'll find 12 floors of retail and wholesale outlets in what is billed as Denver's largest concentration of jewelers since 1924. 910 16th St. ⓒ **303/534-6270.**

John Atencio   A highly regarded Colorado artist, John Atencio has received several awards for his unique jewelry designs. Located on historic Larimer Square, his store offers 14- and 18-karat gold jewelry accented with high-quality stones, plus special collections such as "Elements," which features unusual combinations of gold, sterling silver, and stones. 1440 Larimer St. (on Larimer Sq.). ⓒ **303/534-4277.**

MALLS & SHOPPING CENTERS

Cherry Creek Shopping Center   Saks Fifth Avenue, Neiman Marcus, Foley's, and Lord and Taylor anchor this deluxe million-square-foot mall, with more than 160 shops, restaurants (including a new one owned by Denver Broncos Hall of Famer John Elway), and services, including an eight-screen movie theater. Across the street is Cherry Creek North, an upscale retail neighborhood. The mall is open Monday through Friday from 10am to 9pm, Saturday from 10am to 8pm, and Sunday from 11am to 6pm. 3000 E. 1st Ave. (between University Blvd. and Steele St.). ⓒ **303/388-3900.**

Denver Pavilions   Opened in 1998, the Pavilions are several massive retail structures on the southern end of the 16th Street Mall. The three-level complex jammed with entertainment and dining options features Denver's only Hard Rock and Wolfgang Puck cafes, a movie-plex, and Nike Town, Virgin Records, and Barnes & Noble megastores (see "Books," above). Store hours are Monday to Thursday from 10am to 9pm, Friday and Saturday from 10am to 10pm, and Sunday from 11am to 6pm; the restaurants and movie theaters are open later. 500 16th St. (between Welton and Tremont sts.). ⓒ **303/260-6000.**

Larimer Square   This restored quarter of old Denver (see "More Attractions," earlier in this chapter) includes numerous art galleries, boutiques, restaurants, and nightclubs. Most shops are open Monday through Thursday from 10am to 7pm, Friday and Saturday from 10am to 6pm, and Sunday from noon to 5pm. Restaurant and nightclub hours vary, and hours are slightly shorter during the winter. 1400 block of Larimer St. ⓒ **303/534-2367.**

Mile High Flea Market   Just 10 minutes northeast of downtown Denver, this huge market attracts more than 1.5 million shoppers a year to its 80 paved acres. Besides close-outs, garage sales, and seasonal merchandise, it has more than a dozen places to eat and snack, plus family rides. It's open year-round on Wednesday, Saturday, and Sunday from 7am to 5pm. Admission is $2 Saturday, $3 Sunday, $1 Wednesday, and always free for children under 12. 7007 E. 88th Ave. (at I-76), Henderson. ⓒ **303/289-4656.**

Park Meadows Retail Resort   Located at the C-470/I-25 interchange south of Denver, this is the largest shopping center in Colorado, and now the heart of a mind-boggling retail area. Very posh and upscale—the interior is reminiscent of a luxurious mountain lodge—Park Meadows features Nordstrom, Dillard's, Foley's, and 160 specialty shops and restaurants. Stores are open Monday through Saturday from 10am to 9:30pm, Sunday from 11am to 6pm. 8401 Park Meadows Center Dr. (south of C-470 on Yosemite St.), Littleton. 𝄏 303/792-2533.

The Outlets at Castle Rock   This outlet mall between Denver and Colorado Springs, about 30 minutes south of Denver, has well over 100 stores, including Levi's, Van Heusen, Eddie Bauer, Bass, Nike, Big Dog, Gap, and Toy Liquidators, plus a food court. Camp Coleman has practically every camping supply you can imagine, all manufactured by the reliable Coleman company. Wheelchair and stroller rentals are available. Open Monday through Saturday from 10am to 9pm and Sunday from 11am to 6pm. I-25 exit 184. 𝄏 303/688-4494.

SPORTING GOODS

Those in need of a bike should talk to the experts at **Campus Cycles,** 2102 S. Washington St. (𝄏 303/698-2811), which carries the Gary Fisher, Raleigh, and Giant brands. Sports fans looking for that Rockies cap or Broncos shirt will have no trouble finding it at the appropriately named **Sportsfan,** 1962 Blake St., across from Coors Field (𝄏 303/295-3460; www.sportsteams.com). There are several other locations in the Denver area, and mail orders are accepted.

For information on where to rent sporting-goods equipment, see the "Outdoor Activities" section, earlier in this chapter.

Gart Sports Castle   Active travelers will be pleased to discover that Denver has the world's largest sporting-goods store—this five-story monster. With everything from footballs to golf clubs to tents, the selection is comprehensive. Extras include a driving cage for golfers, ball courts on the roof, and the annual Sniagrab (that's bargains spelled backwards), featuring rock-bottom prices on ski equipment every Labor Day weekend. There are also a number of Gart outlets in the Denver area. 1000 Broadway. 𝄏 303/861-1122. www.gartsports.com.

REI ★★   While the Seattle-based co-op has several stores in the metro area, its flagship store, a beautifully restored redbrick just west of downtown, is one of the country's best and biggest outdoor-oriented retailers. (It is one of only three flagship stores; the others are in Seattle and the Minneapolis area.) This is the place to go before heading for an excursion in the Rockies. The gargantuan store features a climbing wall, an outdoor bike-testing area, a kayaking area on adjacent Cherry Creek, and a "cold room" to try out outerwear and sleeping bags. 1416 Platte St. 𝄏 303/756-3100. www.rei.com.

TOYS & HOBBIES

Caboose Hobbies   Model-train buffs should plan to spend at least half a day here. Billed as the world's largest train store, it stocks electric trains, accessories, books, and so much train-related stuff that it's hard to know where to start. The knowledgeable employees seem just as happy to talk about trains as to sell them. Naturally, there are model trains of every scale winding through the store, as well as test tracks so that you can check out a locomotive before purchasing it. There are also mugs, patches, and decals from just about every railroad line that ever existed in North America. 500 S. Broadway. 𝄏 303/777-6766. www.caboosehobbies.com.

Wizard's Chest *Kids*   This store's magical design—a castle with drawbridge and moat—and legendary wizard out front are worth the trip alone, but be sure to go inside. The Wizard's Chest is paradise for kids of all ages, specializing in games, toys, and puzzles. The costume department is fully stocked with attire, wigs, masks, and professional makeup. 230 Fillmore St. in Cherry Creek N. 𝄏 303/321-4304.

8 Denver After Dark

The anchor of Denver's performing arts scene, an important part of this increasingly sophisticated city, is the 4-square-block **Denver Performing Arts Complex,** located downtown just a few blocks from major hotels. The complex houses nine theaters, a concert hall, and what may be the nation's first symphony hall in the round. It is home to the Colorado Symphony, Colorado Ballet, Opera Colorado, and the Denver Center for the Performing Arts (an umbrella organization for resident and touring theater companies).

Denver has some 30 theaters, more than 100 cinemas, and dozens of concert halls, nightclubs, discos, and bars. Clubs offer country-and-western music, jazz, rock, and comedy.

Current entertainment listings appear in special Friday-morning sections of the two daily newspapers, the *Denver Post* and *Rocky Mountain News. Westword,* a weekly newspaper distributed free throughout the city every Wednesday, has perhaps the best listings: It focuses on the arts, entertainment, and local politics.

You can get tickets for nearly all major entertainment and sporting events from **Ticketville USA,** 101 W. 84th Ave., Denver, CO 80260 (℃ **303/430-1100;** www.ticketvilleusa.com), which offers delivery to hotels. Also try **Ticketmaster** (℃ **303/830-TIXS**), which has several outlets in the Denver area.

THE CLUB & MUSIC SCENE
ROCK, JAZZ & BLUE

Bluebird Theater This historic theater, built in 1913 to show silent movies, has been restored and now offers a diverse selection of rock, alternative, and other live music, as well as films. The performers generally target teens and 20-somethings. Tickets usually run $7 to $20. 3317 E. Colfax Ave. (at Adams St.). ℃ **303/322-2308.** www.nipp.com.

The Church Located just a few blocks southeast of downtown, this former church features three dance floors and several bars (including wine and sushi bars) scattered around a bizarre configuration—it's easy to get lost here. The semi-religious decor and diverse crowd, in conjunction with the loud music, make for near sensory overload. 1160 Lincoln St. ℃ **303/832-3528.**

El Chapultepec Denver's oldest jazz club, the "Pec" offers live jazz nightly in a noisy, friendly atmosphere. You'll often find standing-room only, not to mention a hearty helping of local color—young and old, poor and rich, in equal measure. A small burrito kitchen and poolroom adjoin the club. 1962 Market St. ℃ **303/295-9126.** No cover.

Gothic Theatre One of metro Denver's best-looking (and best-sounding) midsize venues, the Gothic is light-years beyond the heavy-metal dive it was in the 1980s. Both local and national acts play the stage here. Tickets usually cost $7 to $30. 3263 S. Broadway, Englewood. ℃ **303/380-2333.** www.nipp.com.

Larimer Lounge This bar on old Larimer Street has been serving drinks since 1892 and serving loud punk rock and alternative music since 2003. The place is out of the hustle and bustle of LoDo, in an old neighborhood east of Broadway, and has seen such national acts as J Mascis and Black Rebel Motorcycle Club take the stage. The average patron is young, tattooed, and a bit rough around the edges. 2721 Larimer St. ℃ **303/291-1007.**

Mercury Cafe It's hard to classify the Mercury as specializing in any genre of music, but there's always something exciting happening, even on poetry night. It attracts a casual, eclectic clientele. Offerings usually range from avant-garde jazz to classical violin and harp to big band to progressive rock. A healthful-oriented restaurant is also here. 2199 California St. (at 22nd St.). ℂ 303/294-9258. www.mercurycafe.com. Cover free to $10.

COUNTRY MUSIC

Grizzly Rose ⋆   Known to locals as "the Griz" or "the Rose," its 5,000-square-foot dance floor beneath a 1-acre roof draws such national acts such as George Thorogood, Garth Brooks, Willie Nelson, Don Williams, LeAnn Rimes, Tanya Tucker, and Johnny Paycheck. There's live music Tuesday through Saturday; Sunday is family night. The cafe serves a full-service menu, and dance lessons are available. 5450 N. Valley Hwy., at I-25 exit 215. ℂ 303/295-1330 or 303/295-2353. www.grizzlyrose.com.

Stampede   This colossal nightclub offers free country-western dance lessons on Friday and Saturday, a huge solid oak dance floor, pool tables, a restaurant, and seven bars. It's off I-225 exit 4 (north on Parker Rd. about 2 miles to Havana St.). Closed Sunday through Tuesday. 2430 S. Havana St. (at Parker Rd.), Aurora. ℂ 303/337-6909.

THE BAR SCENE

The first permanent structure on the site of modern Denver was supposedly a saloon, and the city has built on that tradition ever since. Today, there are sports bars, dance bars, lots of brewpubs, outdoor cafe bars, English pubs, Old West saloons, city-overlook bars, Art Deco bars, gay bars, and a few bars we don't want to discuss here.

Appropriately, the newest Denver "in" spot for barhopping is also the oldest part of the city—LoDo—which has been renovated and upgraded, and now attracts all the smart Generation-Xers and other young professionals. Its

> **Bottoms Up!**
> More beer is brewed in metro-politan Denver than in any other city in the United States.

trendy nightspots are often noisy and crowded, but if you're looking for action, this is where you'll find it.

Glendale, an enclave surrounded by southeastern Denver where Colorado Boulevard crosses Cherry Creek, is another well-established hangout for Denver's party set. In recent years, however, as Glendale has become the Denver area's nexus for topless bars, the other bars have suffered.

Other popular "strips" are along North and South Broadway, and along East and West Colfax Avenue. For those who prefer caffeine to alcohol, there are also a number of good coffee bars throughout downtown Denver, as well as the Capitol Hill and uptown neighborhoods.

The following are among the popular bars and pubs, but there are plenty more, so be sure to check out the publications mentioned at the beginning of this section.

BJ's Carousel   Decorated with miniature and full-size carousel horses (but, alas, no carousel), this longstanding south Denver gay bar features drag enter-tainment on Fridays and Saturdays and free popcorn all the time. The restaurant serves dinner and Sunday brunch, and Wednesday is karaoke night. 1380 S. Broadway. ℂ 303/777-9880.

Bull & Bush Pub & Brewery   A neighborhood hangout in Cherry Creek, this re-creation of a famous London pub always has about ten of its own award-win-ning beers on tap—its IPA won the silver medal at the 2003 Great American

Finds Brewery Tours

Whether or not you drink beer, it can be fun to look behind the scenes and see how beer is made. Denver's first modern microbrewery, the **Wynkoop Brewing Co.**, 1634 18th St., at Wynkoop Street (✆ **303/297-2700**), offers tours every Saturday between 1 and 5pm. Housed in the renovated 1898 J. S. Brown Mercantile Building across from Union Station, the Wynkoop is also a popular restaurant (see "Where to Dine," in chapter 4). At least 10 beers are always on tap, including a few exotic recipes—the spicy chile beer is our favorite. If you can't decide which one to try, the "taster set" provides a nice sampling: nine 4-ounce glasses of different brews. For non–beer drinkers, the Wynkoop offers some of the best root beer in town. On the second floor is a top-notch pool hall with billiards, snooker, and darts.

Since it opened in 1991, **Rock Bottom Brewery**, 1001 16th St. (✆ **303/534-7616**), has been one of the leading brewpubs in the area. Tours, which are given upon request, offer great views of the brewing process, plus a sampling of the product. The Rock Bottom also has eight billiard tables and a good menu, starting at $8.

Breckenridge Brewery, 471 Kalamath St. (✆ **303/623-BREW**), a mile south of downtown, also lets you see the brewing process. Free brewery tours are given by appointment. In addition to its award-winning ales, the brewery serves traditional pub fare. Breckenridge also has a downtown tasting room at 2220 Blake St., across from Coors Field (✆ **303/297-3644**).

In Cherry Creek, **Bull & Bush Pub & Brewery**, 4700 Cherry Creek Dr. S. (✆ **303/759-0333**), produces about ten handcrafted ales and will give tours of its facilities upon request. Northwest of Denver, the **Cheshire Cat**, 7803 Ralston Rd., Arvada (✆ **303/431-9000**), is an authentic English pub in a historic building (1891) that offers tours on request.

Those who are really serious about visiting Colorado's microbreweries should consider an organized tour with **Actually Quite Nice Brew Tours** (✆ **303/431-1440**). Participants sample the beers at Denver- and Boulder-area microbreweries on lunch and dinner tours that last 4 to 5 hours. Full-day excursions visit breweries in Breckenridge and other mountain towns, or the Front Range cities of Colorado Springs and Fort Collins. Prices range from $50 to $75, and include beer samples and lunch or dinner. Custom tours are also available.

For a look at the other side of the coin, take a trip to nearby Golden for a look at **Coors,** the world's largest single-site brewery (see "A Side Trip to Colorado's Gold Circle Towns," later in this chapter).

Beer Festival. On Sunday evening, there's traditional jazz by regional groups. A full brew-house menu is available. 4700 Cherry Creek Dr. S., Glendale. ✆ **303/759-0333.**

Charlie Brown's Bar & Grill Just south of downtown, Charlie Brown's is a popular piano bar, some version of which has been in existence since 1927. The atmosphere is casual, with Elvis decanters, a baby grand piano, and a large central bar that attracts a diverse array of Denverites. The grill serves breakfast, lunch, and dinner, inside and out on a great patio. 980 Grant St. (at 10th Ave.). ℂ 303/860-1655.

Churchill Bar   You'll find an excellent selection of fine cigars, single-malt Scotch, and after-dinner drinks at this refined cigar bar, which caters to older, well-to-do Establishment types. In the Brown Palace Hotel, 321 17th St. ℂ 303/297-3111.

Cruise Room Bar   Modeled after a 1930s-era bar aboard the *Queen Mary*, the Cruise Room opened in 1933 on the day Prohibition ended. Recently restored to its Art Deco best, it draws a sophisticated, fairly young crowd with a free jukebox and one of the best martinis in town. In the Oxford Hotel, 1600 17th St. (at Wazee St.). ℂ 303/825-1107.

Falling Rock Tap House   Comfy, woody, and just down the street from Coors Field, this LoDo pub has 69 beers on tap—the best selection of good beer in Denver. You'll also find darts and pool, happy hours, and occasional live music. 1919 Blake St. ℂ 303/293-8338.

Herb's Hideout   Herb's is a downtown bar with an atmosphere steeped in nostalgia. The checkerboard floors, dim lighting, lengthy bar, and intimate booths give the bar a retro aura, making Herb's a haven for the young and hip. There is live jazz, rock, and blues, as well as regular DJs spinning records. Closed Monday. 2057 Larimer St. ℂ 303/299-9555.

My Brother's Bar   A Platte Valley fixture since the Beat Generation, this is the locals' choice for big, juicy burgers, wrapped in wax paper and served with an array of condiments and a side helping of friendly, unpretentious vibes. 2376 15th St. ℂ 303/455-9991.

Samba Room   The atmosphere at the Samba Room—Cuban murals, booming Latin music, a fashionable young clientele—is right up there with Denver's flashiest nightclubs. The menu of Latin-Caribbean fusion, albeit a bit pricey and uneven, adds to the theme. 1460 Larimer St. ℂ 720/956-1701.

Sing Sing   A noisy, eclectic crowd dominates the scene at this LoDo hot spot, located beneath the Denver ChopHouse & Brewery (see "Where to Dine" in chapter 4). You'll often find low-priced beer specials, which encourage the hard-partying college types to sing along (loudly and badly) with the dueling pianos. A fun place, but hang on tight. Closed Sunday. 1735 19th St. ℂ 303/291-0880.

Wynkoop Brewing Company   Many suds aficionados say this, Denver's first modern brewpub, is still the city's best. Among its most interesting offerings are India pale ale, chile beer, and Scotch ale, but you really can't go wrong with any of the selections. An added attraction is a large upstairs pool hall, which generally attracts a more party-hearty crowd than the restaurant and bar. 1634 18th St. (at Wynkoop St.). ℂ 303/297-2700.

THE PERFORMING ARTS
CLASSICAL MUSIC & OPERA

Colorado Symphony Orchestra   This international-caliber orchestra performs more than 100 classical, pops, and family concerts each year at locations throughout the metropolitan area, mostly at the Denver Center for the Performing Arts. Tickets run $15 to $70. 821 17th St., #700. ℂ 303/893-4100. www.denvercenter.org.

Opera Colorado   The company stages three operas (four performances each) with English super-titles each season at the Denver Performing Arts Complex. Internationally renowned singers and local favorites sing the lead roles. The typical schedule is three evening performances and one matinee each week from February through May. Tickets usually cost $30 to $120. 695 S. Colorado Blvd., #20. ℂ 303/893-4100 or 303/778-1500. www.operacolorado.org.

THEATER & COMEDY

Comedy Works   Considered one of the region's top comedy clubs for more than 20 years, this is your best bet for seeing America's hot comics at work— Dave Chappelle and Lewis Black recently took to the stage. Admission is $7 to $10 on weekdays, more on weekends and for marquee performers. Several shows a week are nonsmoking. 1226 15th St. ℂ 303/595-3637. www.comedyworks.com.

Denver Center for the Performing Arts   An umbrella organization for resident and touring theater, youth outreach, and conservatory training, the DCPA includes the **Denver Center Theatre Company,** the largest professional resident theater company in the Rockies. With 40 artists on its payroll, the troupe performs about 10 plays in repertory from October through June, including classical and contemporary dramas, musicals, and premieres of new plays. Tickets cost roughly $30 to $50. **Denver Center Attractions** brings in over 10 touring Broadway productions annually. Tickets run $20 to $65. For both companies, many shows sell out well in advance. 14th and Curtis sts. ℂ 800/641-1222 or 303/893-4100, or 303/893-DCPA for recorded information. www.denvercenter.org.

Denver Civic Theatre   A recently restored 1921 gem, the Denver Civic Theatre is a burgeoning outlet for touring productions, typically a bit edgy. Tickets usually cost $30 to $40. 721 Santa Fe Dr. ℂ 303/309-3773. www.denvercivic.com.

El Centro Su Teatro   A Hispanic theater and cultural center, El Centro presents bilingual productions on a regular basis. Tickets cost $10 to $15. 4725 High St. ℂ 303/296-0219. www.suteatro.org.

Germinal Stage Denver   This 100-seat theater presents works by modern playwrights such as Brecht, Albee, and Pinter. Tickets generally cost $13 to $18. 2450 W. 44th Ave. ℂ 303/455-7108. www2.privatei.com/~gsden.

Hunger Artists Ensemble Theatre   This award-winning theater group presents contemporary and children's works at the LIDA Project. Tickets run $16 or $17. 2180 Stout St. ℂ 303/893-5438. www.hungerartists.org.

Rattlebrain Theater   A new—and quite hilarious—entry in Denver's comedy scene, the Rattlebrain players perform sketch and improv shows Thursday through Saturday on a stage in the landmark D & F Tower on the 16th Street Mall. Shows often sell out, so reservations are key; tickets cost $15 to $30. In the D & F Tower, 1601 Arapahoe St. ℂ 720/932-7384. www.rattlebraintheater.com.

DANCE

Cleo Parker Robinson Dance   A highly acclaimed multicultural modern-dance ensemble and school, the Cleo Parker Robinson group performs a varied selection of programs each year, both on tour around the world and at several Denver locations. Tickets usually run $25 to $35. 119 Park Ave. W. ℂ 303/893-4100 or 303/295-1759. www.cleoparkerdance.org.

Colorado Ballet   The state's premier professional resident ballet company performs at various theaters downtown. The company presents four productions during its fall-through-spring season—a balance of classical and contemporary

Travel Tip: He who finds the best hotel deal has more to spend on facials involving knobbly vegetables.

Hello, the Roaming Gnome here. I've been nabbed from the garden and taken round the world. The people who took me are so terribly clever. They find the best offerings on Travelocity. For very little cha-ching. And that means I get to be pampered and exfoliated till I'm pink as a bunny's doodah.

travelocity®

1-888-TRAVELOCITY / travelocity.com / America Online Keyword: Travel

works that always includes *The Nutcracker* at Christmastime. Tickets range from $15 to $55. 1278 Lincoln St. ☎ 303/837-8888. www.coloradoballet.org.

MAJOR CONCERT HALLS & AUDITORIUMS

Arvada Center for the Arts & Humanities   This multidisciplinary arts center is in use almost every day of the year for performances by internationally known artists and its own theater companies, its historical museum and art gallery exhibitions, and hands-on education programs for all ages. In addition, the children's theater program performs in front of an annual audience of 60,000. A new, fully accessible playground features a 343-foot sea creature by the name of Squiggles. The 2003–04 theater season included *Pinocchio, Jekyll & Hyde, the Musical,* and *The Women.* Visiting musicians included Dave Brubeck, Michelle Shocked, and Brazilian jazz songbird Claudia Villela. The indoor theater seats 500 and the outdoor amphitheater seats 1,200. 6901 Wadsworth Blvd., Arvada (2½ miles north of I-70). ☎ 720/898-7200. www.arvadacenter.org.

Coors Amphitheatre   Formerly Fiddler's Green, alfresco summer concerts here feature national and international stars of rock, jazz, classical, and country music. The amphitheater has about 6,500 reserved seats and room for 10,000 more on its spacious lawn. Located in the southwestern section of the metropolitan area, just west of I-25 between Arapahoe and Orchard roads, it's open from May through September. 6350 Greenwood Plaza Blvd., Englewood. ☎ **303/220-7000.**

Denver Performing Arts Complex   Covering 4 square downtown blocks, from Speer Boulevard to 14th Street and Champa to Arapahoe streets, the Center for the Performing Arts (called the "Plex" by locals) is impressive even to those not attending a performance. Its numerous theaters seat from 157 to 2,800, and there's also a restaurant and shopping promenade. 14th and Curtis sts. ☎ **800/641-1222** or 303/893-4100, or 303/893-DCPA for recorded information. www.denver center.org.

Fillmore Auditorium   The 3,600-seat Fillmore is the former Mammoth Gardens, which was recently renovated by proprietors of the legendary Fillmore in San Francisco. The slickly remodeled venue is now one of Denver's best, loaded with bars and countless vintage rock photos. It attracts national rock acts from Ween to Bob Dylan, as well as many jam bands. Tickets generally cost $20 to $50. 1510 Clarkson St. ☎ **303/860-7181.** www.fillmoreauditorium.com.

Paramount Theatre   A performing-arts center since 1929, this restored 2,000-seat downtown theater is a wonderful place to enjoy jazz, pop, and folk performances, as well as comedy, lectures, and theater. Recent bookings have included Tom Waits and Diana Krall. 1621 Glenarm Place. ☎ **303/825-4904.**

Red Rocks Amphitheatre ★★★   Quite possibly the country's best and most beautiful venue for top-name outdoor summer concerts, Red Rocks is in the foothills of the Rocky Mountains, 15 miles southwest of the city. Four-hundred-foot-high red sandstone rocks flank the 9,000-seat amphitheater, a product of the Civilian Conservation Corps. At night, with the lights of Denver spread across the horizon, the atmosphere is magical.

The Beatles performed here, as have Jimi Hendrix, Paul Simon, the Grateful Dead, Sting, Bonnie Raitt, Lyle Lovett, and Willie Nelson and top symphony orchestras from around the world. Renovated in 2002–03, the venue now has a sparkling new **visitor center** at the amphitheater's apex, which affords amazing views and displays detailing the varied performances that have taken place here since it opened in 1941. There's also a restaurant. The **trading post** carries a good selection of American-Indian jewelry and pottery, plus a variety of other curios and souvenirs. I-70 exit 259 S., 16351 County Rd. 93, Morrison. © 303/295-4444. www.redrocksonline.com/.

Universal Lending Pavilion   This 5,000-seat outdoor amphitheater on the southwest side of the Pepsi Center is the largest outdoor venue in the downtown area. An eclectic range of performers (from Travis Tritt to comedian Dave Chappelle in 2004) takes the stage here. 1700 7th St. © 303/405-1111.

9 A Side Trip to Colorado's Gold Circle Towns

Golden, Idaho Springs, and **Georgetown** make up most of the fabled Gold Circle—those towns that boomed with the first strikes of the gold rush in 1859. Central City, once the richest of the four towns but now the least attractive, completes the circle. Central City is trying to relive its glory days with a return to gambling, largely supported by locals from Denver, and although the exteriors of its historic buildings remain appealing, the rows of electronic slot machines and other gambling devices inside are a turn-off. Visitors to the area might like to make a brief stop and then move on to Idaho Springs.

GOLDEN 🏞🏞
Golden, 15 miles west of downtown Denver by way of U.S. 6 or Colo. 58 off I-70, is better known for the Coors Brewery (founded in 1873) and the Colorado School of Mines (established in 1874) than for its years as territorial capital.

For tourist information, contact the **Greater Golden Area Chamber of Commerce,** 1010 Washington Ave. (P.O. Box 1035), Golden, CO 80402 (© **303/279-3113;** www.goldencochamber.org).

WHAT TO SEE & DO
Historic downtown Golden centers on the **Territorial Capitol** in the **Loveland Building,** 12th Street and Washington Avenue. Built in 1861, it housed the first state legislature from 1862 to 1867, when the capital was moved to Denver. Today it contains offices and a restaurant. The **Armory,** 13th and Arapahoe streets, is probably the largest cobblestone structure in the United States; 3,300 wagonloads of stone and quartz went into its construction. **The Rock Flour Mill Warehouse,** 8th and Cheyenne streets, dates from 1863; it was built with red granite from nearby Golden Gate Canyon and still has its original cedar beams and wooden floors.

In addition to the attractions listed below, see the section on Golden Gate State Park in the Denver "Outdoor Activities" section, earlier in this chapter.

Astor House Museum   This handsome native stone structure, believed to be the first stone hotel built west of the Mississippi River, was constructed in 1867 to house legislators when Golden was the territorial capital. Scheduled for demolition to make space for a parking lot, the Astor House was instead restored in the 1970s and is now listed on the National Register of Historic Places. Today the Western-style Victorian hotel offers glimpses into life in Golden during the town's heyday in the late 19th century. Allow 30 to 60 minutes.

While there, you can obtain a walking-tour guide for the 12th Street Historic District or visit the Victorian Gift Shop, whose proceeds benefit the museum.
822 12th St. © 303/278-3557. www.astorhousemuseum.org. Admission $3 adults ($4.50 for combo ticket that also includes Clear Creek History Park), $2 children under 13 ($3 combo ticket). Tues–Sat 10am–4:30pm.

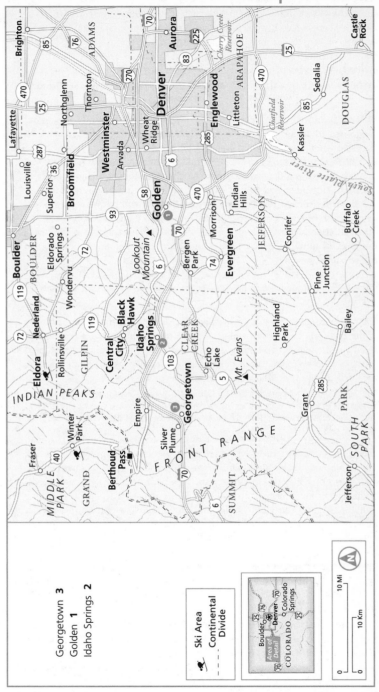

Georgetown **3**
Golden **1**
Idaho Springs **2**

Ski Area
Continental Divide

10 Mi
10 Km

Area of Detail
Boulder
Denver
Colorado Springs
COLORADO

Boettcher Mansion   This historic Jefferson County estate was built by Charles Boettcher in 1917 as a summer home and hunting lodge. It contains displays of furnishings and other items from the American Arts and Crafts period of the late 1800s and early 1900s. Other exhibits explore the history of Golden and the Boettcher family. Allow 1 hour.

900 Colorow Rd. (on Lookout Mountain). ℂ 303/526-0855. http://mansion.co.jefferson.co.us. Free admission, donations accepted. Mon–Fri 8am–5pm, or by appointment.

Buffalo Bill Museum & Grave ★ *Kids*   William Frederick Cody, the famous Western scout, is buried atop Lookout Mountain, south of Golden. (Some folks claim that friends stole Cody's body after his sister sold it to the City of Denver and the *Denver Post,* hightailed it north, and buried it in Wyoming, but we were assured that this was the real McCoy.) The museum contains memorabilia from the life and legend of Buffalo Bill, who rode for the Pony Express, organized buffalo hunts for foreign royalty, and toured the world with his Wild West Show. There are also displays of American Indian artifacts, guns, and Western art; an observation deck provides a great view of Denver. The museum is in 66-acre **Lookout Mountain Park,** a Denver municipal park popular for picnicking. Allow 1 to 1½ hours.

987½ Lookout Mountain Rd. ℂ 303/526-0747. www.buffalobill.org. Admission $3 adults, $2 seniors, $1 children 6–15, free for children under 6. May–Oct daily 9am–5pm; Nov–Apr Tues–Sun 9am–4pm. Closed Dec 25. I-70 exit 256.

Clear Creek History Park   This 3-acre creek-side park illustrates the history of the area's ranching, with two log cabins, several animal barns, a blacksmith's shop, and a one-room schoolhouse from the 1870s. The buildings were moved to this site to save them from development in nearby Golden Gate Canyon, their original location. Allow about an hour.

11th and Arapahoe sts. in downtown Golden. ℂ 303/278-3557. www.clearcreekhistorypark.org. Admission $3 adults ($4.50 for combo ticket that also includes the Astor House Museum), $2 children under 13 ($3 combo ticket). June–Aug Tues–Sat 10am–4:30pm; May and Sept Sat 10am–4:30pm. Closed Oct–Apr.

Colorado Railroad Museum ★   Housed in a replica of an 1880 railroad depot, this museum 2 miles east of Golden is a must-see for railroad buffs. On display are more than four dozen narrow- and standard-gauge locomotives and cars, plus other historic equipment, artifacts, photos, documents, and model trains. The exhibits cover 12 acres, including the two-story depot and a working roundhouse. You can climb into many of the old locomotives and wander through the parlor cars. The excellent gift-and-souvenir shop sells hundreds of railroad-related items, from coffee mugs to posters to T-shirts. Allow 1 to 2 hours.

17155 W. 44th Ave. ℂ 800/365-6263 or 303/279-4591. www.crrm.org. Admission $7 adults, $6 seniors over 60, $4 children under 16, children under 2 free, $16 families. June–Aug daily 9am–6pm; Sept–May daily 9am–5pm. Closed Jan 1, Thanksgiving, and Dec 25. Follow signs from I-70 exit 265 westbound, exit 266 eastbound.

Colorado School of Mines Geology Museum ★   Exhibits here help explain the history of mining in Colorado with a replica of a uranium mine and other displays. On exhibit are some 50,000 minerals, gems, fossils, and artifacts from around the world, plus displays on geology, earth history, and paleontology. There's also a kids' corner. The Colorado School of Mines, founded in 1874, has an enrollment of about 3,000. Allow 1 hour.

13th and Maple sts. ℂ 303/273-3815. Free admission. School year Mon–Sat 9am–4pm, Sun 1–4pm; summer Mon–Sat 9am–4pm. Closed Colorado School of Mines holidays.

Coors Brewing Company   Reputedly the world's largest single-site brewery, this facility produces 1.5 million gallons of beer each day. Coors conducts free public tours, followed by free samples of the various beers produced. The entire presentation lasts about 1½ hours. Tours leave a central parking lot at 13th and Ford streets, where visitors board a bus for a short drive through historic Golden before arriving at the brewery. There, a 30-minute walking tour covers the history of the Coors family and company, the barley malting process, the 13,640-gallon gleaming copper kettles, and the entire production process all the way to packaging. Children are welcome, and arrangements can be made for visitors with disabilities and non–English speakers. There's also a gift shop and an interactive time line in the reception area. Allow about 2 hours. *Note:* Visitors 18 and under must be accompanied by an adult.

13th and Ford sts. ✆ **303/277-2337.** www.coors.com. Free admission. Tours Mon–Sat 10am–4pm; shop Mon–Sat 10am–5pm. Closed holidays. Visitors under 18 must be accompanied by an adult.

Foothills Art Center   Housed in an 1872 Gothic-style Presbyterian church (which is on the National Historic Register), this exhibition center evolved from the annual Golden Sidewalk Art Show and features changing national and regional exhibits. A gift shop next door—Foothills Two—sells crafts by local artisans. Allow 30 minutes.

809 15th St. ✆ **303/279-3922.** www.foothillsartcenter.org. Free admission. Mon–Sat 10am–5pm; Sun 1–5pm.

Golden Pioneer Museum   This museum exhibits an impressive collection of furniture, household articles, photographs, and other items, including a re-created 19th-century parlor and boudoir. Especially impressive is its collection of 200 American-Indian dolls, representing 39 different groups from all around North America. There are also a genealogical and historic research library and a small gift shop. Allow 1 hour.

923 10th St. ✆ **303/278-7151.** www.goldenpioneermuseum.com. Free admission. Mon–Sat 10am–4:30pm; Memorial Day to Labor Day also Sun 11am–5pm. Closed major holidays.

Heritage Square *Kids*   A family-oriented shopping, dining, and entertainment village with a Wild West theme, Heritage Square features some Victorian specialty shops, a Ferris wheel, a stocked fishing pond, and a dinner theater. Warm-weather activities include go-carts, bumper boats, and a 2,350-foot alpine slide with bobsled-style carts. Heritage Square Music Hall offers shows for adults and children, and there's a nostalgic ice-cream parlor. Allow 1 to 2 hours.

18301 Colfax Ave. (U.S. 40). ✆ **303/279-2789.** www.heritagesquare.info. Free admission; separate charges for individual activities. Memorial Day to Labor Day Mon–Sat 10am–8pm, Sun noon–8pm; rest of year Mon–Sat 10am–6pm, Sun noon–6pm. I-70, exit 259.

Lookout Mountain Nature Center *Kids*   A 1½-mile self-guided nature trail winds through this 110-acre preserve among ponderosa pines and pretty mountain meadows. A free trail guide is available at the Nature Center when it's open, and a map is on display at a kiosk for those walking the trail at other times. The nonprofit Nature Center has displays on the pine beetle, pollination, and Colorado wildlife, plus an interactive exhibit on the ponderosa pine forest. The building is also worth a look—it's constructed of used and recycled materials such as ground-up plastic soda containers and the pulp of aspen trees. The center schedules free naturalist-guided environmental education activities year-round. Topics vary, but could include the flowers, butterflies, or wildlife of the area, or a look at the night sky. Advance registration is required for most programs, and age restrictions may apply. Call for details. Allow at least 1 hour.

910 Colorow Rd. (on Lookout Mountain). ℂ **303/526-0594.** Free admission. Trail daily 8am–dusk; Nature Center Tues–Sun 10am–4pm.

Mother Cabrini Shrine   A 22-foot statue of Jesus stands at the top of a 373-step stairway adorned by carvings representing the stations of the cross and mysteries of the rosary. Terra-cotta benches provide rest stops along the way. The shrine is dedicated to the country's first citizen saint, St. Frances Xavier Cabrini, who founded the Order of the Missionary Sisters of the Sacred Heart. The order has a convent here with a gift shop that's open from 9am to 5pm daily. Allow 45 to 90 minutes.

20189 Cabrini Blvd. (I-70 exit 259), Lookout Mountain. ℂ **303/526-0758.** www.den-cabrini-shrine.org. Free admission, donations welcome. Summer daily 7am–7:30pm; winter daily 7am–5:30pm; masses daily 7:30am, Sun 11am.

National Earthquake Information Center   The U.S. Geological Survey operates this facility to collect rapid earthquake information, transmit warnings over the Earthquake Early Alerting Service, and publish and disseminate earthquake data. Tours of 30 to 45 minutes can be scheduled by appointment when a guide is available. They include information about the NEIC, the Earthquake Early Alerting Service, and earthquakes in general.

1711 Illinois St. ℂ **303/273-8500.** http://neic.usgs.gov. Free admission. Tues–Thurs 9–11am and 1–3pm, by appointment only.

Rocky Mountain Quilt Museum   This museum presents changing exhibits, including works from its permanent collection of some 250 quilts. Consigned works are for sale in the gift shop. Allow 30 minutes.

1111 Washington Ave. ℂ **303/277-0377.** www.rmqm.org. Admission $4 adults, $3 seniors, $1 children 6–12, free for children under 6. Mon–Sat 10am–4pm.

WHERE TO STAY & DINE

La Quinta Inn—Golden, just off I-70 exit 264, at 3301 Youngfield Service Rd. (ℂ **800/531-5900** or 303/279-5565), is a dependable choice, with 129 units and rates of $89 for a double room. **Table Mountain Inn,** 1310 Washington Ave. (ℂ **800/762-9898** or 303/277-9898; www.tablemountaininn.com), is a smaller, slightly more expensive alternative, with 65 standard rooms and 9 suites. Rates are $122 to $147 single or double, $167 to $207 suite. The place is loaded with Southwest charm, featuring beautiful views of the surrounding mesas and a good restaurant.

For a good meal in a historic setting, try the **Old Capitol Grill** in downtown Golden, 1122 Washington Ave. at 12th Street (ℂ **303/279-6390**), offering steak and burgers plus a good selection of sandwiches. Located in the Territorial Capitol Building constructed in 1862, the restaurant is open daily for lunch and dinner, with dinner prices in the $8-to-$18 range. A more upscale dinner choice is **Coburn's,** in the Coburn Hotel, 800 11th St. (ℂ **303/279-0100**). It serves creative regional fare in the $16-to-$23 range.

IDAHO SPRINGS ⚓

For visitor information, contact the **Idaho Springs Chamber of Commerce,** P.O. Box 97, Idaho Springs, CO 80452 (ℂ **303/567-4382;** www.idahosprings chamber.com). Information on Idaho Springs and the nearby towns of Empire, Georgetown, and Silver Plume is available from the **Clear Creek County Tourism Board,** P.O. Box 100, Idaho Springs, CO 80452 (ℂ **800/88-BLAST** or 303/567-4660; www.clearcreekcounty.org).

WHAT TO SEE & DO

The scenic "Oh My God" dirt road, a steep, winding thoroughfare, runs from Central City through Virginia Canyon to Idaho Springs, although most visitors prefer to take I-70 directly to this community 35 miles west of Denver. Site of a major gold strike in 1859, today Idaho Springs beckons visitors to try their luck at panning for any gold that may remain. The quaint Victorian downtown is worth a look; don't miss the Bridal Veil Falls tumbling through the largest waterwheel in Colorado, right across from City Hall.

The **Argo Gold Mine, Mill, and Museum,** 2350 Riverside Dr. (© **303/567-2421;** www.historicargotours.com), is listed on the National Register of Historic Places, and offers tours daily from mid-April through October from 9am to 6pm. Visitors can see the Double Eagle Gold Mine, relatively unchanged since the early miners first worked it more than 100 years ago, and the mill, where ore was processed into gold. Everyone is welcome to take part in gold- and gemstone-panning. Admission is $13 for adults, $7.50 for children 7 to 12, and free for kids under 7. Allow at least 45 minutes.

At the **Phoenix Gold Mine** ☆, on Trail Creek Road (© **303/567-0422**), you can don a hard hat and follow a working miner through narrow tunnels to see what mining 100 years ago was all about. You can also pan for gold on the property and relax in the picnic area. Weather permitting, the mine is open daily from 10am to 6pm in the summer (until 5pm in the winter); the tours are informal and entertaining. Cost is $10 for adults, $9 for seniors, $5 for children 5 to 11, and free for children under 5. Allow about 1 hour.

Just outside Idaho Springs is **Indian Springs Resort,** 302 Soda Creek Rd. (© **303/567-2191** or 303/989-6666; www.indianspringsresort.com), a fine spot for a relaxing soak in the hot springs after a long day of skiing or hiking. The resort has a covered swimming pool, indoor and outdoor private baths, and a vapor cave with soaking pools. Rates are $16 to $23 per person for an hour in the private baths or all-day use of the vapor cave, $12 to $14 for all-day use of the pool, and $12 for a mud bath in "Club Mud." Lodging ($60–$125 for two), meals, and weekend entertainment are also offered. The resort is open daily from 7:30am to 10:30pm year-round.

Idaho Springs is the starting point for a 28-mile drive to the summit of 14,260-foot **Mount Evans** ☆☆. From I-70 exit 240, follow Colo. 103—also called Mt. Evans Highway—as it winds along Chicago Creek through Arapahoe National Forest to **Echo Lake Park,** another Denver mountain park with fireplaces, hiking trails, and fishing. From here, Colo. 5—the highest paved auto road in North America—climbs to the Mount Evans summit. Views along this highway are of spectacular snowcapped peaks even in June, and you're likely to see mountain goats, bighorn sheep, marmots, eagles, and other wildlife. The road is generally open from Memorial Day to Labor Day. Allow at least 4 hours.

Another way to see this area's great scenery is by horseback. **A&A Historical Trails Stables,** 5 miles up Virginia Canyon from Idaho Springs (© **303/567-4808;** www.aastables.com), offers a variety of trail rides, including breakfast and moonlight rides. Rides are usually offered from May through November, weather permitting. A 1-hour ride costs $25 per person, and a 2-hour ride costs $45.

WHERE TO STAY & DINE

H&H Motor Lodge, 2445 Colorado Blvd. (P.O. Box 1359), Idaho Springs, CO 80452 (© **800/445-2893** or 303/567-2838; www.hhlodge.com), is a mom-and-pop motel on the east side of town. It offers bright and cheery rooms,

TVs with HBO, a hot tub, and a sauna. The 34 rooms and suites include several larger family units. Rates are $59 double for a standard room, kitchenettes $10 to $20 extra; two-bedroom suites start at $69. Pets are accepted for a $5 nightly fee.

Beau Jo's Colorado Style Pizza, 1517 Miner St. (© **303/567-4376**), offers a wide variety of so-called mountain pizzas, including standard pepperoni; "Skier Mike's," with Canadian bacon, green peppers, and chicken breast; and a roasted garlic and veggie combo. Sandwiches are also available, plus a salad bar set up in a pair of old claw-foot bathtubs. The bill usually comes out to $7 to $12 per person. Smoking is not permitted.

GEORGETOWN ⊛

A pretty village of Victorian-era houses and stores, Georgetown, 45 miles west of Denver on I-70 at an elevation of 8,500 feet, is named for an 1860 gold camp. Among the best preserved of the foothill mining towns, Georgetown is one of the few that didn't suffer a major fire during its formative years. Perhaps to acknowledge their blessings, townspeople built eye-catching steeples on top of their firehouses, not their churches.

For information on attractions and travel services, drop by or contact the **Georgetown Visitors Center,** 613 6th St. (P.O. Box 444), Georgetown, CO 80444 (© **800/472-8230** or 303/569-2888), which runs a visitor information center at 6th and Argentine streets across from the Georgetown post office; or **Historic Georgetown, Inc.,** 15th and Argentine streets, P.O. Box 667, Georgetown, CO 80444-0667 (© **303/569-2840;** www.historicgeorgetown.org).

WHAT TO SEE & DO

The Georgetown–Silver Plume Mining Area was declared a National Historic Landmark District in 1966, and more than 200 of its buildings have been restored.

A convenient place to begin a **walking tour** is the Old County Courthouse, 6th and Argentine streets. Now the community center and tourist information office, it was built in 1867. Across Argentine Street is the Old Stone Jail (1868); 3 blocks south, at 3rd and Argentine, is the Hamill House (see below).

Sixth Street is Georgetown's main commercial strip. Walk east from the Old Courthouse. On your left are the Masonic Hall (1891), the Fish Block (1886), the Monti and Guanella Building (1868), and the Cushman Block (1874); on your right, the Hamill Block (1881) and the Kneisel & Anderson Building (1893). The Hotel de Paris (see below) is at the corner of 6th and Taos. Nearly opposite, at 6th and Griffith, is the Star Hook and Ladder Building (1886), along with the town hall and marshal's office.

If you turn south on Taos Street, you'll find Grace Episcopal Church (1869) at 5th Street, and the Maxwell House (1890) a couple of steps east on 4th. Glance west on 5th to see Alpine Hose Company No. 2 (1874) and the Courier Building (1875). North on Taos Street from the Hotel de Paris are the Old Georgetown School (1874) at 8th Street, First Presbyterian Church (1874) at 9th, Our Lady of Lourdes Catholic Church (1918) at 9th, and the Old Missouri Firehouse (1870) at 10th and Taos.

If you turn west on 9th at the Catholic church, you'll find two more historic structures: the Bowman-White House (1892) at Rose and 9th, and the Tucker-Rutherford House (ca. 1860), a miner's log cabin with four small rooms and a trapper's cabin in back, on 9th Street at Clear Creek.

Georgetown Energy Museum   This small museum is dedicated to educat-
ing people about the history of hydropower in Georgetown and Colorado.
Located at Georgetown's power plant—built in 1900 and still operating—the
museum allows visitors an up-close look at a pair of hydroelectric-generating
units in action. The museum also features photographic and text displays detailing the history of similar plants in the region, as well as a collection of antiques:
washing machines, stoves, and generator meters. Allow 30 minutes.

600 Griffith St. ☎ **303/569-3557**. www.georgetownenergymuseum.org. Free admission, donations
accepted. June–Sept Mon–Sat 10am–4pm, Sun noon–4pm; Oct–May by appointment only.

Hamill House   Built in Country Gothic Revival style, this house dates from
1867, when silver speculator William Hamill owned it. When Historic Georgetown, Inc., acquired it in 1971, the house had its original woodwork, fireplaces,
and wallpaper. A delicately carved outhouse had two sections: one with walnut
seats for the family; the other with pine seats for servants. Allow 30 to 60
minutes.

305 Argentine St. ☎ **303/569-2840**. Admission $5 adults, $4 seniors 60 and older, $4 students, free for chil-
dren under 6. Memorial Day to Sept daily 10am–4pm; Oct–Dec Sat–Sun noon–4pm. Closed Jan to late May
except for prearranged tours.

Hotel de Paris ☆   The builder of the hotel, Louis Dupuy, once explained his
desire to build a French inn so far away from his homeland: "I love these mountains and I love America, but you will pardon me if I bring into this community
a remembrance of my youth and my country." The hotel opened in 1875 and
soon became famous for its French provincial luxury.

Today it's a historic museum run by the National Society of Colonial Dames
of America, embellished with many of its original furnishings, including Havi-
land china, a big pendulum clock, paintings and etchings, photographs by
William Henry Jackson, and carved walnut furniture. The kitchen contains an
antique stove and other cooking equipment, and the wine cellar houses early
wine barrels, with their labels still in place. Allow 45 to 60 minutes.

409 6th St. (at Taos St.). ☎ **303/569-2311**. www.hoteldeparismuseum.org. Admission $4 adults, $3 seniors
60 and older, $2 children 6–16, free for children under 6. Memorial Day to Labor Day daily 10am–4:30pm;
early Sept to Dec and Apr Sat–Sun noon–4pm, weather permitting. Closed Jan–Apr and major holidays.

WHERE TO STAY & DINE

Colorado's oldest continuously operating hotel, about 5 minutes from Georgetown, is the **Peck House Hotel and Restaurant,** 83 Sunny Ave. (P.O. Box 428),
on U.S. 40 off I-70 exit 232, Empire, CO 80438 (☎ **303/569-9870;** fax
303/569-2743; www.thepeckhouse.com). Established in 1862 as a stagecoach
stop for travelers and immigrants from the East Coast, the hotel has an antique-
filled parlor lined with photos of the Peck family and their late-19th- and early-
20th-century guests. The rooms are comfortable and quaint (claw-foot tubs
grace many bathrooms). One of the best parts of a stay here is the fine
panoramic view of the Empire Valley afforded by the wide veranda. There are 11
rooms (9 with private bathroom), and rates for two are in the $65-to-$100
range. The hotel's excellent **restaurant** serves fish and steak entrees and seriously
delicious hot-fudge cake and raspberries Romanoff. The restaurant serves dinner
daily year-round; prices for entrees are $20 to $30.

Back in Georgetown, **The Happy Cooker,** 412 6th St. (☎ **303/569-3166**),
serves unusual soups, sandwiches on homemade breads, crepes, quiches, and
more substantial fare such as frittatas and eggs Benedict, in a converted home in

Georgetown's historic business district. It's open Monday through Friday from 7am to 4pm, Saturday and Sunday from 7am to 5pm. Prices are in the $4-to-$8 range, and breakfast is served all day. For a beer, a burger, and a dose of local color, head to the **Red Ram Restaurant & Saloon,** 606 6th St. (© **303/569-2300**). The menu also has Mexican plates and slow-cooked baby back ribs; prices run $6 to $15 for a main course.

Boulder

Although Boulder is known primarily as a college town (the University of Colorado is here), it would be inaccurate to begin and end the description there. Sophisticated and artsy, Boulder is home to numerous high-tech companies and research concerns; it also attracts countless outdoor sports enthusiasts with its delightful climate, vast open spaces, and proximity to Rocky Mountain National Park.

Set at the foot of the Flatirons of the Rocky Mountains, just 30 miles northwest of downtown Denver and only 74 feet higher than the Mile High City, Boulder was settled by hopeful miners in 1858 and named for the large rocks in the area. Welcomed by Chief Niwot and the resident southern Arapaho, the miners struck gold in the nearby hills the following year. By the 1870s, Boulder had become a regional rail and trade center for mining and farming. The university, founded in 1877, became the economic mainstay of the community after mining collapsed around the beginning of the 20th century.

In the 1950s, Boulder emerged as a center for scientific and environmental research. The National Center for Atmospheric Research and the National Institute of Standards and Technology are located here, as are dozens of high-tech and aerospace companies. Alongside the ongoing high-tech boom, the university and attendant vibrant culture have attracted a diverse mix of intellectuals, individualists, and eccentrics. Writers William S. Burroughs, Jr., Stephen King, and Allen Ginsberg, founder of the city's Naropa Institute, all called Boulder home at one time or another.

Today's residents are a mix of students attending the University of Colorado (called CU by locals); employees of the many computer, biotech, and research firms; and others attracted by the casual, bohemian, environmentally aware, and otherwise hip lifestyles that prevail here. Whatever differences exist among the residents, they are united by a common love of the outdoors. Boulder has 30,000 acres of open space within its city limits, 56 parks, and 200 miles of trails. On any given day, seemingly three-quarters of the population is outside making great use of this land, generally from the vantage point of a bicycle seat, the preferred mode of transport—there are about 100,000 bicycles in Boulder, which has a human population of roughly 95,000.

1 Orientation

ARRIVING
BY PLANE

Boulder doesn't have a commercial airport. Air travelers must fly into Denver International Airport, then make ground connections to Boulder, a trip of about an hour.

GETTING TO & FROM THE AIRPORT   The **SuperShuttle Boulder** (© **800/525-3177** or 303/444-0808; www.supershuttle.com) leaves Denver hourly from 7:00am to 11pm, and Boulder hourly between 4am and 10pm, with fewer departures on holidays. Scheduled pickups in Boulder are at the University of Colorado campus and area hotels; pickups from other locations are made on call. The one-way fare from a scheduled pickup point to the airport is $20 per person, or $26 for residential pickup service from other points; children 8 and under ride free. **Boulder Express** (© **303/457-4646**) offers airport shuttle service to and from the Boulder area for $18 to $25 one-way, $32 to $40 round-trip.

Boulder Yellow Cab (© **303/777-7777**) charges $70 one-way to the airport for up to five passengers.

Buses operated by the **Regional Transportation District,** known locally as **RTD** (© **800/366-7433** or 303/299-6000, TDD 303/299-6089; www.rtd-denver.com), charge $10 for a one-way trip to the airport (exact change required). Buses leave from, and return to, the main terminal at 14th and Walnut streets daily every hour from 6am to 11pm.

Boulder Limousine Service (© **800/910-7433** or 303/449-5466; www.whitedovelimo.com) charges $100 to $250 to take up to three people from Boulder to Denver International Airport in a limousine or minibus. Charter services are also available.

BY CAR

The Boulder Turnpike (U.S. 36) branches off I-25 north of Denver and passes through the suburbs of Westminster, Broomfield, and Louisville before reaching Boulder. The trip takes about 30 minutes. If you are coming from Denver International Airport, E-470 west to I-25 south is the best route to U.S. 36.

If you're arriving from the north, take the Longmont exit from I-25 and follow Colo. 119 all the way. Longmont is 7 miles due west of the freeway; Boulder is another 15 miles southwest on the Longmont Diagonal Highway.

VISITOR INFORMATION

The **Boulder Convention and Visitors Bureau,** 2440 Pearl St. (at Folsom St.), Boulder, CO 80302 (© **800/444-0447** or 303/442-2911; www.bouldercoloradousa.com), is open Monday through Thursday from 8:30am to 5pm, Friday from 8:30am to 4pm, and can provide excellent maps, brochures, and general information on the city.

There are also visitor information kiosks on **Pearl Street Mall** and at the **Davidson Mesa overlook,** several miles southeast of Boulder on U.S. 36. Brochures are available at both sites year-round.

CITY LAYOUT

The north–south streets increase in number going from west to east, beginning with 3rd Street. (The eastern city limit is at 61st St., although the numbers continue to the Boulder County line at 124th St. in Broomfield.) Where U.S. 36

Fun Fact **A Job Well Done**

The National Trust for Historic Preservation has named Boulder one of the nation's "dozen distinctive destinations" for preserving historic sites, managing growth, and maintaining a vibrant downtown.

enters Boulder (and does a 45-degree turn to the north), it becomes 28th Street, a major commercial artery. The Longmont Diagonal Highway (Colo. 119) enters Boulder from the northeast and intersects 28th Street at the north end of the city.

To reach downtown Boulder from U.S. 36, turn west on Canyon Boulevard (Colo. 119 west) and north on Broadway, which would be 12th Street if it had a number. It's 2 blocks to the Pearl Street Mall, a 4-block, east–west pedestrian-only strip from 11th to 15th streets that constitutes the historic downtown district. Boulder's few one-way streets circle the mall: 13th and 15th streets are one-way north, 11th and 14th one-way south, Walnut Street (a block south of the mall) one-way east, and Spruce Street (a block north) one-way west.

Broadway continues across the mall, eventually joining U.S. 36 north of the city. South of Arapahoe Avenue, Broadway turns southeast, skirting the University of Colorado campus and becoming Colo. 93 (the Foothills Hwy. to Golden) after crossing Baseline Road. Baseline follows a straight line from east Boulder, across U.S. 36 and Broadway, past Chautauqua Park and up the mountain slopes. To the south, Table Mesa Drive takes a similar course.

The Foothills Parkway (not to be confused with the Foothills Hwy.) is the principal north–south route on the east side of Boulder, extending from U.S. 36 at Table Mesa Drive to the Longmont Diagonal; Arapahoe Avenue, a block south of Canyon Boulevard, continues east across 28th Street as Arapahoe Road.

2 Getting Around

BY PUBLIC TRANSPORTATION

The **Regional Transportation District,** known as the **RTD** (© **800/366-7433** or 303/299-6000; www.rtd-denver.com), provides bus service throughout Boulder as well as the Denver greater metropolitan area. The Boulder Transit Center, 14th and Walnut streets, is open Monday through Friday from 5am to midnight and Saturday and Sunday from 6am to midnight. Fares within the city are $1.25 for adults and children, (65¢ for seniors and passengers with disabilities; children under 6 ride free). Schedules are available at the Transit Center, the Chamber of Commerce, and other locations. Buses are wheelchair accessible.

The city of Boulder runs a shuttle bus service called the **HOP** (© **303/ 447-8282**), connecting downtown, University Hill, the University of Colorado, and 30th and Pearl. The HOP operates Monday through Thursday from 7am to 10pm, Friday and Saturday from 9am to 10pm, and Sunday from 10am to 6pm. While the University of Colorado is in session, the night HOP runs Friday through Saturday from 10pm to 3am. Buses run about every 8 to 15 minutes during the day, every 15 to 20 minutes at night; the fare is $1.25 (65¢ for seniors).

The RTD runs a complementary local shuttle, the **SKIP,** Monday through Friday from 5:12am to 12:30am, Saturday from 7am to 12:30am, and Sunday from 7am to 11pm. Buses run north and south along Broadway, with a loop through the west Table Mesa neighborhood, every 6 to 10 minutes during peak weekday times and less frequently in the evenings and on weekends.

BY CAR

The **American Automobile Association (AAA)** has an office at 1933 28th St., #200 (© **303/753-8800**). It's open Monday through Friday from 8:30am to 5:30pm, Saturday from 9am to 1pm.

CAR RENTALS   Most people who fly to Colorado land at Denver International Airport and rent a car there. To rent a car in Boulder, contact **Avis** (© 800/331-1212), **Budget** (© 800/527-0700), **Dollar** (© 800/800-4000), **Enterprise** (© 800/736-8222), **Hertz** (© 800/654-3131), or **National** (© 888/227-7368).

PARKING   Most downtown streets have parking meters, with rates of about 25¢ per 20 minutes. Downtown parking lots cost $1 to $3 for 3 hours. Parking can be hard to find around the Pearl Street Mall, but new lots have eased the pain. Outside downtown, free parking is generally available on side streets.

BY BICYCLE
Boulder is a wonderful place for bicycling; there are bike paths throughout the city and an extensive trail system leading for miles beyond Boulder's borders (see "Bicycling" under "Sports & Outdoor Activities," later in this chapter).

You can rent and repair mountain bikes and buy trail and city maps at **University Bikes,** 839 Pearl St., about 2 blocks west of the Pearl Street Mall (© **303/444-4196;** www.ubikes.com), and **Full Cycle,** 1211 13th St., near the campus (© **303/440-7771**). Bike rentals cost $20 to $30 daily. Maps and other information are also available at the **Boulder Convention and Visitors Bureau,** 2440 Pearl St. (© **303/442-2911**).

BY TAXI
Boulder Yellow Cab (© **303/777-7777**) operates 24 hours, but you need to call for service—there are no taxi stands, and taxis won't stop for you on the street. Another company that serves Boulder is **Metro Taxi** (© **303/333-3333**).

ON FOOT
You can walk to most of what's worth seeing in downtown Boulder, especially around the Pearl Street Mall and University of Colorado campus. **Historic Boulder, Inc.** (© **303/444-5192;** www.historicboulder.org), can provide advice about exploring the city's historic neighborhoods on foot. It prints a brochure, *Walking Tours of Boulder,* that's available for $3 at the Convention and Visitors Bureau, 2440 Pearl St.

FAST FACTS: Boulder

Area Code   Area codes are **303** and **720,** and local calls require 10-digit dialing. See the "Telephone, Telegraph, Telex & Fax" section under "Fast Facts," in chapter 3.

Babysitters   The front desk at a major hotel often can make arrangements on your behalf. Boulder's **Child Care Referral Service** (© **303/441-3180**) can also help if you call in advance.

Business Hours   Most banks are open Monday through Friday from 9am to 5pm, and some have Saturday hours, too. Major stores are open Monday through Saturday from 9 or 10am until 5 or 6pm, and often Sunday from noon until 5pm. Department and discount stores often have later closing times.

Car Rentals   See "Getting Around," above.

Drugstores   Reliable prescription services are available at the Medical Center Pharmacy in the **Boulder Medical Center,** 2750 N. Broadway

(✆ 303/440-3111). The pharmacy at **King Soopers Supermarket**, 1650 30th St., in Sunrise Plaza (✆ **303/444-0164**), is open from 8am to 9pm weekdays, 9am to 6pm Saturdays, and 10am to 6pm Sundays.

Emergencies For police, fire, or medical emergencies, call ✆ **911**. For the **Poison Control Center**, call ✆ **800/332-3073** or 303/739-1123. For the **Rape Crisis Hotline**, call ✆ **303/443-7300**.

Eyeglasses You can get fast repair or replacement of your glasses at **Boulder Optical**, 1928 14th St. (✆ **303/442-4521**), or **Aspen Eyewear**, 2525 Arapahoe Ave. (✆ **303/447-0210**).

Hospitals Full medical services, including 24-hour emergency treatment, are available at **Boulder Community Hospital**, 1100 Balsam Ave., at North Broadway (✆ **303/440-2273**).

Newspapers & Magazines Newspaper options include Boulder's award-winning *Daily Camera* and the new *Boulder Weekly*. Many townspeople also read the campus paper, the *Colorado Daily*, available all over town. Both Denver dailies—the *Denver Post* and *Rocky Mountain News*—are available at newsstands throughout the city. You can also find the *New York Times, Wall Street Journal*, and *Christian Science Monitor* at many newsstands. The free *Boulder* magazine, published three times a year, lists seasonal events and other information on restaurants and the arts.

Photographic Needs For standard processing requirements (including 2-hr. slide processing), as well as custom lab work, contact **Photo Craft**, 3550 Arapahoe Ave. (✆ **303/442-6410**). For equipment, supplies, and repairs, visit **Mike's Camera**, 2500 Pearl St. (✆ **303/443-1715**; www.mikes camera.com).

Post Office The main downtown post office is at 15th and Walnut streets. Contact the U.S. Postal Service (✆ **800/275-8777**; www.usps.com) for hours and other locations.

Safety Although Boulder is generally a safe city—safer than Denver, for instance—it is not crime-free. Many locals avoid walking alone late at night along the Boulder Creek Path because of the transients who tend to hang out there.

Taxes State and city sales taxes total almost 7%.

Useful Telephone Numbers Call ✆ **303/639-1111** for **road conditions**; ✆ **303/825-7669** for **ski reports**; and ✆ **303/494-4221** for **weather reports**.

3 Where to Stay

You'll find a good selection of comfortable lodgings in Boulder, with a wide range of rates to suit almost every budget. Be aware, though, that the town literally fills up during the popular summer season, making advance reservations essential. It's also almost impossible to find a place to sleep during any major event at the University of Colorado, particularly graduation. Those who do find themselves in Boulder without lodging can check with the Boulder Convention and Visitors Bureau (see "Visitor Information," under "Orientation," above), which keeps track of availability. You can usually find a room in Denver, a half-hour or so away. Rates listed below do not include the 9.7% accommodations tax. Parking is free unless otherwise specified.

Boulder Accommodations & Dining

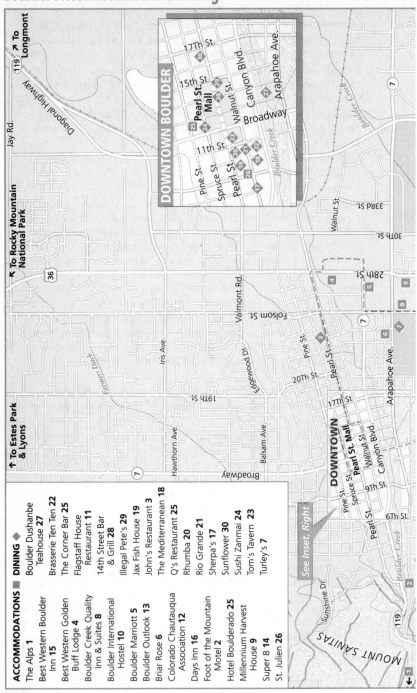

ACCOMMODATIONS ■

The Alps **1**
Best Western Boulder Inn **15**
Best Western Golden Buff Lodge **4**
Boulder Creek Quality Inn & Suites **8**
Boulder International Hostel **10**
Boulder Marriott **5**
Boulder Outlook **13**
Briar Rose **6**
Colorado Chautauqua Association **12**
Days Inn **16**
Foot of the Mountain Motel **2**
Hotel Boulderado **25**
Millennium Harvest House **9**
Super 8 **14**
St. Julien **26**

DINING ◆

Boulder Dushanbe Teahouse **27**
Brasserie Ten Ten **22**
The Corner Bar **25**
Flagstaff House Restaurant **11**
14th Street Bar & Grill **28**
Illegal Pete's **29**
Jax Fish House **19**
John's Restaurant **3**
The Mediterranean **18**
Q's Restaurant **25**
Rhumba **20**
Rio Grande **21**
Sherpa's **17**
Sunflower **30**
Sushi Zanmai **24**
Tom's Tavern **23**
Turley's **7**

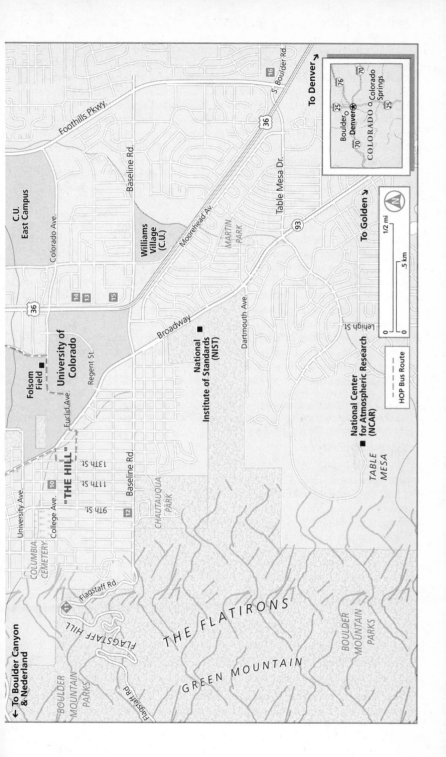

Major chains and franchises that provide reasonably priced lodging in Boulder include **Best Western Golden Buff Lodge,** 1725 28th St., Boulder, CO 80301 (© **800/528-1234** or 303/442-7450), with 112 units, charging $94 to $114 double; **Best Western Boulder Inn,** 770 28th St., Boulder, CO 80303 (© **800/233-8469** or 303/449-3800), with 98 units and rates of $66 to $104 double; **Boulder Creek Quality Inn and Suites,** 2020 Arapahoe Ave., Boulder, CO 80302 (© **888/449-7550** or 303/449-7550), with 46 units and rates of $99 to $160 double; **Super 8,** 970 28th St., Boulder, CO 80303 (© **800/525-2149** or 303/443-7800), with 71 units and rates of $70 to $90 double; and **Days Inn,** 5397 S. Boulder Rd., Boulder, CO 80303 (© **800/329-7466** or 303/499-4422), with 78 units and rates of $69 to $109 double.

VERY EXPENSIVE

St. Julien ★★   The first new hotel in downtown Boulder since the Boulderado opened in 1909, the $24 million St. Julien first welcomed guests in early 2005. The flagstone and Norman brick exterior (accented by patina copper and red roof tiles) sheaths 200 exquisite guest rooms, averaging a healthy 400 square feet each. Everything from the luxurious linens to the premium bath amenities to the in-room artwork is first rate. Honeyed tones and French doors accent the guest rooms, which feature either one California king or two queens. The bathrooms are the best in town; there are separate tubs and showers in every granite-laden one. The facilities include a restaurant, a bar (T-Zero, named for a local climbing route), a two-lane lap pool, and a spa that offers "indigenous therapies" using local minerals and plants. Expect to be wowed.

900 Walnut St., Boulder, CO 80302. © **877/303-0900** or 720/406-9696. Fax 720/406-9668. www.stjulien. com. 200 units, including 15 suites. $245 double; $285–$300 suite. Lower weekend rates. AE, DC, DISC, MC, V. **Amenities:** Restaurant (American); lounge; indoor heated pool; outdoor heated pool; fitness center; spa; bike rentals; concierge; business center; dry cleaning. *In room:* A/C, cable TV w/pay movies, high-speed wireless Internet, coffeemaker, hair dryer, iron, safe.

EXPENSIVE

The Alps ★★ *Finds*   A stage stop in the late 1800s, this historic log lodge sits on a mountainside about 7 minutes west of downtown Boulder. Converted into a beautiful bed-and-breakfast decorated with Arts and Crafts and Mission furnishing by owners Jeannine and John Vanderhart, the Alps is ideal for travelers planning to split time between Boulder and its outlying wilderness and scenery. Each room here is different and named after a Colorado mining town, including Magnolia, Solina, and Wall Street. All have functional fireplaces with Victorian mantels, queen beds with down comforters, and individual thermostats. Most are spacious, with a claw-foot or double whirlpool tub plus a double shower, and many have private porches. Shared spaces include a beautiful lounge with a huge rock fireplace and VCR, plus delightful gardens and patio areas. The entrance is the original log cabin built in the 1870s. Smoking is not permitted.

38619 Boulder Canyon Dr., Boulder, CO 80302. © **800/414-2577** or 303/444-5445. Fax 303/444-5522. www.alpsinn.com. 12 units. $139–$225 double. Rates include full breakfast. AE, DC, DISC, MC, V. **Amenities:** Jacuzzi; concierge; activities desk; in-room massage. *In room:* A/C, TV, dataport, hair dryer, iron.

Boulder Marriott ★   Until the St. Julien came along, the Marriott was the newest full-service hotel in the city. It is conveniently located just a block off 28th Street (U.S. 36), providing great access to everything in town. Furnished with Southwestern touches, the rooms are geared to the business traveler, with multi-line phones, large work desks, and ergonomic chairs. Local and toll-free calls cost $1. Half of the rooms are on two concierge levels, which have a private lounge; rates include continental breakfast, happy hour, and hors d'oeuvres. Three-quarters of the rooms feature mountain views.

2660 Canyon Blvd., Boulder, CO 80302 (1 block west of Canyon and 28th St.). © **303/440-8877.** Fax 303/440-3377. www.marriott.com/DENBO. 155 units. $109–$209 double; $139–$239 suite. AE, DC, DISC, MC, V. Free valet and self-parking. **Amenities:** Restaurant (steakhouse); lounge; indoor heated pool; exercise room; spa; Jacuzzi; 24-hr. business center; shopping arcade; limited room service; massage; laundry service; dry cleaning; executive level. *In room:* A/C, cable TV w/pay movies, dataport, coffeemaker, hair dryer, iron, safe.

Briar Rose ★★   A country-style brick home built in the 1890s, this midcity bed-and-breakfast might remind you of Grandma's place. Every room is furnished with antiques, from the bedrooms to the parlor to the sunny back porch, and the lovely gardens offer a quiet escape. Several rooms have business amenities, such as modem hookups, large worktables, and super lighting. A fax/copy machine is also available.

Two of the six units in the main house have fireplaces; four in a separate cottage come with either a patio or a balcony. All are furnished with feather comforters. The suite, designed for extended executive stays, is also popular with families. It can sleep four, and features a full kitchen and dining room. Weekly and monthly rates are available.

The continental breakfast is gourmet quality: yogurt, homemade granola, fresh nut breads, yogurt with fruit, and much more. Refreshments are available in the lobby from 8am to 9pm. Smoking is permitted only in the outside garden areas.

2151 Arapahoe Ave., Boulder, CO 80302. © **303/442-3007.** Fax 303/786-8440. www.briarrosebb.com. 10 units (6 with shower only). May–Oct $134–$164 double, $199 suite; Nov–Apr $149–$164 double, $129–$199 suite. Rates include continental breakfast. AE, DC, MC, V. *In room:* A/C, dataport.

Hotel Boulderado ★★   Opened on January 1, 1909, this elegant and historic hotel still has the same Otis elevator that wowed visiting dignitaries that day. The colorful leaded-glass ceiling and cantilevered cherrywood staircase are other reminders of days past, along with the rich woodwork of the balusters around the mezzanine and the handsome armchairs and settees in the main-floor lobby. The hotel's Christmas tree, a 35-footer with 1,000 white lights, is a Boulder tradition, and the setting for afternoon tea on the mezzanine in December.

Five stories tall and just a block off the Pearl Street Mall, this contemporary of Denver's Brown Palace has 42 original guest rooms, all bright and cozy, and each a little bit different. Although the rooms are continuously renovated and refurbished, they retain a Victorian flavor, with lush floral wallpapering, candlewick-knit spreads, and furnishings alternately stately and plush. The construction of a spacious North Wing in 1989 almost quadrupled the number of rooms; while these are larger and more typical of a modern hotel, they also embody the early-20th-century theme. All units have a few high-tech touches: electronic locks and two-line phones with voice mail; some rooms have refrigerators, and a few have jetted tubs.

2115 13th St. (at Spruce St.), Boulder, CO 80302. © **800/433-4344** or 303/442-4344. Fax 303/442-4378. www.boulderado.com. 160 units. $185–$215 double; $275–$325 suite. AE, DC, DISC, MC, V. **Amenities:** 2 restaurants (contemporary American, see "Where to Dine," below); 2 lounges; access to nearby health club; business center; laundry service. *In room:* A/C, cable TV, dataport, high-speed Internet access, coffeemaker, hair dryer, iron.

Millennium Harvest House *Kids*   The Harvest House is exceptional: a full-service hotel with spacious and lovely grounds. Located on the west side of U.S. 36 on the south side of Boulder, the former Regal Harvest House looks like

---

Kids Family-Friendly Hotels

Millennium Harvest House (p. 139)   A good place to stay with the kids, especially in the summer. The Harvest House has a nice swimming pool and lots of nearby green space; it's also next to the Boulder Creek Path and within walking distance of the Crossroads Mall.

Foot of the Mountain Motel (p. 141)   There's lots of space here where the kids can expend their energy. Across the street is a lovely park with a playground, as well as the Boulder Creek Path.

Boulder Outlook (see below)   At this former "Holidome," kids can use the pool and play inside even when the weather is bad, and the diversions are many (bouldering rocks, game room, dog park).

---

almost any other four-story hotel from the front—but its backyard melts into a park that surrounds the east end of the 10-mile Boulder Creek Path (see "Attractions," later in this chapter), where bike rentals are available.

All rooms hold one king-size or two double beds, a lounge chair and ottoman, remote-control cable TV, and direct-dial phone. Spacious VIP Tower accommodations provide upgraded amenities such as hair dryers and bathrobes, and some rooms have high-speed Internet access. Rates for these units include continental breakfast and evening hors d'oeuvres in the Millennium Club Lounge. Our favorite rooms here are the two dozen that look out on the Boulder Creek Path.

1345 28th St., Boulder, CO 80302. © 800/545-6285 or 303/443-3850. Fax 303/443-1480. www.millennium hotels.com. 268 units. $129–$145 double; $175–$395 suite. AE, DC, DISC, MC, V. **Amenities:** Restaurant (American); 2 lounges; indoor lap pool; outdoor heated swimming pool; 15 tennis courts (5 indoor); fitness center; 2 Jacuzzis (indoor and outdoor); bike rental; game room; airport shuttle; business center; limited room service; on-call masseur; valet and self-service laundry; executive level. *In room:* A/C, cable TV w/pay movies, coffeemaker, hair dryer, iron.

MODERATE

Boulder Outlook ★★ *Kids* *Value*   The proprietors of this former Ramada and Holidome have outdone every chain motel in town. The Outlook is fun, fresh, and definitively Boulder, with such unique perks as two bouldering rocks (one is 11 ft. high, the other 4 ft.), a fenced, 4,000 square foot dog run, and discounts on bike rentals and other activities. The brightly painted motel has 40 rooms which have an outdoor entrance; the rest are accessed indoors. Overall, the rooms are larger than average and contemporary; the baths nicely tiled. In-room recycling containers and all-natural bath amenities are two more distinctly Boulder touches. The indoor pool is superb, complete with a waterfall and a mural of a cloud-speckled sky, and the bar and grill here features bluegrass on Fridays.

800 28th St., Boulder, CO 80303. © 800/542-0304 or 303/443-3322. Fax 303/449-5130. www.boulder outlook.com. 162 units. $89–99 double; lower rates off season. Rates include continental breakfast. AE, DC, DISC, MC, V. Pets accepted, $10/night. **Amenities:** Restaurant (American); lounge; indoor heated pool; exercise room; Jacuzzi; men's and women's saunas; game room; activities desk; 24-hr. business center; limited room service, massage; coin-op washers and dryers; dry cleaning, executive level. *In room:* A/C, cable TV, dataport, coffeemaker, hair dryer, iron, safe.

Colorado Chautauqua Association ★ *Finds*   During the late 19th and early 20th centuries, more than 400 Chautauquas—adult education and cultural entertainment centers—sprang up around the United States. This 26-acre park, at the foot of the Flatiron Mountains, is one of the few remaining. In summer, it hosts a wide-ranging arts program, including the Colorado Music Festival (see "Boulder After Dark," later in this chapter).

Lodging is in attractive cottages and in rooms and apartments in two historic lodges. All units were outfitted with new furnishings in 2003 and come with linens and towels. They have balconies or porches, and either private or shared kitchens. Cottages range from efficiencies to three-bedroom, two-bathroom units. Larger groups might take the newly restored Mission House, which has eight bedrooms, a kitchen, and a screened-in porch and rents for $967 a night. From September to May, many cottages and apartments are rented by the month or longer, but nightly accommodations are generally available.

Guests have access to the park's playgrounds, picnic grounds, and hiking trailheads. The historic Chautauqua Dining Hall, which opened on July 4th, 1898, serves three moderately priced meals a day year-round.

900 Baseline Rd. (at 9th St.), Boulder, CO 80302. ℂ 303/442-3282, ext. 11 for lodging, 303/440-3776 for restaurant. Fax 303/449-0790. www.chautauqua.com. 87 units. $69–$114 lodge room; $89–$104 efficiency cottage; $114–$124 1-bedroom cottage; $129–$169 2- or 3-bedroom cottage. MC, V. Bus: 203. Pets accepted in cottages for a nonrefundable $100 fee. Pets not accepted in lodges. **Amenities:** Restaurant (creative American); 4 tennis courts; children's programs during summer; self-service laundry. *In room:* Kitchen, coffeemaker, no phone.

Foot of the Mountain Motel *(Kids)* *(Value)* This motel, a series of connected, cabin-style units with bright red trim near the east gate of Boulder Canyon, dates from 1930 but has been fully modernized. The location is inspiring, on the west edge of town where city meets mountains, and right across the street is the top end of the Boulder Creek Path and the trailhead that leads to the summit of Flagstaff Mountain. The pleasant pine-walled cabins are furnished with queen or double beds and individual water heaters; two suites (converted manager's quarters) are big enough for families and outfitted with full kitchens.

200 Arapahoe Ave., Boulder, CO 80302. ℂ 866/773-5489 or 303/442-5688. www.footofthemountainmotel. com. 20 units (2 with shower only), including 2 suites. $85 double; $165–$175 suite. AE, DISC, MC, V. Pets accepted for $5 nightly fee and a $50 refundable deposit. *In room:* Cable TV, kitchen, fridge.

INEXPENSIVE

Boulder International Hostel *(Value)* As at most hostels, guests come here expecting to share—and they do. The toilets, showers, kitchen, laundry, and TV room are communal. Individual phones can be arranged for private rooms (with a deposit), but others share a phone. Just 2 blocks from the University of Colorado campus, the hostel is open for registration daily from 8am to 11pm. To stay in a bunk, you must present identification proving you are not a resident of Colorado.

1107 12th St., Boulder, CO 80302-7029. ℂ 888/442-0522 or 303/442-0522. Fax 303/442-0523. 50 units. $17 dorm bed; $35–$45 private unit. AE, DISC, MC, V. *In room:* No phone.

4 Where to Dine

Partly because Boulder is a young, hip community, it has attracted a variety of small, with-it restaurants. At these chef-owned and -operated establishments, innovative and often-changing cuisine is the rule. You'll find a lot of California influences here, as well as a number of top-notch chefs doing their own thing.

A Boulder city ordinance prohibits smoking inside restaurants.

VERY EXPENSIVE

Flagstaff House Restaurant ★★★ *(Moments)* NEW AMERICAN/ REGIONAL   Named for its perch on Flagstaff Mountain, this restaurant attracts patrons from across the state and nation with excellent cuisine and service, and the spectacular nighttime view of the lights of Boulder spread out 1,000 feet below. A local institution since 1951, this family-owned and -operated restaurant has an elegant, candlelit dining room with glass walls that maximize the view. The prices aren't for the budget-minded, but those seeking a romantic setting and superlative food can't miss with the Flagstaff House.

The menu, which changes daily, offers an excellent selection of seafood and Rocky Mountain game, all prepared with a creative flair. Typical appetizers include smoked rabbit or duck, oysters, wild mushrooms, and cheeses. Entrees, many of which are seasonal, might include Colorado buffalo, ahi tuna, Canadian halibut, and soft-shell crabs. The restaurant also boasts dessert soufflés, a world-renowned wine cellar (at, 20,000 bottles, undoubtedly the best in Colorado), and an impressive selection of after-dinner drinks.

1138 Flagstaff Rd. (west up Baseline Rd.). (ℂ) 303/442-4640. Reservations recommended. Main courses $25–$60. AE, DC, MC, V. Sun–Fri 6–10pm; Sat 5–10pm.

EXPENSIVE

John's Restaurant ★★★ *(Finds)* CONTINENTAL/MEDITERRANEAN This funky but elegant converted house has set the pace for the Boulder dining scene for nearly 30 years. The emphasis here is squarely on the food. Chef-owner Corey Buck (who bought the place from founder John Bizzarro in 2003) starts with the classic cuisine of southern Europe, but adds his own creative signature spin to each dish; compared to Bizzarro, Buck prepares bigger plates and is more fond of game dishes. For starters, apple Stilton pecan salad and ricotta-and-spinach gnocchi verde set the stage for the continually changing main-course offerings. Menu mainstays include filet mignon with Stilton ale sauce, surrounded by grilled Bermuda onions; chile-crusted pork tenderloin with cranberry-orange sauce; and a variety of fresh seafood dishes—chowder and several succulent plates featuring plump Gulf shrimp are always available. The menu also includes vegetarian items, and the homemade desserts (still by John's daughter Stella) include caramel cheesecake that verges on transcendental. There's a full bar as well.

2328 Pearl St. (ℂ) 303/444-5232. Reservations recommended. Main courses $19–$35. AE, DISC, MC, V. Tues–Sat from 5:30pm.

Q's Restaurant ★★ CONTEMPORARY AMERICAN   The historic ambience that makes the Hotel Boulderado such a delightful place to stay also makes its way into Q's, the hotel's main restaurant. The dining room combines the old—rich polished wood and stained glass—with the comfortable, casually elegant feel of today. Of course, the important thing is the food, and chef-owner John Platt does an excellent job, using locally grown organic vegetables whenever possible.

Platt, who claims seafood as his specialty after years on Cape Cod, always includes several fresh fish selections on the menu, such as grilled ahi tuna served with potato-leek purée with roasted cauliflower, apple-smoked bacon, and a sweet pepper salad. Rotisseried meats often include allspice-cured pork loin served with shoestring onions, whipped potatoes, and BBQ jus. You'll also likely find several pasta dishes, roasted chicken and quail, venison, and beef.

In the Hotel Boulderado, 2115 13th St. (at Spruce St.). © **303/442-4880**. Reservations recommended. Main courses $5–$10 breakfast, $8–$16 lunch, $16–$27 dinner. AE, DC, DISC, MC, V. Mon–Fri 6:30–11am and 11:30am–2pm; Sat–Sun 7am–2pm; daily 5–10pm.

Sushi Zanmai ⭐ *(Kids)* SUSHI/JAPANESE   Boulder is a hot spot for great sushi: Zanmai is a go-to stalwart but faces stiff competition from a number of like-minded upstarts. We still prefer the place for its festive atmosphere, impeccable service, and traditional sushi. Prepared while you watch—at the sushi bar or table-side—the options include everything from tuna and trout to sea urchin and octopus, with such exotic rolls as Colorado (raw filet mignon), Z-No. 9 (shrimp tempura, avocado, salmon, and eel sauce), and LSD (lettuce shrimp deluxe). There are lunch specials as well as sushi happy-hour specials during lunch and dinner. Karaoke sing-along takes place every Saturday from 10pm to midnight.

1221 Spruce St. (at Broadway). © **303/440-0733**. Reservations recommended for groups of 4 or more. Main courses $7.50–$13 lunch, $15–$26 dinner; sushi rolls $2–$12. AE, DC, MC, V. Mon–Fri 11:30am–2pm; Sun–Fri 5–10pm; Sat 5pm–midnight.

MODERATE

Boulder Dushanbe Teahouse ⭐⭐ *(Finds)* ETHNIC WORLD CUISINE   In 1990, 200 crates were shipped to Colorado as a gift from Dushanbe, Tajikistan, Boulder's sister city. From the ornately hand-carved and painted pieces of a Persian teahouse in the crates, the building was assembled at its present site with help from four Tajik artisans. It's the only teahouse of its kind in the Western Hemisphere. Lavishly and authentically decorated, the teahouse holds 14 pillars carved from Siberian cedar, and a grand central fountain. The cuisine includes traditional ethnic dishes from the Middle East, Asia, and elsewhere, including several noodle and vegetarian options. There are even a few Tajik specialties, often a lamb dish. Pastries, coffees, and more than 70 teas are also available. There is a full bar on-site as well.

1770 13th St. © **303/442-4993**. Main courses $6–$13 lunch, $8–$18 dinner. AE, DISC, MC, V. Mon–Fri 8am–10:30am and 11am–3pm; Sat–Sun 8am–3pm; daily 5–10pm. Tea and coffee bar daily 8am–10pm.

Brasserie Ten Ten ⭐⭐ FRENCH BISTRO   From the same folks who brought you The Med across the street, Brasserie Ten Ten is a more than respectable sequel. The breezy bistro, done up with frosted glass, brick walls, and a handsome marble bar, serves delectable oysters (both raw and Rockefeller are quite good) for starters, and some well thought out variations on French standbys, such as a scrumptious lamb shank braised with burgundy and poblano pepper and a nice skirt steak with *pommes frites* (yep, french fries). We recommend the brique de poulet, a salt- and rosemary-crusted chicken cooked with the help of a perfectly shaped stone. The duck breast salad is excellent, as are the baked

(Kids) **Family-Friendly Restaurants**

Sushi Zanmai (see above)   Flashing knives and table-side cooking keep kids fully entertained.

Turley's (p. 146)   Breakfast is served all day, plus there are fresh-squeezed juices, soups, salads, interesting entrees, burgers, and sandwiches. There's a great kids' menu and a sunny, social atmosphere.

goods and the desserts, both made in-house at a bakery that also supplies The Med.

1011 Walnut St. ℂ **303/998-1010.** Reservations accepted. Main courses $5–$11 brunch, $5–$11 lunch, $9–$27 dinner. AE, DC, DISC, MC, V. Mon–Wed 11am–10pm; Thurs–Fri 11am–11pm; Sat 9am–11pm; Sun brunch 9am–3pm.

14th Street Bar & Grill ✦ CONTEMPORARY AMERICAN   An open restaurant with large windows facing the street, this is a great spot for people-watching as well as dining. The open wood grill and pizza oven, the long, crowded full-service bar, and a changing display of abstract art let you know that this is a fun place. The menu centers around what chef-owner Kathy Andrade calls "American grill" cuisine, which includes grilled sandwiches, Southwestern chicken salads, and unusual homemade pizzas, such as a pie topped with chorizo sausage, garlic, and roasted green chiles. A variety of pasta dishes are also offered, plus changing dinner specials such as beef tenderloin stuffed with cheese and cilantro.

1400 Pearl St. (at 14th St.). ℂ **303/444-5854.** Main courses $9–$22. AE, MC, V. Daily 11:30am–10pm.

Jax Fish House ✦ SEAFOOD   Fresh seafood is flown in daily from the East and West coasts to supply this restaurant, a lively space with colored chalk graffiti and oceanic art on its brick walls, social patrons, and a booming stereo system. At patio, bar, and table seating, you can order one of the house specialties—the Mississippi catfish skillet is a good bet—or simply slurp down raw oysters and martinis to your heart's content. Entrees usually include shrimp, New Zealand bluenose, Rocky Mountain trout, and ahi tuna, along with lobster and soft-shell crab when available. Or try a smoked salmon carpaccio or clam, rock shrimp, catfish, or calamari po' boy, with slaw and your choice of a side. Those who prefer beef can choose from New York strip steak and all-natural burgers.

928 Pearl St. (1 block west of the mall). ℂ **303/444-1811.** Main courses $8–$24. AE, DC, MC, V. Mon–Thurs 4–10pm; Fri–Sat 4–11pm; Sun 4–9pm.

The Mediterranean ✦ (Value) MEDITERRANEAN/TAPAS   Known as "The Med," this local favorite is designed as an homage to the casual eateries of Spain and Italy. With a multihued tile interior and an enjoyable breezy patio, the Med draws a bustling after-work drinking crowd for its weekday tapas hour (3–6:30pm), which includes such delicacies as fried artichoke hearts, risotto-and-crab fritters, and hummus for very reasonable prices. (A few shared tapas can prove a fairly satisfying meal for two or three people.) For a full dinner, the selection is extensive, ranging from pasta to poultry, steaks to gourmet wood-fired pizzas, with several vegetarian dishes to please the health-conscious Boulder crowd. Our favorite: the delectable *paellas,* traditional Spanish rice dishes that come in five varieties. The lunch menu is similar, with a nice selection of panini sandwiches (including lamb, salmon, and vegetarian). There are also several daily specials.

1002 Walnut St. ℂ **303/444-5335.** Main courses $7–$13 lunch, $9–$19 dinner; most tapas $3–$5. AE, DC, DISC, MC, V. Mon–Wed 11am–10pm; Thurs–Sat 11am–11pm; Sun 4–10pm.

Rhumba ✦ SEAFOOD   A loud and lively Caribbean cafe, Rhumba has earned a loyal following since it opened in 1999. With a curved bar that abuts a popular patio and plenty of plants, sun, and original art, this hip eatery dishes out plates of jerked pork and chicken, noodle bowls, and curried dishes, served with such sides as black beans, sweet potato hash browns, and grilled flatbread. More exotic offerings include the seviche of the day, conch chowder, and seared calamari. Even the cheeseburgers have an island flavor when doused with Rhumba's banana-guava ketchup. There is spice aplenty for fiery-foods fanatics, but there are also plenty of dishes that won't set meeker mouths afire. The cocktail of choice is the mojito: silver rum, fresh mint and lime, sugar, and soda water. There is live music (reggae, Latin, jazz, and funk) on a regular basis.

950 Pearl St. © 303/442-7771. Main courses $10–$19. AE, DC, MC, V. Mon–Thurs 4–10pm; Fri 11:30am–10pm; Sat–Sun 1–10pm.

Sunflower ★★ *Finds* CONTEMPORARY/ORGANIC   This pleasant contemporary eatery, eclectically decorated with murals, rotating local art, and a flagstone floor, touts itself as "Boulder's most unique restaurant," based on its dedication to healthy cuisine. The ingredients include certified organic produce and free-range, hormone-free poultry and game. Owner-chef Jon Pell takes a multicultural approach: Sunflower features a diverse selection of dinner entrees, including grilled ahi tuna served with a coconut-lemongrass infusion; seared elk tenderloin with raspberry-vermouth coulis; and tempeh scallopini with wine, lemon, and fresh herbs. Lunch includes fresh variations on sandwiches—such as a blackened salmon burger—as well as specialties like pad Thai and penne pomodoro. An all-you-can-eat organic salad buffet is served daily until 4pm, and there's a popular weekend brunch.

1701 Pearl St. (2 blocks east of the mall). © 303/440-0220. Main courses $7–$12 lunch, $13–$26 dinner. AE, MC, V. Tues–Fri 11am–2:30pm; Sat–Sun brunch 10am–3pm; dinner Tues–Sun 5–10pm.

INEXPENSIVE

In addition to the choices below, try a slice of Boulder's best New York–style pie at any **Abo's Pizza** location: 1110 13th St. (© **303/443-3199**), 1911 Broadway (© **303/443-9113**), 2761 Iris Ave. (© **303/443-1921**), and 637 S. Broadway (© **303/494-1274**). Another Boulder mainstay, for plump, tasty bagels, strong coffee, and trademark Boulder vibe, is **Moe's Broadway Bagel,** with locations at 2650 Broadway (© **303/442-3252**) and 3075 Arapahoe Ave. (© **303/442-4427**).

Corner Bar ★ CONTEMPORARY AMERICAN   With the same chef as the highly rated Q's Restaurant (see above), the Hotel Boulderado's Corner Bar is far above your average sandwich shop, although sandwiches and burgers are on the menu, too. Here you can savor a grilled-salmon sandwich, served with red-onion marmalade, spinach, and horseradish aioli. Or you might try a roast turkey BLT with herbed mayo, or pan-roasted halibut with avocado, tomato, orange, and a black-bean cake. Those not in search of a full meal can opt for an appetizer, such as Chesapeake Bay oysters baked with spinach, calamari, or Boulderado nachos.

In the Hotel Boulderado, 2115 13th St. (at Spruce St.). © 303/442-4560. Main courses $7–$14. AE, DC, DISC, MC, V. Daily 11am–midnight.

Illegal Pete's *Value* MEXICAN   Located at the far east end of the Pearl Street Mall, Illegal Pete's is renowned locally for its creative, healthy burritos, packed with chicken, steak, veggies, or fish. The menu also includes a similar range of tacos, as well as salads, quesadillas, and chili. Margaritas and domestic and Mexican beers are available, as are takeout and delivery.

1447 Pearl St. © 303/440-3955. Menu items $4–$6. AE, DISC, MC, V. Sun–Thurs 11am–10pm; Fri–Sat 11am–2:30am.

Rio Grande MEXICAN   This popular neighborhood restaurant and bar, just south of the Pearl Street Mall, is probably best known for its huge, award-winning margaritas—so potent that the staff enforces a strict limit of three.

Frequented by college students and Boulder's under-30 crowd, the Rio is bustling for reasons beyond its alcoholic concoctions—the loud, social atmosphere and the food, a good variety of oversize Mexican entrees and combos. Our favorites are hearty fajitas (steak or veggie, with handmade tortillas), zesty Yucatan shrimp, and creative chiles rellenos.

1101 Walnut St. © 303/444-3690. Meals $6–$14. AE, MC, V. Mon–Thurs 11am–2pm; Mon–Wed 5–10pm; Thurs 5–10:30pm; Fri–Sun 11am–10:30pm.

Sherpa's ★ *Finds* TIBETAN/NEPALI   Owned by Pemba Sherpa—a native of Nepal who in fact is a sherpa, or Himalayan mountain guide—Sherpa's is located in a converted Victorian house just southwest of the Pearl Street Mall. Decorated with Himalayan relics and photography of the peaks of Nepal and Tibet, the restaurant serves up food to match: Tibetan dishes like *thupka* (noodle bowls) and sherpa stew as well as spicier Nepali and Indian cuisine, including saag (creamed spinach with garlic, cumin, ginger, and your choice of veggie or meat) and curry dishes. There are lunch specials daily, as well as a comfortable bar with a library full of climbing tomes.

825 Walnut St. © 303/440-7151. Reservations accepted. Main courses $5–$9 lunch, $6–$13 dinner. AE, DISC, MC, V. Daily 11am–3pm; Sun–Thurs 5–9:30pm; Fri–Sat 5–10pm.

Tom's Tavern ★ AMERICAN   Boulder's most popular place for a good hamburger, Tom's has been a neighborhood institution owned by local politician Tom Eldridge for almost 40 years. Located in an early-20th-century building that once housed an undertaker, the tavern has vinyl-upholstered booths and patio seating. Besides the ⅓-pound burgers (made from all-organic Coleman beef) and other sandwiches, you can get a 10-ounce steak, fried chicken, or a veggie burger, not to mention a variety of BBQ plates. Tom's serves dinner anytime.

1047 Pearl St. © 303/443-3893. Menu items $6–$12. AE, DC, DISC, MC, V. Mon–Thurs 10am–10pm; Fri–Sat 10am–11pm; Sun 12:30–8:30pm.

Turley's *Kids* AMERICAN   A feel-good family restaurant with a healthier menu than the norm, Turley's is a Boulder landmark. Its sunny atmosphere and friendly staff provide a pleasant, homey backdrop for any meal, and breakfast is served all day. The bars serve everything from wheat grass juice to martinis. A menu featuring omelets, burgers, sandwiches, fresh fish, and dinner entrees ranging from buffalo meatloaf to tofu scramble ensures that everyone's tastes will be satisfied. Turley's moved from its longtime Arapahoe Avenue location to Pearl Street in March 2004.

2805 Pearl St. (at 28th St.) © 303/442-2800. Most menu items $4–$15. AE, DC, DISC, MC, V. Mon–Sat 6:30am–10pm; Sun 7am–9pm.

ESPRESSO BARS, COFFEEHOUSES & RELATED ESTABLISHMENTS

Espresso fans will have no problem finding a decent espresso, cappuccino, or latte: Boulder has a number of **Starbucks** establishments, as well as many more interesting independent coffeehouses. Many of the independents, located near the Pearl Street Mall, provide outdoor seating in nice weather. Attached to the Boulder Book Store, the **Bookend Cafe,** 1115 Pearl St. (© **303/440-6699**), offers a variety of coffee drinks and a delightful array of baked goods, soups, and pies. At the east end of the mall (at 18th St.) is the somewhat bohemian **Penny Lane** (© **303/443-9516**), a gathering place for talking, playing chess, or reading while you sip regular coffee, espresso, cappuccino, or a latte, and munch on a bagel or muffin. There's a wide variety of newspapers and nightly live entertainment, including poetry, an open stage, and a diverse range of music by local and regional performers. See also "Boulder After Dark," later in this chapter. **Trident Booksellers & Café,** 940 Pearl St. (© **303/443-3133**), features indoor and outdoor seating as well as a comprehensive selection of used books. The **Boulder Dushanbe Teahouse,** 1770 13th St. (© **303/442-4993;** p. 143), offers an authentic Persian setting for quaffing more than 70 varieties of tea and a good selection of coffees from 8am to 10pm daily. Homemade baked goods are also available.

5 Attractions

THE TOP ATTRACTIONS

Boulder Creek Path ⭐⭐ *Kids*   Following Boulder Creek, this nature corridor provides about a 16-mile-long oasis and recreation area through the city and west into the mountains. With no street crossings (there are bridges and underpasses instead), the path is popular with Boulder residents, especially on weekends, when you'll see numerous walkers, runners, bicyclists, and in-line skaters. (Walkers should stay to the right; the left lane is for faster traffic.) The path links the CU campus, several city parks, and office buildings. Near the east end, watch for deer, prairie-dog colonies, and wetlands, where some 150 species of birds have been spotted. You might see Canada geese, mallard ducks, spotted sandpipers, owls, and woodpeckers.

At 30th Street, south of Arapahoe Road, the path cuts through **Scott Carpenter Park** (named for the astronaut and Colorado native), where you can enjoy swimming in summer and sledding in winter. Just west of Scott Carpenter Park, you'll find **Boulder Creek Stream Observatory,** which is adjacent to and maintained by the Millennium Harvest House (see "Where to Stay," earlier in this chapter). In addition to observing trout and other aquatic wildlife, you're invited to feed the fish with trout food purchased from a vending machine (25¢). **Central Park,** at Broadway and Canyon Boulevard, preserves some of Boulder's history with a restored steam locomotive. The **Boulder Public Library** is also in this area.

Traveling west, watch for the **Charles A. Heartling Sculpture Garden** (with the stone image of local Indian chief Niwot) and the **Kids' Fishing Ponds;** the Boulder Fish and Game Club stocks the ponds, which are open only to children under 12, who can fish for free and keep what they catch. Near 3rd Street and Canyon Boulevard, you'll find the **Xeriscape Garden,** where drought-tolerant plants are tested for reduced water intake.

The **Eben G. Fine Park** is named for the Boulder pharmacist who discovered Arapaho Glacier on nearby Arapaho Peak. To the west, **Red Rocks Settlers' Park** marks the beginning of the **Boulder Canyon Pioneer Trail,** which leads to a continuation of Boulder Creek Path. The park is named for Missouri goldseekers who camped at this spot in 1858 and later found gold about 12 miles farther west. Watch for explanatory signs along the 1¼-mile path. The **Whitewater Kayak Course** has 20 slalom gates for kayakers and canoeists to use free; to the west, **Elephant Buttresses** is one of Boulder's more popular rock-climbing areas. The path ends at **Four Mile Canyon,** the old town site of Orodell.

Note: Although the path is generally well populated and quite safe, Boulderites warn against using it late at night if you are alone; one of the problems is the number of transients who take refuge there.

Boulder Attractions

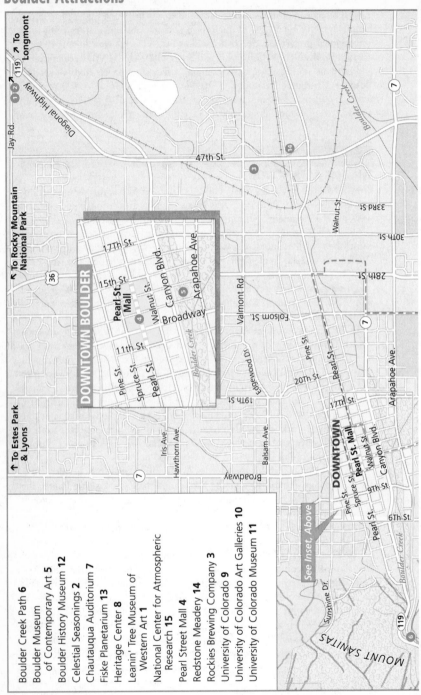

Boulder Creek Path **6**
Boulder Museum
of Contemporary Art **5**
Boulder History Museum **12**
Celestial Seasonings **2**
Chautauqua Auditorium **7**
Fiske Planetarium **13**
Heritage Center **8**
Leanin' Tree Museum of
Western Art **1**
National Center for Atmospheric
Research **15**
Pearl Street Mall **4**
Redstone Meadery **14**
Rockies Brewing Company **3**
University of Colorado **9**
University of Colorado Art Galleries **10**
University of Colorado Museum **11**

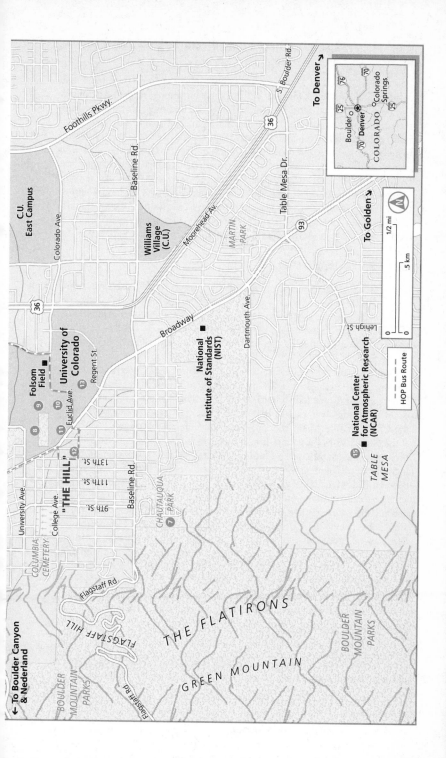

55th St. and Pearl Pkwy., to the mouth of Boulder Canyon. © 303/413-7200. Free admission. Daily 24 hr. Bus: HOP.

Pearl Street Mall ★★ *Kids*   This 4-block-long tree-lined pedestrian mall marks Boulder's downtown core and its center for dining, shopping, strolling, and people-watching. Musicians, mimes, jugglers, and other street entertainers hold court on the landscaped mall day and night, year-round. Buy your lunch from one of the many vendors and sprawl on the grass in front of the courthouse to relax and eat. Locally owned businesses and galleries share the mall with trendy boutiques, sidewalk cafes, and major chains including Peppercorn, Banana Republic, and Abercrombie & Fitch. There's a wonderful play area for youngsters, with climbable boulders set in gravel. Don't miss the bronze bust of Chief Niwot (of the southern Arapaho) in front of the Boulder County Courthouse between 13th and 14th streets. Niwot, who welcomed the first Boulder settlers, was killed in southeastern Colorado during the Sand Creek Massacre of 1864.

Pearl St. from 11th to 15th sts. Bus: HOP.

University of Colorado ★   The largest university in the state, with nearly 29,000 students (including about 4,600 graduate students), "CU" dominates the city. Its student population, cultural and sports events, and intellectual atmosphere have helped shape Boulder into the city it is today. The school boasts 16 alumni astronauts who have flown in space and three Nobel laureates on the faculty.

Old Main, on the Norlin Quadrangle, was the first building erected after the university was established in 1876; at that time, it housed the entire school. Later, pink-sandstone Italian Renaissance–style buildings came to dominate the campus. Visitors may want to take in the university's **Heritage Center,** on the third floor of Old Main; the **University of Colorado Museum** (see "More Attractions," below), a natural-history museum in the Henderson Building on Broadway; the **Mary Rippon Outdoor Theatre,** behind the Henderson Building, site of the annual Colorado Shakespeare Festival; **Fiske Planetarium,** between Kittredge Loop Drive and Regent Drive on the south side of campus; and the **Norlin Library,** on the Norlin Quadrangle, the largest research library in the state, with extensive holdings of American and English literature. Other attractions include the CU Art Museum, University Memorial Center (the student center), and the Integrated Teaching and Learning Laboratory in the College of Engineering. Prospective students and their parents can arrange campus tours by contacting the admissions office (© 303/492-6301).

Tours are available weekdays at the **Laboratory for Atmospheric and Space Physics** (© 303/492-6412), on the east campus, with at least 1 week's advance notice. The **Sommers-Bausch Observatory** (© 303/492-6732 during the day, 303/492-2020 at night) offers tours and Friday-evening open houses. Among the telescopes there are 16-, 18-, and 24-inch Cassegrain reflectors and a 10-inch aperture heliostat.

East side of Broadway, between Arapahoe Ave. and Baseline Rd. © 303/492-1411. www.colorado.edu. Bus: HOP, SKIP, STAMPEDE, and Denver buses.

National Center for Atmospheric Research ★ *Finds*   Inspired by the cliff dwellings at Mesa Verde National Park, I. M. Pei designed this striking pink-sandstone building, which overlooks Boulder from high atop Table Mesa in the southwestern foothills. (You might recognize the center from Woody Allen's *Sleeper;* scenes were shot here.) Scientists study such phenomena as the

---

Impressions

If heaven has a college town, it's probably as beautiful as Boulder.

—*Sunset Magazine*

---

greenhouse effect, wind shear, and ozone depletion to gain a better understanding of the earth's atmosphere. Among the technological tools on display are satellites, weather balloons, interactive computer monitors, robots, and supercomputers that can simulate the world's climate. There are also hands-on, weather-oriented exhibits from the San Francisco Exploratorium Museum, now on permanent display. The **Walter Orr Roberts Weather Trail** outside the building's west doors takes visitors on a 0.4-mile, wheelchair-accessible loop along a path with interpretive signs describing various aspects of weather and climate plus the plants and animals of the area. The center also houses a changing art exhibit and a science-oriented gift shop. Allow 1 to 2 hours.

1850 Table Mesa Dr. ℂ 303/497-1174. www.ncar.ucar.edu. Free admission. Self-guided tours daily 8am–5pm; holidays 9am–4pm. 1-hr. guided tours daily at noon; there is also a self-guided audio tour. Take Broadway heading southwest out of town to Table Mesa Dr., and follow it west to the center.

MORE ATTRACTIONS
INDUSTRIAL TOURS
Beyond the attractions listed below, the **Boulder Creek Winery,** 6440 Odell Place (ℂ **303/516-9031;** www.bouldercreekwine.com) offers a complimentary tasting on Fridays through Sundays from noon to 5pm.

Celestial Seasonings 🅡 *Value*   The nation's leading producer of herbal teas, housed in a modern building in northeastern Boulder, offers tours that are an experience for the senses. The company, which began in a Boulder garage in the 1970s, now produces more than 50 varieties of tea from more than 75 different herbs and spices imported from 35 foreign countries. You'll understand why the company invites you to "see, taste, and smell the world of Celestial Seasonings" as you move from a consumer taste test in the lobby to marketing displays, and finally into the production plant where 9 million tea bags roll off the line daily. The overpowering "Mint Room" is a highlight. The tour lasts about 45 minutes, and there is a cafe on-site.

4600 Sleepytime Dr. ℂ 303/581-1202. www.celestialseasonings.com. Free admission. Mon–Sat 10am–3pm; Sun 11am–3pm; tours on the hour. Reservations required for groups of 8 or more. Exit Colo. 119, Longmont Diagonal, at Jay Rd. and go east to Spine, then north on Spine. Bus: J.

Redstone Meadery 🅡 *Finds*   Drunk by Beowulf and Shakespeare, mead is the original fermented beverage. There are about 60 active meaderies in the United States, including this standout in Boulder. Founded by David Myers in 2000, the meadery crafts several beverages (ranging from sparkling to port-like) that quickly demonstrate why this amateur mead maker turned pro. The meadery offers free 30-minute tours and tasting, and sells its wares ($15–$25 for a liter) and other regional foods and gifts. The meadery is the host of the International Mead Festival, held annually in the fall.

4700 Old Pearl St., #2A. ℂ 720/406-1125. www.redstonemeadery.com. Free admission. Tours Mon–Fri 3pm, Sat 12:30pm; tasting room Mon–Fri 3:30–6:30pm, Sat 1–5pm. Located 1 block northeast of the Pearl St. exit off Foothills Pkwy.

Rockies Brewing Company   From the grinding of the grain to the bottling of the beer, the 25-minute tour of this attractive "designer" microbrewery ends as all brewery tours should: in the pub. Tours pass by glistening copper vats that turn out hundreds of kegs of Boulder Beer a day. The pub is a restaurant that overlooks the bottling area, so even if you visit without taking a tour, you still get a good view of the brewing process. The menu includes burgers, burritos, salads, and appetizers; entrees run $6 to $8.

2880 Wilderness Place. (𝓒 303/444-8448. www.boulderbeer.com. Free admission. Tours Mon–Sat 2pm; pub Mon–Fri 11am–9pm. Take U.S. 36 north to Valmont Rd., then head east to Wilderness Place.

MUSEUMS & GALLERIES

There are three art galleries on the University of Colorado campus, all with free admission. The **CU Art Museum,** in the Sibell Wolle Fine Arts Building near Euclid Avenue and Broadway (𝓒 303/492-8300), displays the work of CU students and faculty as well as pieces from the Colorado Collection, about 5,000 works by international artists including Warhol, Dürer, Rembrandt, Tiepolo, Hogarth, Hiroshige, Matisse, and Picasso. There are also rotating exhibits. The gallery is open Monday to Friday from 10am to 5pm, Tuesday 10am to 7pm, and Saturday from noon to 4pm. Bus: HOP, SKIP.

At the University Memorial Center, the **UMC Art Gallery** (𝓒 303/492-7465) organizes and hosts a variety of exhibitions featuring regional and national artists. In the music-listening rooms, visitors can peruse current periodicals while listening to modern and classical music. The gallery is on the second floor of the center, just left of the information desk; it's open Monday to Friday from 9am to 6pm. Bus: HOP, SKIP, STAMPEDE.

The **Andrew J. Macky Gallery** (𝓒 303/492-8423), at the main entrance of Macky Auditorium, shows touring exhibits and works by local artists. It's open Wednesday from 9am to 4pm. Bus: HOP, SKIP, STAMPEDE.

There are also studios and a gallery at the **Dairy Center for the Arts,** 2590 Walnut St. (𝓒 303/440-7826; www.thedairy.org), which also houses two theaters, classrooms, and several dance, theater, and arts organizations. See "Theater & Dance," later in this chapter.

Boulder Museum of Contemporary Art   This multidisciplinary art center, created in 1972 to exhibit the work of local artists, has evolved into an exciting venue where one can expect to see almost anything art-related, from the lighthearted to the elegant, political to religious, by local, regional, and international contemporary artists. There are special programs for young children and a variety of other events throughout the year. Performing arts—from poetry and dance to music and drama—are presented in the museum's award-winning "black box" performance venue, featuring local, national, and international performers. Allow 30 to 45 minutes. In addition, on Saturday evenings in summer, classic movies such as *Citizen Kane* and cult classics are shown outside ($5 per person). Take a lawn chair or blanket.

1750 13th St. (𝓒 303/443-2122. www.bmoca.org. Admission $4 adults, $3 students and seniors, free for children under 12. Wed–Fri noon–6pm; Sat 9am–4pm; Sun noon–4pm. Hours change seasonally; call ahead for current information. Closed Mon–Tues and major holidays. Bus: HOP, SKIP.

Boulder History Museum ✦   Ensconced on University Hill in the 1899–1900 Harbeck-Bergheim House, a Victorian mansion with a Dutch-style front door and Italian tile fireplaces, the museum houses one of the most comprehensive local-history collections in the region. There are more than 30,000 artifacts (from snake oil to sidesaddles), plus hundreds of thousands of photographs and historical documents from Colorado's early days to the present.

Semi-permanent exhibits include "Storymakers: A Boulder History," featuring a rich collection of oral histories and late-19th-to-early-20th-century photographs. There are also rotating exhibits that stay up for 6 to 10 months. The museum also hosts numerous lectures, programs, tours, and community events, including the Great Boulder Pie Festival and Quilt Raffle in July, Northern Arapaho Pow Wow in June, and Boulder History Day in May. Allow 1 to 2 hours.

1206 Euclid Ave. © 303/449-3464. www.boulderhistorymuseum.org. Admission $5 adults, $3 seniors, $2 children and students, free for children under 5. Tues–Fri 10am–4pm; Sat noon–4pm. Guided tours by appointment. Closed Sun–Mon and major holidays. Bus: HOP.

Heritage Center   Located in the oldest building on campus, this museum reflects the history of the university. Its seven galleries hold exhibits on early student life (together with a complete set of yearbooks), CU's contributions to space exploration, campus architecture, distinguished alumni, and an overview of the university's history. Allow 30 minutes; a lot more if you're an alum.

3rd floor of Old Main, University of Colorado. © 303/492-6329. Free admission. Mon–Fri 10am–4pm; Sat 10am–2pm. Bus: HOP, SKIP, STAMPEDE.

Leanin' Tree Museum of Western Art   You may know Leanin' Tree as the world's largest publisher of Western-art greeting cards. What's not so well known is that the company's headquarters houses an outstanding 400-piece collection of original paintings and bronze sculptures by contemporary artists. All depict scenes from the Old or New West, including a collection of humorous cowboy art. Some of the works have been reproduced on the company's greeting cards, which are for sale in the gift shop. Free guided tours are available. Allow 1 hour.

6055 Longbow Dr. (exit Jay Rd. and Longmont Diagonal). © 800/777-8716 or 303/530-1442, ext. 299. www.leanintree.com. Free admission. Mon–Fri 8am–4:30pm; Sat–Sun 10am–4pm. Bus: 205.

University of Colorado Museum (Kids)   The natural history and anthropology of the Rocky Mountains and Southwest are the focus of this campus museum, founded in 1902. Featured exhibits include Ancestral Puebloan pottery and collections pertaining to dinosaurs, geology, paleontology, botany, entomology, and zoology. A children's area has interactive exhibits, and one gallery is devoted to special displays that change throughout the year. Allow 1 to 3 hours.

University of Colorado, Henderson Bldg., Broadway at 15th St. © 303/492-6892. Free admission, donations accepted. Mon–Fri 9am–5pm; Sat 9am–4pm; Sun 10am–4pm. Bus: HOP.

ESPECIALLY FOR KIDS

City parks (see "Sports & Outdoor Activities," below) offer the best diversions for children.

On the **Boulder Creek Path** (see "The Top Attractions," earlier in this chapter), the underwater fish observatory behind the Millennium Harvest House fascinates youngsters. They can feed the huge trout swimming behind a glass barrier on the creek (machines cough up handfuls of fish food for 25¢). Farther up the path, on the south bank around 6th Street, Kids' Fishing Ponds, stocked by the Boulder Fish and Game Club, are open to children under 12. There's no charge for either activity.

The **Fiske Planetarium** (© 303/492-5001) offers visitors a walk through the solar system. Dedicated to the memory of CU alumnus Ellison Onizuka and the six other astronauts who died in the space shuttle *Challenger* explosion, the outdoor scale model begins at the entrance to the planetarium with the sun and inner planets, and continues across Regent Drive to the outer planets, located along the walkway to the Engineering Center. Admission is free; allow at least a half-hour. The planetarium offers after-school and summer discovery programs for kids, star shows, and other programs where you get a chance to look at the sky through the planetarium's telescopes. Admission for these events is usually $2 to $4; call for the latest schedule. Bus: HOP.

6 Sports & Outdoor Activities

Boulder is one of the leading spots for outdoor sports in North America. The city manages over 38,000 acres of parklands, including more than 200 miles of hiking trails and bicycle paths. Several canyons lead down from the Rockies directly into Boulder, attracting mountaineers and rock climbers. Families enjoy picnicking and camping in the beautiful surroundings. It seems that everywhere you look, people of all ages are running, walking, biking, skiing, or engaged in other active sports.

The **Boulder Parks and Recreation Department** (© **303/413-7200;** www.ci.boulder.co.us/parks-recreation) manages many of the outdoor facilities and schedules a variety of year-round activities for children as well as adults. Seasonal booklets on activities and city parks are available free from the Chamber of Commerce office and through the parks and recreation department's website (see above). Although many of the programs last for several weeks or months, some are half- or full-day activities that visiting children can join, usually at a slightly higher price than that for city residents. The department sponsors hikes, fitness programs, ski trips, watersports, special holiday events, performances in local parks, and even operates a skate park and a pottery lab. (TV trivia buffs, take note: Mork of *Mork and Mindy* first touched down on Planet Earth in Chautauqua Park, on the city's south side, and the house used as their residence's exterior is at 1619 Pine St.).

One destination where you can enjoy several kinds of outdoor activities is **Eldorado Canyon State Park** . This mountain park, just 5 miles southwest of Boulder in Eldorado Springs, is a favorite of technical rock climbers, but the 850-foot-high canyon's beauty makes it just as popular with hikers, picnickers, and others who want to get away from it all. The 1,448-acre park features 9 miles of hiking and horseback-riding trails, plus 7½ miles of trails suitable for mountain bikes; fishing is permitted, but camping is not. An exhibit at the brand-new visitor center describes the history of the park; there's also a bookstore and rotating displays covering topics from wildflowers to climbing. Admission is $5 to $6 per vehicle and $2 to $3 per pedestrian; the park is open daily from dawn to dusk. For further information, contact Eldorado Canyon State Park, Box B, Eldorado Springs, CO 80025 (© **303/494-3943;** www.parks. state.co.us).

BALLOONING   Float above the majestic Rocky Mountains in a hot-air balloon, watching as the early morning light gradually brightens to full day. Flights often include champagne and an elaborate continental breakfast or brunch. **Fair Winds Hot Air Balloon Flights** (© **303/939-9323;** www.fairwindsinc.com)

Impressions

This is Mork from Ork signing off from Boulder, Colorado. Nanu, Nanu!
—Mork from Ork (Robin Williams), on TV's *Mork & Mindy,*1978–82

flies 7 days a week year-round, weather permitting. Prices are $175 to $200 per person, and include a certificate, T-shirt, and photograph.

BICYCLING   On some days, you can see more bikes than cars in Boulder. Paths run along many of the city's major arteries, and local racing and touring events are scheduled year-round. Bicyclists riding at night are required to have lights; perhaps because of the large number of bicyclists in Boulder, the local police actively enforce traffic regulations that apply to them. Generally, bicyclists must obey the same laws that apply to operators of motor vehicles.

For current information on biking events, tips on the best places to ride, and equipment sales and repairs, check with **University Bicycles,** 839 Pearl St., about 2 blocks west of the Pearl Street Mall (© **303/444-4196;** www. ubikes.com), and **Full Cycle,** 1211 13th St., near the campus (© **303/440-7771;** www.fullcycleboulder.com). University Bikes rents bikes for $15 to $20 per day, and has maps of the city's 90 miles of bike lanes, paths, and routes. See also "By Bicycle" under "Getting Around," earlier in this chapter.

CLIMBING & BOULDERING   If you would like to tackle the nearby mountains and cliffs with ropes and pitons, contact **Mountain Sports,** 2835 Pearl St. (© **303/442-8355**), which sells clothing and technical equipment, and can also provide maps and advice on climbing and trail running. Other good information sources are **Colorado Athletic Training School,** 2800 30th St. (© **303/939-9699**), and the **Boulder Rock Club,** 2829 Mapleton Ave. (© **303/447-2804;** www.boulderrock.com). The latter houses 10,000 square feet of indoor climbing surfaces and offers guide services.

Boulderers (those who climb without ropes) should check out **The Spot,** the country's largest bouldering gym at 3240 Prairie Ave. (© **303/379-8806;** www. thespotgym.com). Lessons and guiding service are available, and there is a cafe and a yoga studio on-site.

The Flatiron Range (easily visible from downtown Boulder) and nearby Eldorado Canyon are two favorite destinations for expert rock scalers. The "amphitheater" in the Flatirons is among the most revered of the nearby climbing areas. For bouldering, Carter Lake (30 miles north on U.S. 36) and Boulder Canyon (west of the city on Canyon Blvd.) are two of the top spots.

FISHING   Favored fishing areas near Boulder include **Boulder Reservoir,** North 51st Street, northeast of the city off the Longmont Diagonal, where you can try your luck at walleye, catfish, largemouth bass, bluegill, crappie, and carp. The Boulder Parks and Recreation Department (© **303/441-3461**) manages the reservoir. Other favorite fishing holes include **Lagerman Reservoir,** west of North 73rd Street off Pike Road, about 15 miles northeast of the city, where only non-motorized boats can be used; **Barker Reservoir,** just east of Nederland on the Boulder Canyon Drive (Colo. 119), for bank fishing; and **Walden Ponds Wildlife Habitat,** about 6 miles east of downtown on North 75th Street. Fly-fishing is also popular in the area; guide service is available through **Kinsley Outfitters,** 1155 13th St. (© **800/442-7420** or 303/442-6204), for $225 for one person for a full day or $295 for two. Kinsley's fly shop offers a good selection of supplies.

GLIDER FLYING & SOARING   The atmospheric conditions generated by the peaks of the Front Range are ideal for year-round soaring and gliding. **Mile High Gliding,** 5534 Independence Rd. (© **303/527-1122**), offers rides and lessons on the north side of Boulder Municipal Airport, 2 miles northeast of downtown. Rides for one person range from $60 to $200 and last from 15 minutes to an hour or more; a 25-minute ride for two costs $160.

GOLF   Local courses include the 18-hole **Flatirons Golf Course** (run by Boulder Parks and Recreation), 5706 E. Arapahoe Ave. (© **303/442-7851**), and the nine-hole **Haystack Mountain Golf Course,** 5877 Niwot Rd. in Niwot., 5 miles north of Boulder (© **303/530-1400**). Nonresident greens fees range from $15 to $32.

HIKING & BACKPACKING   There are plenty of opportunities in the Boulder area—the Boulder Mountain Parks system includes 4,625 acres bordering the city limits, including the Flatirons and Flagstaff Mountain. You can obtain a map with descriptions of more than 60 trails from the **Boulder Convention and Visitors Bureau,** 2440 Pearl St. (© **303/442-2911**).

Numerous Roosevelt National Forest trailheads leave the Peak-to-Peak Scenic Byway (Colo. 72) west of Boulder. Check with the **U.S. Forest Service,** Boulder Ranger District, 2140 Yarmouth Ave. (© **303/541-2500**), for hiking and backpacking information. During dry weather, check on possible fire and smoking restrictions before heading into the forest. The trailheads leading to Long, Mitchell, and Brainard lakes are among the most popular, as is the 2-mile hike to Isabel Glacier.

About 70 miles west of Boulder, on the Continental Divide, is the **Indian Peaks Wilderness Area** (© **303/541-2500**). More than half of the area is fragile alpine tundra; a $5 permit is required for camping from June 1 to September 15. North of Boulder, via Estes Park, is **Rocky Mountain National Park** (© **970/586-1206**), one of the state's prime destinations for hikers and those seeking beautiful mountain scenery. The 2.5-mile **Mills Lake Trail** ✸, one of our favorites, is here; see "A Side Trip to Rocky Mountain National Park," later in this chapter. Another good hike is the 6-mile Mesa Trail, which departs from the Bluebell Shelter in Chautauqua Park.

RUNNING   The Boulder Creek Path (see "The Top Attractions," earlier in this chapter) is one of the most popular routes for runners in Boulder. A good resource for the traveling runner is **Boulder Road Runners** (© **303/499-2061; www.boulderroadrunners.org**). They organize group runs in the area and can provide information. The **Bolder Boulder** (© **303/444-RACE; www.bolder boulder.com**), held every Memorial Day, attracts about 50,000 runners who circle its 6¼-mile course. The **Boulder Running Company,** 2775 Pearl St. (© **303/786-9255**), sells a wide variety of running shoes and gear, going as far as analyzing customers' strides on a treadmill to find the perfect shoe.

SKIING   Friendly **Eldora Mountain Resort,** P.O. Box 1697, Nederland, CO 80466 (© **888/235-3672** or 303/440-8700; fax 303/440/8797; www.eldora. com), is just 21 miles west of downtown Boulder. It's about a 40-minute drive on Colo. 119 through Nederland. RTD buses leave Boulder for Eldora four times daily during ski season. For downhill skiers and snowboarders, Eldora has 53 trails, rated 30% novice, 50% intermediate, and 20% expert terrain on 680 acres. It has snowmaking on 320 acres and a terrain park with a 600-foot super-pipe. The area has two quad lifts, two triple and four double chairlifts, four surface lifts, and a vertical rise of 1,500 feet. Lift tickets (2003–04 rates) are $49 for adults, $20 for children 6 to 12 and seniors 65 to 69, and just $5 for those under 6 and over 69. There are also discount packages that include lessons and rental equipment for both skiers and snowboarders. Snowshoeing is also gaining popularity in the area. The season runs from mid-November to mid-April, snow permitting.

For cross-country skiers, Eldora has 28 miles of groomed and backcountry trails, and an overnight hut available by reservation. About 15% of the trails are rated easy, 50% intermediate, and 35% difficult. The trail fee is $14, or $8 for children 6 to 12 and seniors 65 to 69.

You can rent all your ski, snowboard, and snowshoeing equipment at the ski-rental center, and Nordic equipment at the Eldora Nordic Center. A free base-area shuttle runs throughout the day from the lodge to the Little Hawk area and the Nordic Center.

In Boulder, you can rent or buy telemark and alpine touring equipment from **Mountain Sports,** 2835 Pearl St. (© **303/442-8355**) or **Eldora Mountain Sports,** 2775 Canyon Blvd. (© **303/447-2017**).

SWIMMING   Five public pools are located within the city. Indoor pools, all open daily year-round, are at the newly renovated **North Boulder Recreation Center,** 3170 N. Broadway (© **303/413-7260**); the **East Boulder Community Center,** 5660 Sioux Dr. (© **303/441-4400**); and the **South Boulder Recreation Center,** 1360 Gillaspie Dr. (© **303/441-3448**). The two outdoor pools (both open daily from Memorial Day to Labor Day) are **Scott Carpenter Pool,** 30th Street and Arapahoe Avenue (© **303/441-3427**), and **Spruce Pool,** 2102 Spruce St. (© **303/441-3426**). Swimming fees for all municipal pools are $5.50 adults, $3.50 seniors, $3 teens, and $2.75 children 4 to 12.

TENNIS   There are more than 30 public courts in the city. The North and South Boulder Recreation centers (see "Swimming," above) each have four lighted courts and accept reservations ($8 an hour). The North Boulder Recreation Center also has two platform tennis courts. Play is free if you arrive and there's no one using the courts or with a reservation. For locations of other public tennis courts, contact the Boulder Parks and Recreation Department (© **303/413-7200**).

WATERSPORTS   For both motorboating and human-powered boating, sailboard instruction, or swimming at a sandy beach, head for the square-mile **Boulder Reservoir** (© **303/441-3461**), on North 51st Street off the Longmont Diagonal northeast of the city. Human-powered boats and canoes (no personal watercraft) can be rented at the **boathouse** (© **303/441-3456**). Rates start at $35 per full day, with sailboards at $65 per full day. There's also a boat ramp and other facilities.

SPECTATOR SPORTS

The major attractions are **University of Colorado football, women's volleyball,** and **men's and women's basketball.** For tickets, contact the Ticket Office, Campus Box 372, Boulder, CO 80309 (© **303/49-BUFFS;** www.cubuffs.com). Football tickets sometimes sell out early, particularly for homecoming and games with Nebraska and Oklahoma, so it would be wise to make reservations in advance.

7 Shopping

For the best shopping in Boulder, head to the **Pearl Street Mall** (see "The Top Attractions," earlier in this chapter), where you'll find not only shops and galleries galore but also street entertainers.

The indoor-outdoor, 1½-million-square-foot **FlatIron Crossing** (🕐 **720/ 887-9900;** www.flatironcrossing.com), an upscale mall featuring Nordstrom, Dillard's, and Lord & Taylor among its 200 shops, is a more comprehensive option for the devout shopper. It's 9 miles southeast of Boulder off U.S. 36 in Broomfield. Hours are 10am to 9pm Monday through Saturday and 11am to 6pm on Sunday.

Crossroads Mall, at 28th and Pearl sts. in Boulder, has long been nearly vacant. At press time, it looked like a redevelopment plan for a new indoor-outdoor retail center would go forward, called **29th Street,** but nothing was finalized.

SHOPPING A TO Z
ARTS & CRAFTS

Art Source International   Natural-history prints, maps, and other items relevant to Western Americana, mainly from the 18th and 19th centuries, are the specialty here, along with collections of hundred-year-old Colorado photographs, maps, and prints. The store also features a great selection of new globes, as well as a few reproductions. 1237 Pearl St. 🕐 303/444-4080.

Boulder Arts & Crafts Cooperative   This is a good place to find a unique gift or souvenir. The shop, owned and operated by its artist members since 1971, features a wide variety of original handcrafted works. Pieces range from watercolors, serigraphs, and other fine art to top-quality crafts, including blown glass, stained glass, handmade jewelry, and functional pottery. Many of the items are made in Colorado or the Rocky Mountain region. 1421 Pearl St. 🕐 303/443-3683.

Niwot Antiques *(Finds)*   With dozens of dealers (including New England antiques specialist Elysian Fields), this antiques mall, in business since the 1950s, is the area's best, and a good excuse to make a trip to Niwot, 5 miles north of Boulder on the Longmont Diagonal. 136 2nd Ave., Niwot. 🕐 303/652-2587.

BOOKS

Being a college town, Boulder is one of the best cities in the world for a browsing bookworm. It reportedly has more used-book stores per capita than any other U.S. city. Chain outlets include **Barnes & Noble,** 2915 Pearl St. (🕐 **303/442-1665**), and **Borders,** 1600 Pearl St. (🕐 **720/565-8266**). The independents run the gamut from the Kerouac and Burroughs specialists at **Beat Bookshop,** 1713 Pearl St. (🕐 **303/444-7111**), to the lesbian/feminist/gay selection at **Word Is Out,** 2015 10th St. (🕐 **303/449-1415**). **Trident Booksellers,** 940 Pearl St. (🕐 **303/443-3133**), is a good used-book shop with a coffeehouse attached.

Boulder Book Store   This meandering, four-story, 20,000-square-foot bookstore has been locally owned and operated since the 1970s. It attracts students, bohemians, and businesspeople alike with its homey vibe, and features great selections of Buddhism tomes and travel guides. It is attached to a coffeehouse with patio seating on the Pearl Street Mall, The Bookend Cafe (see "Espresso Bars, Coffeehouses & Related Establishments," earlier in this chapter). 1107 Pearl St. 🕐 303/447-2074. www.boulderbookstore.com.

FASHION

Alpaca Connection   Come here for natural-fiber clothing from around the world, including alpaca-and-wool sweaters from South America. 1326 Pearl St. 🕐 303/447-2047.

Rocky Mountain Kids   Offering clothing for newborns to 12-year-olds, this bright store specializes in quality brands and is known for its kid-friendliness: complimentary animal crackers and plenty of toys in the box. 2525 Arapahoe Ave. ℂ 303/447-2267.

Weekends   The selection of men's and women's fashions is somewhat pricey but chosen for comfort and style—and it shows. 1101 Pearl St. ℂ 303/444-4231.

FOOD & DRINK

Boulder Wine Merchant   This store has a solid selection of wines from around the world, plus knowledgeable salespeople (and more than one master sommelier) who can help you make the right choice. 2690 Broadway. ℂ 303/443-6761.

Liquor Mart   Here you'll find a huge choice of discounted wine and liquor, with more than 5,000 wines and 900 beers, including a wide selection of imported and microbrewed beers. 1750 15th St. (at Canyon Blvd.). ℂ 303/449-3374.

Whole Foods   The latest and greatest of Boulder's organic supermarkets, this huge store—part of the national chain—has a wide-ranging, fresh inventory, and is a favorite lunch spot of locals. Offerings include a deli, soup and salad bar, sushi, and more free samples than you could possibly eat. It's also 100% wind-powered. 2905 Pearl St. ℂ 303/545-6611.

GIFTS & SOUVENIRS

The best stops for T-shirts, University of Colorado paraphernalia, and other Boulder souvenirs are **Jackalope and Company,** 1126 Pearl St. (ℂ **303/939-8434**); **Where the Buffalo Roam,** 1320 Pearl St. (ℂ **303/938-1424**); and the **CU Bookstore,** 1111 Broadway (ℂ **303/442-5051**).

HARDWARE

McGuckin Hardware   McGuckin's claims to have the world's largest hardware selection, with more than 200,000 items in stock. In addition to the nuts, bolts, brackets, paints, tools, and assorted whatchamacallits that most hardware stores carry, you'll also find sporting goods, kitchen gizmos, automotive supplies, stationery, some clothing, electronics, outdoor furniture, fresh flowers, and a whole lot of other stuff. 2525 Arapahoe Ave. ℂ 303/443-1822 or 86-MCGUCKIN. www.mcguckin.com.

JEWELRY

El Loro   Distinctively Boulder, this bohemian jewelry shop has been a Pearl Street Mall resident for more than 25 years. Aside from a nice selection of sterling silver items with semiprecious stones, El Loro also sells clogs and incense. 1416 Pearl St. ℂ 303/449-3162.

KITCHENWARE

Peppercorn   From cookbooks to pasta makers, you can find anything and everything for the kitchen here at "the Smithsonian of cookstores." In business since 1977, this vast store (12,000 sq. ft.!) has hundreds of kitchen gadgets and appliances—everything you might need to prepare, serve, and consume the simplest or most exotic meal. 1235 Pearl St. ℂ 800/447-6905 or 303/449-5847.

SPORTING GOODS

Gart Sports, 3320 N. 28th St. (ℂ **303/449-9021**), is a good all-purpose source, while the following are more specialized—and interesting—retail outlets.

Boulder Army Store   Just east of the Pearl Street Mall, this shop has the best inventory of camping gear in the city, along with a limited amount of fishing equipment. There is also a good supply of outdoor clothing and military surplus items such as fatigues, helmets, and that disarmed hand grenade you've always wanted. 1545 Pearl St. ⒸⒸ 303/442-7616.

Mountain Sports   This shop, which opened in 1958, boasts of being Boulder's oldest mountaineering shop. It specializes in equipment, clothing, and accessories for backpacking, camping, rock and ice climbing, mountaineering, backcountry skiing, and snowshoeing. Equipment rentals include sleeping bags, tents, backpacks, and snowshoes; backcountry and telemark ski packages are available. Mountain Sports also sells maps and guidebooks, and the knowledgeable staff—which includes several trained guides—can help you plan your trip. 2835 Pearl St. Ⓒ 303/442-8355.

8 Boulder After Dark

As a cultured and well-educated community (59% of adult residents have at least one college degree), Boulder is especially noted for its summer music, dance, and Shakespeare festivals. Major entertainment events take place year-round, both downtown and on the University of Colorado campus. There's also a wide choice of nightclubs and bars, but it hasn't always been so: Boulder was dry for 60 years, from 1907 (13 years before national Prohibition) to 1967. The first new bar in the city opened in 1969, in the Hotel Boulderado. The notoriously healthy city banned smoking in 1995; only a few establishments allow patrons to ignore the policy.

Entertainment schedules can be found in the *Daily Camera*'s weekly *Friday Magazine;* in either of the Denver dailies, the *Denver Post* or the *Rocky Mountain News;* in *Westword,* the Denver weekly; or in the free *Boulder Weekly.*

THE CLUB & MUSIC SCENE

Boulder Theater *Finds*   Rock, folk, bluegrass, jazz, hip-hop, comedy, and who knows what else—performed by musicians such as Lou Reed, Bill Maher, Herbie Hancock, and Norah Jones—takes the stage here. During the week, you'll also find independent and otherwise alternative films. 14th and Pearl sts. Ⓒ 303/786-7030. www.bouldertheater.com.

The Catacombs   This popular bar books live blues and jazz by local and regional performers. The loud, somewhat raucous atmosphere (and smoking room) draws a crowd of CU students and an eclectic mix of locals and traveling businesspeople. A limited pub menu is served. In the basement of the Hotel Boulderado, 13th and Spruce sts. Ⓒ 303/443-0486.

Fox Theatre and Cafe *Finds*   A variety of live music (including, but not limited to, bluegrass, funk, blues, hip-hop, reggae, and punk) is presented here 5 or 6 nights a week, featuring a mix of local, regional, and national talent. You'll find three bars at this converted movie theater, which is revered for its great acoustics. 1135 13th St. Ⓒ 303/443-3399 or 303/447-0095. www.foxtheatre.com.

Penny Lane Coffee House   By day a bohemian gathering place for talking, playing chess, or reading while sipping espresso, this Greenwich Village–style coffeehouse comes alive at night. There's usually a poetry reading on Monday, 1 night of live jazz each week, several open-stage evenings, and a diverse mixture of live music by local and regional artists on Friday and Saturday. See also

"Espresso Bars, Coffeehouses & Related Establishments," earlier in this chapter. Pearl and 18th sts. ✆ 303/443-9516.

'Round Midnight A hip basement joint on the Pearl Street Mall, 'Round Midnight specializes in malt scotch, good beer, and dancing. An eclectic array of performers (hip-hop, techno, jazz, rock) take the stage here on weekends and DJs during the week. 1005 Pearl St. ✆ 303/442-2176.

Trilogy Wine Bar This hip venue is tucked in the back of a stylish restaurant with a diverse international menu and a great wine list. Performers include reggae bands, acid and Latin jazz acts, DJs, and hip-hop acts. 2017 13th St. ✆ 303/473-WINE. www.trilogywinebar.com.

THE BAR SCENE

Barrel House Consistently voted the number-one sports bar in Boulder by local newspaper readers, the Barrel House offers a choice of 25 beers on tap, mostly Colorado microbrews. There are close to 40 TVs, including four big-screen sets, and a huge menu of burgers, pizza, sandwiches, and Mexican dishes. The bar is a traditional pre-game meeting place for University of Colorado football fans. 2860 Arapahoe Ave. ✆ 303/444-9464.

Conor O'Neill's *Finds* Everything in this pub—from the bar to the art to the timber floors—was designed and built in Ireland. The atmosphere is rich, with a "shop pub" up front and two back rooms centered on a pair of fireplaces that were constructed by visiting Irish stonemasons. There are over a dozen beers on tap, primarily from (where else?) Ireland, and the pub menu features fish and chips, burgers, and a mean shepherd's pie. There is live music (surf to Celtic) every night of the week except Mondays, which feature a popular trivia game, and Irish music Sunday afternoons. 1922 13th St. ✆ 303/449-1922.

Mountain Sun Pub & Brewery An English-style neighborhood pub and microbrewery, Mountain Sun produces dozens of barrels of beer each week and provides tours on request during the day. The mostly made-from-scratch menu features soups, salads, burgers, sandwiches, and a few Mexican dishes. There's live folk, acoustic, and bluegrass music on Sunday night. 1535 Pearl St. (east of the mall). ✆ 303/546-0886.

The Republic of Boulder Subtitled "The People's Pub," the former Oasis has been rethought to reflect the passions and quirks of its home city—in the form of hemp fan blades, a large dance floor, and creative but affordable eats. The cavernous pub also produces its own beer and has a full array of bar games: pool, darts, and retro video games like Ms. Pac-Man. 1095 Canyon Blvd. ✆ 303/443-1460.

The Sink *Finds* This off-campus establishment opened in 1923 (CU dropout Robert Redford was once the janitor) but has been updated with new spacey wall murals that help make it one of Boulder's funniest—and most fun—nightspots. There's a full bar with more than a dozen regional microbrews, live music, and fare such as Sinkburgers and "ugly crust" pizza. 1165 13th St. ✆ 303/444-SINK. www.thesink.com.

Sundown Saloon This raucous dive is a CU institution. In a spacious basement on the west end of the Pearl Street Mall, pool is the pastime of choice and the drinks are reasonably priced. The Sundown Saloon has the largest and most popular smoking room in town (legal under Boulder's smoking ban), resulting in one of the smokiest rooms known to humankind. 1136 Pearl St. 303/449-4987.

Tips **Lyons: On the Beaten Path**

Most tourists driving U.S. 36 to Rocky Mountain National Park from Boulder or Denver blaze through the dinky town of Lyons without even bothering to slow down. They're missing some top-drawer diversions in the process. For beer and music aficionados, **Oskar Blues Grill & Brew,** 303 Main St. (© **303/823-6685;** www.oskarblues.com) is a fun and—to say the least—eclectically decorated place for lunch and a beer, or a blues, rock, or rockabilly show come nighttime. Oskar Blues owns a distinction in the fact that it was the first craft brewery in the country to can its beer (Dale's Pale Ale and our favorite, Old Chub); visitors can even can a six-pack themselves at certain times. The restaurant is open daily from 11am to 11pm; the bar is open until midnight Sunday through Thursday and 2am on Friday and Saturday. Also worth a look is the **Lyons Pinball Arcade,** 339-A Main St. (© **303/823-6100;** www.lyonspinball.com), with 30 pinball machines dating from the 1970s and more recent decades, including Kiss, Black Knight, and Addams Family. For silverball fiends, it's a real trip down memory lane.

Downtown Lyons is a historic district marked by 16 Victorian sandstones, and just outside of town, the fishing and hiking are excellent. For additional information, contact the **Lyons Chamber of Commerce** (© **303/823-5215;** www.lyons-colorado.com).

Walnut Brewery   In a historic brick warehouse a block from the Pearl Street Mall, this large restaurant/bar/microbrewery is popular with the after-work crowd, both young and old. 1123 Walnut St. (near Broadway). © **303/447-1345.**

West End Tavern   A 2004 makeover of this popular neighborhood bar left the brick walls and the classic bar intact, but gave the rest of the joint a contemporary shot in the arm and a slick look. Beyond the 48 bourbons stocked by the bar, fare includes a different specialty burger every day, barbecue, and more upscale items. The tavern's roof garden is an ideal spot to unwind and enjoy some of the best views in town and outdoor cinema on certain summer nights. 926 Pearl St. © **303/444-3535.**

THE PERFORMING ARTS
Music, dance, and theater are important aspects of life for Boulder residents. Many of these activities take place at **Macky Auditorium** at the University of Colorado (© **303/492-8008;** www.colorado.edu/music) and other campus venues, as well as the **Chautauqua Auditorium,** 900 Baseline Rd. (© **303/442-3282**), and the **Dairy Center for the Arts,** 2590 Walnut St. (© **303/440-7826;** www.thedairy.org).

CLASSICAL MUSIC & OPERA
Boulder Bach Festival   First presented in 1981, this celebration of the music of Johann Sebastian Bach includes not only a late-January festival but also concerts and other events year-round. Tickets run $10 to $30. Series tickets are also available. P.O. Box 1896, Boulder, CO 80306. © **303/494-3159.** www.boulderbachfest.org.

Boulder Philharmonic Orchestra   This acclaimed community orchestra performs an annual fall-to-spring season, primarily at Macky Auditorium, with world-class artists who have included singer Marilyn Horne, guitarist Carlos Montoya, cellist Yo-Yo Ma, and violinist Itzhak Perlman. Tickets cost $10 to $65, more for concerts that feature premier performers. P.O. Box 4626, Boulder, CO 80306. ℂ **303/449-1343.** www.peakarts.org.

Colorado MahlerFest Begun in 1988, this international festival is the only one of its kind in the world. For a week each January it celebrates the work of Gustav Mahler with a performance of one of his symphonies as well as chamber concerts, films, discussions, seminars, and other musical programs. Most events are free; admission to symphony concerts ranges from $8 to $25. P.O. Box 1314, Boulder, CO 80306. ℂ **303/447-0513** for information, 303/449-1343 for box office. www. mahlerfest.org.

Colorado Music Festival *(Finds* Begun in 1976, this series is the single biggest annual arts event in Boulder, with visiting musicians from around the world performing in the acoustically revered Chautauqua Auditorium. The festival presents works of the classical through modern eras, such as Bach, Beethoven, Mozart, Dvorak, and Gershwin, plus living composers. It usually runs from mid-June to mid-August, with symphony orchestra performances Thursday and Friday, chamber-orchestra concerts Sunday, and a chamber-music series Tuesday; all shows start at 7:30pm. There's also a children's concert in late June and a free Independence Day concert at CU's Folsom Field. Adult ticket prices range from $10 to $37. 900 Baseline Rd., cottage 100, Boulder, CO 80302. ℂ **303/449-1397** for general information, 303/440-7666 or visit website for tickets. www.coloradomusicfest.org.

CU Concerts The university's College of Music presents the Artist Series, Music, Theatre, University of Colorado Summer Opera, Takács String Quartet Series, and Holiday Festival at Macky Auditorium and Grusin Music Hall. General admission tickets usually cost $10 to $38. The Artist Series features an outstanding lineup of classical soloists, jazz artists, dance companies, and multidisciplinary events. Call early for tickets for performances of the renowned Takács String Quartet. The annual Holiday Festival includes the University Symphony Orchestra, university choirs, several smaller ensembles, and soloists from the College of Music's student body and faculty. University of Colorado. ℂ **303/492-8008.** www.cuconcerts.org.

THEATER & DANCE

Colorado Shakespeare Festival *(Moments* Considered one of the top three Shakespearean festivals in the United States, this 2-month annual event attracts more than 40,000 theatergoers between late June and late August. Held since 1958 in the University of Colorado's Mary Rippon Outdoor Theatre, and indoors at the University Theatre Main Stage, it offers more than a dozen performances of each of four plays. Actors, directors, designers, and everyone associated with the productions are fully schooled Shakespearean professionals. Tickets run from $10 to $50 for single performances, with series packages also available. Campus Box 277, University of Colorado, Boulder, CO 80309. ℂ **303/492-0554** for information and the box office. www.coloradoshakes.org.

Nomad Theatre Boulder's only resident professional theater, the Nomad has presented a mix of classic and contemporary dramas, comedies, and musicals since the curtains first opened in 1951. Recent productions have included *Wit, Alarms & Excursions,* and *Darwin in the Dreamtime.* Tickets cost $18 to $22. 1410 Quince Ave. ℂ **303/443-7510** or 303/774-4037 (box office). www.nomadstage.com.

Upstart Crow Theatre Company   Specializing in Shakespeare and more contemporary classics, the Upstart Crow is the resident theater companies at the Dairy Center for the Arts. They perform on two stages: a 99-seat theater (where no seat is more than three rows from the stage) and an 86-seat proscenium theater. Dairy Center for the Arts, 2590 Walnut St. (C) **303/258-7939** or 303/449-5151. www. theupstartcrow.org.

9 A Side Trip to Rocky Mountain National Park

44 miles NW of Boulder, 71 miles NW of Denver

The northern half of the Colorado Rockies is the country's ultimate mountain wilderness, the crown on the head of the great range that dominates the American West. This is rugged beauty at its best, extending on either side of the meandering Continental Divide down sawtooth ridgelines, through precipitous river canyons, and across broad alpine plains. Here, snowfall is measured in feet, not inches, and when spring's sun finally melts away the frost, amazing arrays of alpine wildflowers herald the new beginning. There's no better place to experience this spectacular scenery than at Rocky Mountain National Park. Although it can be a fairly easy day trip from Boulder or Denver, we highly recommend spending at least 2 or 3 days here, perhaps making the gateway community of Estes Park your base of operations while exploring the trails and spectacular views of the national park.

ROCKY MOUNTAIN NATIONAL PARK ★★★

Snow-covered peaks—17 mountains above 13,000 feet—stand over lush valleys and shimmering alpine lakes in the 415 square miles (265,727 acres) of Rocky Mountain National Park. The highest, at 14,255 feet, is Longs Peak.

What really sets the park apart (after all, this sort of eye-popping beauty is not unusual in the Rockies) is its variety of distinct ecological zones. As you rise and descend in altitude, the landscape of the park changes dramatically. In relatively low areas, from about 7,500 to 9,000 feet, a lush forest of ponderosa pine and juniper cloaks the sunny southern slopes, with Douglas fir on the cooler northern slopes. Thirstier blue spruce and lodgepole pine cling to stream sides, with occasional groves of aspen. Elk and mule deer thrive. On higher slopes, a subalpine ecosystem exists, dominated by forests of Engelmann spruce and subalpine fir, but interspersed with wide meadows alive with wildflowers during spring and summer. This is also home to bighorn sheep, which have become unofficial mascots of the park. Above 11,500 feet, the trees become increasingly gnarled and stunted, until they disappear altogether and alpine tundra predominates. Fully one-third of the park is at this altitude; in this bleak, rocky world, many of the plants are identical to those found in the Arctic.

Trail Ridge Road, which cuts west through the middle of the park from Estes Park, then south down its western boundary to Grand Lake, is one of America's great alpine highways. Climbing to 12,183 feet near Fall River Pass, it's the highest continuous paved highway in the United States. The road is usually open from Memorial Day into October, depending on the snowfall. The 48-mile scenic drive from Estes Park to Grand Lake takes about 3 hours, allowing for stops at numerous scenic outlooks. Exhibits at the **Alpine Visitor Center** at Fall River Pass, 11,796 feet above sea level, explain life on the alpine tundra.

Fall River Road, the original park road, leads to Fall River Pass from Estes Park via Horseshoe Park Junction. West of the Endovalley picnic area, the road is one-way uphill, and closed to trailers and motor homes. As you negotiate its

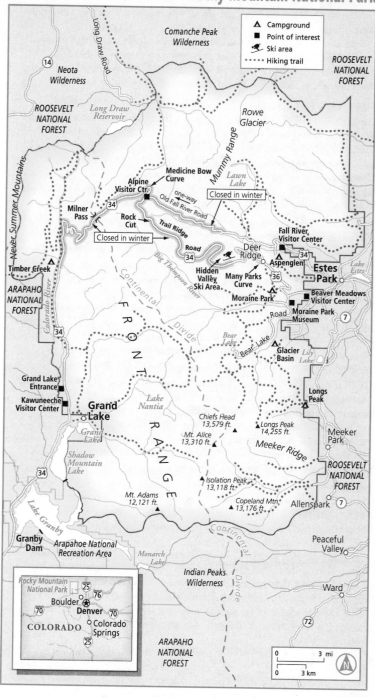

Legend:
- △ Campground
- ■ Point of interest
- 🎿 Ski area
- ····· Hiking trail

Comanche Peak Wilderness

14 Neota Wilderness

ROOSEVELT NATIONAL FOREST

Long Draw Road

Long Draw Reservoir

Rowe Glacier

ROOSEVELT NATIONAL FOREST

Never Summer Mountains

Medicine Bow Curve

Alpine Visitor Ctr.

one-way Old Fall River Road

Lawn Lake

Closed in winter

Mummy Range

Milner Pass

Rock Cut

Trail Ridge

Closed in winter

Continental Divide

Big Thompson River

Road 34

Deer Ridge

Fall River Visitor Center

34

Lake Estes

Timber Creek

ARAPAHO NATIONAL FOREST

Colorado River

Hidden Valley Ski Area

Many Parks Curve

Moraine Park

Aspenglen

36

Estes Park

Beaver Meadows Visitor Center

Moraine Park Museum

7

34

Road

Bear Lake

Bear Lake

Glacier Basin

Lily Lake

F R O N T

Grand Lake Entrance

Kawuneeche Visitor Center

Grand Lake

Lake Nantia

Longs Peak

Grand Lake

Chiefs Head 13,579 ft.

Longs Peak 14,255 ft.

Meeker Park

R A N G E

Mt. Alice 13,310 ft.

Meeker Ridge

ROOSEVELT NATIONAL FOREST

34

Shadow Mountain Lake

Isolation Peak 13,118 ft.

Mt. Adams 12,121 ft.

Copeland Mtn. 13,176 ft.

Allenspark

7

Lake Granby

Granby Dam

Arapahoe National Recreation Area

Monarch Lake

Indian Peaks Wilderness

Continental Divide

Peaceful Valley

Ward

Rocky Mountain National Park

25

76

Boulder

70 Denver 70

COLORADO

Colorado Springs

25

72

ARAPAHO NATIONAL FOREST

0   3 mi
0   3 km

gravelly switchbacks, you get a clear idea of what early auto travel was like in the West. This road, too, is closed in winter.

One of the few paved roads in the Rockies that leads into a high mountain basin is **Bear Lake Road;** it is open year-round, with occasional half-day closings to clear snow. Numerous trails converge at Bear Lake, southwest of the Beaver Meadows Visitor Center, on the other side of Moraine Park.

JUST THE FACTS

GETTING THERE By Car The most direct route to Estes Park (and Rocky Mountain National Park) is U.S. 36 from Denver and Boulder. At Estes Park, U.S. 36 joins U.S. 34, which runs up the Big Thompson Canyon from I-25 and Loveland, and continues through Rocky Mountain National Park to Granby. An alternative scenic route to Estes Park is Colo. 7, the "Peak-to-Peak Scenic Byway" that goes, under different designations, through Central City (Colo. 119), Nederland (Colo. 72), and Allenspark (Colo. 7).

By Plane Visitors can fly into Denver International Airport, then rent a car or contact **Estes Park Shuttle** (© **970/586-5151;** www.estesparkshuttle.com), which connects Estes Park with Boulder and Denver. Rates to Denver International Airport are $39 one-way and $75 round-trip.

ENTRY POINTS Entry into the park is from the east (through Estes Park) or the west (through Grand Lake). **Trail Ridge Road** connects the two sides. Most visitors enter the park from the Estes Park side. The **Beaver Meadows entrance,** west of Estes Park on U.S. 36, is the national park's main entrance. U.S. 34 west from Estes Park takes you to the **Fall River entrance** (north of the Beaver Meadows entrance). Those entering the park from the west side should take U.S. 40 to Granby, then follow U.S. 34 north to the **Grand Lake entrance.**

GETTING AROUND In summer, a free national park **shuttle bus** runs from Moraine Park Campground, Moraine Park Museum, and the Glacier Basin parking area to Bear Lake, with departures every 10 to 20 minutes.

There's year-round taxi service by **Estes Park Shuttle** (see "Getting There," earlier in this chapter), which also provides tours into Rocky Mountain National Park during the summer.

VISITOR CENTERS & INFORMATION For information on where to stay and eat and what to do in the gateway community of Estes Park, contact the **Estes Park Chamber of Commerce,** 500 Big Thompson Ave., Estes Park, CO 80517 (© **800/378-3708** or 970/586-4431; www.estesparkresort.com). It has a visitor center on U.S. 34, just east of its junction with U.S. 36, with access from both highways.

Unless otherwise noted, call the main park number (© **970/586-1206**) for information on the following visitor centers.

Entering the park from Estes Park, the **Beaver Meadows Visitor Center,** U.S. 36, west of Colo. 66, has knowledgeable people to answer questions and give advice, a wide choice of books and maps for sale, and interpretive exhibits, including a relief model of the park. It's open year-round daily from 8am to 6pm.

Outside the park, just east of the Fall River entrance, is the **Fall River Visitor Center.** Located in a beautiful mountain lodge–style building, it was built with private funds but is staffed by park rangers and volunteers from the Rocky Mountain Nature Association. It contains exhibits on park wildlife, including some spectacular full-size bronzes of elk and other animals, plus a children's Discovery Room, information desk, and a bookstore. Next door is a large (but somewhat pricey) souvenir-and-clothing shop plus a cafeteria-style restaurant with snacks and sandwiches. It's open daily from 9am to 6pm spring through fall.

Near the park's west side entrance is the **Kawuneeche Visitor Center** (© **970/586-1513**), open daily from 8am to 6pm year-round. Located high in the mountains (11,796 ft. above sea level) is the **Alpine Visitor Center,** at Fall River Pass, open from late June through early October, daily from 9am to 5pm (with shorter hours at the end of the season); exhibits here explain life on the alpine tundra. Visitor facilities are also available at the **Moraine Park Museum** on Bear Lake Road, open late June to late August daily from 9am to 5pm.

For more specifics on planning a trip, contact Rocky Mountain National Park, 1000 U.S. 36, Estes Park, CO 80517-8397 (© **970/586-1206** or 970/586-1333 for recorded information; www.nps.gov/romo). You can also get detailed information from the **Rocky Mountain Nature Association,** Rocky Mountain National Park, Estes Park, CO 80517 (© **800/816-7662;** www.rmna.org), which sells a variety of maps, guides, books, and videos (including some in PAL format).

FEES & REGULATIONS   Park admission for up to 7 days is $15 per vehicle, $5 per person for bicyclists, motorcyclists, and pedestrians.

As in many national parks, wilderness permits are required for all overnight backpacking trips, and camping is allowed only in specified campsites. Pets must be leashed at all times and are not permitted on trails or in the backcountry. Both motor vehicles and bicycles must remain on the roads or in parking areas. Do not feed or touch any park animals, and do not pick any wildflowers.

SEASONS   Even though the park is technically open daily year-round, Trail Ridge Road, the main east–west thoroughfare through the park, is almost always closed in winter. The road is usually open by late May (after the snow has been cleared) and closes between mid- and late October. However, it is not uncommon for snowstorms to close the road for several hours or even a full day at any time, especially in early June and October. The high country is open during the summer and as snow conditions permit in winter.

AVOIDING THE CROWDS   Because large portions of the park are closed half the year, practically everyone visits during the spring and summer. The busiest period is from mid-June to mid-August—essentially during school vacations. In order to avoid the largest crowds, try to visit just before or just after that period. For those who don't mind chilly evenings, late September and early October are less crowded and can be beautiful, although there's always the chance of an early winter storm. Regardless of when you visit, the absolute best way to avoid crowds is by putting on a backpack or climbing onto a horse. Rocky Mountain has over 350 miles of trails leading into all corners of the park (see "Sports & Outdoor Activities In & Around the Park," later in this section).

RANGER PROGRAMS   Each visitor center offers campfire talks and other programs between June and September. Consult the park's free *High Country Headlines* newspaper for scheduled activities, which vary from photo walks to fly-fishing and orienteering.

SEEING THE HIGHLIGHTS

Although Rocky Mountain National Park is generally considered the domain of hikers and climbers, it's surprisingly easy to thoroughly enjoy this park without working up a sweat. For that we can thank **Trail Ridge Road.**

Built in 1932 and undoubtedly one of America's most scenic highways, it provides expansive and sometimes dizzying views in all directions. The drive from Estes Park to Grand Lake covers some 48 miles through the park, rising above 12,000 feet in elevation and crossing the Continental Divide. It offers spectacular vistas of snowcapped peaks, deep forests, and meadows of wildflowers, where bighorn sheep, elk, and deer browse. Allow at least 3 hours for the drive, and possibly more if you'd like to take a short hike from one of the many vista points.

TRAIL RIDGE ROAD ⊛

Along Trail Ridge Road are numbered signs, from 1 to 12, starting on the east side of the park and heading west. These stops are described below, and the route is also discussed in a brochure available at park visitor centers (25¢). Motorists starting from the west side of the park will begin at number 12 and count down.

Stop No. 1: Deer Ridge Junction. This spot offers views of the Mummy Mountain Range to the north. It is the official beginning of Trail Ridge Road,

---

Tips **Old Fall River Road: A Step Back in Time**

For those who find Trail Ridge Road too civilized or too easy, there is an alternative: The park's original road still exists, and it's still mostly dirt, still steep, and just as narrow and winding as ever. Covering 11 miles (2 paved and 9 gravel), from Horseshoe Park to Fall River Pass, this one-way (west) road climbs 3,200 feet. It provides today's visitors with a glimpse into the experiences of those who explored this rugged land in Model T Fords and Stanley Steamers during its early years as a national park.

Even before the establishment of Rocky Mountain National Park in 1915, there was interest in building a road through the mountains. In July 1913, work began with the arrival of 38 convicts from the Colorado State Penitentiary. The road was finally dedicated on September 14, 1920, and until Trail Ridge Road was built in 1932, Old Fall River Road was the only route from the east into the heart of the national park. Although the grading was new, the route of Old Fall River Road was not—it followed what Arapahos called the Dog's Trail, a path where they used dogs to pull crude V-shaped sleds through the mountains.

Today this road remains much as it was in the 1920s, with numerous drop-offs and switchbacks—not for anyone with a serious fear of heights! As you drive it, you'll see boulder fields, riparian areas, and cascading waterfalls, as well as some of the most rugged high-elevation sections of the park. Watch for the stone walls along the roadsides that were built during the 1920s in an often-unsuccessful effort to keep the road from being washed away. Snowmelt, freezing and thawing, and thunderstorms often caused damage to the road. A mudslide in July 1953 did so much harm that the park service was ready to give up on the road; public pressure led to a change of heart, and the historic Old Fall River Road reopened in 1968.

the highest continuous paved road in the United States, reaching an elevation of 12,183 feet. Here you're at a mere 8,940 feet.

Stop No. 2: Hidden Valley. Formerly the site of a downhill ski area, this scenic subalpine valley boasts forests of Engelmann spruce and fir. The elevation is 9,240 feet.

Stop No. 3: Many Parks Curve. This delightfully scenic stop, with one of the best roadside views in the park, is also a good location for birders, who are likely to spot the noisy Steller's jay and Clark's nutcracker. The term "park" is used in the sense of a level valley between mountain ranges (often an open, grassy area), which in this case was carved by glaciers some 10,000 years ago. The elevation is 9,620 feet.

Stop No. 4: Rainbow Curve. Just past a sign announcing your position 2 miles above sea level is Rainbow Curve, an area known for colorful rainbows that are often seen after thunderstorms. It's also famous for ferocious winds and brutal winters. Take a look at the trees that have branches only on their downwind side,

Passing through three ecosystems, the relatively short, slow drive provides a cross-section view of Rocky Mountain National Park, its plants and animals, its forests and valleys, and its famous alpine tundra, quite likely the bleakest but most fascinating terrain most people will ever see. Open only in summer, Old Fall River Road begins at an elevation of 8,558 feet in the **montane** ecosystem. One of the milder sections of the park, it is home to ponderosa pine, Douglas fir, quaking aspen, numerous birds, and a wide variety of mammals, ranging from cotton-tail rabbits to elk and mountain lions. Continue your drive and you'll soon ease into the **subalpine** ecosystem, which is cooler and moister than the montane, with forests of Engelmann spruce, Colorado blue spruce, and subalpine fir. You'll find birds such as Clark's nutcracker, and mule deer, long-tailed weasels, and elk.

The upper limit of the subalpine ecosystem is at about 11,000 feet. Then there's a transition zone, where the same trees as in the subalpine ecosystem exist, but in a smaller size. Finally you're there—the end of the world. At almost 12,000 feet elevation, the **alpine tundra** has no trees, and many of its other plants are almost too tiny to see. The wildlife includes golden eagles, hawks, mice and other rodents, and yellow-bellied marmots, plus bighorn sheep and elk.

Old Fall River Road ends at Fall River Pass at the Alpine Visitor Center—watch for elk as you approach the visitor center. There it joins Trail Ridge Road, which you can take back to the east side of the park, or go west to cross the Continental Divide at Milner Pass and continue into the park's western section. Old Fall River Road is open to motor vehicles and mountain bikes; trailers and motor homes over 25 feet long are wisely prohibited.

where their trunks protect them from the elements. The excellent view from the overlook here extends past Longs Peak and into Hidden Valley and Horseshoe Park, where you can see rock, gravel, and other rubble left by a flood that struck in 1982 after a dam broke. The elevation is 10,829 feet.

Stop No. 5: Forest Canyon Overlook. From this stop's parking area, a short, paved walkway leads to an observation platform offering a beautiful but dizzying view into vast Forest Canyon, where the erosion work of glaciers is clearly evident. The peaks of the Continental Divide appear beyond. Near the overlook, watch for pikas (relatives of rabbits), marmots, and other small mammals. The elevation is 11,716 feet.

Stop No. 6: Rock Cut. Practically the highest point along Trail Ridge Road, this is alpine tundra at its harshest. Winds can reach 150 mph, winter blizzards are frequent, and temperatures in midsummer frequently drop below freezing. You'll have splendid views of the glacially carved peaks along the Continental Divide, and on the ½-mile **Tundra World Nature Trail,** you'll find signs identifying and discussing the hardy plants and animals that inhabit this cold and barren region. The elevation is 12,110 feet.

Stop No. 7: Lava Cliffs. Here you'll see a dark cliff, created by the carving action of glacial ice through a thick layer of tuff (volcanic ash and debris) that was deposited here about 28 million years ago during volcanic eruptions in the Never Summer Range, located about 8 miles west. If you look just below the cliff, you'll see a pretty meadow that is a popular grazing spot for elk. The elevation is 12,080 feet.

Stop No. 8: Fall River Pass. At this spot you'll get a good view of a huge amphitheater, and you can take a break at the Alpine Visitor Center. A viewing platform at the rear of the visitor center offers vistas of a wide, glacially carved valley of grasses, wildflowers, shrubs, and small trees where you're practically guaranteed to see elk grazing. This is also the junction of Trail Ridge Road and Old Fall River Road. The elevation is 11,796 feet.

Stop No. 9: Medicine Bow Curve. Views of a vast subalpine forest of spruce and fir and the distant Cache la Poudre River give way to the Medicine Bow Mountains, which extend into Wyoming. The elevation is 11,640 feet.

Stop No. 10: Milner Pass. This is the Continental Divide, the backbone of North America. From this point, water flows west to the Pacific or east toward the Atlantic. The divide also affects the park's weather—the west side is usually colder, is less windy, and receives much more precipitation than the east side. The elevation is 10,758 feet.

Stop No. 11: Farview Curve. This aptly named overlook provides a look at the beginnings of the Colorado River as it carves its way through the Kawuneeche Valley 1,000 feet below the overlook, before flowing some 1,400 miles to the Gulf of California. There are also panoramic views of the Never Summer Mountains. Looking west from this point, you can see the Grand Ditch, which carries water across the Continental Divide to Colorado's thirsty eastern plains. Engelmann spruce and lodgepole pine grow here, and you'll see ground squirrels and chipmunks scurrying among the rocks. The elevation is 10,120 feet.

Stop No. 12: Holzwarth Trout Lodge Historic Site. Just past the Timber Creek Campground, this stop provides access to a short trail to **Holzwarth Trout Lodge Historic Site,** an early-20th-century homestead that started out as a working cattle ranch and soon evolved into a dude ranch. Rangers give talks and guided walks here during the summer. The elevation is 8,884 feet.

SPORTS & OUTDOOR ACTIVITIES IN & AROUND THE PARK

In addition to Rocky Mountain National Park, many activities take place just outside the park in the 1,240-square-mile Roosevelt National Forest. Obtain information on hiking, horseback riding, fishing, and other activities in advance from the **Canyon Lakes Ranger District Office,** 1311 S. College Ave., Fort Collins, CO 80524 (℃ **970/498-2770;** www.fs.fed.us/r2). In Estes Park, a **Forest Service Information Center** is at 161 2nd St. (℃ **970/586-3440**); it's usually open daily 9am to 5pm in summer.

BICYCLING   Bicyclists will have to share the roadways with motor vehicles along narrow roads with 5% to 7% grades. As in most national parks, bikes are not permitted off established roads. However, bicyclists still enjoy the challenge and scenery. One popular 16-mile ride is the **Horseshoe Park/Estes Park Loop,** which goes from Estes Park west on U.S. 34 past Aspenglen Campground and the park's Fall River entrance, then heads east at the Deer Ridge Junction, following U.S. 36 through the Beaver Meadows park entrance. There are plenty of beautiful mountain views; allow 1 to 3 hours. A free park brochure provides information on safety, regulations, and other suggested routes. Tours, rentals, and repairs are available at **Colorado Bicycling Adventures,** 184 E. Elkhorn Ave., Estes Park (℃ **970/586-4241;** www.coloradobicycling.com). Bike rentals range from $15 to $40 for a half-day and $23 to $60 for a full day, depending on the type of bike. The company offers guided downhill trips in the park for about $65 per person, and also leads a variety of free group bike rides in the Estes Park area from May through September (call or check the website for the current schedule).

CLIMBING & MOUNTAINEERING   **Colorado Mountain School,** 341 Moraine Ave. (P.O. Box 1846), Estes Park, CO 80517 (℃ **888/267-7783** or 970/586-5758; www.cmschool.com), is an AMGA accredited year-round guide service, and the sole concessionaire for technical climbing and instruction in Rocky Mountain National Park. The school has programs for all ages; cost for a 2-day excursion is about $350. The school also offers lodging in a hostel-type setting, at about $25 per night per person. (See also "Hiking & Backpacking," below.) Be sure to stop at the ranger station at the Longs Peak trailhead for current trail and weather information before attempting to ascend Longs Peak.

EDUCATIONAL PROGRAMS   The **Rocky Mountain Nature Association** (see contact information under "Visitor Centers & Information," earlier in this chapter), offers a wide variety of seminars and workshops, ranging from 1 full day to several days. Subjects vary but might include songbirds, flower identification, edible and medicinal herbs, painting, wildlife photography, tracking park animals, and edible mushrooms. Rates are about $35 for a half-day program, $65 for a full-day program, $135 for 2-day programs, and $165 for 3-day programs. There are also kids' programs; prices start at $15.

FISHING   Four species of trout are fished in national park and national forest streams and lakes: brown, rainbow, brook, and cutthroat. A state fishing license is required, and only artificial lures or flies are permitted in the park. A number of lakes and streams in the national park are closed to fishing, including Bear Lake. A free park brochure that's available at visitor centers lists open and closed bodies of water, plus regulations and other information.

HIKING & BACKPACKING Park visitor centers sell U.S. Geological Survey topographic maps and guidebooks, and rangers can direct you to lesser-used trails. Keep in mind that all trails here start at over—sometimes well over—7,000 feet elevation, and even the easiest and flattest walks will likely be tiring for those accustomed to lower elevations.

One particularly enjoyable (and easy) hike is the **Alberta Falls Trail** from the Glacier Gorge Parking Area (½ mile one-way), which rises in elevation only 160 feet as it follows Glacier Creek to pretty Alberta Falls.

A slightly more difficult option is the **Bierstadt Lake Trail,** accessible from the north side of Bear Lake Road about 6⅕ miles from Beaver Meadows. This 1⅗-mile (one-way) trail climbs 566 feet through an aspen forest to Bierstadt Lake, where you'll find excellent views of Longs Peak.

Starting at Bear Lake, the trail up to **Emerald Lake** offers spectacular scenery en route, past Nymph and Dream lakes. The ½-mile hike to Nymph Lake is easy, climbing 225 feet; from there the trail is rated moderate to Dream Lake (another ½ mile) and then on to Emerald Lake (another ¾ miles), which is 605 feet higher than the starting point at Bear Lake. Another moderate hike is the relatively uncrowded **Ouzel Falls Trail,** which leaves from Wild Basin Ranger Station and climbs about 950 feet to a picture-perfect waterfall. The distance one-way is 2¾ miles.

Among our favorite moderate hikes here is the **Mills Lake Trail** ⭐, a 2½-mile (one-way) hike, with a rise in elevation of about 700 feet. Starting from Glacier Gorge Junction, the trail goes up to a picturesque mountain lake, nestled in a valley among towering mountain peaks. This lake is an excellent spot for photographing dramatic Longs Peak, especially in late afternoon or early evening, and it's the perfect place for a picnic.

If you prefer a more strenuous adventure, you'll work hard but be amply rewarded with views of timberline lakes and alpine tundra on the **Timber Lake Trail,** in the western part of the park. It's 4¾ miles one-way, with an elevation gain of 2,060 feet. Another strenuous trail, only for experienced mountain hikers and climbers in top physical condition, is the 8-mile (one-way) **East Longs Peak Trail,** which climbs some 4,855 feet along steep ledges and through narrows to the top of Longs Peak.

Backcountry permits (required for all overnight hikes) can be obtained at Park Headquarters and ranger stations (in summer) for $20 from May through October, free from November through April. For information, call ✆ **970/586-1242.** There is a 7-night backcountry camping limit from June to September, with no more than 3 nights at any one spot. Tents are not permitted in the backcountry in summer.

HORSEBACK RIDING Many of the national park's trails are open to horseback riders. Several outfitters provide guided rides inside and outside the park, ranging from 1 hour (about $25) to all day (about $100), plus breakfast and dinner rides and multi-day pack trips. Recommended companies include S.K. Horses (www.cowpokecornercorral.com), which operates **National Park Gateway Stables,** at the Fall River entrance of the national park on U.S. 34 (✆ **970/586-5269**), and the **Cowpoke Corner Corral,** at Glacier Lodge, 3 miles west of town, 2166 Colo. 66 (✆ **970/586-9272**). **Hi Country Stables** (www.colorado-horses.com/highcountrystables) operates two stables inside the park: **Glacier Creek Stables** (✆ **970/586-3244**) and **Moraine Park Stables** (✆ **970/586-2327**).

SKIING & SNOWSHOEING   Much of the park is closed to vehicular travel during the winter, when deep snow covers roads and trails. Snow is usually best from January through March. A popular spot for cross-country skiing and snow-shoeing in the park is Bear Lake, south of the Beaver Meadows entrance. A lesser-known area of the park is Wild Basin, south of the park's east entrances off Colo. 7, about a mile north of the community of Allenspark. A 2-mile road, closed to motor vehicles for the last mile in winter, winds through a subalpine forest to the Wild Basin Trailhead, which follows a creek to a waterfall, a rustic bridge, and eventually to another waterfall. Total distance to the second falls is 2¾ miles. Along the trail, your chances are good for spotting birds such as Clark's nutcrackers, Steller's jays, and the American dipper. On winter weekends, the Colorado Mountain Club often opens a warming hut at the Wild Basin Ranger Station.

Before you set forth, stop by a visitor center for maps, information on where the snow is best, and a permit if you plan to stay out overnight. Ski rentals, instruction, and guide service are available from **Colorado Mountain School** (see contact information under "Climbing & Mountaineering," above). Rangers often lead guided snowshoe walks on winter weekends.

WILDLIFE VIEWING & BIRD-WATCHING   Rocky Mountain National Park is a premier wildlife-viewing area; fall, winter, and spring are the best times, although we saw plenty of elk and squirrels, plus a few deer, a marmot, and a coyote during a recent mid-July visit. Large herds of elk and bighorn sheep can often be seen in the meadows and on mountainsides. In addition, you may spot mule deer, beavers, coyotes, and river otters. Watch for moose among the wil-lows on the west side of the park. In the forests are lots of songbirds and small mammals; particularly plentiful are gray and Steller's jays, Clark's nutcrackers, chipmunks, and golden-mantled ground squirrels. There's a good chance of see-ing bighorn sheep, marmots, pikas, and ptarmigan along Trail Ridge Road. For detailed and current wildlife-viewing information, stop by one of the park's vis-itor centers, and check on the many interpretive programs, including bird walks. Rangers stress that it is both illegal and foolish to feed any wildlife.

CAMPING

The park has five campgrounds with a total of almost 600 sites. Nearly half are at **Moraine Park;** another 150 are at **Glacier Basin.** Moraine Park, **Timber Creek** (98 sites), and **Longs Peak** (26 tent sites) are open year-round; Glacier Basin and **Aspenglen** (54 sites) are seasonal. Camping in summer is limited to 3 days at Longs Peak and 7 days at other campgrounds; the limit is 14 days at all the park's campgrounds in winter. Arrive early in summer if you hope to snare one of these first-come, first-served campsites. Reservations for Moraine Park and Glacier Basin are accepted from Memorial Day through early September and are usually completely booked well in advance. However, any sites not reserved—as well as sites at Timber Creek, Longs Peak, and Aspenglen—are available on a first-come, first-served basis. Make reservations with the **National Park Reservation Service** (✆ **800/365-2267**). Campsites cost $20 per night during the summer, $12 in the off season when water is turned off. No showers or RV hookups are available.

There are also a number of commercial campgrounds in Estes Park, just out-side the national park. All offer RV hookups and clean bathhouses, and are open from late spring through early fall only. They include **Estes Park KOA,** 2051 Big Thompson Ave., Estes Park, CO 80517 (✆ **800/562-1887** for reservations, or 970/586-2888; www.estes-park.com/koa), with RV rates for two of $30 to $35; **Mary's Lake Campground,** 2120 Mary's Lake Rd. (P.O. Box 2514), Estes Park, CO 80517 (ⓒ **800/445-6279** for reservations, or 970/586-4411; www. maryslakecampground.com), with RV rates for two of $36 to $39; and **Spruce Lake R.V. Park,** 1050 Mary's Lake Rd., Estes Park, CO 80517 (ⓒ **800/536-1050** or 970/586-2889; www.sprucelakerv.com), charging $35 to $37 for an RV site for two people. Estes Park KOA and Mary's Lake Campground also have tent sites at lower rates; Spruce Lake does not permit tents.

ESTES PARK

Located just outside the east entrances to Rocky Mountain National Park, literally within a stone's throw, the community of Estes Park provides most of the lodging, dining, and other services for park visitors (there are no lodging facilities within the park boundaries). Unlike other Colorado mountain towns, most of which began as mining communities, Estes Park (elevation 7,522 ft.) has always been a resort town. Long known by the Utes and Arapahos, this area was explored in 1859 by rancher Joel Estes. But the growth of Estes Park is inextricably linked with two individuals: Freelan Stanley and Enos Mills. Stanley, a Bostonian who, with his brother Francis, invented the kerosene-powered Stanley Steamer automobile in 1899, settled in Estes Park in 1907, launched a Stanley Steamer shuttle service from Denver, and in 1909 built the landmark Stanley Hotel. Mills, an innkeeper turned conservationist, was one of the prime advocates for the establishment of Rocky Mountain National Park. President Woodrow Wilson signed the bill creating the 400-square-mile park in 1915; today it attracts some three million visitors annually.

FAST FACTS   In an **emergency,** dial ⓒ **911.** The hospital, **Estes Park Medical Center,** which has a 24-hour emergency room, is at 555 Prospect Ave. (ⓒ **970/586-2317**). The **post office** is at 215 W. Riverside Dr. (ⓒ **800/275-8777**). For statewide **road conditions,** call ⓒ **303/639-1111.** For **local weather,** call ⓒ **970/586-5555.**

WHERE TO STAY

For help in finding accommodations, call the **Estes Park Chamber of Commerce Lodging Referral Service** (ⓒ **800/379-3708;** www.estesparkresort. com). National chains here include **Best Western Silver Saddle,** 1260 Big Thompson Hwy. (U.S. 34), Estes Park, CO 80517 (ⓒ **800/WESTERN** or 970/586-4476), with rates of $99 to $199 double from June to mid-September, $79 to $149 double off season; **Super 8,** 1040 Big Thompson Ave., Estes Park, CO 80517 (ⓒ **800/800-8000** or 970/586-5338), charging $72 to $90 double in summer, $52 to $64 double off season; and **Travelodge,** 1220 Big Thompson Ave., Estes Park, CO 80517 (ⓒ **800/578-7878** or 970/586-4421), charging $85 to $189 double in summer, $59 to $149 double off season.

   Although many lodging facilities in the Estes Park area do not have air-conditioning, it is seldom needed at this elevation. Unless otherwise noted, pets are not permitted at the following properties.

All Budget Inn *Value*   This pleasant motel, smack against Rocky Mountain National Park, offers simple rooms with homey touches such as fresh flowers, and nature prints adorning the white walls. The units, which sleep from two to six people each, have firm queen or king beds and tub/shower combos. Some have kitchenettes and private balconies. There's also a picnic area with barbecue grills.

945 Moraine Ave., Estes Park, CO 80517. ☏ **800/628-3438** or 970/586-3485. www.allbudgetinn.com. 22 units. Summer $89–$130 double, $130–$250 suite or condominium; off season $69–$98 double, $110–$175 suite or condominium. MC, V. Pets accepted. **Amenities:** Outdoor hot tub. *In room:* A/C, cable TV, fridge, coffeemaker, hair dryer, microwave.

Allenspark Lodge Bed & Breakfast 🐾🐾 *(Finds* We love historic properties, and this one has just the right ambience for a visit to Rocky Mountain National Park. The three-story lodge was built in 1933 of hand-hewn ponderosa-pine logs, and holds a large native stone fireplace. Located 16 miles south of Estes Park, in a tiny village at the southeast corner of the national park, all lodge rooms offer mountain views and original handmade 1930s pine furniture. At the top end is the Hideaway Room, with a queen-size brass bed, bear-claw-footed tub, fine linens, and gas-log stove. Guests share the large sunroom, the stone fireplace in the Great Room, videos in the recreation room, and books in the library. Rates include a hot family-style breakfast, afternoon and evening coffee, tea, and cookies. There's also a hot tub, conference rooms, espresso coffee shop, and wine-and-beer bar. Horseback riding is available within walking distance in summer.

184 Main St., Colo. 7 Business Loop (P.O. Box 247), Allenspark, CO 80510. ☏ **303/747-2552.** www.allensparklodge.com. 13 units (7 with bathroom). $75–$145 double. Rates include full breakfast. DISC, MC, V. Children under 14 not accepted. **Amenities:** Hot tub. *In room:* No phone.

Boulder Brook 🐾🐾 It would be hard to find a more beautiful setting for lodging than this. Surrounded by tall pines and cradled in a ruggedly majestic valley two miles from the park entrance, all suites face the Fall River, and all have private riverfront decks and full or partial kitchens. The spa suites are equipped with two-person spas, fireplaces, sitting areas with cathedral ceilings, and king-size beds. One-bedroom suites hold king-size beds, window seats, two TVs, and bathrooms with whirlpool tub/shower combinations. The grounds, a serene jumble of forest, rock, and running water, include an outdoor hot tub and barbecue area. Smoking is not allowed.

1900 Fall River Rd., Estes Park, CO 80517. ☏ **800/238-0910** or 970/586-0910. Fax 970/586-8067. www.boulderbrook.com. 19 units. $109–$225 double. AE, DISC, MC, V. **Amenities:** Year-round outdoor hot tub; large free video library. *In room:* Cable TV, DVD/VCR, kitchen.

Glacier Lodge *(Kids* Deer and elk frequently visit these lovely cottages, which spread across 19 acres of woodland along the Big Thompson River. There are poolside chalets; cozy, homey river duplexes with outside decks overlooking the stream; and river triplexes range from earthy to country quaint in decor. All have a porch or patio, and almost all feature kitchens and fireplaces, with a bundle of wood delivered daily. Facilities include a sport court, playground, fishing, gift shop, ice-cream shop, and stables. Breakfast cookouts, barbecues, and special kids' activities take place in summer, at an extra charge. Four large lodges that sleep 12 to 30 are available for groups (call for rates).

Colo. 66 (P.O. Box 2656), Estes Park, CO 80517. ☏ **800/523-3920** or 970/586-4401. www.glacierlodge.com. 26 units. Early June to late Aug $80–$218; mid-May to early June and late Aug to late Sept $60–$150; late Sept to mid-Oct $50–$130. Rates are per unit (2 to 5 people). Minimum stays of 2 to 4 nights may be required. DISC, MC, V. Closed mid-Oct to mid-May. **Amenities:** Outdoor pool. *In room:* TV, no phone.

WHERE TO DINE

In addition to the restaurants described here, we like the family-oriented **Lazy B Ranch,** 1915 Dry Gulch Rd. (☏ **800/228-2116** or 970/586-5371; www.lazy branchinestespark.homestead.com), which serves a chuck-wagon supper (chicken or beef, beans, potatoes, peach halves, biscuits, and spice cake) with a show of live cowboy music and comedy. There's also a program on the history of Western music. Cost is $17 for people over 12, $15 for those 10 to 12 years old, $10 for children 3 to 9, and free for kids under 3. To reach Lazy B, take U.S. 34 east from Estes Park about 1½ miles, turn left at Sombrero Stables, and follow the signs. The ranch is open from late May through September, but the schedule varies. Call for specifics.

Dunraven Inn ★★ ITALIAN   This is a great spot to celebrate a special occasion in an intimate setting, but not so fancy that you wouldn't want to take the (well-behaved) kids. The decor is eclectic, to say the least: Images of the *Mona Lisa* are scattered about, ranging from a mustachioed lady to opera posters, and autographed dollar bills are posted in the lounge area. House specialties include shrimp scampi, lasagna, and our favorite, the Dunraven Italiano (an 11-oz. charbroiled sirloin steak in a sauce of peppers, onions, and tomatoes). There's a wide choice of pastas, fresh seafood, vegetarian plates, and desserts, plus a children's menu. Another Dunraven (same owner, but smaller and more casual) is downtown at 101 W. Elkhorn Ave. (© **970/586-3818**).

2470 Colo. 66. © **970/586-6409**. Reservations recommended. Main courses $8–$34. AE, DISC, MC, V. Sun–Thurs 5–10pm; Fri–Sat 5–10pm; closes slightly earlier in winter.

Grumpy Gringo ★ *Kids* MEXICAN   Dine in style at this classy Mexican restaurant without breaking the bank. The private booths, whitewashed plaster walls, green plants, bright poppies, and a few choice sculptures provide a posh atmosphere. And although the food is excellent and portions are large, the prices are surprisingly low. Our choice here is a burrito, but which one to choose? We also recommend the huge enchilada olé. It's actually three enchiladas: one each of cheese, beef, and chicken. The fajitas—either chicken or beef—are delicious. There are six sauces from which to choose, each homemade, and rated mild, semihot, or hot. Burgers and sandwiches are also offered. The house specialty drink is the Gringo Margarita, made with Sauza Gold tequila from an original (and secret) recipe.

1560 Big Thompson Ave. (U.S. 34). © **970/586-7705**. Main courses $4.95–$15. AE, DISC, MC, V. Daily 11am–10pm summer, 11am–8pm off season. Closed last week of Jan, 1st week of Feb. On U.S. 34, 1 mile east of the junction of U.S. Hwy. 34 and Hwy. 36.

Molly B ★ *Finds* AMERICAN   It's hard to not feel right at home at this busy restaurant, where the atmosphere is casual and the staff treats you like an old friend. Located in an older downtown building, the dining room has light-colored pine walls and tables that add to the down-home atmosphere. Molly B is especially popular at breakfast, with specialties such as our favorite, the sunrise stuffer—a large tortilla filled with scrambled eggs, potatoes, cheese, and spicy chorizo. Lunch and dinner selections include vegetarian entrees, fresh seafood (we suggest the grilled Rocky Mountain trout), pasta, and steak. Desserts are made in-house—try the mud pie: chocolate and mocha ice cream in an Oreo cookie crust, topped with fudge. Patio seating, providing good people-watching along the noisy street, is available in warm weather.

200 Moraine Ave. © **970/586-2766**. Reservations recommended for dinner. Main courses $3–$7 breakfast, $5–$8 lunch, $8–$17 dinner. AE, MC, V. Year-round Thurs–Tues 6:30am–3pm; May–Oct also 4–9pm.

Colorado Springs

Magnificent scenic beauty, a favorable climate, and dreams of gold have lured visitors to Colorado Springs and neighboring Pikes Peak Country for well over 100 years.

Nearly 2 centuries ago, in 1806, army Lt. Zebulon Pike led a company of soldiers on a trek around the base of an enormous mountain. He called it "Grand Peak," declared it unconquerable, and moved on. Today, the 14,110-foot mountain we know as Pikes Peak has been conquered so often that an auto highway and a cog railway take visitors to the top.

Unlike many Colorado towns, neither mineral wealth nor ranching was the cornerstone of Colorado Springs' economy during the 19th century—tourism was. In fact, Colorado Springs, founded in 1871, was the first genuine resort community west of Chicago. Gen. William J. Palmer, builder of the Denver & Rio Grande Railroad, established the resort on his rail line, at an elevation of 6,035 feet. The state's growing reputation as a health center, with its high mountains and mineral springs, convinced him to build at the foot of Pikes Peak. In an attempt to lure affluent easterners, he named the resort Colorado Springs, because most fashionable eastern resorts were called "springs." The mineral waters at Manitou Springs were only 5 miles away, and soon Palmer exploited them by installing a resident physician, Dr. Samuel Solly, who exuberantly trumpeted the benefits of Manitou's springs both in print and in person.

The 1890s gold strikes at Cripple Creek, on the southwestern slope of Pikes Peak, added a new dimension to life in Colorado Springs. Among those who cashed in on the boom was Spencer Penrose, a middle-aged Philadelphian and Harvard graduate who arrived in 1892, made some astute investments, and became quite rich. Penrose, who believed that the automobile would revolutionize life in the United States, promoted the creation of new highways. To show the effectiveness of motorcars in the mountains, he built (from 1913–15) the Pikes Peak highway, using more than $250,000 of his own money. Then, during World War I, at a cost of more than $2 million, he built the luxurious Broadmoor hotel at the foot of Cheyenne Mountain. World War II brought the military and defense industry to this area, and in 1958 the $200-million U.S. Air Force Academy opened.

Modern Colorado Springs is a growing city of 358,000, with over half a million people in the metropolitan area. The majority of its residents are conservative (one-third are active or retired military personnel), and in recent years it has developed a reputation for right-wing political activism. The city is also home to some of the country's largest nondenominational churches and conservative groups.

To many visitors, the city retains the feel and mood of a small Western town. Most tourists come to see the Air Force Academy, marvel at the scenery at Garden of the Gods and Pikes Peak, and explore the history of America's West. We're pleased to report that Colorado Springs also has some of the best lodging and dining in the state.

1 Orientation

ARRIVING

BY PLANE

Major airlines offer nearly 100 flights a day to **Colorado Springs Airport,** located north of Drennan Road and east of Powers Boulevard in the southeastern part of the city (© **719/550-1972;** www.flycos.com).

Airlines serving Colorado Springs include **Allegiant** (© 888/594-6937), **American** (© 800/433-7300; www.aa.com), **America West** (© 800/235-9292; www.americawest.com), **Continental** (© 800/525-0280; www.flycontinental.com), **Delta** (© 800/221-1212; www.delta.com), **Mesa** (© 800/637-2247; www.mesa-air.com), **Northwest** (© 800/225-2525; www.nwa.com), and **United** (© 800/241-6522; www.ual.com).

GETTING TO & FROM THE AIRPORT   Several companies provide airport shuttle services; call © **719/550-1930** for information.

BY CAR

The principal artery to and from the north and south, I-25, bisects Colorado Springs. Denver is 70 miles north; Pueblo, 42 miles south. U.S. 24 is the principal east–west route through the city.

Visitors arriving on I-70 from the east can take exit 359 at Limon and follow U.S. 24 into the Springs. Arriving on I-70 from the west, the most direct route is exit 201 at Frisco, then Colo. 9 through Breckenridge 53 miles to U.S. 24 (at Hartsel), and then east 66 miles to the Springs. This route is mountainous, so check road conditions before setting out in winter.

VISITOR INFORMATION

The **Colorado Springs Convention and Visitors Bureau** is at 515 S. Cascade Ave., Colorado Springs, CO 80903 (© **800/888-4748** or 719/635-7506; fax 719/635-4968; www.coloradosprings-travel.com). Ask for the free *Official Visitor Guide to Colorado Springs and the Pikes Peak Region,* a colorful booklet with a comprehensive listing of accommodations, restaurants, and other area visitor services, as well as a basic but efficient map. Inquire at the Visitor Information Center or local bookstores for more detailed maps. An excellent one is the Pierson Graphics Corporation's *Colorado Springs and Monument Valley Street Map.*

Heads Up

At an elevation of 6,035 feet, Colorado Springs has two-thirds the oxygen found at sea level; Pikes Peak, at 14,110 feet, has only one-half the oxygen.

The **Visitor Information Center,** at the southeast corner of Cascade Avenue and Cimarron Street, is open from 8:30am to 5pm daily in summer, Monday through Friday in winter. From I-25, take the Cimarron Street exit (exit 141), and head east about 4 blocks. The center also operates a weekly events line with a 24-hour recording (© **719/635-1723**).

Visitors to Manitou Springs—every Colorado Springs visitor should also get to Manitou Springs—can get information from the **Manitou Springs Chamber of Commerce & Visitors Bureau,** 354 Manitou Ave., Manitou Springs,

CO 80829 (© **800/642-2567** or 719/685-5089; www.manitousprings.org). You can also contact the **Pikes Peak Country Attractions Association** at the same address (© **800/525-2250** or 719/685-5894; www.pikes-peak.com).

CITY LAYOUT

It's easy to get around central Colorado Springs, which is laid out on a classic grid pattern.

If you focus on the intersection of I-25 and U.S. 24, downtown Colorado Springs lies in the northeast quadrant, bounded on the west by I-25 and on the south by U.S. 24 (Cimarron St.). Boulder Street to the north and Wahsatch Avenue to the east complete the downtown frame. Nevada Avenue (Bus. 25 and U.S. 85) parallels the freeway for 15 miles through the city, intersecting it twice; Tejon Street and Cascade Avenue also run north–south through downtown between Nevada Avenue and the freeway. **Colorado Avenue** and **Platte Avenue** are the busiest east–west downtown cross streets.

West of downtown, Colorado Avenue extends through the historic Old Colorado City district and the quaint foothill community of **Manitou Springs,** rejoining U.S. 24—a busy but less interesting artery—as it enters Pike National Forest.

South of downtown, **Nevada Avenue** intersects **Lake Avenue,** the principal boulevard into the Broadmoor hotel, and proceeds south as Colo. 115 past Fort Carson.

North and east of downtown, **Academy Boulevard** (Colo. 83) is the street name to remember. From the south gate of the Air Force Academy north of the Springs, it winds through residential hills, crosses Austin Bluff Parkway, then runs without a curve 8 miles due south, finally bending west to intersect I-25 and Colo. 115 at Fort Carson. U.S. 24, which exits downtown east as Platte Avenue, and Fountain Boulevard, which leads to the airport, are among its cross streets. Austin Bluffs Parkway extends west of I-25 as **Garden of the Gods Road,** leading to that natural wonder.

City street addresses are divided by Pikes Peak Avenue into north and south; by Nevada Avenue into east and west.

2 Getting Around

Although Colorado Springs has public transportation, most visitors prefer to drive. Parking and roads are good, and some of the best attractions, such as the Garden of the Gods, are accessible only by car (or foot or bike for the truly ambitious).

BY CAR

For regulations and advice on driving in Colorado, see "Getting Around the Front Range," in chapter 2. The **American Automobile Association (AAA)** maintains an office in Colorado Springs at 3525 N. Carefree Circle (© **800/283-5222** or 719/591-2222; www.aaa.com), open Monday through Friday from 8:30am to 5:30pm and Saturday from 9am to 1pm.

CAR RENTALS   Car-rental agencies in Colorado Springs, some of which have offices in or near downtown as well as at the airport, include **Advantage** (© 800/777-5500 or 719/574-1144), **Alamo** (© 800/462-5366 or 719/574-8579), **Avis** (© 800/831-2847 or 719/596-2751), **Budget** (© 800/527-7000 or 719/473-6535), **Enterprise** (© 800/736-8222 or 719/636-3900), **Hertz** (© 800/654-3131 or 719/596-1863), **National** (© 866/342-0717 or 719/596-1519), and **Thrifty** (© 800/367-2277 or 719/390-9800).

PARKING   Most downtown streets have parking meters; the rate is 25¢ for a half-hour. Look for city-run parking lots, which charge 25¢ per half-hour and also offer day rates. Outside of downtown, free parking is generally available on side streets.

BY BUS

Colorado Springs Transit (📞 719/385-7433; www.springsgov.com) provides city bus service. Buses operate Monday through Friday from 5:20am to 10:40pm and Saturday from 7am to 6pm, except holidays. Fares on in-city routes are $1.25 for adults; 95¢ students; 60¢ for children 6 to 11, seniors, and passengers with disabilities; and free for children under 6. Fares for routes outside the city limits are 35¢ higher, except for free trolley service in Manitou Springs. Bus schedules can be obtained at terminals, city libraries, and the Colorado Springs Convention and Visitors Bureau.

BY TAXI

Call **Yellow Cab** (📞 **719/634-5000**) for taxi service.

ON FOOT

Each of the main sections of town can easily be explored without a vehicle. It's fun, for instance, to wander the winding streets of Manitou Springs or explore the Old Colorado City "strip." Between neighborhoods, however, distances are considerable. Unless you're particularly fit, it's wise to drive or take a bus or taxi.

FAST FACTS: **Colorado Springs**

American Express To report a lost card, call 📞 **800/528-4800;** to report lost traveler's checks, call 📞 **800/221-7282.**

Area Code The telephone area code is **719.**

Babysitters Front desks at major hotels often can make arrangements.

Business Hours Most banks are open Monday through Friday from 9am to 5pm, and some have Saturday hours. Major stores are open Monday through Saturday from 9 or 10am until 5 or 6pm (sometimes until 9pm Fri), and often Sunday from noon until 5pm. Stores that cater to tourists are usually open longer in the summer, with shorter hours in winter.

Car Rentals See "Getting Around," above.

Dentists For referrals for dentists who accept emergency patients, contact the **Colorado Springs Dental Society** (📞 **719/598-5161**).

Doctors For referrals and other health information, call **Healthlink** (📞 **719/444-2273**).

Drugstores **Walgreens,** 920 N. Circle Dr. (📞 **719/473-9090**), has a 24-hour prescription service.

Emergencies For police, fire, or medical emergencies, dial 📞 **911.** To reach **Poison Control,** call 📞 **800/332-3073.**

Eyeglasses You can get 1-hour replacement of lost or broken glasses at **Pearle Vision Express** in Citadel Mall (📞 **719/597-0757**) and **LensCrafters,** in Erindale Centre on North Academy Boulevard (📞 **719/548-8650**).

Hospitals **Memorial Hospital,** 1400 E. Boulder St. (© **719/365-5000**), offers full medical services, including 24-hour emergency treatment, as does **Penrose Hospital,** 2215 N. Cascade Ave. (© **719/776-5000**).

Newspapers & Magazines The *Gazette* (www.gazette.com), published daily in Colorado Springs, is the city's most widely read newspaper. The *Denver Post* is also available at newsstands throughout the city. The glossy *Springs* magazine and the politically oriented *Independent* are other free local periodicals. *USA Today* and the *Wall Street Journal* can be purchased on the street and at major hotels.

Photographic Needs There are dozens of photo-finishing outlets throughout the city, including **Walgreens** and **Shewmaker's Camera Shop,** in the Woodmen Valley Shopping Center, 6902 N. Academy Blvd. (© **719/598-6412**). For camera and video supplies and repairs as well as photo finishing, go to the central location of **Shewmaker's Camera Shop,** 30 N. Tejon St., downtown (© **719/636-1696;** www.shewmakers.com).

Post Office The main post office is downtown at 201 E. Pikes Peak Ave. Contact the U.S. Postal Service (© **800/275-8777;** www.usps.com) for hours and locations of other post offices.

Safety Although Colorado Springs is generally a safe city, it is not crime-free. Try to be aware of your surroundings at all times, and ask at your hotel or the visitor center about the safety of neighborhoods you plan to explore, especially after dark.

Taxes Total taxes on retail sales in Colorado Springs amount to about 6.4%; room taxes total about 9%. Rates in Manitou Springs are a bit higher.

Useful Telephone Numbers For **weather and road conditions,** including road construction, throughout the state, call © **303/639-1111** or visit www.cotrip.org.

3 Where to Stay

You'll find a wide range of lodging possibilities here, from Colorado's ritziest resort—The Broadmoor—to basic budget motels. There are also several particularly nice bed-and-breakfasts. The rates listed here are the officially quoted prices ("rack rates") and don't take into account individual or group discounts. Generally, rates are highest from Memorial Day to Labor Day, and lowest in the spring. During graduation and other special events at the Air Force Academy, rates can be absolutely ridiculous, and you may have trouble finding a room at any price. Rates listed below do not include the lodging tax (about 9% in Colorado Springs, almost 10% in Manitou Springs).

In addition to the accommodations described below, a number of moderately priced chain and franchise motels offer reliable lodging. These include the economical **Best Western Pikes Peak Inn,** 3010 N. Chestnut St., Colorado Springs, CO 80907 (© **800/223-9127** or 719/636-5201), which charges $49 to $99 double; **Econo Lodge Downtown,** 714 N. Nevada Ave., Colorado Springs, CO 80903 (© **800/553-2666** or 719/636-3385), with rates from $35 to $85 double; and **Super 8,** 4604 Rusina Rd., Colorado Springs, CO 80907 (© **800/800-8000** or 719/594-0964), which charges $45 to $70 double.

Colorado Springs Accommodations & Dining

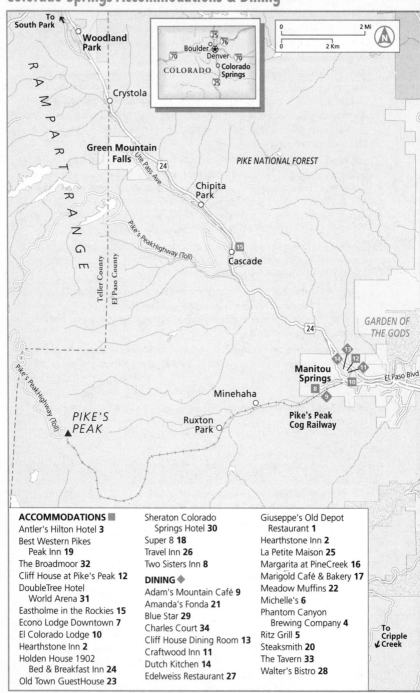

ACCOMMODATIONS ■
Antler's Hilton Hotel **3**
Best Western Pikes
 Peak Inn **19**
The Broadmoor **32**
Cliff House at Pike's Peak **12**
DoubleTree Hotel
 World Arena **31**
Eastholme in the Rockies **15**
Econo Lodge Downtown **7**
El Colorado Lodge **10**
Hearthstone Inn **2**
Holden House 1902
 Bed & Breakfast Inn **24**
Old Town GuestHouse **23**

Sheraton Colorado
 Springs Hotel **30**
Super 8 **18**
Travel Inn **26**
Two Sisters Inn **8**

DINING ◆
Adam's Mountain Café **9**
Amanda's Fonda **21**
Blue Star **29**
Charles Court **34**
Cliff House Dining Room **13**
Craftwood Inn **11**
Dutch Kitchen **14**
Edelweiss Restaurant **27**

Giuseppe's Old Depot
 Restaurant **1**
Hearthstone Inn **2**
La Petite Maison **25**
Margarita at PineCreek **16**
Marigold Café & Bakery **17**
Meadow Muffins **22**
Michelle's **6**
Phantom Canyon
 Brewing Company **4**
Ritz Grill **5**
Steaksmith **20**
The Tavern **33**
Walter's Bistro **28**

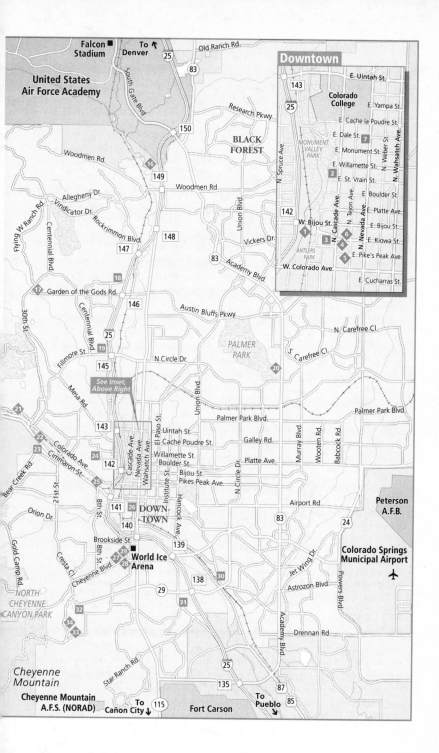

Falcon Stadium ■

To ↑ Denver

Old Ranch Rd.

25

83

United States Air Force Academy

South Gate Blvd.

Research Pkwy.

150

BLACK FOREST

Woodmen Rd.

16

149

Woodmen Rd.

Allegheny Dr.

Vindicator Dr.

Rockrimmon Blvd.

Union Blvd.

Vickers Dr.

148

147

83

Academy Blvd.

Flying W Ranch Rd.

Centennial Blvd.

18

17

Garden of the Gods Rd.

146

Austin Bluffs Pkwy.

30th St.

Centennial Blvd.

25

19

145

N. Circle Dr.

PALMER PARK

20

N. Carefree Cl.

S. Carefree Cl.

Mesa Rd.

Fillmore St.

Union Blvd.

Palmer Park Blvd.

21

See Inset, Above Right

143

Palmer Park Blvd.

Galley Rd.

Murray Blvd.

Wooten Rd.

Babcock Rd.

22

Colorado Ave.

23

Cimarron St.

24

142

Cascade Ave.

Nevada Ave.

Wahsatch Ave.

El Paso St.

Uintah St.

E. Cache Poudre St.

Willamette St.

Boulder St.

Bijou St.

Pikes Peak Ave.

Platte Ave.

N. Circle Dr.

Beer Creek Rd.

21st St.

25

8th St.

Institute St.

141

26

DOWN-TOWN

Hancock Ave.

Airport Rd.

83

24

Peterson A.F.B.

Orion Dr.

Cresta Cl.

140

Colorado Springs Municipal Airport ✈

Gold Camp Rd.

Brookside St.

8th St.

Cheyenne Blvd.

141

139

29

25

27

28

■ **World Ice Arena**

138

30

Jet Wing Dr.

Astrozon Blvd.

Academy Blvd.

Powers Blvd.

NORTH CHEYENNE CANYON PARK

32

34

33

31

Drennan Rd.

Cheyenne Mountain

Star Ranch Rd.

25

135

87

85

Cheyenne Mountain A.F.S. (NORAD)

To Cañon City ↓

115

Fort Carson

To Pueblo ↘

Downtown

E. Uintah St.

143

25

Colorado College

E. Yampa St.

E. Cache la Poudre St.

E. Dale St.

7

MONUMENT VALLEY PARK

E. Monument St.

2

E. Willamette St.

N. Spruce Ave.

E. St. Vrain St.

E. Boulder St.

142

N. Cascade Ave.

N. Tejon Ave.

N. Nevada Ave.

N. Weber St.

N. Wahsatch Ave.

W. Bijou St.

1

3

6

E. Bijou St.

4

E. Kiowa St.

ANTLERS PARK

5

E. Pike's Peak Ave.

W. Colorado Ave.

E. Cucharras St.

Those looking for a more upscale chain won't go wrong with the **Doubletree Hotel World Arena,** 1775 E. Cheyenne Mountain Blvd. (I-25 exit 138), Colorado Springs, CO 80906 (© **800/222-TREE** or 719/576-8900); or the **Sheraton Colorado Springs Hotel,** 2886 S. Circle Dr. (I-25 exit 138), Colorado Springs, CO 80906 (© **800/981-4012** or 719/576-5900).

VERY EXPENSIVE

The Broadmoor ⭐⭐⭐ (Kids)   We thought The Broadmoor couldn't get much better, but it's amazing what a mere $75 million can do. A massive renovation and restoration project, completed in spring 2002, has taken it to new heights of luxury, and also restored much of the historic building's grandeur. The Broadmoor is a sprawling resort complex of historic pink Mediterranean-style buildings with modern additions, set at the foot of Cheyenne Mountain on magnificently landscaped 3,000-acre grounds about 3½ miles southwest of downtown Colorado Springs. The Italian Renaissance–style Broadmoor opened in 1918. Its marble staircase, chandeliers, Italian tile, hand-painted beams and ceilings, and carved-marble fountain remain spectacles today. The priceless art collection features original work by Toulouse-Lautrec and Ming dynasty ceramicists. The first names entered on the guest register were those of John D. Rockefeller, Jr., and his party.

Behind the main building is lovely Cheyenne Lake; a swimming pool almost seamlessly attached to the west end looks like a part of the lake. This swimming complex will make you think you're at an oceanside beach resort, with water slides, 2 outdoor hot tubs, 13 cabanas, and an outdoor cafe.

The guest rooms occupy a series of separate buildings centered on the lake and pool area. The spacious, luxurious rooms are beautifully decorated in European style, with chandeliers, Italian fabrics, rich wood, and limited-edition works of art. Most units hold two double beds or one king-size bed, desks and tables, plush seating, and two-line portable phones, dataports, and Internet access through Web TV. Many rooms contain large soaking tubs and separate marble showers. The service is impeccable: The hotel averages two employees for every guest.

Lake Circle, at Lake Ave. (P.O. Box 1439), Colorado Springs, CO 80901. © **800/634-7711** or 719/634-7711. Fax 719/577-5700. www.broadmoor.com. 700 units. May–Oct $325–$470 double, $800 standard suite; Nov–Apr $225–$345 double, $295–$635 standard suite; year-round up to $3,100 large suite. AE, DC, DISC, MC, V. Free parking. **Amenities:** 11 restaurants (all Continental, American, or both); 4 lounges; outdoor pool cafe; 3 swimming pools (indoor, outdoor with water slide, outdoor lap pool); 2 outdoor hot tubs; 2 18-hole golf courses (3 in spring 2006); 9 all-weather tennis courts; state-of-the-art fitness center and full-service spa with aerobics classes, saunas, and whirlpool tubs; paddleboats; bicycle rentals; children's programs (summer); riding concierge; car-rental agency; shopping arcade; 24-hr. room service; in-room massage; valet laundry; stables; fly-fishing school; movie theater; shuttle bus between buildings; service station. *In room:* A/C, cable TV, dataport, minibar, coffeemaker, hair dryer, iron, safe.

EXPENSIVE

Antlers Hilton Hotel ⭐⭐   The Antlers has been a Colorado Springs landmark for more than a century, and remains a most impressive facility that is a cut above other high-end chain properties. Although the Antlers is in many ways geared to business travelers, for vacationers it offers first-rate accommodations within a short walking distance of many of Colorado Springs' major attractions and restaurants. There have been three different Antlers on this site. The first, a turreted Victorian showcase built in 1883, was named for General William Palmer's collection of deer and elk trophies. After it was destroyed by fire in 1898, Palmer built an extravagant Italian Renaissance–style building that survived until 1964, when it was leveled to make room for the more contemporary Antlers Plaza, set off from the street and featuring a modern, 13-story hotel with a rich marble- and woodwork-laden lobby.

Antique black-walnut nightstands from the previous incarnation provide a touch of historic continuity to the spacious guest rooms, which are handsomely decorated in earth tones with rich wood furnishings. Each room has two telephones, dataports, voice mail, a large working desk, and ample closet space. The corner rooms are larger, and we prefer the west-side rooms, which provide great views of Pikes Peak. On-site is Colorado Springs' first microbrewery: Judge Baldwin's Brewing Company.

4 S. Cascade Ave., Colorado Springs, CO 80903. © 877/754-9940 or 719/473-5600. Fax 719/389-0259. www.antlers.com. 292 units. Summer $129–$240 double; $250–$750 suite. Off-season discounts (10–30%) available. AE, DC, DISC, MC, V. Self-parking $8; valet $12. **Amenities:** 2 restaurants (American); indoor pool; fitness center; whirlpool; salon; room service (6:30am–11pm); laundry. *In room:* A/C, cable TV, coffeemaker, hair dryer, iron.

Cliff House at Pikes Peak ★★ *(Finds*   Striving to compete with the best that Colorado has to offer (and doing a pretty good job), the Cliff House is an old yet new facility. Built in 1874, it was designated a National Historic Landmark in 1980, and has hosted such eminent guests as Theodore Roosevelt, Clark Gable, and Thomas Edison. A major fire forced the Cliff House to close in 1982, and it remained closed until a massive reconstruction in 1997. The project incorporated several pieces of the hotel's original decor, including ornate woodwork and a tile fireplace, and what the fire destroyed was replicated with an emphasis on attention to detail. Once again a grand and luxurious hotel, the Cliff House reopened in July 1999.

Today, the lovely, uniquely decorated accommodations vary in size and personality, although the overall decor is Queen Anne–Victorian. Units range from average-size, relatively simple studios to large, luxurious celebrity suites named for former guests. Some units have gas fireplaces, two-person spas, steam showers, and terrific views of the mountains. All have live flowering plants, robes, heated toilet seats, working desks, and high-speed Internet access. We wouldn't turn down any room at the Cliff House, but our favorite is definitely the Clark Gable Suite ($475 double in summer), which is decorated in subdued Hollywood style—if you can call leopard-print wallpaper subdued—and contains a shower for two, a jetted tub, a wet bar and refrigerator, two TVs, a gas fireplace, and photos of Clark, who stayed at the hotel in the early 1940s.

There's a fine dining restaurant (see "Where to Dine," below), and the entire property is nonsmoking.

306 Cañon Ave., Manitou Springs, CO 80829. © 888/212-7000 or 719/685-3000. Fax 719/685-3913. www.thecliffhouse.com. 55 units. $145–$200 double; $189–$475 suite. Children under 13 stay free in parent's room. Rates include breakfast buffet. AE, DC, DISC, MC, V. **Amenities:** Restaurant (American); bar; small fitness center; concierge; activities desk; airport pickup; room service 7am–11pm; on-call massage; valet laundry service. *In room:* A/C, cable TV, VCR, CD player, dataport, coffeemaker, hair dryer, iron, safe.

Old Town GuestHouse ★★   Just a half-block south of the main street of Colorado Springs' historic Old Colorado City stands this three-story redbrick inn. It may appear to be from the 19th century, but innkeepers Kaye and David Caster designed and built it in 1997 to provide all the modern amenities in a warm and inviting atmosphere. The spacious rooms and modern conveniences make it an especially good choice for vacationers who will be doing a little work during their R and R.

All eight of the individually decorated rooms are named for flowers: for example, Colorado Columbine, with an attractive red, white, and blue quilt on the king bed; Moroccan Jasmine, with a Sahara Desert theme; Oriental Poppy, decorated with collectibles from the Orient; and romantic Victorian Rose. Each room has individual climate control, robes, and a queen or king bed. Several have gas-log fireplaces, seven have a private porch or balcony, and some have steam showers for two or private outdoor hot tubs. There's an elevator, and one room is Americans with Disabilities Act compliant.

The attractive library has a fireplace, music, and overstuffed chairs. Downstairs is a game room with pool table and exercise equipment, plus wireless Web access throughout the inn. On many weekends, Dave parks his 1936 Cadillac in front to add a festive historic touch.

115 S. 26th St., Colorado Springs, CO 80904. ℂ **888/375-4210** or 719/632-9194. Fax 719/632-9026. www. oldtown-guesthouse.com. 8 units. $99–$205 double. AE, DISC, MC, V. Off-road parking. Children under 12 not accepted. *In room:* A/C, cable TV, VCR, CD player, fridge, coffeemaker, hair dryer, iron.

MODERATE

Eastholme in the Rockies 🏵   Nestled in the quaint Pikes Peak mountain village of Cascade, 10 miles west of downtown Colorado Springs, this Victorian B&B gives guests an opportunity to see the city and get away from it all in the same day. Originally built in 1885 as a resort hotel, this property has a storied history that includes a stint as a boarding house before becoming a guest inn in 1988. Today it is a favorite of vacationers who want to be within striking distance of city attractions, but whose main interests lay in the Rockies.

The parlor holds a bay window, fireplace, and antiques. Most of the inn's large rooms feature 10-foot ceilings, and all provide plush quilts and remarkable views. The Marriott and Eisenhower suites feature original furnishings and a plethora of antiques, and the cottages offer VCRs, fireplaces, and spacious bathrooms with whirlpool tubs.

Breakfasts include freshly baked breads, pastries, and entrees such as soufflés or frittatas. The mountainous pine scenery of the Pike National Forest surrounds Eastholme, and stargazers love the views from the second-floor balcony, free of the light pollution of Colorado Springs. Guest amenities include a pleasant gazebo, shared kitchen, and library. Smoking is not permitted.

4445 Hagerman Ave. (P.O. Box 98), Cascade, CO 80809. ℂ **800/672-9901** or 719/684-9901. www.east holme.com. 8 units (6 with bathroom), including 2 cottages. $75–$120 double; $120 suite; $150 cottage. Rates include full breakfast. AE, DISC, MC, V. Free parking. 10 miles west of I-25, about 1 mile off U.S. 24. **Amenities:** Hot tub. *In room:* Cable TV w/VCR, fridge, coffeemaker, hair dryer.

Hearthstone Inn 🏵🏵   Among our top choices in Colorado Springs is this comfortably elegant small downtown lodging, a true old world–style inn that combines the allure of a grand, historic hotel with the intimacy of a small B&B. Actually two connected historic homes, built in 1885 and 1900, the Hearthstone is listed on the National Register of Historic Places and has won numerous preservation awards. Old photographs, numerous antiques, and reproductions decorate the inn. Some of the rooms can accommodate three or four people, and each unit has its own personality. The Study, for instance, is a parlor-style room with built-in bookcases and a fireplace. The Solarium features an open-air latticed porch, and the third-floor Loft has three dormer windows, a queen-size brass bed, and a tiny child's bed with a child-size rocking chair. Three rooms have fireplaces, and five have telephones with dataports. Breakfasts are wonderful, offering a choice of a half-dozen or so items such as breakfast burritos, and eggs Benedict. The restaurant, which is open to the public (see

Kids Family-Friendly Hotels

The Broadmoor (p. 184)   A lake and pool area with a terrific water slide, plus tennis, golf, riding stables, and a great summer kids' program that includes a visit to the Cheyenne Mountain Zoo all add up to a wonderful family experience.

Sheraton Colorado Springs Hotel (p. 184)   Two swimming pools, a separate children's pool, shuffleboard, and a putting green should keep most kids occupied.

"Where to Dine," below), also serves lunch and dinner. A common parlor has games, a piano, and fresh coffee. Children of all ages are welcome. Smoking is not permitted.

506 N. Cascade Ave., Colorado Springs, CO 80903. © **800/521-1885** or 719/473-4413. Fax 719/473-1322. www.hearthstoneinn.com. 25 units, 2 with shared bathroom. $99–$159 double with private bathroom, $69 double with shared bathroom; $199 suite. Rates include full breakfast. AE, DISC, MC, V. Free off-street lighted parking. Small, well-behaved pets accepted. **Amenities:** Restaurant (American). *In room:* A/C.

Holden House 1902 Bed & Breakfast Inn ★★   Innkeepers Sallie and Welling Clark restored this storybook 1902 Colonial Revival–style Victorian house and its adjacent carriage house, and filled the rooms with antiques and family heirlooms. Located near Old Colorado City, the inn has a living room with a tile fireplace, a front parlor with a TV, verandas, and a gazebo out back in a lovely garden. Guests enjoy 24-hour coffee and tea service with a bottomless cookie jar, plus a gourmet breakfast in the formal dining room. Smoking is not allowed and pets are not permitted—there are two resident cats, Mingtoy and Muffin.

Two rooms are in the main house and two are in the adjacent carriage house. Each guest room bears the name of a Colorado mining area and contains memorabilia of that district. All have sitting areas, queen-size beds, fireplaces, CD players, and tubs for two. The Cripple Creek suite features Victorian fretwork in the sitting area, a mahogany fireplace, and a magnificent Roman marble tub. The Independence Suite, in the adjacent building, is accessible to guests with disabilities and is cat-free for those with allergies.

1102 W. Pikes Peak Ave., Colorado Springs, CO 80904. © **888/565-3980** or 719/471-3980. Fax 719/471-4740. www.holdenhouse.com. 5 suites. $125–$150 double. Rates include full breakfast. AE, DC, DISC, MC, V. Children not accepted. *In room:* A/C, TV w/DVD player, fridge; hair dryer, iron.

Two Sisters Inn ★★   Built by two sisters in 1919 as a boarding house, this splendid bed-and-breakfast has been owned and operated by two women—sisters in spirit if not in blood—since 1990. Wendy Goldstein and Sharon Smith have furnished the four bedrooms and separate honeymoon cottage with family heirlooms and photographs, in a style best described as informal elegance. The rooms in the main house feature Victorian frills and furnishings, such as quilts and claw-foot bathtubs. The two rooms that share a bathroom are only rented together ($69 for the second bedroom), which is a great choice for two couples or for parents traveling with teenagers. Across a splendid garden area, the small cottage, with a separate bedroom and living room, has a feather bed, gas-log fireplace, refrigerator, and shower with skylight. Fresh flowers adorn each room, and homemade chocolates and baked goods are served upon arrival. The rooms are great, but we especially like the breakfasts, which the proprietors describe as "healthy decadence." They often cook with herbs and vegetables from their garden, and do some marvelous things with fruit. In the summer, Wendy and Sharon's lemonade, made fresh with naturally sparkling Manitou Springs water, is the perfect refreshment. Smoking is not permitted.

10 Otoe Place, Manitou Springs, CO 80829. ✆ 800/2SISINN or 719/685-9684. www.twosisinn.com. 5 units. $105 double; $125 cottage. Rates include full breakfast. DISC, MC, V. Children under 11 not accepted. Located 1 block south of the town clock on Manitou Ave.

INEXPENSIVE

El Colorado Lodge   While not particularly ritzy, El Colorado is an economical lodging and more interesting than a standard motel. The Southwestern-style cabins are a tad dated, but all of them have fireplaces and beamed ceilings, and nine have kitchens. Each holds one to three rooms and can accommodate two to six people. The lodge boasts the largest outdoor swimming pool in Manitou Springs and an outdoor pavilion for groups. Complimentary coffee is served during the summer.

23 Manitou Ave., Manitou Springs, CO 80829. ✆ 800/782-2246 or 719/685-5485. Fax 719/685-4699. www.pikes-peak.com/elcolorado. 26 cabins (6 with shower only). Summer $69–$125 cabin. Winter discounts available. AE, DC, DISC, MC, V. Free parking. **Amenities:** Large outdoor pool. *In room:* A/C, cable TV, kitchen, fridge, microwave.

Travel Inn *(Value)*   Popular with both business travelers and vacationers on a budget, the Travel Inn offers a comfortable place to sleep at very reasonable rates. The two-story motel with bright turquoise trim is conveniently located near downtown Colorado Springs, with easy access to all the area attractions on I-25 and U.S. 24. The recently remodeled rooms are simple and comfortable, with white stucco walls and dark-wood furnishings. There is one apartment with a kitchenette that is designed for longer stays.

512 S. Nevada Ave., Colorado Springs, CO 80903. ✆ 719/636-3986. Fax 719/636-3980. 34 units (most with shower only). Summer $45–$52 double; winter $32–$37 double. Rates include continental breakfast. AE, DC, DISC, MC, V. Free parking. **Amenities:** Coin-op laundry. *In room:* A/C, cable TV, kitchenette.

CAMPING

Also see the section on **Mueller State Park** under "Parks & Zoos," later in this chapter.

Garden of the Gods Campground   Located near Garden of the Gods (see "Attractions," p. 198), this large, tree-shaded campground offers 250 full RV hookups (30- and 50-amp service, some with modems and phones), and additional tent sites. Facilities include tables, barbecue grills, bathhouses, a grocery store, Internet cafe, laundry, heated swimming pool, whirlpool tub, playground, and clubhouse with pool tables and game room. The 12 camping cabins, which share the campground's bathhouse, rent for $40 double. Tours are also offered (see "Organized Tours," later in this chapter).

3704 W. Colorado Ave., Colorado Springs, CO 80904. ✆ 800/248-9451 or 719/475-9450. www.coloradocampground.com. $28–$38 for 2 people. Extra person $3. DISC, MC, V. Take I-25 exit 141, head west on U.S. 24, then north (right) on 31st St., then left on Colorado Ave. for 6 blocks (keep right), and turn right to gate.

4 Where to Dine

Colorado Springs has an excellent variety of above-average restaurants, with a good sampling of continental cuisine, Mexican restaurants, and steak joints. See also the section on dinner theaters in "Colorado Springs After Dark," later in this chapter. A good online resource for information on area restaurants and nightlife is www.sceneinthesprings.com.

VERY EXPENSIVE

Charles Court ★★ PROGRESSIVE AMERICAN   The English country-manor atmosphere of this outstanding restaurant at The Broadmoor resort, with picture windows looking across Cheyenne Lake to the renowned hotel, lends itself to a fine dining experience. The creative American menu, which changes seasonally, has a decidedly Rocky Mountain emphasis. You'll usually find such delicacies as Colorado rack of lamb, beef tenderloin, salmon filet, grilled ahi tuna, and a wild-game selection such as Colorado elk. The wine list includes more than 600 selections, service is superlative, and the desserts are extraordinary. A seasonal outdoor patio provides splendid views of the mountains across the lake.

Broadmoor W., in The Broadmoor, Lake Circle. ✆ **719/634-7711.** Reservations recommended. Breakfast $7.75–$16; dinner main courses $18–$36. AE, DC, DISC, MC, V. Daily 7–11am and 6–10pm.

Cliff House Dining Room ★★ AMERICAN   The Cliff House Dining Room is an excellent choice for a romantic occasion. The Villeroy & Boch china, damask linen, crystal glassware, and 19th-century tiled fireplace evoke the charm of the Victorian era. Dinners are the main event; old favorites expertly prepared in new ways. We recommend the filet mignon, charbroiled with roasted garlic pepper, and the seafood (trout to scallops and prawns), but everything is quite good. As would be expected, service is impeccable. The breakfast menu offers traditional American selections, plus a nifty wild-mushroom Florentine with smoked bacon, and lunches are upscale sandwiches and entrees like quiche du jour and blackened ruby red trout. The excellent wine list includes some 600 selections.

Cliff House Inn, 306 Cañon Ave., Manitou Springs. ✆ **719/785-2415.** Reservations recommended. Lunch main courses $7–$24; fixed-price lunch $18; dinner main courses $24–$32. AE, DC, DISC, MC, V. Daily 6:30–10:30am, 11:30am–2:30pm, and 5:30–9:30pm.

Craftwood Inn ★★★ *Finds* COLORADO CUISINE   Ensconced in an English Tudor building with beamed ceilings, stained-glass windows, and a copper-hooded fireplace, the casually elegant Craftwood Inn, built in 1912, was originally a coppersmith's shop. Today this excellent restaurant specializes in regional game and also offers steak, seafood, and vegetarian dishes. The extensive selection of game—elk, venison, pheasant, quail, caribou, antelope, wild boar, ostrich, and buffalo—attracts the most acclaim. We especially recommend grilled Rocky Mountain elk steak (when available), marinated in herb and smoke-infused oil, and served with wild-mushroom ragout, cabernet sauvignon glace, and cheddar-sage whipped potatoes. The adventurous might opt for the wild grill: grilled North American elk, seared loin of antelope, and braised venison sausage, served with pear potato. Be sure to save room for one of the superb—and somewhat unusual—desserts, such as jalapeño white-chocolate mousse with raspberry sauce, or prickly pear sorbet. The outdoor patio provides wonderful views of Pikes Peak.

404 El Paso Blvd., Manitou Springs. ✆ **719/685-9000.** Reservations recommended. Main courses $18–$38. AE, DC, DISC, MC, V. Daily 5:30–8:30pm. Turn north off Manitou Ave. onto Mayfair Ave., go uphill 1 block, and turn left onto El Paso Blvd.; the Craftwood is on your right.

Walter's Bistro ★★★ CONTINENTAL   Slick but not stuffy, Walter's manages to be classy, casual, and classic, all at once. Proprietor Walter Iser, a native of Salzburg, Austria, has long worked the front of the house in various upscale properties in the Springs and environs, but he's truly hit his stride with Walter's, which opened in 1999 and relocated to a handsome new location in 2004. Watching over four dining areas—including a richly decorated "red room" and a chef's table beneath windows into the kitchen—Iser's gracious style and steady direction leads right into an expertly prepared menu of continental staples that manage to simultaneously taste traditional and completely original. The menu changes regularly, but our visit included a terrific rack of lamb, herb-roasted and served with a creamy English pea risotto, pan-roasted Chilean sea bass, and a truly phenomenal bone-in filet mignon with an equally superlative bread pudding with wild mushrooms and andouille sausage. Desserts are decadent, including a chocolate "bag" filled with tiramisu, and the wine list is long and varied.

136 E. Cheyenne Mountain Blvd. (C) **719/630-0201.** Reservations recommended. Lunch main courses $7–$24; fixed-price lunch $18; dinner main courses $24–$32. AE, DC, DISC, MC, V. Mon–Fri 11am–2pm; Sun–Thurs 5:30–9pm; Fri–Sat 5:30–10pm; Sun brunch 10:30am–2pm.

EXPENSIVE

Blue Star ★★ MEDITERRANEAN   In a quiet area just south of downtown, Blue Star is one of the most popular eateries in Colorado Springs, and deservedly so. The menu changes weekly, but it always includes filet mignon, fresh fish (flown in daily), pasta, pork, and chicken, prepared with a nose for invention. The culinary inspiration from both Mediterranean and Pacific Rim cultures; the restaurant might serve Thai beef tips one week and beef bourguignon the next. Standing-room-only on weekends, the bar features sleek wood-and-metal decor and well-lighted artwork on the walls, while the dining room's atmosphere is milder with an open kitchen. Each serves its own menu: The bar one is "eating" (i.e., lunch, dinner, tapas, live jazz Mondays, dancing on weekends) and the main room is serious "dining," dinner only, as the proprietors say. Blue Star won *Wine Spectator*'s "Best of" award with its 6,000-bottle cellar in 2003.

1645 S. Tejon St. (C) **719/632-1086.** Reservations recommended. Main courses $7–$13 lunch, $15–$24 dinner. AE, MC, V. Dining room Sun–Thurs 5:30–9pm; Fri–Sat 5:30–10pm. Bar open during restaurant hours; bar food service Mon–Fri 11:30am–midnight.

Hearthstone Inn ★ AMERICAN   Located in one of our favorite Colorado Springs inns, this restaurant offers a splendid atmosphere and equally splendid food. The dining room, like the rest of the historic Hearthstone Inn, is decorated in elegant yet comfortable Victorian style. The cuisine is innovative American—you'll always recognize what you're eating, but you've likely never seen or tasted it quite this way before. The breakfast menu includes well-prepared standards and more exotic dishes such as blue-crab fritters with jalapeño hollandaise and sweet-potato scallion cakes. At lunch, try cayenne-dusted rainbow trout, served with simmered black beans and green chile polenta. Dinners include mostly beef and seafood. Grilled New York strip steak with bourbon sauce is quite good, and we also recommend pan-roasted North Atlantic salmon with cranberry-tarragon aioli and goat cheese polenta.

506 N. Cascade Ave. (C) **800/521-1885** or 719/473-4413. Main courses $7–$12 lunch, $12–$25 dinner. AE, DISC, MC, V. Mon–Tues 7am–2pm; Wed–Thurs and Sun 7am–7pm; Fri–Sat 7am–9pm.

La Petite Maison ★★ FRENCH/CONTEMPORARY   This delightful 1894 Victorian cottage houses a gem of a restaurant. It serves a blend of classic French and eclectic modern cuisine in a friendly, intimate setting with jazz playing in the background. The food is innovative, interesting, and well presented; service is impeccable. This is where locals go to celebrate special occasions. An attractive patio is open in warm weather, and the luncheon/patio menu is available anytime the patio is open (until 11pm in summer). The menus change monthly; if they're available, we suggest curried chicken salad with cashews and grapes, and crab cakes with corn pico de gallo. Being beefeaters, we especially like a dinner of grilled Black Angus filet with fresh horseradish and peppercorn crust and shallot jus. Another good dinner item is nut-crusted duck breast with brandy-infused cherries. There's also usually a handmade vegetarian pasta of the day. Desserts, all made in-house, might include white-chocolate mousse with fresh berries, fresh fruit tart with almond paste, or crème brûlée.

1015 W. Colorado Ave. ℂ **719/632-4887.** Reservations recommended. Main courses $8–$15 patio/lunch, $17–$28 dinner. AE, DC, DISC, MC, V. Mon–Fri 11am–2pm; Mon–Sat 5–10pm.

Margarita at PineCreek ★★ ECLECTIC A delightful spot to sit and watch the sun setting over Pikes Peak, the Margarita is tucked away above two creeks on the north side of the city. The decor is attractively simple, with tile floors and stucco walls; a tree-shaded outdoor patio is open in summer. Saturday evenings bring live harpsichord music in the dining room, and Friday nights often feature live acoustic music—bluegrass to Celtic.

Although the style of cooking may vary, depending on the chef's whim, the emphasis is on fresh ingredients, and everything is prepared from scratch, including breads and stocks. Lunches feature a choice of soup (usually a broth and a bisque), salad, and fresh bread; there's also a Southwestern special. Six-course dinners offer three entree choices, usually fresh fish, veal, steak, pasta, lamb, or duckling.

7350 Pine Creek Rd. ℂ **719/598-8667.** Reservations recommended. Fixed-price lunch $9.50; fixed-price dinner $30–$35; brunch $10–$15. AE, DISC, MC, V. Tues–Fri 11:30am–2pm; Tues–Sat 5:30–9pm; Sun 10:30am–2pm.

Steaksmith ★★ STEAK/SEAFOOD The Steaksmith serves some of the best steaks and seafood in the region, and is our choice for an evening of serious beef-eating. Lots of wood and hanging plants give the dining room a comfortable, relaxing atmosphere, and a big fireplace is the centerpiece of the lounge. This is the place to come for top-quality choice-aged, house-cut beef. We especially recommend cracked-peppercorn top sirloin, served on a bed of demi-glace with cognac cream sauce. Not keen on sauces on your steak? You won't be sorry trying rib-eye, broiled under high heat. The Steaksmith also offers excellent fresh fish and seafood; if it's on the menu, you can't miss with wild-caught Alaskan king salmon. The Mexican jumbo shrimp plate, either broiled or deep-fried, is also something special. Be warned that some items often sell out early in the evening—a sure sign of success. The menu, much of which changes daily, also may include Colorado lamb chops, vegetarian entrees, homemade soups, and delicious homemade desserts. There's a full-service bar and an extensive wine list. Smoking is allowed only in the fireside cocktail lounge.

3802 Maizeland Rd. (at Academy Blvd.). ℂ **800/201-2736** or 719/596-9300. Reservations recommended. Main courses $14–$35. AE, DISC, MC, V. Daily 5–10pm. Bar opens at 4:30pm.

The Tavern ★★ STEAK/SEAFOOD Authentic Toulouse-Lautrec lithographs on the walls and knotty pine furniture and paneling mark the Tavern as a restaurant with unusual ambience. In the front dining room, a four-piece ensemble follows piano music nightly—guests are welcome to take a turn around the dance floor between courses. The quieter garden room, with luxuriant tropical foliage, gives the feeling of outdoor dining without being outdoors. Service in both rooms is impeccable.

Many selections are prepared in the restaurant's stone grill, and the emphasis is on fresh ingredients and classic cuisine. The lunch menu features changes seasonally, but typically includes steaks, gourmet burgers, crab cakes, and a variety of sandwiches and salads. Dinners are more elaborate: Choose from slow-roasted prime rib, filet mignon, blackened or broiled salmon, or half a roast duck or chicken. All entrees come with a selection of homemade breads.

Broadmoor Main, at The Broadmoor, Lake Circle. ℂ 719/634-7711. Reservations recommended. Main courses $7.50–$17 lunch, $17–$35 dinner. AE, DC, DISC, MC, V. Daily 11am–11pm.

MODERATE

Edelweiss Restaurant ✮ (Kids) GERMAN The Edelweiss occupies an impressive stone building with a trio of fireplaces and an outdoor patio. It underscores its Bavarian atmosphere with strolling folk musicians on weekends, which gives it a party feel that makes this a fun place for kids. It offers a hearty menu of Jägerschnitzel, Wiener schnitzel, sauerbraten, bratwurst, and other old-country specials, as well as New York strip steak, fresh fish, and chicken. The fruit strudels are excellent, and there are some great German beers.

34 E. Ramona Ave. (southwest of I-25, 1 block west of Nevada Ave.). ℂ 719/633-2220. Reservations recommended. Main courses $6–$8.25 lunch, $9.75–$19.95 dinner. AE, DC, DISC, MC, V. Tues–Fri 11:30am–9pm; Sat 5–9pm; Sun noon–9pm.

Giuseppe's Old Depot Restaurant ✮ (Kids) ITALIAN/AMERICAN Located in a restored Denver & Rio Grande train station with glass ticket windows lining the walls, Giuseppe's is a fun place with a lot of historic ambience. You can see freight trains going by just outside the windows. The same extensive menu is served all day. Spaghetti, lasagna (vegetarian spinach or spicy sausage and ground beef), and stone-baked pizza are house specialties. American dishes include our favorite—baby back pork ribs, smothered in Giuseppe's secret sauce—plus prime rib, grilled salmon filet, and fried chicken.

10 S. Sierra Madre St. ℂ 719/635-3111. Menu items $5–$23; pizzas $10–$15. AE, DC, DISC, MC, V. Sun–Thurs 11am–9pm; Fri–Sat 11am–10pm.

Marigold Café and Bakery ✮ INTERNATIONAL This bustling restaurant and bakery is known for its fresh ingredients and homemade breads and pastries. A low wall separates the bakery counter from the cafelike dining area. Breakfast and lunch are casual, featuring traditional menus and gourmet-savvy items such as Greek pizzas and innovative sandwiches served on fresh breads. The restaurant takes on a more refined atmosphere at dinner, when the menu

---

(Kids) Family-Friendly Restaurants

Edelweiss Restaurant (see above) Kids will enjoy the strolling musicians who play German folk music on weekends, and they'll love the apple and cherry strudels.

Giuseppe's Old Depot Restaurant (see above) An original locomotive stands outside this old Denver & Rio Grande Railroad station. Most kids will adore the spaghetti and pizza.

Meadow Muffins (p. 194) The junk-store appearance and kid-friendly food (like a burger with peanut butter) make this place a hit with the younger set.

reflects a wide range of international influences. Favorites include *culotte* of beef (grilled sirloin steak with shallot red-wine sauce) and papillotte salmon, baked with sun-dried-tomato pesto, fresh lemon, dill, and leeks. The bakery counter bustles through the early afternoon, offering splendid breads, pastries, and sandwiches. Box lunches, coffee, lattes, and cappuccinos are also available.

4605 Centennial Blvd. (at Garden of the Gods Rd.). ✆ 719/599-4776. Main courses $5.50–$10 lunch, $9.25–$23 dinner. AE, DC, DISC, MC, V. Restaurant Mon–Sat 7–10:30am, 11am–2:30pm, and 5–9pm. Coffee bar and bakery Mon–Fri 6am–9pm; Sat 7am–9pm. Closed Sun.

Phantom Canyon Brewing Co. ⋆ CONTEMPORARY AMERICAN   This popular, busy, noisy brewpub is in the Cheyenne Building, home to the Chicago Rock Island & Pacific Railroad in the early 1900s. On any given day, 8 to 10 of Phantom Canyon's specialty beers are on tap, including homemade root beer. The signature beer is the Phantom, a traditional India pale ale; others include an amber ale, a light ale called Queen's Blonde, and Zebulon's Peated Porter.

The dining room is large and wide open, with ceiling fans, hardwood floors, and the large brewing vats, visible in the corner. Lunch is typical but well-prepared brewpub fare: wood-fired pizzas, hearty salads, half-pound beef or buffalo burgers, fish-and-chips, and the like. The dinner menu is varied and more innovative, with choices such as sesame chicken stir-fry with sticky rice, or brie-stuffed top sirloin, or even macaroni and smoked gouda cheese tossed with bacon, spinach, and shiitake mushrooms. The menu changes periodically. On the second floor is a billiard hall with its own menu of pizza, calzones, salad, and appetizers. See also "Colorado Springs After Dark," later in this chapter.

2 E. Pikes Peak Ave. ✆ 719/635-2800. Main courses $7.25–$11 lunch, $9.95–$19 dinner. AE, DC, DISC, MC, V. Mon–Thurs 11am–10pm; Fri–Sat 11am–midnight; Sun 9am–10pm.

Ritz Grill ⋆ NEW AMERICAN   This lively restaurant-lounge with a large central bar is where it's at for many of the city's young professionals. The decor is Art Deco, the service fast and friendly. The varied, trendy menu offers such specialties as Garden Ritz veggie pizza, with fresh spinach, sun-dried tomatoes, bell peppers, onions, mushrooms, fresh pesto, and three cheeses; and Chinese chicken salad—served with rice noodles, tomatoes, water chestnuts, and other veggies. For beefeaters, we recommend the mesquite-grilled 8-ounce center-cut filet mignon, served on a bed of raspberry-chipotle demi-glace, or the semolina-crusted salmon with shrimp and spinach nantua sauce. See also "Colorado Springs After Dark," later in this chapter.

15 S. Tejon St. ✆ 719/635-8484. Main courses $6–$12 brunch and lunch, $10–$25 dinner. AE, MC, V. Mon–Thurs 11am–midnight; Fri–Sat 11am–1am; Sun 9:30am–midnight. Bar open later with a limited menu.

INEXPENSIVE

Adam's Mountain Cafe ⋆⋆ *Finds* AMERICAN/VEGETARIAN   Not strictly vegetarian, Adam's Mountain Cafe is one of the best restaurants in the area for those seeking vegetarian or what we might call health food. Exposed brick and stone, antique tables and chairs, fresh flowers, and original works by a local artist create a country French–Victorian appearance. The menu includes grilled items, fresh fish, and many Mediterranean-style entrees. Breakfast specialties include orange-almond French toast, our top choice, and the P. W. Busboy Special, consisting of two whole-grain pancakes, two scrambled eggs, and slices of fresh fruit. Lunch offerings include sandwiches, soups, salads, fresh pasta, and Southwestern plates. We recommend the harvest crepes, packed with roasted butternut squash and finished with a vegetarian red chile, and the Caribbean jerked chicken.

110 Cañon Ave., Manitou Springs. ℂ **719/685-1430.** Main courses $4.50–$7.50 breakfast and lunch, $7–$16 dinner. AE, DISC, MC, V. Daily 8am–3pm; Tues–Sat 5–9pm.

Amanda's Fonda ⭐ *Finds* AMERICAN   Our pick for Mexican food in Colorado Springs, Amanda's Fonda is the handiwork of a family that has owned Mexican restaurants for five generations. Clearly they've honed the art of making remarkable chile in that time: Both the chile Colorado and the green chile are excellent; the former is red with big hunks of steak, the latter spicier with pork. The burritos, spinach-and-mushroom enchiladas, and seafood are also quite tasty, and the menu includes both menudo and pozole on weekends. The interior of the place is a funky maze, one part log cabin, one part suburban family restaurant, and one part Mexican bar and grill.

3625 W. Colorado Ave. ℂ **719/227-1975.** Main courses $6–$12. AE, DISC, MC, V. Mon–Sat 11:30–9pm; Sun noon–9pm.

Dutch Kitchen ⭐ *Value* AMERICAN   Good homemade food served in a casual, friendly atmosphere is the draw at this relatively small restaurant, which the Flynn family has owned and operated since 1959. We especially like the corned beef, pastrami, and ham sandwiches, and if you're there in summer, be sure to try the fresh rhubarb pie. Other house specialties include buttermilk pie and homemade soups.

1025 Manitou Ave., Manitou Springs. ℂ **719/685-9962.** Main courses $4.25–$7.10 lunch, $6.15–$12.65 dinner. No credit cards. Sat–Thurs 11:30am–3:30pm and 4:30–8pm. Closed Thurs in spring and fall. Closed Dec–Feb.

Meadow Muffins ⭐ *Value* *Kids* AMERICAN   A fun spot for a good, inexpensive meal in a lively atmosphere, Meadow Muffins is a boisterous bar packed with movie memorabilia and assorted oddities. The decorations range from two buckboard wagons (hung from the ceiling near the front door) that were supposedly used in *Gone with the Wind* to a 5-ton cannon used in a number of war movies. The menu includes chicken wings, onion rings, sandwiches, salads, and the like. The burgers are especially good—just ask anyone in the Springs—but we have to admit that we couldn't bring ourselves to try the Jiffy Burger: a large ground-beef burger topped with bacon, provolone cheese, and—believe it or not—peanut butter. On most days, there are great food and drink specials. See also "Colorado Springs After Dark," later in this chapter.

2432 W. Colorado Ave., in Old Colorado City. ℂ **719/633-0583.** Most menu items $4.25–$6.75. AE, DISC, MC, V. Daily 11am–2am (or earlier, depending on business).

Michelle's ⭐ *Value* AMERICAN/GREEK/SOUTHWESTERN   The menu is eclectic, but it's amazing how many different dishes Michelle's prepares well—and at such reasonable prices. Since it opened in 1952, this charming little diner and candy store hasn't changed much: It's long been known for its excellent handmade chocolates, fresh-churned ice cream, and Greek specialties such as gyros and spanakopita. It also serves good burgers, croissant sandwiches, a half-dozen salads, numerous omelets, and a delicious breakfast burrito. A three-page ice-cream menu includes everything from a single scoop of vanilla to the "Believe It or Not Sundae" featured in *Life* magazine in November 1959: It weighs 42 pounds and includes every flavor of ice cream Michelle's makes!

122 N. Tejon St. ℂ **719/633-5089.** Reservations not accepted. Lunch and dinner $5–$8.50. AE, DC, DISC, MC, V. Mon–Thurs 9am–11pm; Fri–Sat 9am–midnight; Sun 10am–11pm.

5 Attractions

Most of the attractions of the Pikes Peak region fit in two general categories: natural, such as Pikes Peak, Garden of the Gods, and Cave of the Winds, and historic/educational, including the Air Force Academy, Olympic Complex training center, museums, historic homes, and art galleries. There are also gambling houses in Cripple Creek.

If you visit Colorado from a sea-level area, you might want to schedule mountain excursions, such as the cog railway to the top of Pikes Peak, at the end of your stay. This will give your body time to adapt to the lower oxygen level at these higher elevations. See also "Health & Safety," in chapter 2.

SUGGESTED ITINERARIES

If You Have 1 Day

Begin your day early by visiting the **Garden of the Gods,** a unique geological site with red sandstone pillars, then go on to the **Cave of the Winds,** an underground cavern. Afterward, head downtown to the **Colorado Springs Pioneers Museum** for an overview of the history of the region. After lunch, tour the **Air Force Academy.** If time remains, visit the **Pro-Rodeo Hall of Fame.**

If You Have 2 Days

Spend your first day as suggested above. Begin day 2 with a 1-hour tour of the **Olympic Complex training center,** followed by stops at **Ghost Town** and **Van Briggle**

Art Pottery. After lunch, visit **Old Colorado City, McAllister House,** the **Fine Arts Center,** and the **Museum of the American Numismatic Association.**

If You Have 3 Days

Spend your first 2 days as suggested above. On day 3, head to **Manitou Springs** for a self-guided mineral-springs historical walking tour; information is available at the visitor center. Then go to **Miramont Castle** and the **Manitou Cliff Dwellings.** Check out the Manitou Springs shops and galleries, enjoy lunch, and then hop aboard the **cog railway** for a trip to the top of **Pikes Peak.**

THE TOP ATTRACTIONS

United States Air Force Academy ★★   Colorado Springs' pride and joy got its start in 1954 when Congress authorized the establishment of a U.S. Air Force Academy and chose this 18,000-acre site from among 400 prospective locations. The first class of cadets enrolled in 1959, and each year since, about 4,000 cadets have enrolled for the 4 years of rigorous training required to become Air Force officers.

The academy is 12 miles north of downtown; enter at the North Gate, off I-25 exit 156B. Soon after entering the grounds, at the intersection of North Gate Boulevard and Stadium Boulevard, you'll see an impressive outdoor B-52 bomber display. Where North Gate Boulevard becomes Academy Drive (in another mile or so), look to your left to see the Cadet Field House, where the basketball and ice hockey teams play (see "Spectator Sports," later in this chapter), and the Parade Ground, where you can sometimes spot cadets marching.

Academy Drive soon curves to the left. Six miles from the North Gate, signs mark the turnoff to the Barry Goldwater Air Force Academy Visitor Center. Open daily, it offers a variety of exhibits and films on the academy's history and cadet life, extensive literature and self-guided tour maps, and the latest information and schedules on academy activities. There's also a large gift shop and coffee shop.

Colorado Springs Attractions

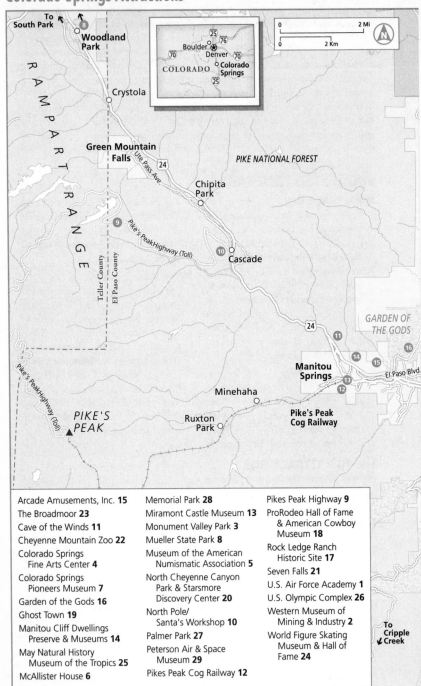

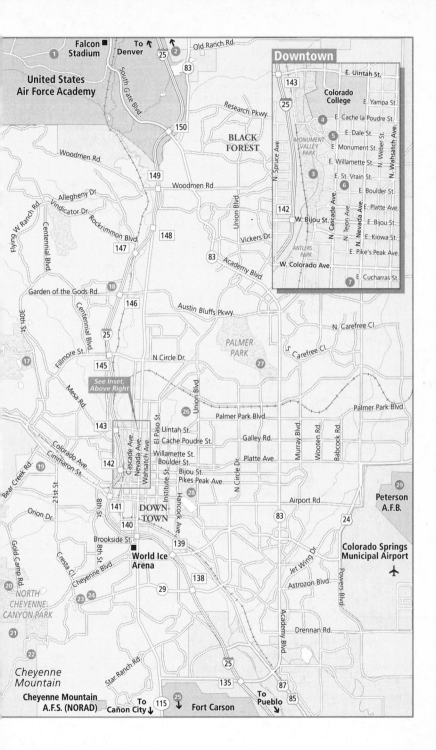

Falcon Stadium ■
① To ↖ Denver ↑ Old Ranch Rd.
25 2

United States
Air Force Academy

South Gate Blvd.

83

Research Pkwy.

150

BLACK FOREST

149

Woodmen Rd.
Woodmen Rd.

Allegheny Dr.
Vindicator Dr.
Rockrimmon Blvd.

Flying W Ranch Rd.
Centennial Blvd.

148

147

Union Blvd

Vickers Dr.

83 Academy Blvd

⑱
Garden of the Gods Rd.
146

Centennial Blvd.
Austin Bluffs Pkwy.

30th St.
Fillmore St.
25
145

⑰

N Circle Dr.
PALMER PARK
②⑦

Mesa Rd.
See Inset,
Above Right

143
26
Union Blvd

Palmer Park Blvd.
Palmer Park Blvd.

N Circle Dr.
Murray Blvd.
Wooten Ave.
Babcock Rd.

Uintah St.
Cascade Ave.
Nevada Ave.
Wahsatch Ave.
El Paso St.
Cache Poudre St.

Colorado Ave.
Cimmaron St.
⑲

142
Willamette St.
Boulder St.
Bijou St.
Galley Rd.

Platte Ave.

Bear Creek Rd.
21st St.
Pikes Peak Ave.
Institute St.

28
Airport Rd.

141
DOWN-
TOWN
Hancock Ave.

83
24

Orion Dr.
8th St.
140

Peterson A.F.B.
29

Colorado Springs
Municipal Airport
✈

Brookside St.
139

World Ice
Arena

Gold Camp Rd.
Cresta Ci.
8th St.
Cheyenne Blvd.
138
Jet Wing Dr.

⑳
NORTH CHEYENNE CANYON PARK
23 24
29
Astrozon Blvd.

Academy Blvd.

②①

②②

Drennan Rd.
Powers Blvd.

Cheyenne Mountain

Cheyenne Mountain
A.F.S. (NORAD)
To
Cañon City ↓
115
25 ↓
Fort Carson
Star Ranch Rd.
25
135
87
85
To Pueblo ↓

Downtown

143
E. Uintah St.
25
Colorado College
E. Yampa St.
④ E. Cache la Poudre St.
MONUMENT VALLEY PARK
⑤ E. Dale St.
N. Spruce Ave.
E. Monument St.
③
E. Willamette St.
N. Weber St.
N. Wahsatch Ave.
⑥ E. St. Vrain St.
E. Boulder St.
142
W. Bijou St.
E. Platte Ave.
N. Cascade Ave.
N. Tejon Ave.
N. Nevada Ave.
E. Bijou St.
E. Kiowa St.
ANTLERS PARK
E. Pike's Peak Ave.
W. Colorado Ave.
⑦ E. Cucharras St.

197

Fun Fact **Fit for the Gods**

In 1859 large numbers of pioneers were arriving in Colorado hoping to find gold (their motto: "Pikes Peak or Bust"). Many of them established communities along what is now called the Front Range, including Colorado City, which was later incorporated within Colorado Springs.

Legend has it that certain pioneers who explored the remarkable sandstone formations in the area wanted to establish a beer garden there. However, one Rufus Cable objected: "Beer Garden! Why this is a fit place for a Garden of the Gods!"

Fortunately for posterity, Charles Elliott Perkins (head of the Burlington Railroad) bought the area some 20 years later and kept it in its natural state. Upon Perkins's death in 1907, his heirs gave the remarkable area to Colorado Springs on the condition that it be preserved as a park and open to the public. The park was dedicated in 1909 and is now a Registered National Landmark.

A short trail from the visitor center leads to the Cadet Chapel. Its 17 gleaming aluminum spires soar 150 feet, and within the building are separate chapels for the major Western faiths as well as an "all-faiths" room. The public can visit Monday through Saturday from 9am to 5pm; Sunday services at 10am are open to the public. The chapel is closed for 5 days around graduation and during special events.

Also within easy walking distance of the visitor center are the Academy Planetarium, a classroom for astronomy, physics, and navigation classes that offers periodic free public programs; Arnold Hall, the social center that houses historical exhibits, a cafeteria, and a theater featuring a variety of public shows and lectures; and Harmon Hall, the administration building, where prospective cadets can obtain admission information.

After leaving the visitor center, continue south, then east, on Academy Drive to Stadium Boulevard; you will see Falcon Stadium on your right. Turn right on Stadium Boulevard and follow it out to South Gate Boulevard, which leaves the academy grounds at I-25 exit 150B. En route, you'll pass the Thunderbird Airmanship Overlook, where you might be lucky enough to see cadets parachuting, soaring, and practicing their takeoffs and landings in U.S. Air Force Thunderbirds.

Off I-25 exit 156B. © 719/333-8723. www.usafa.af.mil. Free admission. Summer daily 9am–6pm; winter daily 9am–5pm; additional hours for special events.

Garden of the Gods ★★★ *Value* One of the West's unique geological sites, the 1,300-acre Garden of the Gods is a giant rock garden composed of spectacular red sandstone formations sculpted by rain and wind over millions of years. Located where several life zones and ecosystems converge, the beautiful city-run park harbors a variety of plant and animal communities. The oldest survivors are the ancient, twisted junipers, some 1,000 years old. The strangest animals are the honey ants, which gorge themselves on honey in the summer and fall, becoming living honey pots to feed their colonies during winter hibernation.

The park has a number of hiking trails—mostly easy to moderate—that offer great scenery and an opportunity to get away from the crowds. Leashed dogs are permitted on trails (owners should clean up after their pets). Many trails are also open to horseback riding and mountain biking. You can get trail maps for the park at the **Visitor Center,** which also offers exhibits on the history, geology, plants, and wildlife of the area; a cafeteria; and other conveniences.

A 12-minute multimedia theater presentation, *How Did Those Red Rocks Get There?* ($2 adults, $1 children 5–12, free for children under 5), is a fast-paced exploration of the geologic history of the area. In summer, park naturalists lead free 45-minute walks through the park and conduct free afternoon interpretive programs. You can also take a 20-minute bus tour of the park ($3.75 adults, $2.50 children under 13). You may spot technical rock climbers on some of the park spires; they are required to register at the visitor center.

Also in the park is the **Rock Ledge Ranch Historic Site** (see "More Attractions," below).

1805 N. 30th St. (C) **719/634-6666.** www.gardenofgods.com or www.springsgov.com (follow links). Free admission. Park May–Oct daily 5am–11pm; Nov–Apr daily 5am–9pm. Visitor Center June–Aug daily 8am–8pm; Sept–May 9am–5pm. Take Garden of the Gods Rd. west from I-25 exit 146 and turn south on 30th St.

Pikes Peak Cog Railway ★★   For those who enjoy rail travel, spectacular scenery, and the thrill of mountain climbing without all the work, this is the trip to take. The first passenger train climbed Pikes Peak on June 30, 1891, and diesel slowly replaced steam power between 1939 and 1955. Four custom-built Swiss twin-unit rail cars, each seating 216 passengers, went into service in 1989. The 9-mile route, with grades up to 25%, takes 75 minutes to reach the top of 14,110-foot Pikes Peak; the round-trip requires 3 hours and 10 minutes (including a 40-min. stopover at the top). Runs depart between 8am and 5pm in midsummer, with shorter hours at other times.

The journey is exciting from the start, but passengers really begin to ooh and aah when the track leaves the forest, creeping above timberline at about 11,500 feet. The view from the summit takes in Denver, 75 miles north; New Mexico's Sangre de Cristo range, 100 miles south; the Cripple Creek mining district, on the mountain's western flank; wave after wave of Rocky Mountain subranges to the west; and the seemingly endless sea of Great Plains to the east. This is also where you'll want to watch for Rocky Mountain bighorn sheep and yellow-bellied marmots. The Summit House at the top of Pikes Peak has a restaurant (sandwiches, snacks, beverages, and box lunches) and a gift shop.

Take a jacket or sweater—it can be cold and windy on top, even on warm summer days. This trip is not recommended if you have cardiac or respiratory problems. Even those in good health may feel faint or light-headed.

515 Ruxton Ave., Manitou Springs. (C) **719/685-5401.** www.cograilway.com. $26–$27 adults, $14–$15 children under 12, free for children under 3 held on an adult's lap. Mid-Apr to early Jan, with 2 to 8 departures daily; call or check schedules online. Closed Jan to mid-Apr. Reservations required (available online). Take I-25 exit 141 west on U.S. 24 for 4 miles, turn onto Manitou Ave. west and go 1½ miles to Ruxton Ave., turn left and go about ½ mile.

(**Fun Fact** **Top of the Charts**

Teacher Katharine Lee Bates (1859–1929) wrote the patriotic song "America the Beautiful" after an 1895 wagon trip to the top of Pikes Peak.

Pikes Peak Highway   Perhaps no view in Colorado equals the 360-degree panorama from the 14,110-foot summit of Pikes Peak. Whether you go by cog railway (see above) or private vehicle, the ascent is a spectacular, exciting experience—although not for those with heart or breathing problems or a fear of heights. The 19-mile toll highway (paved for 7 miles, all-weather gravel thereafter) starts at 7,400 feet, some 4 miles west of Manitou Springs. There are numerous photo stops as you head up the mountain, and deer, mountain sheep, marmots, and other animals often appear on the slopes, especially above timberline (around 11,500 ft.). This 156-curve road is the site of the annual Pikes Peak International Hill Climb (see "Spectator Sports," later in this chapter). Allow 3 hours minimum.

Off U.S. 24 at Cascade Ave. (℃ 800/318-9505 or 719/385-7325. www.pikespeakcolorado.com. Admission $10 adults, free for children under 16, or $35 per car. Memorial Day–Labor Day daily 7am–7pm; Labor Day to late Sept daily 7am–5pm; Oct to Memorial Day daily 9am–3pm, weather permitting. Take I-25 exit 141 west on U.S. 24 about 10 miles.

Colorado Springs Pioneers Museum ★★ (Value)   Housed in the former El Paso County Courthouse (1903), which is on the National Register of Historic Places, this museum is an excellent place to begin your visit to Colorado Springs. Exhibits depict the community's rich history, including its beginning as a fashionable resort, the railroad and mining eras, and its growth and development in the 20th century. Also here are the Victorian home of writer Helen Hunt Jackson; an exhibit on the city's dental, medical, and pharmaceutical industry; and early-20th-century toys, quilts, and clothing.

You can ride an Otis birdcage elevator, which dates to the early 1900s, to the restored original courtroom, where several *Perry Mason* episodes were filmed. A recent renovation uncovered intriguing gold and silver images of goddesses, painted on the courtroom walls in part to represent the two key resources of the state's economy at the time. However, it's believed that they were also painted as a subtle protest when the country was changing from a gold and silver standard to a gold-only monetary standard. Another series of murals depict over 400 years of Pikes Peak region history.

Changing exhibit areas house traveling shows such as quilts, historic photographs, aviation, American-Indian culture, and art pottery. The museum has hosted a wide range of events, including lectures on the American cowboy, antique-auto shows, jazz concerts, and Hispanic celebrations. The historic reference library and archives are available by appointment. Allow 1 to 3 hours.

215 S. Tejon St. (℃ 719/385-5990. www.cspm.org. Free admission, donations accepted. Year-round Tues–Sat 10am–5pm; Jun–Aug Sun 1–5pm. Take I-25 exit 141 east to Tejon St., turn right and go 4 blocks.

United States Olympic Complex   So you think your local fitness center is state-of-the-art? Check out the 37-acre United States Olympic Complex, a sophisticated center where thousands of athletes train each year in a variety of Olympic sports. Free guided tours, available daily, take about an hour, and include a film depicting the U.S. Olympic effort. Visitors may also see athletes in training. The visitor center includes the U.S. Olympic Hall of Fame, interactive kiosks on Olympics subjects, various other displays, and a gift shop that sells Olympic-logo merchandise.

The complex includes the **Olympic Sports Center I,** with five gymnasiums and a weight-training room; **Sports Center II,** which accommodates 14 sports; the **Indoor Shooting Center,** the largest facility of its kind in the Western Hemisphere, with areas for rifle and pistol shooting, rapid-fire and women's sport pistol bays, running-target rifle ranges, and air-rifle and pistol-fire points;

and the **Aquatics Center,** which contains a 50-by-25-meter pool with two movable bulkheads, 10 50m and 20 25m lanes, and more than 800,000 gallons of water. The U.S. Olympic Committee also operates the **7-Eleven Velodrome,** with a banked track for bicycle and roller speed skating, about 1 mile south of the Olympic Complex, in Memorial Park (see "Parks & Zoos," later in this chapter) off Union Boulevard. Olympic figure skaters train at the **World Arena,** southwest of downtown. Allow 1 to 2 hours.

1 Olympic Plaza, corner of Boulder St. (entrance) and Union Blvd. ✆ 888/659-8687 or 719/866-4618. www.usolympicteam.com. Free admission. Complex daily 9am–6pm. Guided tours begin every half-hour 9am–5pm; reservations required for groups of 10 or more (✆ 719/866-4656). From I-25, take exit 143.

MORE ATTRACTIONS
ARCHITECTURAL HIGHLIGHTS
The Broadmoor   This famous Italian Renaissance–style resort hotel has been a Colorado Springs landmark since Spencer Penrose built it in 1918. (See "Where to Stay," earlier in this chapter.)

Lake Circle, at Lake Ave. ✆ 719/634-7711. www.broadmoor.com. Free admission. Daily year-round.

Miramont Castle Museum   Architecture buffs will love this place. Built into a hillside by a wealthy French priest as a private home in 1895 and converted by the Sisters of Mercy into a sanatorium in 1907, this unique Victorian mansion has always aroused curiosity. The structure incorporates at least nine identifiable architectural styles in its 4 stories, 46 rooms, 14,000 square feet of floor space, and 2-foot-thick stone walls. If you like tiny stuff, don't miss the room housing the miniatures museum. In summer, light meals and tea are served Tuesday through Saturday from 11am to 4pm in the Queen's Parlour. The museum lies on the route from Manitou Avenue to the Pikes Peak Cog Railway. Allow at least 1 hour.

9 Capitol Hill Ave., Manitou Springs. ✆ 888/685-1011 or 719/685-1011. www.pikes-peak.com. Admission $5 adults, $4.50 seniors 60 and over, $1 children 6–11, free for children under 6. Memorial Day to Labor Day Tues–Sun 10am–5pm; Apr to late May and early Sept to mid-Dec Tues–Sun 11am–4pm; mid-Dec to Mar Tues–Sun noon–3pm. Located 1 block west of the intersection of Manitou and Ruxton aves.

HISTORIC BUILDINGS
McAllister House   This Gothic cottage, listed on the National Register of Historic Places, is a good place for a quick look at the Colorado of the late 19th century. It was built in 1873, and the builder, an army major named Henry McAllister, decided to construct the house with brick when he learned that the local wind was so strong it had blown a train off the tracks nearby. The house has many original furnishings, including three marble fireplaces. It is now owned by the Colonial Dames of America, whose knowledgeable volunteers lead guided tours. Allow about 1 hour.

423 N. Cascade Ave. (at St. Vrain St.). ✆ 719/635-7925. www.oldcolo.com/~mcallister. Admission $5 adults, $4 seniors 62 and older, $3 children 6–12, free for children under 6. Summer Wed–Sat 10am–4pm, Sun noon–4pm; winter Thurs–Sat 10am–4pm. Take I-25 exit 141 east to Cascade Ave., go left and continue for about 6 blocks.

Rock Ledge Ranch Historic Site   Visitors can explore the history of three pioneer eras at this living-history farm at the east entrance to Garden of the Gods park. Listed on the National Register of Historic Places, the ranch presents the rigors of the homestead era at the 1860s Galloway Homestead, the agricultural difficulties of the working-ranch era at the 1880s Chambers Farm and Blacksmith Shop, and the more sophisticated estate period at the 1907 Orchard House. Special events, which take place frequently, include an old-fashioned

Fourth of July celebration, an 1860s vintage baseball game in late summer, a Victorian Halloween party, and holiday celebrations from Thanksgiving through Christmas. The General Store stocks a wide selection of historic reproductions, books, and gift items, and the proceeds help with preservation and restoration of the ranch. Allow 1 to 2 hours.

Gateway Rd., Garden of the Gods. ⓒ 719/578-6777. www.springsgov.com (follow links). Admission $5 adults, $3 seniors 55 and older and students 13–18, $1 children 6–12, free for children under 6. June to Labor Day Wed–Sun 10am–5pm; early Sept to Dec Sat 10am–4pm, Sun noon–4pm. Closed Jan–May. Take I-25 exit 146, then follow signs west to Garden of the Gods.

HISTORIC NEIGHBORHOODS

Manitou Springs, which centers on Manitou Avenue off U.S. 24 West, is a separate town with its own government. It is one of the country's largest National Historic Districts. Legend has it that Utes named the springs Manitou, their word for "Great Spirit," because they believed that the Great Spirit had breathed into the waters to create the natural effervescence of the springs. Pikes Peak soars above the town nestled at its base.

Today, the community offers visitors a chance to step back to a slower and quieter time. It boasts numerous elegant Victorian buildings, many of which house delightful shops, galleries, restaurants, and lodgings. Manitou Springs is also home to many fine artists and artisans, whom you might spot painting or sketching about town. A small group of sculptors began the Manitou Art Project in 1992; it installed over 20 sculptures in various locations downtown and in the parks, creating a large sculpture garden for all to enjoy. The works, which stay on display for a year, are for sale, with 25% of the proceeds used to purchase permanent sculpture for the city. Five pieces have been purchased to date.

Visitors are encouraged to take the self-guided tour of the nine restored mineral springs of Manitou. Pick up the *Manitou Springs Visitor's Guide,* which contains a map and descriptions to help you find each spring. It's available at the Manitou Springs Chamber of Commerce & Visitors Bureau, 354 Manitou Ave. (ⓒ **800/642-2567** or 719/685-5089; www.manitousprings.org), which is open daily.

Old Colorado City, Colorado Avenue between 21st and 31st streets, was founded in 1859, 12 years before Colorado Springs. The town boomed in the 1880s after General Palmer's railroad came through. Tunnels led from the respectable side of town to this saloon and red-light district so that the city fathers could carouse without being seen coming or going—or so the legend goes. Today this historic district has an interesting assortment of shops, galleries, and restaurants.

MUSEUMS & GALLERIES

Colorado Springs Fine Arts Center ✪   The center's permanent collection includes works by Georgia O'Keeffe, John James Audubon, John Singer Sargent, Charles Russell, Albert Bierstadt, Nicolai Fechin, and other famed painters and sculptors, as well as a world-class collection of American Indian and Hispanic works. Opened in 1936, the center also houses a 450-seat performing-arts theater, a 32,000-volume art-research library, the Bemis Art School, a tactile gallery for those who are visually impaired, and a delightful sculpture garden. Changing exhibits showcase local collections as well as touring international exhibits. Designed by renowned Santa Fe architect John Gaw Meem, the Art Deco–style building reflects Southwestern mission and Pueblo influences. Allow 1 to 3 hours.

30 W. Dale St. (west of N. Cascade Ave.). ℂ **719/634-5581.** www.csfineartscenter.org. Admission to galleries and museum $5 adults, $3 seniors and children 6–16, free for children under 6. Free to all Sat 9am–5pm. Separate admission for performing-arts events. Galleries and museum Mon–Sat 9am–5pm, Sun 1–5pm. Open the 1st Thurs of every month until 8pm. Closed federal holidays. Take I-25 exit 143 east to Cascade St., turn right to Dale St., and then turn right again.

Ghost Town *Kids*   A fun place to take the family, Ghost Town is part historic attraction but more theme park. Made up of authentic 19th-century buildings relocated from other parts of Colorado, this "town" is sheltered from the elements in Old Colorado City. There's a sheriff's office, jail, saloon, general store, livery stable, blacksmith shop, rooming house, and assay office. Animated frontier characters tell stories of the Old West, while a shooting gallery, antique arcade machines, and nickelodeons provide additional entertainment. During the summer you can even pan for real gold. Allow about 2 hours.

400 S. 21st St. (on U.S. 24). ℂ **719/634-0696.** www.ghosttownmuseum.com. Admission $6 adults, $3 children 6–16, free for children under 6. June–Aug Mon–Sat 9am–6pm, Sun 11am–6pm; Sept–May Mon–Sat 10am–5pm, Sun 11am–5pm. Take I-25 exit 141; town is just west of exit.

Manitou Cliff Dwellings Preserve & Museums ⭐ *Kids*   The cliff dwelling ruins here are real, although originally they were located elsewhere. This put us off at first—they would be more authentic if they were in their original location—but the move here may have saved them. In the early 1900s, archaeologists, who saw such dwellings being plundered by treasure hunters, dismantled some of the ancient buildings, gathered artifacts found there, and hauled them away. Some of these ruins, constructed from 1100 to 1300 A.D., can be seen here, in a village reconstructed by archaeologists. There are also two museums with exhibits on prehistoric American Indian life, and several gift shops that sell Indian-made jewelry, pottery, and other crafts, plus Colorado souvenirs. American-Indian dancers perform during the summer. Allow 2 hours.

U.S. 24, Manitou Springs. ℂ **800/354-9971** or 719/685-5242. www.cliffdwellingsmuseum.com. Admission $8 adults, $7 seniors 60 and over, $6 children 7–11, free for children under 7. May–Sept daily 9am–6pm; Oct–Apr daily 9am–5pm. Closed Thanksgiving and Dec 25. Take I-25 exit 141, go west on U.S. 24 about 5 miles.

May Natural History Museum of the Tropics *Kids*   Here you'll find one of the world's best public collections of giant insects and other tropical invertebrates. James F. W. May (1884–1956) spent more than half a century exploring the world's jungles while compiling his illustrious collection, which has grown to more than 100,000 invertebrates, about 8,000 of which are on display at any given time. The specimens are irreplaceable, because many came from areas that are now so politically unstable that no one is willing or able to explore the backcountry to collect them again. Exhibits change periodically.

Also on the grounds is the **Museum of Space Exploration,** where you can take a pictorial trip through the history of space exploration, beginning with man's first attempts to fly and continuing through the most recent photos from NASA. Also on display are numerous models of early aircraft, World War II planes, and spacecraft. Take time to view one or more of the NASA space films, which include the first moon landing. Allow 2 to 3 hours for both museums. There's also a 500-site campground ($20–$22 for campsites) with hiking trails, fishing, and a playground area.

710 Rock Creek Canyon Rd. ℂ **719/576-0450.** Admission (includes Museum of Space Exploration) $4.50 adults, $3.50 seniors 60 and older, $2.50 children 6–12, free for children under 6. May–Sept daily 9am–6pm. Closed Oct–Apr except for groups of 10 or more. Take Colo. 115 and drive southwest out of Colorado Springs for 9 miles; watch for signs and the Hercules Beetle of the West Indies that mark the turnoff to the museum.

Museum of the American Numismatic Association ★ *(Finds)* The largest collection of its kind west of the Smithsonian Institution, this museum consists of four galleries of coins, tokens, medals, and paper money from around the world. Of special note is the earliest *reale* (Spanish coin) struck in the New World, struck in Mexico in 1536. There's also an 1804 dollar, a 1913 'V' nickel, and a nice collectors' library. Allow 1 hour.

818 N. Cascade Ave., on the campus of Colorado College. ⓒ 719/632-2646. www.money.org. Free admission, donations welcome. Tues–Fri 9am–4pm; Sat 10am–4pm. Take I-25 exit 143 east to Cascade Ave., then turn right and go about 6 blocks.

Peterson Air & Space Museum Through its exhibits, this museum traces the history of Peterson Air Force Base, NORAD, the Air Defense Command, and Air Force Space Command. Of special interest are 17 historic aircraft, including P-47 Thunderbolt and P-40 Warhawk fighters from World War II, plus four missiles and jets from the Korean War to the present. To mark the 50th anniversary of the U.S. Air Force, a memorial grove of 58 conifer trees honoring the USAF Medal of Honor recipients was planted. There's also a small gift shop. Allow 1 to 2 hours. *Note:* Visitors must have a military ID or give administration at least 3 days' advance notice to get on the base.

Peterson Air Force Base main gate, off U.S. 24. ⓒ 719/556-4915. www.petemuseum.org. Free admission. Tues–Sat 8:30am–4:30pm. Closed holidays and occasionally during military exercises; call ahead. Take I-25 exit 141, then follow U.S. 24 east about 7½ miles.

ProRodeo Hall of Fame & American Cowboy Museum ★★ *(Kids)* No rhinestone cowboys here. This is the real thing, with exhibits on the development of rodeo, from its origins in early ranch work to major professional sport. You'll learn about historic and modern cowboys, including those brave (or crazy) enough to climb onto bucking broncos and wild bulls, in Heritage Hall. The Hall of Champions displays photos, gear, personal memorabilia, and trophies honoring rodeo greats. There are two multimedia presentations, and the museum features changing exhibits of Western art. Outside you'll find a replica rodeo arena, live rodeo animals, and a sculpture garden. Allow 2 hours.

101 ProRodeo Dr. (off Rockrimmon Blvd.). ⓒ 719/528-4764. www.prorodeo.com. Admission $6 adults, $5 seniors 55 and older, $3 children 6–12, free for children under 6. Daily 9am–5pm. Closed Jan 1, Easter, Thanksgiving, and Dec 25. Take I-25 to exit 147.

Western Museum of Mining & Industry ★★ Machines are fun, and the bigger the better. Historic hard-rock mining machinery and other equipment from Cripple Creek and other late-19th-century Colorado gold camps form the basis of this museum's 4,000-plus-item collection. Visitors can see an operating Corliss steam engine with a 17-ton flywheel (now that's big!), a life-size underground mine reconstruction, and an exhibit on mining-town life showing how early Western miners and their families lived. You can also pan for gold—there's a wheelchair-accessible trough—and view a 23-minute video presentation on life in the early mining camps. Various hands-on family activities focus on themes such as life in a mining town, minerals in everyday products, and recycled art. Free guided tours are available; call for information and times. Allow at least 2 hours.

1025 North Gate Rd., at I-25 exit 156A (off Gleneagle Dr. just east of the north gate of the U.S. Air Force Academy). ⓒ 719/488-0880. www.wmmi.org. Admission $7 adults, $5 seniors 60 and older and students 13–17, $3 children 3–12, free for children under 3. Mon–Sat 9am–4pm. Guided tours begin at 10am and 1pm. Located just east of I-25 via Gleneagle Dr.

World Figure Skating Museum & Hall of Fame This is the only museum of its kind in the world, exhibiting 1,200 years of ice skates—from early versions of carved bone to highly decorated cast-iron examples and finally the steel blades of today. There are also skating costumes, medals, and other memorabilia, changing exhibits, films, a library, and a gift shop. A gallery displays skating-related paintings, including works by the 17th-century Dutch artist Pieter Brueghel and Americans Winslow Homer and Andy Warhol. The museum is recognized by the International Skating Union, the international governing body, as the repository for the history and official records of figure skating and the sport's official hall of fame. Here also are the U.S. national, regional, sectional, and international trophies. Allow 1 to 2 hours.

20 1st St. ✆ 719/635-5200. www.worldskatingmuseum.org. Admission $3 adults, $2 seniors 60 and over and children 6–12, free for children under 6. Year-round Mon–Sat 10am–4pm. Closed major holidays. Take I-25 exit 138, west on Lake Ave.; just before The Broadmoor, turn right onto 1st St.

NATURAL ATTRACTIONS

Cave of the Winds 🛝 Discovered by two boys on a church outing in the 1880s, this impressive underground cavern has offered public tours for well over a century. It provides a good opportunity to see the beauty of the underworld. The 45-minute Discovery Tour takes visitors along a well-lit ¾-mile passageway through 20 subterranean chambers, complete with classic stalagmites, stalactites, crystal flowers, and limestone canopies. In the Adventure Room, modern lighting techniques return visitors to an era when spelunking was done by candle and lantern. The 1½-hour Lantern Tour follows unpaved and unlighted passageways and corridors. This tour is rather strenuous, with some stooping required in areas with low ceilings; it might muddy your shoes, but not your clothes.

Kids especially like the outdoor laser shows (with stereophonic sound) presented nightly during the summer at 9pm ($10 adults, $5 children 6–15, free for children under 6).

U.S. 24, Manitou Springs. ✆ 719/685-5444. www.caveofthewinds.com. Discovery Tour $15 adults, $8 children 6–15, free for children under 6. Tours depart every 15–30 min. Memorial Day to Labor Day daily 9am–9pm; early Sept to Apr daily 10am–5pm. Lantern Tours (3 times daily in summer and on weekends; other times by reservation) $18 adults, $9 children 6–15, not recommended for children under 6. Visitors with heart conditions, visual impairment, or other physical limitations are advised not to take Lantern Tour and may not take Explorer Tour. Take I-25 exit 141, go 6 miles west on U.S. 24.

Seven Falls This is a good choice for those who have not yet gotten their fill of Colorado's spectacular mountain scenery. A picturesque 1-mile drive through a box canyon takes you between the Pillars of Hercules, where the canyon narrows to just 42 feet, ending at these cascading falls. Seven separate waterfalls dance down a granite cliff, cascading some 181 feet. A free elevator takes visitors to the Eagle Nest viewing platform. A mile-long trail atop the plateau passes the grave of 19th-century novelist Helen Hunt Jackson, the author of *Ramona*, and ends at a panoramic view of Colorado Springs. Watch for birds and other wildlife along the way. Allow 2 hours.

At the end of S. Cheyenne Canyon Rd. ✆ 719/632-0765. www.sevenfalls.com. Day admission $8.25 adults, $7.25 seniors, $5.25 children 6–15, free for children under 6; night admission $9.75 adults, $8.75 seniors, $6.25 children 6–15, free for children under 6; lower rates in winter. Mid-May to early June and mid-Aug to early Sept daily 8:30am–9:30pm; early June to mid-Aug daily 8:30am–10:30pm; early Sept to mid-May daily 9am–5:15pm. Christmas lighting Dec 16–26 5–9:30pm. Closed major holidays. Take I-25 exit 141, head west on U.S. 24, turn south on 21st St. for about 3 miles, turn west on Cheyenne Blvd., and then left onto S. Cheyenne Canyon Rd.

Impressions
The air is so refined that you can live without much lungs.
  —Shane Leslie, *American Wonderland,*1936

PARKS & ZOOS

Cheyenne Mountain Zoo ★★ *(Kids* On the lower slopes of Cheyenne Mountain at 6,800 feet above sea level, this medium-size zoological park is our top choice for a family outing. The zoo's 650-plus animals, many in "natural" environments, include wolves, lions, leopards, red pandas, elephants, hippos, monkeys, giraffes, reptiles, snakes, and lots of birds. Rocky cliffs have been created for the mountain goats; there's a pebbled beach for penguins and a new animal-contact area for children. The zoo is home to more than 30 endangered species, including the Siberian tiger, Amur leopard, and black-footed ferret. The zoo's giraffes are the most prolific captive herd in the world; there have been 180 live births since the 1950s. Visitors can actually feed the long-necked beasts.

There's also a colorful antique carousel, built in 1926, the year the zoo was founded. A stroller- and wheelchair-accessible tram makes a full loop of the zoo in about 15 minutes; it operates from Memorial Day to Labor Day, and you can ride all day for $1. Admission to the zoo includes road access to the nearby **Will Rogers Shrine of the Sun,** a granite tower built in 1937, with photos and information on the American humorist. The tower also affords great views of the city and surrounding countryside. Strollers, double strollers, wheelchairs, and wagons are available for rent at Thundergod Gift and Snack Shop. Allow 2 to 4 hours for the zoo and an extra 45 minutes for the shrine.

4250 Cheyenne Mountain Zoo Rd. ℂ 719/633-9925. www.cmzoo.org. Admission $12 adults, $10 seniors 65 and over, $6 children 3–11, free for children under 3. Summer daily 9am–6pm; off season daily 9am–5pm. Take I-25 exit 138, drive west to The Broadmoor hotel and follow signs.

Memorial Park One of the largest parks in the city, Memorial is home to the Mark "Pa" Sertich Ice Center and the Aquatics and Fitness Center, as well as the famed 7-Eleven Velodrome, which is used for world-class bicycling events. Other facilities include baseball and softball fields, volleyball courts, tennis courts, a bicycle criterium, and jogging trails. The park also stages a terrific fireworks display on Independence Day. See the sections on ice-skating, swimming, and tennis under "Outdoor Activities," below.

1605 E. Pikes Peak Ave. (between Hancock Ave. and Union Blvd.). ℂ 719/385-5940. www.springsgov.com (follow links). Free admission. Daily year-round. Located 1 mile east of downtown.

Monument Valley Park This long, slender park follows Monument Creek through downtown Colorado Springs. At its south end are formal zinnia, begonia, and rose gardens, and in the middle are demonstration gardens of the Horticultural Art Society. Facilities include softball and baseball fields, a swimming pool (open daily in summer; $4 adults, $2.50 children), volleyball and tennis courts, children's playgrounds, and picnic shelters. Also in the park are the 4¼-mile Monument Creek Trail for walkers, runners, and cyclists, and the 1-mile Monument Valley Fitness Trail at the north end, beside Bodington Field.

170 W. Cache La Poudre Blvd. ℂ 719/385-5940. www.springsgov.com (follow links). Free admission. Daily year-round.

Mueller State Park ★★★ *(Finds* Somewhat like a junior version of Rocky Mountain National Park, Mueller contains over 5,000 acres of prime scenic beauty along the west slope of Pikes Peak. The 55 miles of trails, designated for hikers, horseback riders, and mountain bikers, afford opportunities to observe elk, bighorn sheep, black bear, and the park's other wildlife. The best times to spot wildlife are spring and fall, just after sunrise and just before sunset. In the summer, rangers lead hikes and offer campfire programs in a 100-seat amphitheater. The park has 132 campsites (℃ **800/678-2267** for reservations), with fees ranging from $12 for walk-in sites to $16 for drive-in sites with electricity; coin-operated pay showers are available from mid-May to mid-October.

P.O. Box 39, Divide, CO 80814. ℃ 719/687-2366. www.parks.state.co.us. Admission $4 per vehicle. Take U.S. 24 west from Colorado Springs to Divide (25 miles), then go 3½ miles south on Colo. 67.

North Cheyenne Cañon Park and Starsmore Discovery Center ★★   A delightful escape on a hot summer day, this 1,600-acre park includes North Cheyenne Creek, which drops 1,800 feet over the course of 5 miles in a series of cascades and waterfalls. The heavily wooded park contains picnic areas and hiking/biking/horseback riding trails. The small visitor center at the foot of scenic Helen Hunt Falls has exhibits on history, geology, flora, and fauna. The **Starsmore Discovery Center,** at the entrance to the park, holds maps, information, and interactive exhibits for both kids and adults, including audiovisual programs and a climbing wall where you can learn about rock climbing. Call for current climbing-wall hours. During the summer, the center schedules a series of free programs on subjects such as rock climbing, butterflies, and humming-birds, and guided walks and hikes (call for the current schedule). The park also has excellent rock-climbing areas for experienced climbers; pick up information at the Starsmore Discovery Center or Helen Hunt Falls visitor center.

2120 S. Cheyenne Cañon Rd. (west of 21st St.). ℃ 719/578-6146. www.springsgov.com (follow links). Free admission. Park May–Oct daily 5am–11pm; Nov–Apr daily 5am–9pm. Starsmore Discovery Center summer daily 9am–5pm; call for hours at other times. Helen Hunt Falls Visitor Center Memorial Day to Labor Day daily 9am–5pm; closed rest of year. Located just west of the Broadmoor Golf Club via Cheyenne Blvd.

Palmer Park   Deeded to the city in 1899 by Colorado Springs founder Gen. William Jackson Palmer, this 737-acre preserve offers hiking, biking, and horse-back riding across a mesa overlooking the city. It boasts a variety of minerals (including quartz, topaz, jasper, and tourmaline), rich vegetation (including a yucca preservation area), and considerable wildlife. The Edna Mae Bennet Nature Trail is a self-guided excursion, and there are numerous other trails. Other facilities include 12 separate picnic areas, softball and baseball fields, and volleyball courts.

3650 Maizeland Rd. off Academy Blvd. ℃ 719/385-5940. www.springsgov.com (follow links). Free admission. Daily year-round. Located 3 miles east of I-25 via Austin Bluffs Pkwy (exit 146).

ESPECIALLY FOR KIDS

In addition to the listings below, children will probably enjoy the **Cheyenne Mountain Zoo, May Natural History Museum,** and **Ghost Town,** described above.

Arcade Amusements, Inc ★ *Kids*   Among the West's oldest and largest amusement arcades, this game complex just might be considered a hands-on arcade museum as well as a fun place for kids of all ages. Some 250 machines range from original working penny pinball machines to modern video games, skee-ball, and 12-player horse racing.

930 Block Manitou Ave., Manitou Springs. ℃ 719/685-9815. Free admission; arcade games from 1¢. Early May to Labor Day daily 10am–10pm. Call for winter hours. Located in downtown Manitou Springs.

North Pole/Santa's Workshop *(Kids)*   A good spot for young kids, Santa's workshop is busy from mid-May right up until Christmas Eve. Not only can kids visit shops where elves have some early Christmas gifts for sale, but they can also see Santa and whisper their requests in his ear. This 26-acre village features numerous rides; including a miniature train, a 60-foot Ferris wheel, and a space shuttle replica that swings to and fro; as well as magic shows and musical entertainment, snack shops, and an ice-cream parlor.

At the foot of Pikes Peak Hwy. off U.S. 24, 5 miles west of Manitou Springs. ✆ 719/684-9432. www.santas-colo.com. Admission (includes all rides, shows, and attractions) $15 ages 2–59, $5.95 seniors 60 and over, free for children under 2. June to mid-Aug daily 9:30am–6pm; mid-May to May 31 and mid-Aug to Dec 24 (weather permitting) Fri–Tues 10am–5pm. Closed Dec 25 to mid-May. Take I-25 exit 141, go west on U.S. 24 about 10 miles.

ORGANIZED TOURS

Half- and full-day bus tours of Colorado Springs, Pikes Peak, the Air Force Academy, and other nearby attractions are offered by **Gray Line of Colorado Springs,** 3704 W. Colorado Ave. (✆ **800/348-6877;** www.coloradograyline. com). From May through October, it offers a variety of other tours, including an excursion to Royal Gorge and white-water rafting trips. Prices range from $30 to $75 per person.

A free downtown **walking tour** brochure, with a map and descriptions of more than 30 historic buildings, is available at the Colorado Springs Convention and Visitors Bureau, as well as at local businesses.

Another free brochure, *Old Colorado City,* shows the location of more than a dozen historic buildings and lists shops, galleries, and other businesses.

The **Manitou Springs Chamber of Commerce & Visitors Bureau** (see "Visitor Information," earlier in this chapter) distributes the free *Manitou Springs Visitor's Guide,* which includes a self-guided walking-tour map of Mineral Springs, as well as information on where to find a variety of outdoor sculptures. See "Historic Neighborhoods," earlier in this chapter.

6 Outdoor Activities

For information on the city's parks and programs, contact the **Colorado Springs Parks and Recreation Department** (✆ 719/385-5940; www.springs gov.com). Most of the state and federal agencies concerned with outdoor recreation are headquartered in Denver. There are branch offices in Colorado Springs for **Colorado State Parks,** 2128 N. Weber St. (✆ **719/471-0900;** www. parks.state.co.us); the **Colorado Division of Wildlife,** 2126 N. Weber St. (✆ **719/227-5200,** or 719/227-5201 for 24-hr. recorded information; www. wildlife.state.co.us); and the **U.S. Forest Service,** Pikes Peak Ranger District of the Pike National Forest, 601 S. Weber St. (✆ **719/636-1602;** www.fs.fed.us/ r2/psicc/pp).

You can get hunting and fishing licenses at many sporting-goods stores, as well as at the Colorado Division of Wildlife office listed above.

AERIAL SPORTS   The **Black Forest Soaring Society,** 24566 David C. Johnson Loop, Elbert, CO 80106 (✆ 303/648-3623; www.serkowski.com/bfss), some 50 miles northeast of Colorado Springs, offers glider rides, rentals, and instruction. Rides cost about $100, with rentals (to those with gliding licenses) running $15 per hour and instruction $24 an hour. Advance reservations are required.

The area's commercial ballooning companies include **High But Dry Balloons,** 4164 Austin Bluffs Pkwy., #146, Colorado Springs, CO 80918 (© **800/897-3066** or 719/260-0011; www.highbutdryballoons.com), for tours, champagne flights, and weddings. Sunrise flights are scheduled daily year-round, weather permitting. Cost depends on the number of passengers, locations, and type of flight, but averages about $150 per person. Generally, flights last 2 or 3 hours, with a minimum of 1 hour. On Labor Day weekend, the **Colorado Springs Balloon Classic** ★★ (© **719/471-4833;** www.balloonclassic.com) sees more than 100 hot-air balloons launched from the city's Memorial Park. Admission is free.

BICYCLING   Aside from the 4¼-mile loop trail around Monument Valley Park (see "Parks & Zoos" under "Attractions," above), there are numerous other urban trails for bikers. You can get information at the city's Visitor Information Center (see "Visitor Information," earlier in this chapter). For guided tours and rentals ($25/day), contact **Challenge Unlimited** (see "Mountain Biking," below).

FISHING   Most serious Colorado Springs anglers drive south 40 miles to the Arkansas River or west to the Rocky Mountain streams and lakes, such as those found in Eleven Mile State Park and Spinney Mountain State Park on the South Platte River west of Florissant. Bass, catfish, walleye pike, and panfish are found in the streams of eastern Colorado; trout is the preferred sport fish of the mountain regions.

Angler's Covey, 917 W. Colorado Ave. (© **800/753-4746** or 719/471-2984; www.anglerscovey.com), is a specialty fly-fishing shop and a good source of general fishing information for southern Colorado. It offers guided half- and full-day trips ($195–$345 for one to three persons), as well as state fishing licenses, rentals, flies, tackle, and so forth.

GOLF   Public courses include the **Patty Jewett Golf Course,** 900 E. Española St. (© 719/385-6950); **Pine Creek Golf Club,** 9850 Divot Trail (© **719/594-9999**); and **Valley Hi Golf Course,** 610 S. Chelton Rd. (© **719/385-6917**). Nonresident greens fees range from $28.50 to $35 for 18 holes (not including a cart).

The finest golf courses in the Colorado Springs area are private. Guests of The Broadmoor hotel can play the 45-hole **Broadmoor Golf Club** (© **719/577-5790**).

HIKING   Opportunities abound in municipal parks (see "Parks & Zoos" under "Attractions," above) and Pike National Forest, which borders Colorado Springs to the west. The U.S. Forest Service district office can provide maps and general information (see address and phone number in the introduction to this section).

Especially popular are the 7½-mile **Waldo Canyon Trail,** with its trailhead just east of Cascade Avenue off U.S. 24; the 6-mile **Mount Manitou Trail,** starting in Ruxton Canyon above the hydroelectric plant; and the 12-mile **Barr Trail**

Impressions

Could one live in constant view of these grand mountains without being elevated by them into a lofty plane of thought and purpose?
—General William J. Palmer, founder of Colorado Springs, 1871

to the summit of Pikes Peak. **Mueller State Park** (℃ **719/687-2366**), 3½ miles south of Divide en route to Cripple Creek, has 55 miles of trails. See "Parks & Zoos" under "Attractions," above.

HORSEBACK RIDING   You'll find good opportunities at city parks, including Garden of the Gods, North Cheyenne Cañon Park, and Palmer Park, plus Mueller State Park (see "Attractions," earlier in this chapter). The **Academy Riding Stables**, 4 El Paso Blvd., near the Garden of the Gods (℃ **888/700-0410** or 719/633-5667; www.academyridingstables.com), offers guided trail rides for children and adults by reservation ($33 for 1 hour, $50 for 2).

ICE-SKATING   The **Mark "Pa" Sertich Ice Center** at Memorial Park (℃ **719/385-5983**) is open daily, offering prearranged instruction and rentals. The U.S. Olympic Complex operates the **Colorado Springs World Arena Ice Hall,** 3185 Venetucci Blvd. (℃ **719/477-2100**; www.worldarena.com), with public sessions daily. Admission is $1 to $2, skate rentals $2. If you have hockey equipment, you can join a pickup game ($5); call for times. To get there, take I-25 exit 138, go west on Circle Drive to Venetucci Boulevard, and south to the arena.

MOUNTAIN BIKING   There are abundant mountain-biking opportunities in the Colorado Springs area; contact the U.S. Forest Service for details (see address and phone number, in the introduction to the section). From May through early October, **Challenge Unlimited,** 204 S. 24th St. (℃ **800/798-5954** or 719/633-6399; www.bikithikit.com), hosts fully equipped, guided rides for every level of experience. Your guide on the 19-mile ride down the Pikes Peak Highway, from the summit at 14,110 feet to the tollgate at 7,000 feet, presents an interpretation of the nature, history, and beauty of the mountain. Participants must be at least 10 years old; advance reservations are advised. Rates are $55 to $100 per person. Challenge Unlimited also rents bikes and guides multi-day excursions.

RIVER RAFTING   Colorado Springs is 40 miles from the Arkansas River near Cañon City. Several licensed white-water outfitters tackle the Royal Gorge. **Echo Canyon River Expeditions,** 45000 U.S. 50 West, Cañon City, CO 81212 (℃ **800/755-3246** or 719/275-3154; www.raftecho.com), offers half-day to 3-day trips on "mild to wild" stretches of river. The company uses state-of-the-art equipment, including self-bailing rafts. Costs range from $41 (half-day, adult) to $95 for a daylong rental of an inflatable kayak. **Arkansas River Tours,** P.O. Box 337, Cotopaxi, CO 81223 (℃ **800/321-4352** or 719/942-4362; www.arkansasrivertours.com), offers white-water trips of lengths from a quarter of a day to all day for $32 to $100, and 2-day trips for about $240.

SWIMMING & TENNIS   Many city parks have pool or lake swimming, for which they charge a small fee, and free tennis courts. Contact the Colorado Springs Parks and Recreation Department (℃ **719/385-5940**) for locations and hours.

7 Spectator Sports

The **Air Force Academy Falcons** football team dominates the sports scene, and there are also competitive baseball, basketball, hockey, and soccer teams. Call for schedules and ticket information (℃ **800/666-USAF** or 719/472-1895; www.airforcesports.com).

AUTO RACING   The **Pikes Peak International Hill Climb** (✆ 719/685-4400; www.ppihc.com), known as the "Race to the Clouds," takes place annually in late June or early July. An international field of drivers negotiates the hairpin turns of the final 12½ miles of the Pikes Peak Highway to the top of the 14,110-foot mountain.

NASCAR and Indy Racing make annual stops at **Pikes Peak International Raceway,** 16650 Midway Ranch Rd., Fountain, CO 80817 (✆ 888/306-7223; www.ppir.com), 15 miles south of Colorado Springs, exit 123 off I-25. The track held its inaugural season in 1997, with a capacity crowd of 40,000. Event tickets usually range from $50 to $100 for a weekend pass, $15 to $60 for a single day. Advance tickets cost less than those bought on race day. The facility also schedules motorcycle races, driving schools, and occasional concerts.

BASEBALL   The **Colorado Springs Sky Sox** of the Pacific Coast League, the AAA farm team for the Colorado Rockies of Denver, play a full 144-game season, with 72 home games at Sky Sox Stadium, 4385 Tutt Blvd., off Barnes Road east of Powers Boulevard (✆ 719/591-7699; www.skysox.com). The season runs from April through Labor Day. Tickets cost $8.50 for adults, $7.50 for children 2 to 12 and seniors 60 and over for reserved box seating; $7.50 and $5, respectively, for upper reserved seats; and $4.25 for general admission.

HOCKEY   In addition to Air Force Academy Hockey (see above), the **World Arena,** 3185 Venetucci Blvd. (✆ 719/477-2100; www.worldarena.com), is home to the Colorado College Tigers (✆ 719/389-6100) and the Colorado Gold Kings (✆ 719/579-9000) of the West Coast Hockey League.

RODEO   The **Pikes Peak or Bust Rodeo,** held annually (since 1941) in early August, is a major stop on the Professional Rodeo Cowboys Association circuit. Its purse of more than $150,000 makes it the second-largest rodeo in Colorado, after Denver's National Western Stock Show. Events are at the **World Arena,** 3185 Venetucci Blvd. (✆ 719/477-2100; www.worldarena.com). Various events around the city, including a parade and a street breakfast, mark rodeo week. In late July the national finals for the **National Little Britches Rodeo** (✆ 719/389-0333) take place at the Penrose Equestrian Center, 1045 W. Rio Grande Ave., off Fountain Creek Boulevard (✆ 719/635-3547; www.coloradospringsrodeo.com).

8 Shopping

Five principal areas attract shoppers in Colorado Springs. The Manitou Springs and Old Colorado City neighborhoods are excellent places to browse for art, jewelry, arts and crafts, books, antiques, and other specialty items. The Chapel Hills and Citadel malls combine major department stores with a variety of national chain outlets. Downtown Colorado Springs also has numerous fine shops.

SHOPPING A TO Z
ANTIQUES
Antique Emporium at Manitou Springs   The shop's 4,000 square feet of floor space provides ample room for displaying its collection of antique furniture, china, glassware, books, collectibles, and primitives. 719 Manitou Ave., Manitou Springs. ✆ 719/685-9195.

Nevada Avenue Antiques This well-established multidealer mall, covering some 7,000 square feet, is filled with a wide variety of antiques and collectibles, including a good selection of lower-priced items. 405 S. Nevada Ave. ✆ 719/ 473-3351.

The Villagers Here you will find a diverse array of quality antiques and collectibles. Volunteers run the shop, and all proceeds go to Cheyenne Village, a community of adults with developmental disabilities. 2514 W. Colorado Ave., Old Colorado City. ✆ 719/632-1400.

ART GALLERIES

Business of Art Center Primarily an educational facility to help artists learn the business end of their profession, the center also has workshops, classes, and lectures, plus numerous artists' studios (open for viewing), six exhibition galleries, and a gift shop. Featured are renowned Colorado artists and juried exhibits of regional art. The shop offers a varied selection of regional artwork, including prints, photographs, jewelry, sculpture, ceramics, wearable art, hand-blown glass, and carved-wood objects. Theater, music, and dance performances are occasionally staged. 513 Manitou Ave., Manitou Springs. ✆ 719/685-1861.

Commonwheel Artists Co-op Original art and fine crafts by area artists fill this excellent gallery, where you'll find a good selection of paintings, photography, sculpture, jewelry, textiles, and other items. 102 Cañon Ave., Manitou Springs. ✆ 719/685-1008. www.commonwheel.com.

Flute Player Gallery This gallery offers contemporary and traditional American Indian silver and turquoise jewelry, Pueblo pottery, Navajo weavings, and Hopi kachina dolls. 2511 W. Colorado Ave., Old Colorado City. ✆ 719/632-7702.

Michael Garman's Gallery *(Kids* A showcase for Garman's sculptures and casts depicting urban and Western life, this gallery also holds "Magic Town," a large model of an old-time inner city, with sculptures and holographic actors. Admission to Magic Town is $3 for adults, $1.50 for children 6 to 13, and free for children under 6. 2418 W. Colorado Ave., Old Colorado City. ✆ 800/731-3908 or 719/471-9391. www.michaelgarman.com.

BOOKS

Book Sleuth *(Finds* For all your mystery needs, visit this bookstore. In addition to a wide selection of mystery novels (including a good stock of out-of-print books), the shop offers numerous puzzles and games. 2501 W. Colorado Ave. #105, Old Colorado City. ✆ 719/632-2727.

CRAFTS

Simpich Character Dolls *(Kids* These exquisite handmade dolls are the creation of Bob and Jan Simpich, who made their first dolls in 1952 as Christmas gifts for their parents. Friends would see the dolls and ask about buying them—and the business grew from there. Today, numerous dolls represent characters from literature, the Victorian era, and early American life. Other creations range from the whimsical—such as leprechauns and elves—to the historical (an Abraham Lincoln bust). Visitors to this gallery and studio can wander through the display and work areas, and watch the process as the dolls are created. 2413 W. Colorado Ave., Old Colorado City. ✆ 719/636-3272. www.simpich.com.

Van Briggle Art Pottery Founded in 1900 by Artus Van Briggle, who applied Chinese matte glaze to Rocky Mountain clays molded into imaginative Art Nouveau shapes, this is one of the oldest active art potteries in the United

States. Artisans demonstrate their craft, from throwing on the wheel to glazing and firing. Free tours are available, and finished works are sold in the showroom. 600 S. 21st St., Old Colorado City. © 800/847-6341 or 719/633-7729. www.vanbriggle.com.

JEWELRY

Manitou Jack's Jewelry & Gifts   Black Hills gold, 10- and 14-karat, is the specialty here. There's also an extensive collection of American-Indian jewelry, pottery, sand paintings, and other art. The shop will create custom jewelry and make repairs. 814 Manitou Ave., Manitou Springs. © 719/685-5004.

Zerbe Jewelers   This well-established downtown Colorado Springs jeweler is known for beautiful custom work and one-of-a-kind designer jewelry. 26 N. Tejon St. © 719/635-3521.

MALLS & SHOPPING CENTERS

Chapel Hills Mall   Foley's, Sears, Mervyn's, JCPenney, and Dillard's are among the 150 stores at this mall, which also houses an ice-skating arena, 40-foot climbing wall, children's play area, 15-screen movie theater, and about two dozen food outlets. 1710 Briargate Blvd. (N. Academy Blvd., at I-25 exit 150A). © 719/594-0111.

The Citadel   This is southern Colorado's largest regional shopping mall, with Dillard's, Foley's, JCPenney, Mervyn's, and more than 170 specialty shops and restaurants. 750 Citadel Dr. E. (N. Academy Blvd. at E. Platte Ave.). © 719/591-5516.

SPORTING GOODS

In business since 1968, the independent **Mountain Chalet,** 226 N. Tejon St. (© 719/633-0732), sells camping gear, outdoor clothing, hiking and climbing gear, and winter sports equipment. Another good source for all sorts of outdoor clothing and equipment is **Gart Sports,** with stores at 7730 N. Academy Blvd. (© 719/532-1020); and 1409 N. Academy Blvd. (© 719/574-1400).

WESTERN WEAR

Lorig's Western Wear ⚡   This Colorado Springs institution is where real cowboys get their hats, boots, jeans, and those fancy belts with the big buckles. 15 N. Union Blvd. © 719/633-4695.

WINE & LIQUOR

Cheers Liquor Mart   This liquor supermarket has a huge selection of beer and wine, including Colorado wines, at good prices. 1105 N. Circle Dr. © 719/574-2244.

The Wines of Colorado   This tasting room and sales outlet offers the greatest number of Colorado wines available for tasting under one roof. There are also gift items, and the restaurant offers a grill menu. 8045 W. U.S. 24, Cascade (about 10 miles west of Colorado Springs). © 719/684-0900.

9 Colorado Springs After Dark

The Colorado Springs entertainment scene spreads throughout the metropolitan area. Pikes Peak Center, the Colorado Springs Fine Arts Center, City Auditorium, Colorado College, and various facilities at the U.S. Air Force Academy are all outstanding venues for the performing arts. The city also supports dozens of cinemas, nightclubs, bars, and other after-dark attractions. Downtown is the major nightlife hub, but Old Colorado City and Manitou Springs also have their fair share of interesting establishments.

Weekly entertainment schedules appear in the Friday *Gazette Telegraph*. Also look at the listings in *Springs* magazine and *The Independent,* free entertainment tabloids. Or call the city's weekly **events line** (© **719/635-1723**). A good online resource for information on events and nightlife, as well as restaurants, is www.sceneinthesprings.com.

Tickets for many major entertainment and sporting events can be obtained from **Ticketmaster** (© **719/520-9090**; www.ticketmaster.com) and **Tickets-West** (© **866/464-2626**; www.ticketswest.com).

THE CLUB & MUSIC SCENE

Cowboys   Two-steppers and country-and-western music lovers flock to this east-side club, which boasts the largest dance floor in the area. It's open Wednesday to Sunday, and dance lessons are available. 3910 Palmer Park Blvd. © 719/596-1212.

Poor Richard's Restaurant   An eclectic variety of performers appears at this bohemian landmark 1 or 2 nights a week, presenting everything from acoustic folk to Celtic melodies to jazz to bluegrass. The menu includes pizza, sandwiches, and the Springs' best nachos (blue corn chips and mozzarella) as well as beer and wine. Adjacent are Poor Richard's Bookstore and Little Richard's Toy Store, all owned by local politico Richard Skorman. 324½ N. Tejon St. © 719/632-7721.

Rum Bay   Located in the renovated Woolworth Building downtown, the lively Rum Bay is a massive nightclub sporting a wall full of rum bottles and a tropical theme. Disc jockeys spin records for two dance floors; there's also a piano bar featuring dueling players. The entire block contains six additional bars under the same management, ranging from "the world's smallest bar" to Rum Bay-like clubs focusing on tequila and bourbon. 20 N. Tejon St. © 719/634-3522.

32 Bleu   This hip downtown nightspot actually has two spaces: a bistro/bar downstairs and the Springs' best midsize live music venue upstairs. Performers are local and national, with steady streams of hip-hop, indie rock, and reggae. 32 S. Tejon St. © 719/955-5664.

Underground Pub   This popular hangout attracts a diverse crowd, from college students and other young people to baby boomers and retirees. Patrons come to dance or just listen to the equally eclectic music (live or recorded), which ranges from rock to jazz to reggae, with some occasional folk. 110 N. Nevada Ave. © 719/633-0590.

THE BAR SCENE

Golden Bee *(Moments*   An opulent 19th-century English pub was disassembled, shipped from Great Britain, and reassembled piece by piece to create this delightful drinking establishment. You can have imported English ale by the yard or half-yard while enjoying steak-and-potato pie, Devonshire cheddar-cheese soup, sandwiches, or other British specialties. Evenings bring a ragtime pianist to enliven the atmosphere; interested guests are given songbooks for sing-along. Lower level entrance of The Broadmoor International Center, Lake Circle. © 719/634-7711.

Hide 'n' Seek   The Hide 'n' Seek, which opened in 1972, is one of the oldest and largest gay bars in the West, covering some 12,500 square feet. It has five bars with country-western and other themes, four dance floors with DJs most nights and live music on weekends, and a restaurant. 512 W. Colorado Ave. © 719/634-9303.

Meadow Muffins   A boisterous barroom packed to the gills with movie memorabilia and assorted knickknacks, Meadow Muffins certainly doesn't lack personality. It features DJs or live music several nights a week. The food is standard bar fare, but the burgers are great. On most days, there are several specials, with happy hour from 4 to 7pm daily and 4pm until closing on Friday. There are also pool tables, a pair of big-screen TVs, and arcade games. See also the restaurant listing on p. 194. 2432 W. Colorado Ave., in Old Colorado City. (C) 719/ 633-0583.

Oscar's   Featuring aquariums above the bar, this downtown hangout shucks more oysters than anyplace in the Springs, including The Broadmoor's eateries. The menu here is Cajun, the crowd eclectic, the music tending towards jazz and blues. 333 S. Tejon St. (C) 719/471-8070.

Phantom Canyon Brewing Co.   This popular brewpub generally offers 8 to 10 of its specialty beers, including homemade root beer. The beers are unfiltered and unpasteurized, served at the traditional temperature for the style. We recommend Railyard Ale, a light amber ale with a smooth, malty taste; Hefeweizen, a traditional German wheat beer; and a very hoppy India pale ale. A billiard hall is on the second floor. See also the restaurant listing on p. 193. 2 E. Pikes Peak Ave. (C) 719/635-2800.

Ritz Grill   Especially popular with young professionals after work and the chic clique later in the evening, this noisy restaurant-lounge, known for its martinis and large central bar, brings an Art Deco feel to downtown Colorado Springs. There's live music (usually rock) starting at 9pm Thursday through Saturday. See also the restaurant listing on p. 193. 15 S. Tejon St. (C) 719/635-8484.

THE PERFORMING ARTS

Among the major venues for performing arts is the 8,000-seat **Colorado Springs World Arena,** 3185 Venetucci Blvd., at I-25 exit 138 ((C) 719/477-2100; www.worldarena.com). The area's newest entertainment center, it presents big-name country and rock concerts and a wide variety of sporting events. Other major facilities include the handsome **Pikes Peak Center,** 190 S. Cascade Ave. ((C) 719/520-7453 for general information, or 719/520-7469 for the ticket office; www.pikespeakcenter.org), a 2,000-seat concert hall in the heart of downtown that has been acclaimed for its outstanding acoustics. The city's symphony orchestra and dance theater call the Pikes Peak Center home, and top-flight touring entertainers, Broadway musicals, and symphony orchestras appear here as well. The **Colorado Springs Fine Arts Center,** 30 W. Dale St. ((C) 719/ 634-5581 for general information, or 719/634-5583 for the box office; www.csfineartscenter.org), is a historic facility (see "Museums & Galleries" under "Attractions," earlier in this chapter) that includes a children's theater program, a repertory theater company, dance programs and concerts, and classic films. Recent productions have included *Annie* and *Oklahoma*. At the historic **City Auditorium,** 221 E. Kiowa St. ((C) 719/578-6652; www.springsgov.com, follow links), you can often attend a trade show or big-name concert—Willie Nelson performed recently—or drop in at the Lon Chaney Theatre, with its resident Star Bar Players (see below) and Pikes Peak Youth Theatre.

THEATER & DANCE

BlueBards   The Air Force Academy's cadet theater group performs Broadway and other productions; it recently staged *Jesus Christ Superstar*. Arnold Hall Theater, U.S. Air Force Academy. (C) 719/333-4497. www.usafa.af.mil/wing/clubs/bluebards.

Colorado Springs Dance Theatre   This nonprofit organization presents international dance companies from September to May at Pikes Peak Center, Colorado College's Armstrong Hall, and other venues. Notable productions have included Mikhail Baryshnikov, Alvin Ailey Repertory Ensemble, Ballet Folklorico of Mexico, and other traditional, modern, ethnic, and jazz dance programs. Each year, three to five performances are scheduled, and master classes, lectures, and other programs often coincide with the performances. 7 E. Bijou St., Suite 209. © **719/630-7434.** www.csdance.org. Tickets $20–$30; senior and student discounts available.

Star Bar Players   Each year, this resident theater company presents several full-length plays, ranging from Greek comedies to modern murder mysteries. Recent productions have included *Arsenic and Old Lace* and Neil Simon's *Lost in Yonkers*. Tickets are typically $10 to $20. Lon Chaney Theatre, City Auditorium, 221 E. Kiowa St. © **719/573-7411.** www.starbarplayers.org.

DINNER THEATERS

Flying W Ranch ⭐   This working cattle and horse ranch just north of the Garden of the Gods encompasses a Western village of more than a dozen restored buildings and a mine train. There are also demonstrations of Navajo weaving and horse shoeing. A Western stage show features bunkhouse comedy, cowboy balladry, and foot-stompin' fiddle, mandolin, and guitar music. From mid-May through September the town opens each afternoon at 4:30pm; a chuck-wagon dinner (barbecued beef or chicken, potatoes, beans, biscuits, and cake) is served ranch-style at 7:15pm, and the show begins at 8:30pm. The winter steakhouse is open October to December and March to May on Friday and Saturday, with seatings at 5 and 8pm and a Western stage show at each seating. 3330 Chuckwagon Rd. © **800/232-FLYW** or 719/598-4000. www.flyingw.com. Reservations recommended. Chuck-wagon dinners $18.50 adults, $8 children under 9; winter steakhouse $21–$22 adults, $7.50 children under 9. MC, V.

Iron Springs Chateau Melodrama ⭐   Located near the foot of the Pikes Peak Cog Railway, this popular comedy and drama dinner theater urges patrons to boo the villain and cheer the hero. Past productions have included *Farther North to Laughter or Buck of the Yukon, Part Two*, and *When the Halibut Start Running or Don't Slam the Door on Davy Jones' Locker*. A family-style dinner, with free seconds, includes oven-baked chicken and barbecued beef brisket, mashed potatoes, green beans almandine, pineapple coleslaw, and buttermilk biscuits. A sing-along and a vaudeville-style olio show follow the performance. Iron Springs Chateau is open from April through September and from late November through December. Dinner is served on Tuesday, Wednesday, Friday, and Saturday between 6 and 6:45pm; the show follows at 8pm. 444 Ruxton Ave., Manitou Springs. © **719/685-5104** or 719/685-5572. www.pikes-peak.com. Reservations required. Dinner and show $24 adults, $23 seniors, $15 children; show only $13 adults, $12.50 seniors, $8.50 children. MC, V.

10 Side Trips to Florissant Fossil Beds National Monument & Cripple Creek

FLORISSANT FOSSIL BEDS NATIONAL MONUMENT ⭐⭐

Approximately 35 miles west of Colorado Springs on U.S. 24 is the small village of Florissant, which means "flowering" in French. It couldn't be more aptly named—every spring its hillsides virtually blaze with wildflowers. Just 2 miles south is one of the most spectacular, yet relatively unknown, fossil deposits in the world, Florissant Fossil Beds National Monument. From Florissant, follow the signs along Teller County Road 1.

The fossils in this 6,000-acre National Park Service property are preserved in the rocks of ancient Lake Florissant, which existed 34 million years ago. Volcanic eruptions spanning half a million years trapped plants and animals under layers of ash and dust; the creatures were fossilized as the sediment settled and became shale.

The detailed impressions, first discovered in 1873, offer the most extensive record of its kind in the world. Scientists have removed thousands of specimens, including 1,100 separate species of insects. Dragonflies, beetles, and ants; more fossil butterflies than anywhere else in the world; plus spiders, fish, some mammals, and birds are all perfectly preserved from 34 to 35 million years ago. Leaves from willows, maples, and hickories; extinct relatives of birches, elms, and beeches; and needles of pines and sequoias are also plentiful. These fossil plants, very different from those living in the area today, show how the climate has changed over the centuries.

Mudflows also buried forests during this long period, petrifying the trees where they stood. Nature trails pass petrified tree stumps; one sequoia stump is 10 feet in diameter and 11 feet high. There's a display of carbonized fossils at the visitor center, which also offers interpretive programs. An added attraction within the monument is the homestead of Adeline Hornbek, who pioneered the area with her children in 1878. The national monument also has some 14 miles of hiking trails.

Nearby, about ½ mile north of the monument, there's superb fishing for German browns and cutthroats at Spinney Mountain Reservoir.

Admission to the monument is $3 per adult and free for children under 17, making a visit here an incredibly affordable outing. It's open from 9am to 5:30pm daily from May to September; 8am to 4:30pm daily October to April. It's closed January 1, Thanksgiving, and December 25. Contact Florissant Fossil Beds National Monument, P.O. Box 185, Florissant, CO 80816-0185 (© 719/748-3253; www.nps.gov/flfo).

CRIPPLE CREEK

This old mining town on the southwestern flank of Pikes Peak was known as the world's greatest gold camp after the precious metal was first discovered here in 1890. During its heyday at the beginning of the 20th century, Cripple Creek (elevation 9,494 ft.) had a stock exchange, 2 opera houses, 5 daily newspapers, 16 churches, 19 schools, and 73 saloons, plus an elaborate streetcar system and a railroad depot that saw 18 arrivals and departures a day. By the time mining ceased in 1961, more than $800 million worth of ore had been taken from the surrounding hills.

Today Cripple Creek has several dozen limited-stakes gambling casinos, most lining Bennett Avenue. They cash in not only on the lure of gambling but also on the nostalgia for the gambling houses that were once prominent throughout the Old West. Although gamblers must be at least 21 years old, some casinos offer special children's areas, along with other family activities. Among the more interesting of the many casinos in town is the **Imperial Casino Hotel,** 123 N. 3rd St. at Bennett Ave. (P.O. Box 869), Cripple Creek, CO 80813 (© **800/ 235-2922** or 719/689-7777; www.imperialcasinohotel.com). Built in 1896 following a disastrous fire that razed most of the city, the fully renovated Imperial offers Victorian accommodations in a handsome historic building, a casino, and several restaurants and bars.

One of the town's unique attractions is a herd of wild donkeys, descendants of the miners' runaways, that roam freely through the hills and into the streets. The year's biggest celebration, **Donkey Derby Days** in late June, culminates with a donkey race.

Although gambling takes place year-round, many of the historic attractions are open in summer only or have limited winter hours. Among those you'll want to check out is the 1891 **Mollie Kathleen Gold Mine,** 1 mile north of Cripple Creek on Colo. 67 (© **719/689-2466;** www.goldminetours.com). It offers visitors a rare chance to join hard-rock miners on a 1,000-foot underground descent into a genuine gold mine and take home a gold-ore specimen as a souvenir. Tours last about 40 minutes; temperatures in the mine are 45°F to 50°F (7°C–10°C), and jackets are provided. Admission is $15 for adults, $7 for children 3 through 11, and free for children under 3. The mine is open from early April through October daily from 9am to 5pm, and usually open Friday through Sunday in winter; call ahead.

The **Cripple Creek District Museum,** at the east end of Bennett Avenue (© **719/689-2634;** www.cripple-creek.org), includes three historic buildings packed with late-19th-century relics, including mining and railroad memorabilia. There's a gold-ore exhibit, Victorian fashions and furniture, exhibits on local wildlife, historic photos, a fully restored Victorian-era flat, and an assay office where fire-testing of local ores took place. The museum is open daily from 10am to 5pm Memorial Day through September, and Friday to Sunday from 11am until 4pm the rest of the year.

The **Cripple Creek & Victor Narrow Gauge Railroad Co.** ★★, at the Midland Terminal Depot, east end of Bennett Avenue at 5th St. (© **719/689-2640;** www.cripplecreekrailroad.com), takes visitors on a 4-mile narrated tour. The route runs past abandoned mines and over a reconstructed trestle to the ghost town of Anaconda, powered by a 15-ton "iron horse" steam locomotive. The train operates daily from mid-June through Labor Day, then on a reduced schedule from mid-May until mid-June and from Labor Day until mid-October. Call for exact times.

Cripple Creek is 45 miles west of Colorado Springs; take U.S. 24 west and Colo. 67 south. For additional information, contact the **Cripple Creek Chamber of Commerce,** P.O. Box 430, Cripple Creek, CO 80813 (© **877/858-4653** or 719/689-3461; www.cripple-creek.co.us).

NEARBY SCENIC DRIVES

When you leave Cripple Creek, two drives of particular beauty offer alternatives to Colo. 67. Neither is paved and both are narrow and winding, but both are usually acceptable for everyday vehicles under dry conditions. Each is roughly 30 miles long but requires about 90 minutes to negotiate. First, take Colo. 67 south out of Cripple Creek for 6 miles to the historic mining town of **Victor,** a delightful, picturesque destination.

The **Gold Camp Road** leads east from Victor to Colorado Springs via the North Cheyenne Cañon. Teddy Roosevelt said that this trip up the old Short Line Railroad bed had "scenery that bankrupts the English language." The **Phantom Canyon Road** leads south from Victor to Florence, following another old narrow-gauge railroad bed known as the Gold Belt Line. A number of ghost towns and fossil areas mark this route.

11 A Side Trip to Royal Gorge

From Colorado Springs, the breathtaking **Royal Gorge** and **Royal Gorge Bridge and Park** and the historic town of Cañon City make an easy day trip. The Royal Gorge, one of the most impressive natural attractions in the state, lies 8 miles west of Cañon City off U.S. 50, at the head of the Arkansas River valley. From the Springs, head southwest on Colo. 115 for about 33 miles, turn west for about 12 miles on U.S. 50 to Cañon City (about 45 miles all together), and then go south to the Royal Gorge.

This narrow canyon, 1,053 feet deep, was cut through solid granite by 3 million years of water and wind erosion. When Zebulon Pike saw the gorge in 1806, he predicted that man would never conquer it. But by 1877 the Denver & Rio Grande Railroad had laid a route through the canyon, and it soon became a major tourist attraction.

The gorge is spanned by what is said to be the world's highest suspension bridge and an aerial tramway, built for no other reason than to thrill tourists. The ¼-mile-long bridge was constructed in 1929, suspended from two 300-ton cables, and reinforced in 1983. An incline railway, believed to be the world's steepest, was completed in 1931; it plunges from the rim of the gorge 1,550 feet to the floor at a 45° angle, giving passengers the view from the bottom as well as the top. The 35-passenger tram added in 1968 provides views of the gorge and the bridge from a height of 1,178 feet above the Arkansas River.

Owned by Cañon City, the park also holds a 260-seat multimedia theater (where visitors can see a video presentation on the area's history and construction of the bridge), miniature railway, trolley, old-fashioned carousel, various thrill rides and children's attractions, restaurants, gift shops, a petting zoo with free burro rides, and herds of tame mule deer. Live entertainment and a variety of special events take place throughout the year.

The park is open year-round, daily from 8:30am to dusk. Admission—$20 for adults, $18 seniors, $16 for children 4 to 11, free for children under 4— includes crossing the bridge and all other park rides and attractions. For information, contact **Royal Gorge Bridge,** P.O. Box 549, Cañon City, CO 81215 (© **888/333-5597** or 719/275-7507; www.royalgorgebridge.com).

An interesting way to view the canyon is from the **Royal Gorge Route Railroad,** 401 Water St. (south of U.S. 50 on 3rd St.), Cañon City, CO 81212 (© **888/RAILS-4U** or 303/569-2403; www.royalgorgeroute.com). The train takes passengers on a 2-hour, 24-mile trip through the canyon. From late May to early September, the train departs daily at 9:30am and 12:30pm; less frequently the rest of the year. Tickets cost $27 for adults, $16.50 for children 3 to 12, and are free for children under 3 who sit on a guardian's lap. Reservations are recommended.

To see this beautiful gorge looking up from the river while also enjoying some thrills, consider a raft trip. Rates for adults run $90 to $100 for a full-day trip, including lunch; a half-day trip is about $50 to $60. Most Royal Gorge raft trips include rough white-water stretches of the river; those preferring calmer sections should inquire with local rafting companies. Major outfitters include **Arkansas River Tours** (© 800/321-4352 or 719/942-4362; www.arkansasrivertours. com), **Echo Canyon River Expeditions** (© 800/748-2953; www.raftecho. com), and **Wilderness Aware Rafting** (© 800/462-7238 or 719/395-2112; www.inaraft.com). See also "River Rafting" under "Outdoor Activities," earlier in this chapter.

OTHER AREA ATTRACTIONS

Cañon City was a popular film setting during the industry's early days, and it was a special favorite of silent screen actor Tom Mix, who reputedly worked as a cowboy in the area before becoming a film star. The drowning death of a prominent actress temporarily discouraged film companies from coming here, but the area's beautiful scenery and Old West heritage lured the industry back in the late 1950s, helped along by the creation of Buckskin Joe, a Western theme park and movie set where dozens of films have been shot, including *How the West Was Won, True Grit,* and *Cat Ballou.*

While movies are rarely shot here nowadays, **Buckskin Joe Frontier Town & Railway** (© 719/275-5149; www.buckskinjoes.com), about 8 miles west of Cañon City on U.S. 50, remains a popular tourist attraction. The authentic-looking Old West town was created from genuine 19th-century buildings relocated from across the state. Visitors can watch gunfights, pan for gold, see a magic show, ride horseback (or in a horse-drawn trolley), and wander through a Western maze. The **Scenic Railway** (© 719/275-5485) offers a 30-minute trip through rugged Royal Gorge country, where you're likely to see deer and other wildlife, to the rim of the Royal Gorge for a panoramic view of the canyon and bridge.

Frontier Town is open from May through September only. Hours are 9am to 6:30pm daily May to August, and Thursday to Tuesday in September. The railway runs from May to September. Hours from Memorial Day to Labor Day are 8am to 6:20pm; call for hours at other times. Combination admission tickets, which include the Scenic Railway, horse-drawn trolley, and all the Frontier Town attractions and entertainment, are $16 for adults, $14 for children 4 to 11, and free for children under 4. Tickets for the railway only are $8 for adults and $7 for children. Expect to spend 2 to 4 hours here.

Other Cañon City attractions include the **Museum of Colorado Prisons** ⚘, 201 N. 1st St. (© 719/269-3015; www.prisonmuseum.org), especially interesting for those with an appreciation of the macabre. Housed in the state's former women's prison, just outside the walls of the original territorial prison that opened in 1871, it contains an actual gas chamber, historic photos of life behind bars, weapons confiscated from inmates, the last hangman's noose used legally in the state, a simulation of a lethal-injection system and of the "Old Gray Mare" (a cruel apparatus used to punish misbehaving prisoners), and other artifacts and exhibits. There's also a gift shop selling arts and crafts made by inmates at a medium-security prison next door. The museum is open May through September daily from 8:30am to 6pm; October through April, Friday through Sunday from 10am to 5pm. Admission is $6 for adults, $5 for seniors 65 and older, $4 for youths 6 to 12, and free for children under 6. Allow about an hour.

Those interested in Colorado history might also enjoy stopping at the **Royal Gorge Regional Museum and History Center,** 612 Royal Gorge Blvd. (© 719/276-5279), which holds displays of American-Indian artifacts, guns, gems, minerals, wild-game trophies, historic photos, old dolls, pioneer household items, and other memorabilia. These are pretty much the kinds of things you'll find in most small-town museums in the American West, but what sets this museum apart somewhat are several renovated and authentically furnished buildings out back. Here are the 1860 log cabin built by Anson Rudd, local blacksmith and first warden of the Colorado Territorial Prison, and the Rudd family's three-story stone house built in 1881, which contains a collection of

Victorian furniture and Western artifacts. Although the museum is closed for renovation until late 2005, it is typically open from 9:30am to 5pm Tuesday through Friday and Mondays 11am to 7pm. It's closed December 24 plus all state and federal holidays. Admission is free. Allow a half-hour.

Another local attraction, especially fascinating for young would-be dinosaur hunters, is **Dinosaur Depot** ⚘, 330 Royal Gorge Blvd. (© **800/987-6379** or 719/269-7150; www.dinosaurdepot.com). The depot's main claim to fame is the dinosaur lab, where paleontologists are working to remove various dinosaur fossils from the rock that has encased them for the last 150 million years. There are also several interpretive exhibits, including fossilized bones that visitors can hold, a fossilized tree, a children's Discovery Room with plenty of hands-on exhibits, and a gift shop. Dinosaur Depot also sells brochures for self-guided tours of the internationally renowned **Garden Park Fossil Area** just north of town, which is the source of many of the museum's exhibits, and to see some 90-million-year-old dinosaur tracks nearby. The museum is open daily from 9am to 6pm June to September; shorter hours the rest of the year. Admission is $3 for adults, $1.50 for children 4 to 12, and free for children under 4. Allow 45 minutes at Dinosaur Depot, and another 1 to 2 hours at Garden Park Fossil Area.

Cañon City has several midprice lodging options, including the **Best Western Royal Gorge Motel,** 1925 Fremont Dr., Cañon City, CO 81212 (© **800/ 231-7317** or 719/275-3377), with double rates ranging from $50 to $100 in summer and $40 to $90 off season; and **Quality Inn & Suites** (formerly the Cañon Inn), 3075 E. U.S. 50, Cañon City, CO 81212 (© **800/525-7727** or 719/275-8676; www.canoninn.com), which has six indoor hot tubs, with rooms priced from $68 to $99 double in summer, and about $20 less in winter. The **Barquero Restaurant** at the Cañon Inn features Mexican and American food; the **True Grit Lounge** has a John Wayne theme. Most dinner entrees cost $8 to $16. Another good dining option is **Merlino's Belvedere,** 1330 Elm Ave. (© **719/275-5558;** www.belvedererestaurant.com), which specializes in gourmet Italian cuisine, steaks, and seafood at lunch and dinner daily. Dinner main courses run $10 to $30.

For more information on where to stay and eat, a walking tour of historic downtown Cañon City, and details on scenic drives and other attractions, contact the **Cañon City Chamber of Commerce,** 403 Royal Gorge Blvd., Cañon City, CO 81212 (© **719/275-2331;** www.canoncitychamber.com).

Appendix A:
Denver, Boulder &
Colorado Springs in Depth

To explore Colorado today is to step into its past, from its dinosaur graveyards and impressive stone and clay cities of the Ancestral Puebloan people (also called the Anasazi) to reminders of the Wild West of Bat Masterson and Doc Holliday and elegant Victorian mansions. The history of Colorado is a testimony to the human ability to adapt and flourish in a difficult environment. This land of high mountains and limited water continues to challenge its inhabitants today.

The earliest people in Colorado are believed to have been nomadic hunters who arrived some 12,000 to 20,000 years ago by way of the Bering Strait, following the tracks of the woolly mammoth and bison. Then, about 2,000 years ago, the people we call the Ancestral Puebloans arrived, living in shallow caves in the Four Corners area, where the borders of Colorado, Utah, Arizona, and New Mexico meet.

These hunters gradually learned farming and basket making, then pottery making and the construction of pit houses—basically large underground pots. Eventually they built complex villages, examples of which can be seen at Mesa Verde National Park. For some unknown reason, possibly drought, they deserted the area around the end of the 13th century, probably moving south into present-day New Mexico and Arizona.

Dateline

- 12,000 B.C. First inhabitants include Folsom Man.
- 3000 B.C. Prehistoric farming communities appear.
- A.D. 1000 Ancestral Puebloan cliff-dweller culture peaks in Four Corners region.
- Late 1500s Spanish explore upper Rio Grande Valley, colonize Santa Fe and Taos, New Mexico, and make forays into what is now southern Colorado.
- 1803 The Louisiana Purchase includes most of modern Colorado.
- 1805 The Lewis and Clark expedition sights the Rocky Mountains.
- 1806–07 Capt. Zebulon Pike leads first U.S. expedition into the Colorado Rockies.
- 1822 William Becknell establishes the Santa Fe Trail.
- 1842–44 Lieutenant John C. Frémont and Kit Carson explore Colorado and American West.
- 1848 Treaty of Guadalupe Hidalgo ends Mexican War, adds American Southwest to the United States.
- 1858 Gold discovered in modern Denver.
- 1859 General William Larimer founds Denver. Major gold strikes in nearby Rockies.
- 1861 Colorado Territory proclaimed.
- 1862 Colorado cavalry wins major Civil War battle at Glorietta Pass, New Mexico. Homestead Act is passed.
- 1863–68 Ute tribe obtains treaties guaranteeing 16 million acres of western Colorado land.

Although the Ancestral Puebloans were gone by the time the Spanish conquistadors arrived in the mid–16th century, in their place were two major nomadic cultures: the mountain dwellers of the west, primarily Ute; and the plains tribes of the east, principally Arapaho, Cheyenne, and Comanche.

Spanish colonists, having established settlements at Santa Fe, Taos, and other upper Rio Grande locations in the 16th and 17th centuries, didn't immediately find southern Colorado attractive for colonization. Not only was there a lack of financial and military support from the Spanish crown, but the freedom-loving, sometimes fierce Comanche and Ute also made it clear that they would rather be left alone.

Nevertheless, Spain held title to southern and western Colorado in 1803, when U.S. President Thomas Jefferson paid $15 million for the vast Louisiana Territory, which included the lion's share of modern Colorado. Two years later the Lewis and Clark expedition passed by, but the first official exploration by the U.S. government occurred when Jefferson sent Capt. Zebulon Pike to the territory. Pikes Peak, Colorado's landmark mountain and a top tourist attraction near Colorado Springs, bears the explorer's name.

As the West began to open up in the 1820s, the Santa Fe Trail was established, cutting through Colorado's southeast corner. Much of eastern Colorado, including what would become Denver, Boulder, and Colorado Springs, was then part of the Kansas Territory. It was populated almost exclusively by plains tribes until 1858, when gold-seekers discovered flakes of the precious metal near the junction of Cherry Creek and the South Platte, and the city of Denver was established, named for Kansas governor James Denver.

- **1864** Hundreds of Cheyenne killed in Sand Creek Massacre. University of Denver becomes Colorado's first institution of higher education.
- **1870** Kansas City–Denver rail line completed. Agricultural commune of Greeley established by Nathan Meeker. Colorado State University opens in Fort Collins.
- **1871** General William Palmer founds Colorado Springs.
- **1876** Colorado becomes 38th state.
- **1877** University of Colorado opens in Boulder.
- **1878** Little Pittsburg silver strike launches Leadville mining boom, Colorado's greatest.
- **1879** Milk Creek Massacre by Ute warriors leads to tribe's removal to reservations.
- **1890** Sherman Silver Purchase Act boosts price of silver. Gold discovered at Cripple Creek, leading to state's biggest gold rush.
- **1893** Women win right to vote. Silver industry collapses following repeal of Sherman Silver Purchase Act.
- **1901–07** President Theodore Roosevelt sets aside 16 million acres of national forest land in Colorado.
- **1906** U.S. Mint built in Denver.
- **1913** Wolf Creek Pass highway is first to cross Continental Divide in Colorado.
- **1915** Rocky Mountain National Park established.
- **1934** Direct Denver–San Francisco rail travel begins. Taylor Grazing Act ends homesteading.
- **1941–45** World War II establishes Colorado as military center.
- **1947** Aspen's first chairlift begins operation.
- **1948–58** Uranium "rush" sweeps western slope.
- **1955** Environmentalists prevent construction of Echo Park Dam in Dinosaur National Monument.
- **1967** Colorado legalizes medically necessary abortions.
- **1988** Senator Gary Hart, a frontrunner for the Democratic presidential nomination, withdraws from race after a scandal.

continues

The Cherry Creek strike was literally a flash in the gold-seeker's pan, but two strikes in the mountains just west of Denver in early 1859 were more significant: one at Clear Creek, near what would become Idaho Springs, and another in a quartz vein at Gregory Gulch, which led to the founding of Central City. The race to Colorado's goldfields had begun.

Abraham Lincoln was elected president of the United States in November 1860, and Congress created the Colorado Territory 3 months later. The new territory absorbed neighboring sections from Utah, Nebraska, and New Mexico to form the boundaries of the state today. Lincoln's Homestead Act of 1862 brought much of the public domain into private ownership and led to the plotting of Front Range townships, starting with Denver.

Controlling the American Indian peoples was a priority of the territorial government. A treaty negotiated in 1851 had guaranteed the entire Pikes Peak region to the nomadic plains tribes, but that had been made moot by the arrival of settlers in the late 1850s. The Fort Wise Treaty of 1861 exchanged the Pikes Peak territory for 5 million fertile acres of Arkansas Valley land, north of modern La Junta. But when the Arapaho and Cheyenne continued to roam their old hunting grounds, conflict became inevitable. Frequent rumors and rare instances of hostility against settlers led the Colorado cavalry to attack a peaceful settlement of Indians—who were flying Old Glory and a white flag—on November 29, 1864. More than 150 Cheyenne and Arapaho, two-thirds of them women and children, were killed in what has become known as the Sand Creek Massacre.

Vowing revenge, the Cheyenne and Arapaho launched a campaign to drive whites from their ancient hunting grounds. Their biggest triumph was the destruction of the northeast

- **1992** Colorado voters approve a controversial state constitutional amendment barring any measures to protect homosexuals from discrimination.
- **1993** Denver becomes 15th U.S. city with three major professional sports teams by adding the Rockies, a new major league baseball franchise.
- **1995** The $4.2-billion state-of-the-art Denver International Airport and $2.16-million Coors Field baseball stadium open. Denver goes sports-crazy with its fourth major professional sports team, the Avalanche of the National Hockey League.
- **1996** The U.S. Supreme Court strikes down Colorado's 1992 constitutional amendment, stating that it could prevent homosexuals from enjoying basic constitutional rights granted to all Americans.
- **1996** The Avalanche win the Stanley Cup, giving Colorado its first championship in any major league.
- **1997** Weather wreaks havoc across the state. First, a summer rainstorm turns a small creek that runs through Fort Collins into a roaring river. Then, in late October, a 24-hour blizzard, the worst October storm in Denver since 1923, virtually shuts down Interstate 25 from Wyoming to New Mexico and strands thousands at Denver International Airport.
- **1997** Gary Lee Davis, convicted of the 1986 abduction and murder of a Colorado farm wife, is executed by lethal injection, the state's first execution in 30 years.
- **1998** The Denver Broncos win the Super Bowl, defeating the Green Bay Packers. The stunning victory saves the Broncos the indignity of becoming the first team to lose five Super Bowls.
- **1999** The Broncos win the Super Bowl again, this time defeating the Atlanta Falcons.
- **1999** The worst school shooting in United States history takes place in suburban Denver inside Columbine high school, leaving 15 dead.
- **2000** Colorado ski resorts report that the 1999–2000 season was the worst in history due to poor snowfall and potential skiers' fears about Y2K problems.

Colorado town of Julesburg in 1865, but the cavalry, bolstered by returning Civil War veterans, managed to force the two tribes onto reservations in Indian Territory in what is now Oklahoma—a barren area that whites thought they would never want.

Also in 1865, a smelter was built in Black Hawk, just west of Denver, setting the stage for the large-scale spread of mining throughout Colorado.

▪ 2002 One of the worst wildfire seasons in history hits Colorado, with about 1,000 fires burning some 364,000 acres across the state. The biggest fire, southwest of Denver, burns 138,000 acres and destroys 133 homes.

▪ 2003 Wynkoop Brewing Company owner John Hickenlooper elected mayor of Denver.

When the first transcontinental railroad was completed in 1869, the Union Pacific went through Cheyenne, Wyoming, 100 miles north of Denver; 4 years later the Kansas City–Denver Railroad linked the line to Denver.

Colorado politicians had begun pressing for statehood during the Civil War, but it wasn't until August 1, 1876, that Colorado became the 38th state. Because it gained statehood less than a month after the 100th birthday of the United States, Colorado became known as the Centennial State.

The state's new constitution gave the vote to blacks but not to women, despite the strong efforts of the Colorado Women's Suffrage Association. In 1893, women finally succeeded in winning the vote, 3 years after Wyoming became the first state to offer universal suffrage.

At the time of statehood, most of Colorado's vast western region was still occupied by some 3,500 mountain and plateau dwellers of a half-dozen Ute tribes. Unlike the plains tribes, their early relations with white explorers and settlers had been peaceful. Chief Ouray, leader of the Uncompahgre Utes, had negotiated treaties in 1863 and 1868 that guaranteed them 16 million acres—most of western Colorado. In 1873, Ouray agreed to sell the United States one-fourth of that acreage in the mineral-rich San Juan Mountains in exchange for hunting rights and $25,000 in annuities.

But a mining boom that began in 1878 led to a flurry of intrusions into Ute territory and stirred up a "Utes Must Go!" sentiment. Two years later the Utes were forced onto small reserves in southwestern Colorado and Utah, and their lands opened to white settlement in 1882.

Colorado's real mining boom began on April 28, 1878, when August Rische and George Hook hit a vein of silver carbonate 27 feet deep on Fryer Hill in Leadville. Perhaps the strike wouldn't have caused such excitement had not Rische and Hook, 8 days earlier, traded one-third interest in whatever they found for a basket of groceries from storekeeper Horace Tabor, the mayor of Leadville and a sharp businessman. Tabor was well acquainted with the Colorado "law of apex," which said that if an ore-bearing vein surfaced on a man's claim, he could follow it wherever it led, even out of his claim and through the claims of others.

Tabor, a legend in Colorado, typifies the rags-to-riches success story of a common working-class man. A native of Vermont, he mortgaged his Kansas homestead in 1859 and moved west to the mountains, where he was a postmaster and storekeeper in several towns before moving to Leadville. He was 46 when the silver strike was made. By age 50, he was the state's richest man and its Republican lieutenant governor. His love affair with and marriage to Elizabeth "Baby Doe" McCourt, a young divorcée for whom he left his wife, Augusta, was a national scandal that became the subject of numerous books and even an opera.

Impressions

I spent a night in a silver mine. I dined with the men down there . . . .
Poems every one of them. A complete democracy underground. I find
people less rough and coarse in such places. There is no chance for rough-
ness. The revolver is their book of etiquette.
                              —Oscar Wilde, quoted in the *Morning Herald,* 1882

Although the silver market collapsed in 1893, gold was there to take its place. In the fall of 1890, a cowboy named Bob Womack found gold in Cripple Creek, on the southwestern slope of Pikes Peak, west of Colorado Springs. He sold his claim to Winfield Scott Stratton, a carpenter and amateur geologist, and Stratton's mine earned a tidy profit of $6 million by 1899, when he sold it to an English company for another $11 million. Cripple Creek turned out to be the richest goldfield ever discovered, ultimately producing $500 million in gold.

Unlike the flamboyant Tabor, Stratton was an introvert and a neurotic. His fortune was twice the size of Tabor's, and it grew daily as the deflation of silver's value boosted that of gold. But he invested most of it back in Cripple Creek, searching for a fabulous mother lode that he never found. By the early 1900s, the price of gold, like silver, began to be driven down by overproduction.

Another turning point for Colorado occurred just after the beginning of the 20th century. Theodore Roosevelt had visited the state in September 1900 as the Republican vice-presidential nominee. Soon after he became president in September 1901 (following the assassination of President McKinley), he began to declare large chunks of the Rockies forest reserves. By 1907, when an act of Congress forbade the president from creating any new reserves by proclamation, nearly one-fourth of Colorado—16 million acres in 18 forests—was national forest. Also during Roosevelt's term was the establishment in 1906 of Mesa Verde National Park, in the state's southwest corner.

Tourism grew hand-in-hand with the setting aside of public lands. Easterners had been visiting Colorado since the 1870s, when General William J. Palmer founded a Colorado Springs resort and made the mountains accessible on his Denver & Rio Grande Railroad.

Estes Park, northwest of Boulder, was among the first resort towns to emerge in the 20th century, spurred by a visit in 1903 by Freelan Stanley. With his brother Francis, Freelan had invented the Stanley Steamer, a steam-powered automobile, in Boston in 1899. Freelan Stanley shipped one of his cars to Denver and drove the 40 miles to Estes Park in less than 2 hours, a remarkable speed for the day. Finding the climate conducive to his recovery from tuberculosis, he returned in 1907 with a dozen Stanley Steamers and established a shuttle service from Denver to Estes Park. Two years later he built the luxurious Stanley Hotel, still a hilltop landmark today.

Stanley befriended Enos Mills, a young innkeeper whose property was more a workshop for students of wildlife than a business. A devotee of conservationist John Muir, Mills believed tourists should spend their Colorado vacations in the natural environment, camping and hiking. As Mills gained national stature as a nature writer, photographer, and lecturer, he urged that the national forest land around Longs Peak, outside Estes Park, be designated a national park. In January 1915, President Woodrow Wilson created the 400-square-mile Rocky Mountain National Park. Today it is one of America's leading tourist attractions, with more than 3 million visitors each year.

The 1920s saw the growth of highways and the completion of the Moffat Tunnel, a 6¼-mile passageway beneath the Continental Divide that in 1934 led to the long-sought direct Denver–San Francisco rail connection. Of more tragic note was the worst flood in Colorado history. The city of Pueblo, south of Colorado Springs, was devastated when the Arkansas River overflowed its banks on June 1, 1921; 100 people were killed, and the damage exceeded $16 million. The Great Depression of the 1930s was a difficult time for many Coloradans, but it had positive consequences. The federal government raised the price of gold from $20 to $35 an ounce, reviving Cripple Creek and other stagnant mining towns.

World War II and the subsequent Cold War were responsible for many of the defense installations that are now an integral part of the Colorado economy, particularly in the Colorado Springs area. The war also indirectly caused the other single greatest boon to Colorado's late-20th-century economy: the ski industry. Soldiers in the 10th Mountain Division, on leave from Camp Hale before heading off to fight in Europe, often crossed Independence Pass to relax in the lower altitude and milder climate of the 19th-century silver-mining village of Aspen. They tested their skiing skills, which they would need in the Italian Alps, against the slopes of Ajax Mountain.

In 1945, Walter and Elizabeth Paepcke—he the founder of the Container Corporation of America, she an ardent conservationist—moved to Aspen and established the Aspen Company as a property investment firm. Skiing was already popular in New England and the Midwest, but had few devotees in the Rockies. Paepcke bought a 3-mile chairlift, the longest and fastest in the world at the time, and had it ready for operation by January 1947. Soon, Easterners and Europeans were flocking to Aspen—and the rest is ski history.

The war also resulted in the overnight creation of what became at the time Colorado's 10th largest city, Amache, located in the southeastern part of the state. Immediately after the bombing of Pearl Harbor, the U.S. government began rounding up Americans of Japanese ancestry and putting them in internment camps, supposedly because the U.S. government feared they would side with the Japanese government against the United States. Although there was a great deal of prejudice against those of Japanese ancestry throughout the United States at the time, Colorado Governor Ralph Carr came to their defense, stating, "They are loyal Americans, sharing only race with the enemy." He welcomed them to the state and authorized the Amache Relocation Center, which at its peak had a population of more than 7,500. Amache was much like other Colorado towns of the time, with a school, post office, hospital, and even its own government, although its residents did not have the freedom to travel.

Colorado continued its steady growth in the 1950s, aided by tourism and the federal government. The $200 million U.S. Air Force Academy, authorized by Congress in 1954 and opened to cadets in 1958, is Colorado Springs' top tourist attraction today. There was a brief oil boom in the 1970s, followed by increasing high-tech development and even more tourism. Colorado made national news in 1967 when it became the first state to legalize abortions, allowing medically necessary abortions with unanimous approval of a panel of three doctors.

Weapons plants, which had seemed like a good idea when they were constructed during World War II, began to haunt Denver and the state in the 1970s and 1980s. Rocky Mountain Arsenal, originally built to produce chemical weapons, was found to be creating hazardous conditions by contaminating the land with deadly chemicals. A massive cleanup began in the early 1980s, and by the 1990s the arsenal was well on its way to accomplishing its goal of converting the 27-square-mile site into a national wildlife refuge.

The story of Rocky Flats, a nuclear weapons facility spurred on by the Cold War, is not so happy. Massive efforts to figure out what to do about contamination caused by nuclear waste have been largely unsuccessful. Although state and federal officials announced in 1996 that they had reached agreement on the means of removing some 14 tons of plutonium, their immediate plan calls for keeping it in Denver until at least 2010, and Department of Energy officials don't know what they'll do with it then. In the meantime, plans are underway to build storage containers that will safely hold the plutonium for up to 50 years.

In 1992, Colorado voters approved a controversial state constitutional amendment that would bar any legal measure that specifically protected homosexuals. The amendment would have nullified existing gay-rights ordinances in Denver, Boulder, and elsewhere. Enforcement was postponed pending judicial review, and in the meantime, gay-rights activists urged tourists to boycott Colorado. (Tourism did decline somewhat, although many Colorado ski resorts posted record seasons.) Then, in May 1996, the U.S. Supreme Court struck down the measure in a 6-to-3 vote, saying that, if enforced, it would have denied homosexuals constitutional protection from discrimination in housing, employment, and public accommodations.

On April 20, 1999, in a suburb of Denver, two students shook the city, state, and nation when they went on a shooting spree through Columbine high school. They killed 12 students and 1 teacher before turning their guns on themselves in the worst school shooting in the nation's history.

Now in the 21st century, the state's attention has turned to controlling population growth. With Colorado's growth rate nearly twice the national average, both residents and government leaders question how this unabated influx of outsiders can continue without causing serious harm to the state's air, water, and general quality of life.

2 Denver, Boulder & Colorado Springs Today

Colorado's major cities retain much of the casual atmosphere that has made them popular through the years, both with tourists and transplants. Many of those moving to Colorado's cities are fleeing the pollution, crime, and crowding of the East and West coasts, and some native and long-term Coloradans have begun to complain that these newcomers are bringing with them the very problems they sought to escape.

There is also a growing effort in Colorado to limit, or at least control, tourism. For instance, in 1995, just as the ski season was winding down, town officials in the skier's mecca of Vail reached an agreement with resort management to limit the number of skiers on the mountain and alleviate other aspects of overcrowding in the village. The word now from Vail and other high-profile Colorado tourist destinations is that visitors will be given incentives, such as discounts, to visit at off-peak times.

Several years ago, Colorado voters approved a measure that effectively eliminated state funding for tourism promotion. That resulted in the creation of the Colorado Tourism Authority, funded by the tourism industry, but debate continues over whether state government should take a more active role. Those in the tourism industry who run small businesses or are located away from the major attractions say they have been hurt by the lack of state promotion, whereas others insist that government assistance for one specific industry is inappropriate and argue that the tourism industry is doing very well on its own—too well, in some areas.

One particular problem is the increasingly popular Rocky Mountain National Park, which is not only attracting increasing numbers of out-of-state visitors, but also becoming a popular day trip for residents of the fast-growing Front Range cities of Denver, Boulder, Colorado Springs, and Fort Collins. During the summer, park roads are packed and parking lots full to overflowing, and in autumn, during the elk-rutting season, hundreds of people make their way to the Moraine Park and Horseshoe Park areas each evening. National park officials say that motor vehicle noise is starting to have a negative effect on the experience, and disappointed visitors are asking where they can go to find serenity. A limited shuttle system has been put into effect in one of the busier areas, and park officials have begun studying ways to expand public transportation in the park, possibly by creating off-premises parking areas where day visitors could leave their vehicles and hop a shuttle.

3 Colorado's Natural Landscape

First-time visitors to Colorado's Front Range are often awed by the looming wall of the Rocky Mountains, which come into sight a good 100 miles away, soon after you cross the border from Kansas. East of the Rockies, a 5,000-foot peak is considered high—yet Colorado has 1,143 mountains above 10,000 feet, including 53 over 14,000 feet! Mount Elbert, which is southwest of Leadville, is the highest of all at 14,433 feet.

The Rockies were formed some 65 million years ago by pressures that forced hard Precambrian rock to break through the earth's surface and push layers of earlier rock up on end. Millions of years of erosion then eliminated the soft surface material, producing the magnificent Rockies of calendar fame.

An almost perfect rectangle, Colorado measures some 385 miles east to west, and 275 miles north to south. The Continental Divide zigzags more or less through the center of the 104,247-square-mile state, eighth largest in the nation.

You can visualize Colorado's basic topography by dividing the state into vertical thirds: The eastern part is plains, the midsection is high mountains, and the western third is mesa.

That's a broad simplification, of course. The central Rockies, though they cover six times the mountain area of Switzerland, are not a single vast highland but consist of a series of high ranges running roughly north to south. East of the Continental Divide, the primary river systems are the South Platte, Arkansas, and Rio Grande, all flowing toward the Gulf of Mexico. The westward-flowing Colorado River system dominates the western part of the state, with tributary networks including the Gunnison, Dolores, and Yampa-Green rivers. In most cases, these rivers are not broad bodies of water such as the Ohio or Columbia, but streams, heavy with spring and summer snowmelt, that shrink to mere trickles during much of the year under the demands of farm and ranch irrigation. Besides agricultural use, these rivers provide necessary water to wildlife and offer wonderful opportunities for rafting, fishing, and swimming.

The forested mountains are essential in that they retain precious water for the lowlands. Eleven national forests cover 15 million acres of land, with an additional 8 million acres controlled by the Bureau of Land Management, also open for public recreation. Another half-million acres are within national parks, monuments, and recreation areas; and there are more than 40 state parks, including about 10 within an hour's drive of Denver, Boulder, or Colorado Springs.

Colorado's name, Spanish for "red," derives from the state's red soil and rocks. Some of the sandstone agglomerates have become attractions in their own right, such as Red Rocks Amphitheatre west of Denver and the startling Garden of the Gods in Colorado Springs.

Of Colorado's almost 4 million people, some 80% live along the I-25 corridor, where the plains meet the mountains. Denver, the state capital, has a population of more than half a million, with about 2.5 million in the metropolitan area. Colorado Springs has the second largest population, with almost 360,000 residents, followed by Fort Collins (120,000), Pueblo (102,000) and Boulder (95,000).

Appendix B:
Useful Toll-Free Numbers & Websites

AIRLINES

Air Canada
© 888/247-2262
www.aircanada.ca

Alaska Airlines
© 800/252-7522
www.alaskaair.com

American Airlines
© 800/433-7300
www.aa.com

America West Airlines
© 800/235-9292
www.americawest.com

British Airways
© 800/247-9297
© 0345/222-111 or
   0845/77-333-77 in Britain
www.british-airways.com

Continental Airlines
© 800/525-0280
www.continental.com

Delta Air Lines
© 800/221-1212
www.delta.com

Frontier Airlines
© 800/432-1359
www.frontierairlines.com

Korean Air
© 800/438-5000
www.koreanair.com

Martinair
© 800/366-4655
www.martinair.com

Mesa
© 800/637-2247
www.mesa-air.com

Mexicana
© 800/531-7921 in U.S.
© 01800/502-2000 in Mexico
www.mexicana.com

Midwest Express
© 800/452-2022
www.midwestexpress.com

Northwest Airlines
© 800/225-2525
www.nwa.com

Southwest Airlines
© 800/435-9792
www.southwest.com

Sun Country
© 800/359-6786
www.suncountry.com

United Airlines
© 800/241-6522
www.united.com

US Airways
© 800/428-4322
www.usairways.com

CAR-RENTAL AGENCIES

Advantage
© 800/777-5500
www.advantagerentacar.com

Alamo
© 800/327-9633
www.goalamo.com

Avis
© 800/331-1212 in Continental U.S.
© 800/TRY-AVIS in Canada
www.avis.com

Budget
✆ 800/527-0700
www.budget.com

Dollar
✆ 800/800-4000
www.dollar.com

Enterprise
✆ 800/325-8007
www.enterprise.com

Hertz
✆ 800/654-3131
www.hertz.com

National
✆ 800/CAR-RENT
www.nationalcar.com

Thrifty
✆ 800/367-2277
www.thrifty.com

MAJOR HOTEL & MOTEL CHAINS

Best Western International
✆ 800/528-1234
www.bestwestern.com

Clarion Hotels
✆ 800/CLARION
www.clarionhotel.com
    or www.hotelchoice.com

Comfort Inns
✆ 800/228-5150
www.hotelchoice.com

Courtyard by Marriott
✆ 800/321-2211
www.courtyard.com
    or www.marriott.com

Days Inn
✆ 800/325-2525
www.daysinn.com

Doubletree Hotels
✆ 800/222-TREE
www.doubletree.com

Econo Lodges
✆ 800/55-ECONO
www.hotelchoice.com

Hampton Inn
✆ 800/HAMPTON
www.hampton-inn.com

Holiday Inn
✆ 800/HOLIDAY
www.basshotels.com

Howard Johnson
✆ 800/654-2000
www.hojo.com

Hyatt Hotels & Resorts
✆ 800/228-9000
www.hyatt.com

ITT Sheraton
✆ 800/325-3535
www.starwood.com

La Quinta Motor Inns
✆ 800/531-5900
www.laquinta.com

Marriott Hotels
✆ 800/228-9290
www.marriott.com

Motel 6
✆ 800/4-MOTEL6
www.motel6.com

Omni
✆ 800/THEOMNI
www.omnihotels.com

Quality Inns
✆ 800/228-5151
www.hotelchoice.com

Radisson Hotels International
✆ 800/333-3333
www.radisson.com

Ramada Inns
✆ 800/2-RAMADA
www.ramada.com

Renaissance
✆ 800/228-9290
www.renaissancehotels.com

Sheraton Hotels & Resorts
✆ 800/325-3535
www.sheraton.com

Super 8 Motels
✆ 800/800-8000
www.super8.com

Travelodge
℃ 800/255-3050
www.travelodge.com

Westin Hotels & Resorts
℃ 800/937-8461
www.westin.com

Wyndham Hotels and Resorts
℃ 800/822-4200 in Continental U.S.
   and Canada
www.wyndham.com

Index

See also Accommodations and Restaurant indexes, below.

ACCOMMODATIONS: DENVER & ENVIRONS

ACCOMMODATIONS: BOULDER & ENVIRONS

Frommer's® Portable Guides

Destinations in a Nutshell

- Frommer's Portable Acapulco, Ixtapa & Zihuatanejo
- Frommer's Portable Amsterdam
- Frommer's Portable Aruba
- Frommer's Portable Australia's Great Barrier Reef
- Frommer's Portable Bahamas
- Frommer's Portable Berlin
- Frommer's Portable Big Island of Hawaii
- Frommer's Portable Boston
- Frommer's Portable California Wine Country
- Frommer's Portable Cancun
- Frommer's Portable Cayman Islands
- Frommer's Portable Charleston
- Frommer's Portable Chicago
- Frommer's Portable Disneyland®
- Frommer's Portable Dominican Republic
- Frommer's Portable Dublin
- Frommer's Portable Florence
- Frommer's Portable Frankfurt
- Frommer's Portable Hong Kong
- Frommer's Portable Houston
- Frommer's Portable Las Vegas
- Frommer's Portable Las Vegas for Non-Gamblers
- Frommer's Portable London
- Frommer's Portable London from $90 a Day
- Frommer's Portable Los Angeles
- Frommer's Portable Los Cabos & Baja
- Frommer's Portable Maine Coast
- Frommer's Portable Maui
- Frommer's Portable Miami
- Frommer's Portable Nantucket & Martha's Vineyard
- Frommer's Portable New Orleans
- Frommer's Portable New York City
- Frommer's Portable New York City from $90 a Day
- Frommer's Portable Paris
- Frommer's Portable Paris from $90 a Day
- Frommer's Portable Phoenix & Scottsdale
- Frommer's Portable Portland
- Frommer's Portable Puerto Rico
- Frommer's Portable Puerto Vallarta, Manzanillo & Guadalajara
- Frommer's Portable Rio de Janeiro
- Frommer's Portable San Diego
- Frommer's Portable San Francisco
- Frommer's Portable Savannah
- Frommer's Portable Seattle
- Frommer's Portable Sydney
- Frommer's Portable Tampa & St. Petersburg
- Frommer's Portable Vancouver
- Frommer's Portable Vancouver Island
- Frommer's Portable Venice
- Frommer's Portable Virgin Islands
- Frommer's Portable Washington, D.C.

Frommer's®

 WILEY

FROMMER'S® COMPLETE TRAVEL GUIDES

Alaska
Alaska Cruises & Ports of Call
American Southwest
Amsterdam
Argentina & Chile
Arizona
Atlanta
Australia
Austria
Bahamas
Barcelona, Madrid & Seville
Beijing
Belgium, Holland & Luxembourg
Bermuda
Boston
Brazil
British Columbia & the Canadian Rockies
Brussels & Bruges
Budapest & the Best of Hungary
Calgary
California
Canada
Cancún, Cozumel & the Yucatán
Cape Cod, Nantucket & Martha's Vineyard
Caribbean
Caribbean Ports of Call
Carolinas & Georgia
Chicago
China
Colorado
Costa Rica
Cruises & Ports of Call
Cuba
Denmark
Denver, Boulder & Colorado Springs
England
Europe
Europe by Rail
European Cruises & Ports of Call

Florence, Tuscany & Umbria
Florida
France
Germany
Great Britain
Greece
Greek Islands
Halifax
Hawaii
Hong Kong
Honolulu, Waikiki & Oahu
India
Ireland
Italy
Jamaica
Japan
Kauai
Las Vegas
London
Los Angeles
Maryland & Delaware
Maui
Mexico
Montana & Wyoming
Montréal & Québec City
Munich & the Bavarian Alps
Nashville & Memphis
New England
Newfoundland & Labrador
New Mexico
New Orleans
New York City
New York State
New Zealand
Northern Italy
Norway
Nova Scotia, New Brunswick & Prince Edward Island
Oregon
Ottawa
Paris
Peru

Philadelphia & the Amish Country
Portugal
Prague & the Best of the Czech Republic
Provence & the Riviera
Puerto Rico
Rome
San Antonio & Austin
San Diego
San Francisco
Santa Fe, Taos & Albuquerque
Scandinavia
Scotland
Seattle
Shanghai
Sicily
Singapore & Malaysia
South Africa
South America
South Florida
South Pacific
Southeast Asia
Spain
Sweden
Switzerland
Texas
Thailand
Tokyo
Toronto
Turkey
USA
Utah
Vancouver & Victoria
Vermont, New Hampshire & Maine
Vienna & the Danube Valley
Virgin Islands
Virginia
Walt Disney World® & Orlando
Washington, D.C.
Washington State

FROMMER'S® DOLLAR-A-DAY GUIDES

Australia from $50 a Day
California from $70 a Day
England from $75 a Day
Europe from $85 a Day
Florida from $70 a Day
Hawaii from $80 a Day

Ireland from $80 a Day
Italy from $70 a Day
London from $90 a Day
New York City from $90 a Day
Paris from $90 a Day
San Francisco from $70 a Day

Washington, D.C. from $80 a Day
Portable London from $90 a Day
Portable New York City from $90 a Day
Portable Paris from $90 a Day

FROMMER'S® PORTABLE GUIDES

Acapulco, Ixtapa & Zihuatanejo
Amsterdam
Aruba
Australia's Great Barrier Reef
Bahamas
Berlin
Big Island of Hawaii
Boston
California Wine Country
Cancún
Cayman Islands
Charleston
Chicago
Disneyland®
Dominican Republic
Dublin

Florence
Frankfurt
Hong Kong
Las Vegas
Las Vegas for Non-Gamblers
London
Los Angeles
Los Cabos & Baja
Maine Coast
Maui
Miami
Nantucket & Martha's Vineyard
New Orleans
New York City
Paris

Phoenix & Scottsdale
Portland
Puerto Rico
Puerto Vallarta, Manzanillo & Guadalajara
Rio de Janeiro
San Diego
San Francisco
Savannah
Vancouver
Vancouver Island
Venice
Virgin Islands
Washington, D.C.
Whistler

FROMMER'S® NATIONAL PARK GUIDES

Algonquin Provincial Park
Banff & Jasper
Family Vacations in the National
   Parks

Grand Canyon
National Parks of the American
   West
Rocky Mountain

Yellowstone & Grand Teton
Yosemite & Sequoia/Kings
   Canyon
Zion & Bryce Canyon

FROMMER'S® MEMORABLE WALKS

Chicago
London

New York
Paris

San Francisco

FROMMER'S® WITH KIDS GUIDES

Chicago
Las Vegas
New York City

Ottawa
San Francisco
Toronto

Vancouver
Walt Disney World® & Orlando
Washington, D.C.

SUZY GERSHMAN'S BORN TO SHOP GUIDES

Born to Shop: France
Born to Shop: Hong Kong,
   Shanghai & Beijing

Born to Shop: Italy
Born to Shop: London

Born to Shop: New York
Born to Shop: Paris

FROMMER'S® IRREVERENT GUIDES

Amsterdam
Boston
Chicago
Las Vegas
London

Los Angeles
Manhattan
New Orleans
Paris
Rome

San Francisco
Seattle & Portland
Vancouver
Walt Disney World®
Washington, D.C.

FROMMER'S® BEST-LOVED DRIVING TOURS

Austria
Britain
California
France

Germany
Ireland
Italy
New England

Northern Italy
Scotland
Spain
Tuscany & Umbria

THE UNOFFICIAL GUIDES®

Beyond Disney
California with Kids
Central Italy
Chicago
Cruises
Disneyland®
England
Florida
Florida with Kids
Inside Disney

Hawaii
Las Vegas
London
Maui
Mexico's Best Beach Resorts
Mini Las Vegas
Mini Mickey
New Orleans
New York City
Paris

San Francisco
Skiing & Snowboarding in the
   West
South Florida including Miami &
   the Keys
Walt Disney World®
Walt Disney World® for
   Grown-ups
Walt Disney World® with Kids
Washington, D.C.

SPECIAL-INTEREST TITLES

Athens Past & Present
Cities Ranked & Rated
Frommer's Best Day Trips from London
Frommer's Best RV & Tent Campgrounds
   in the U.S.A.
Frommer's Caribbean Hideaways
Frommer's China: The 50 Most Memorable Trips
Frommer's Exploring America by RV
Frommer's Gay & Lesbian Europe
Frommer's NYC Free & Dirt Cheap

Frommer's Road Atlas Europe
Frommer's Road Atlas France
Frommer's Road Atlas Ireland
Frommer's Wonderful Weekends from
   New York City
The New York Times' Guide to Unforgettable
   Weekends
Retirement Places Rated
Rome Past & Present